Better Banking

For other titles in the Wiley Finance series
please see www.wiley.com/finance

Better Banking

Understanding and Addressing the Failures in Risk Management, Governance and Regulation

Adrian Docherty and Franck Viort

WILEY

Registered office

John Wiley & Sons Ltd, The Atrium, Southern Gate, Chichester, West Sussex, PO19 8SQ, United Kingdom

For details of our global editorial offices, for customer services and for information about how to apply for permission to reuse the copyright material in this book please visit our website at www.wiley.com.

Library of Congress Cataloging-in-Publication Data

Docherty, Adrian, 1969-
  Better banking : understanding and addressing the failures in risk management, governance and regulation/Adrian Docherty and Franck Viort.
     pages cm
  Includes index.
  ISBN 978-1-118-65130-8 (cloth)
  1. Banks and banking. 2. Banks and banking–Risk management. 3. Banks and banking–State supervision. 4. Bank management. I. Viort, Franck, 1972- II. Title.
  HG1601.D55 2014
  332.1–dc23

                                                            2013043103

A catalogue record for this book is available from the British Library.

ISBN 978-1-118-65130-8 (hbk) ISBN 978-1-118-65132-2 (ebk)
ISBN 978-1-118-65133-9 (ebk) ISBN 978-1-118-65131-5 (ebk)

Set in 10/12 Times LT Std by Aptara, New Delhi, India
Printed in Great Britain by CPI Group (UK) Ltd, Croydon, CR0 4YY

To our wives,
Bénédicte and Justine, and our children:
Agathe, Elise, Lucy, Robin and Sophie.

Contents

Acknowledgements

The concept of this book was driven by our profound belief, formed over many years at the coalface of the banking industry, including during this latest financial crisis, that banking can be truly "better". Events of recent years have exposed massive problems in the banking industry. As practitioners on the ground, we are confident that we understand the root causes: failings in risk management, governance and regulation. We have been frustrated by the incomplete diagnoses that have been published, worried at the prospect of unintended consequences of policy actions and disappointed by the lack of effective dialogue in the industry. We have been encouraged to find that similar views to ours are widely held by many of the people whose opinions we most respect and who, in our opinion, understand what is really going on in banking. This book, therefore, aims to fill an important gap in the literature and give a voice to these crucial, progressive perspectives.

We have written this book in a personal capacity and it expresses our own personal views, rather than the views of anyone else or of our employers. Nevertheless, we have not written the book in a vacuum and so would like to acknowledge the input and support we have received from others.

We would like to thank our editor, Werner Coetzee, for his help and drive in getting this project off the ground, as well as all the excellent professionals at Wiley for their support and assistance. We had the good fortune of being supported greatly by our expert reviewers and friends Julien Carmona and Mark Kibblewhite during the drafting of the book and are supremely grateful to them both for their valuable input and suggestions. We would also like to thank Sonia Peterson and Joaqin Mercado, who helped out on several parts of the book with research and writing. Many other senior industry figures, colleagues, clients, professors and friends have contributed to our efforts and we owe them a sincere "thank you": work on the book has reminded us of the immense intelligence and enthusiasm of the people around us. Lastly, we would like to thank our wives and families for their patience during the drafting of this book and apologise to them for our frequent neglect of familial duties during that period.

1

Introduction

1.1 OVERVIEW AND OBJECTIVES

> If the terrain and the map do not agree, follow the terrain.[1]

Today, the world is in its sixth year of a deep and damaging financial crisis. The cause of this crisis was a massive failure of risk management and governance: quite simply, we lost control of our financial system. As a result, we experienced a debt-fuelled boom that turned rapidly into an economic "bust". Millions are suffering as a consequence: for example, youth unemployment has risen in the last ten years from 17.8% to 22.8% in the EU and from 12.0% to 16.2% in the United States.[2]

The problems could have been greater. The bankruptcy of Lehman Brothers could have led our modern, global economy to freeze. Such problems have been averted by the pumping of huge amounts of extra money into the financial system by central banks at low interest rates. These monetary policies are sure to have painful side-effects in the long term, but they have succeeded in keeping our economies moving and bought time to fix the causes of this financial crisis.

Banks are lead actors in the crisis. In many countries, large swathes of the banking industry failed and had to be supported by the state. In general, banks had been loosely supervised and some had been badly managed. Seeking ever-increasing profits, the banking industry took huge risks that were not apparent at the time but that we can now see were unacceptable. Problems emerged first in the US subprime mortgage market, which enabled poor people to buy expensive homes. New financial products used financial alchemy to turn this high-risk lending activity into seemingly low-risk investments for gullible investors. They were anything but low-risk: one study of $640bn worth of securities shows that investors lost two-thirds of their money.[3] Many of the most gullible investors were banks themselves, often banks outside the USA. The subprime malaise of over-confidence followed by ruinous losses spilled over into other markets and other countries.

Common sense should have told us from the outset that this kind of alchemy was impossible and that someone stood to lose out. In the end, it was society that was bearing those risks unwittingly. When the banks failed, society was forced to stump up the financial resources to prop up the system or face chaos and oblivion.

The public is rightfully angry about the burden of those losses, but also with the odious behaviours in the banking industry that have been uncovered by the financial crisis: greed, incompetence, negligence, arrogance, contempt, deceitfulness. Several of the leaders of the

---

[1] Attributed widely to a Swedish Army training manual.
[2] Labour Force Survey: Unemployment rate for age group under 25 years 2002–12, Eurostat.
[3] Collateral Damage: Sizing and Assessing the Subprime CDO Crisis, Federal Reserve Bank of Philadelphia, May 2012.

banking industry, who had been lauded as superheroes and feted with honours and multi-million dollar bonuses during boom years, turned out to be incompetent or even downright villainous.

No-one disagrees that change is needed, in order to learn the lessons of the current financial crisis and enable us to reduce the likelihood, frequency and impact of future crises. There is a risk, however, that the diagnostic is incomplete and the remedial actions may be ineffective. This book aims to contribute to an improved understanding of the diagnostic as well as offering some additional and alternative proposals for consideration.

Current diagnoses tend to focus on the symptoms of the current financial crisis (e.g. the banks' excessive leverage, weak capital bases, poor funding profiles and insufficient liquidity buffers[4]) or play the blame game, singling out scapegoats in order to make the resolution of the problem punchier and more streamlined. Requiring higher levels of capital and exposing bad behaviour by bankers should solve the matter, apparently, all at little cost to the rest of us.

Such views are incomplete. A better diagnostic should do two things. Firstly, it should recognise the contribution of global macro-economic imbalances – especially the growing indebtedness of western consumer economies – to the current financial crisis. These imbalances are as much political as they are financial. They are also stubbornly difficult to reduce. Secondly, the diagnostic of the banking industry's problems should centre squarely on failings of governance, regulation and risk management. Society failed to control adequately the banks and the banks failed to manage adequately the risks they were running. Problems of excessively aggressive financial profiles, bad behaviours and excessive pay are consequent symptoms of the failure of governance, regulation and risk management. Society – the ultimate owner of the banking industry – must accept its responsibility for heaping praise on the "banker's new clothes", to extend a recently used metaphor.[5]

In order to advance this diagnostic, there is a need to engage a broad audience. A discussion that is restricted to dedicated professionals from the banking industry and the authorities may miss the broader picture and get lost in cul-de-sacs. Certain arcane elements of the regulatory response to the financial crisis (known as Basel III and covered in Section 4.5) indicate that this is the case. "Expert" diagnostics may also fail to achieve acceptance from the public, who are, after all, the "society" that ultimately carries the can. In the spirit of active engagement, therefore, we seek to set out a basic understanding of the nature and fundamentals of banking, to act as a methodological backdrop to the discussion and assist a simultaneous *broadening* and *simplification* of the subject. For example, a basic common understanding of the notions of risk and capital will help any diagnostic on the solvency and resilience of our banks.

An elegant diagnostic and a critique of the current regulatory response would be a noble objective for this book, but it would not be sufficient. Therefore, we have tried to set out some concrete, high-level, novel proposals for "better banking". All of these are to do with bank governance, regulation and risk management. To begin this task, we have had to assume at the outset that politically, a liberal free-market form of capitalism with moderate state oversight

---

[4] Basel III: A global regulatory framework for more resilient banks and banking systems, Basel Committee, December 2010 (revised June 2011).
[5] *The Banker's New Clothes*, Anat Admati and Martin Hellwig, 2013.

is the desired economic framework; and that society's capacity for risk is low enough not to accept anything like the level of risk that was building up in the system in 2005/6. Our thesis is that finance and banking are important features of a modern, democratic society and liberal, capitalist economy. But the risks that are inherent need to be well managed, regulated and supervised. They can be mitigated, never tamed but, if we adopt the wrong approaches, they can be needlessly inflamed. So we propose a vision of a banking industry that is based firmly on free-market principles but supplemented by a benign and competent public authority, which ensures that risk is transparent and confronted through rigorous and intelligent risk management capabilities.

The proposals are set out in the immodestly titled Chapter 7: "A Blueprint for Basel IV". They comprise suggestions on:

- improved risk management processes, including better information and the use of dynamic "wargaming" over "stress testing";
- a hands-on "Guardian Angel" approach to supervision;
- a more impressionistic and subjective approach to capital and funding;
- some radical proposals on deposit funding (effectively, the nationalisation of guaranteed deposits by the central bank) and liquidity management (replacing investments in government bonds with a central bank overdraft);
- increased rigour in governance processes and management accountability structures through the adoption of a meticulous "Centurion approach";
- the active engagement of market forces in bank governance by means of a new "glasnost" approach; and
- relatively liberal and flexible common-sense views on human capital management and industry structure, which should be allowed to find their own form through market forces, good risk management and good governance.

These proposals are meant to be a "strawman": "throw stones and it doesn't hurt". We have put these ideas forward because there are so few, coherent, credible responses to the lessons of the current financial crisis, even those of the most esteemed experts and banking authorities. The debate on the banking industry is polarised and not progressing at a great pace. Banks are engaged in "lobbying" to protect their vested interests; the authorities are keen to be seen as competent and in possession of the magic fix; almost everyone else is frustrated and feels disenfranchised. We do not feel that taking sides is appropriate: this is not a battle between two armies. Society needs banks, banks need to change and society needs to guide that change. There should be no opposing objectives between bankers and banked: there may be multiple viewpoints, but the objectives should be non-controversial. Status quo is not acceptable. To put it bluntly, we feel that the banking industry has still not been fixed and the current reform agenda is not going to change that.

We hope we are not naïve. We are aware of some of the challenges that our proposal would entail and have dedicated Chapter 8 to the consideration of some of these challenges.

The reader should be aware of some questions of style:

- The subject matter is broad and raises many questions. This book skims the surface. We hope that the inquisitive reader will be left with a thirst to dig deeper into several areas.

- We use quotes extensively, to demonstrate the views and nuances of experts in the industry and commentators, as there is no need to "reinvent the wheel" when others have already provided good material.
- Too much of the technical debate on the banking industry is inaccessible: this book hopes to be highly accessible, insofar as that is possible with a highly complex, sophisticated and, let's face it, intangible topic. In order to improve accessibility, we have a glossary of jargon. Data exhibits are kept to a minimum and are included only where they are highly relevant. We don't use maths beyond what's necessary and even then, only very basics of risk management or simple sums.

Thematically, the book has three main parts. Initially, we set out our diagnostic and methodological foundations; then, we consider 14 real-life case studies; lastly, we set out for consideration the proposals for "better banking".

1.2 QUICK START GUIDE TO BANKING CONCEPTS AND REGULATION

The banking industry is huge and important. Due to its central role in the economy, it stores or handles vast sums of money. To give some idea of scale, consider the following statistics in Table 1.1.

These numbers may not mean very much in isolation. But they hopefully illustrate that banks deal with big sums of money and *getting it right* is important. Imperfections or – worse – sloppiness are bound to have a disastrous effect.

Banking is an industry that is at the heart of our capitalist system. On the one hand, banks take money in and safeguard it; on the other hand, banks provide credit for people to buy homes and companies to make investments. Banks act as a bridge between these two needs and their expertise in credit and investment management keeps both sides of the business happy, if everything is working well. Banks also provide payments services to facilitate the transfer of money for purchases, though this aspect of banking is not a focus of this book.

Banking is risky and banking is about risk management. The classic bank product, a loan, consists of the up-front provision of money by the bank to the borrower, who promises to repay the debt within a certain timeframe. How can a bank be certain that the loan will be repaid? What can the bank do to ensure the loan is repaid? And what should the bank do in the event of non-repayment? On the other side of the business, how can a customer be certain that the bank will be able to honour their deposit?

It is an often-overlooked fact that a bank deposit is not backed with cash on reserve or gold. Or, as was said of one of the largest and best regarded banks in the world: "Turns Out Wells Fargo Doesn't Just Keep Your Deposits in a Stagecoach Full of Gold Ingots".[6] In fact, most of any bank's deposit base is lent out to borrowing customers, who may or may not repay their debt.

This intermediation function makes banks fragile. They rely upon the confidence and trust of those who entrust their funds to them. They need to manage their risks sufficiently well to be viable in the long term (solvent) and in the short term (liquid). So risk management rapidly

---

[6] Dealbreaker.com, 3 January 2013.

Table 1.1   Key figures on banking

Penetration	It seems – though admittedly the data is not clear – that around half of the world's population has a bank account. One-third of small businesses have a credit line from a bank.[7] Globally, there is one bank branch for every 6,000 people. This number varies from one branch for every 1,100 people in Spain to one branch for every 150,000 people in Congo.[8]
Size: balance sheet	The balance sheet size of the world's largest 1,000 banks is more than $100,000bn.[9]
Size: deposits	Deposit balances globally are reported to be 44% of world GDP,[10] or around $30,000bn. In richer countries, the average is 84% of GDP.
Size: derivatives	The face value of derivatives contracts is more than $400,000bn[11] (see Section 3.7 for an overview of derivatives).
Volumes	The value of all the payments transactions processed by banks is in the region of £78,000bn in the UK alone,[12] or 50 times the UK's annual GDP. If we gross that up a factor of about 30 (reflecting the UK's share of global GDP[13]), then we would have an estimate equivalent to more than $3,000,000bn in payments globally. In addition to these volumes, the world's currency markets trade some $5,000bn per day[14] or $1,500,000bn per annum.
Market value	The top 55 banks in the world have a market capitalisation of $4,000bn,[15] representing nearly 10% of the entire global stock market capitalisation of listed companies, which is $53,000bn.[16] In China and Australia, large banks make up more than a quarter of the stock market's value.
Profitability	The top 1,000 banks make around $700bn per year in pretax profits.[17] In the USA, financial companies (including insurance companies as well as banks) made up 28% of corporate profits over the last three years.[18]
Big banks	Fifteen banks currently have balance sheets bigger than $2,000bn: ● Europe: Deutsche Bank, HSBC, Barclays, BNP Paribas, Crédit Agricole, Royal Bank of Scotland ● Japan: Mitsubishi UFJ, Mizuho, Japan Post Bank ● China: Industrial & Commercial Bank of China, China Construction Bank, Agricultural Bank of China, Bank of China ● USA: JP Morgan Chase, Bank of America. And a further 11 have balance sheets between $1,000bn and $2,000bn: ● Europe: Banco Santander, Société Générale, ING Group, Groupe BPCE, Lloyds Banking Group, UBS, UniCredit, Credit Suisse Group ● Japan: Sumitomo Mitsui Financial Group ● USA: Citigroup Inc, Wells Fargo.

---

[7] Global Financial Development Database, World Bank, April 2013.   [8] Ibid.

[9] Top 1000 World Banks 2012, *The Banker*, 2 July 2012.

[10] Global Financial Development Database, World Bank, April 2013.

[11] Mid-Year 2012 Market Analysis, ISDA, 20 December 2012.

[12] Payments Council Quarterly Statistical Report, 18 March 2013.

[13] World Bank.   [14] *BIS Quarterly Review*, BIS, March 2012.

[15] World's Largest Banks 2013, relbanks.com, 25 January 2013.

[16] World Bank.   [17] Top 1000 World Banks 2012, *The Banker*, 2 July 2012.

[18] Table 6.16D, Bureau of Economic Analysis, 28 March 2013.

becomes an issue of solvency capital management (being able to absorb losses when they come around, without depositors losing their money) and funding and liquidity management (being able to borrow from – and repay when requested – the bank's depositors and creditors). This is the reason why bank regulation has been focused heavily on capital levels and liquidity measures.

If things don't go well, banks can lose confidence and suffer from bank runs, where depositors try to get their funds out; the bank simply runs out of cash to meet its obligations and is forced to close. Bank runs are fortunately rare, though the current crisis is providing several new case studies. The banking industry can also suffer from system-wide crises, the financial busts that generally follow a period of boom.

If something is important yet fragile, it follows that it needs to be protected. This is why regulation and supervision are important. The regulatory discussion focuses a lot on "Basel", the international club of banking regulators where such issues are managed. A basic understanding of the three Basel regulatory regimes (Basel I, Basel II and Basel III) will help to serve as a backdrop to the more prescriptive chapters later.

Society needs to ensure that the essential functions of banks are preserved, to avoid problems such as a "credit crunch", when certain reasonable needs of the economy cannot find financing. Society also needs a "guardian" to ensure that financial stability is preserved, the value of deposits is safeguarded and banking ethics are applied.

Finally, if something is important and fragile, it needs to be well managed. This is the duty of everyone, from the regulatory and supervisory "guardians" to the owners of banks to the executives and middle-managers of banks. It is also the duty of society itself for – to adapt a well-known quotation – every society gets the banking system it deserves.

The following three chapters give a brief overview of how banks contributed to the current financial crisis, what the basic concepts of banking and risk management entail and the history of banking regulation to the present day.

2
The Global Financial Crisis

The current, ongoing financial crisis has shaken the world economy and the global banking sector. Many publications, of differing quality and emphasis, are available for those who wish to study the factual history of the financial crisis. Here, we consider the crisis more from a *thematic* rather than a *narrative* perspective: the goal is to derive insights into the causes of the crisis that might help us consider improvements in the banking industry, rather than simply recounting facts or telling a sensational story.

2.1 FROM DEREGULATION TO DOTCOM CRASH

The world economy and financial system underwent a major change in the 30 or so years running up to the crisis. Politically, many nations embraced the free-market doctrines of Reagonomics and Thatcherism, which had appeared to triumph over various forms of socialism and centrally planned economies. Logistically, the world became smaller and more integrated through advances in communication and transport. Technologically, rapid increases in computing power enabled vastly enhanced data processing, storage and analytics. These factors shaped developments in the structure and innovation of the banking system.

Arguably, the changes were most pronounced in Europe. Deregulation of banking in the UK (the "Big Bang" of 1986) opened up the industry to new firms from abroad and kick-started a resurgence in London's importance as the pre-eminent global financial centre. At the European level, the Single European Act in 1986 reinforced the concepts of competition, limiting barriers to trade. The foundations for the common currency to become the Euro that were laid during this period followed a similar objective of closer trade integration between members, but also involved the creation of a reserve currency that would compete with the US dollar and provide European borrowers with a vast and liquid capital market. And widespread privatisations in the 1980s and 1990s introduced the culture of share ownership to a European populace whose main financial asset had previously been the traditional bank deposit.

New types of companies entered the banking market. A breed of investment firms emerged that became known as "hedge funds". The archetypal hedge fund was largely unregulated and aimed to exploit market imperfections, by finding trading positions that were offsetting yet differently priced and so certain to make a profit, no matter in which direction the financial markets moved. Hedge funds financed themselves with their founders' and clients' investment capital, together with short-term debt facilities from the banks with whom they traded. Since the hedge funds were active trading customers of the banks, the banks were keen to provide them with loans. The hedge funds employed highly intelligent quantitative analysts, who used the latest databases and computing power to build risk arbitrage models. The funds were hedging their positions and the number-crunchers' models generally showed that the hedges were not perfect – but they were pretty good and only a very odd circumstance would cause problems. The models also demonstrated that such an odd circumstance would only be expected to occur once in every 10,000 years or so. Hence, the hedge funds felt like a pretty safe bet and a good source of earnings for all involved, so long as the disaster of biblical proportions didn't show up.

In 1998, a disaster of biblical proportions did show up. Or at least, something highly unusual occurred, which the models had not anticipated. The financial markets were spooked by the unexpected default by Russia on its international bonds and this triggered a "flight to quality" reaction from international investors. Their sudden and massive shifts in investment preferences, for example moving their portfolios out of thinly-traded or illiquid bonds into safer and more liquid bonds, caused problems for a large hedge fund called "Long Term Capital Management" (LTCM). LTCM had credibility: it counted the winners of the 1997 Nobel Prize in Economic Sciences among its partners. Guided by their strong belief in the power of risk modelling (Myron Scholes and Robert Merton had helped develop the Black–Scholes option pricing model), they had a different way of thinking about the financial world and "by putting numerical odds on its likelihood of loss",[1] they were supposedly able to generate superior trading strategies, certain to win against all the less sophisticated investors. But its trading strategy failed and resulted in massive losses that threatened to destabilise the capital markets through contagion.

> Had the failure of LTCM triggered the seizing up of markets, substantial damage could have been inflicted on many market participants, including some not directly involved with the firm, and could have potentially impaired the economies of many nations, including our own.[2]

The Federal Reserve orchestrated a bail-out by LTCM's lenders, so that the hedge fund did not need to close its positions at "fire sale" prices into fragile markets. A crisis was averted. In the end, LTCM lost "only" around $5bn and its lenders did not need to write off their loans. In retrospect, however, the LTCM episode should have served as a forewarning of the risks that were building up in the financial system.

At the turn of the century, the "dotcom" bubble was a crisis that never happened. Investors chased technology and "new era" stocks higher and higher and were largely wiped out when most of the dotcom businesses failed to convert their concepts into profits and experienced share price crashes. The main benchmark of the dotcom era, the NASDAQ index, peaked above 5,000 in early 2000 having been around 2,000 two years earlier, and fell to just above 1,000 two years later.[3] The value of the stock holdings of US households fell from $18,100bn in early 2000 to $9,900bn in the second half of 2002.[4] Wall Street banks were subsequently investigated by New York Attorney Eliot Spitzer, leading to prosecution and settlement, owing to practices that mismanaged the conflict of interest between research departments and

---

[1] When Genius Failed: The Rise and Fall of Long-Term Capital Management, Roger Lowenstein, 2000.
[2] Private-sector refinancing of the large hedge fund, Long-Term Capital Management, Alan Greenspan testimony before the Committee on Banking and Financial Services, US House of Representatives, 1 October 1998.
[3] From WSJ.com.
[4] Some Reflections on the Crisis and the Policy Response, Ben S. Bernanke, 13 April 2012.

investment banking salespeople. But there was no banking collapse to accompany the collapse of the high-tech sector. This has puzzled some analysts:

> The dotcom crash was of a similar magnitude to the subprime crisis while its output effects were small in comparison.[5]

and

> The fall of dot-com stock prices just a few years earlier, which destroyed as much or more paper wealth – more than $8 trillion – resulted in a relatively short and mild recession and no major financial instability.[6]

Why did the dotcom crash not create a serious crisis? It is true that banks did need to write off some of the dud loans to high-tech companies. For example, WorldCom had debt of $41bn when it went bankrupt in 2002. But the losses on dotcom investments did not cause contagion and second-order problems, because they were, for the most part, not financed by debt. Investors saw their wealth grow, soar, explode and crash, but they were not left with a debt "hangover".

> Bubbles in themselves aren't always bad. But when they leave behind debts, they can be disastrous.[7]

The specific problems and vulnerabilities that led to today's crisis were not present during the dotcom crash. Nevertheless, the authorities were concerned at the economic slowdown that was induced by the end of the dotcom bubble and the terrorist attacks of 11 September 2001.

2.2 THE SEEDS OF A CRISIS

> Had I been in love, I could not have been more wretchedly blind. But vanity, not love, has been my folly,[8]

Greenspan's Low Interest Rates
The response of the authorities to the economic slowdown was to lower interest rates to spur economic activity. At the New York Federal Reserve ("the Fed"), Governor Alan Greenspan lowered interest rates and kept them low. By admitting that the Fed could "mitigate the fallout when it occurs and, hopefully, ease the transition to the next expansion",[9] Greenspan signalled there would be a safety net in case the market crashed, providing justification for a more aggressive approach to risk and "implicitly encouraged bankers to borrow short-term while making long-term loans, confident the Fed would be there if funding dried up".[10]

---

[5] *Bubbles, Banks, and Financial Stability*, Kosuke Aokiy and Kalin Nikolovz, August 2011.
[6] Some Reflections on the Crisis and the Policy Response, Ben S. Bernanke, 13 April 2012.
[7] *Masters of Nothing*, Matthew Hancock and Nadhim Zahami, 2011.
[8] *Pride and Prejudice,* Jane Austen, 1813.
[9] Economic Volatility, Alan Greenspan, 30 August 2002.
[10] *Fault Lines*, R. Rajan, 2010.

American interest rates were below 2% throughout the three years 2002, 2003 and 2004. In retrospect, this overly accommodative monetary policy sowed the seeds of a boom that became the backdrop of the current financial crisis. Holding rates so low for so long was "the original sin of the Bernanke-Greenspan Fed" that was bound to lead to excessive risk-taking.[11]

The other implication of the actions of the authorities, notably the Fed, was to give investors a clear indication that action would always be taken to avoid calamity. The capital markets interpreted this as an implicit backstop to risk, a guarantee that distressed markets would be revived by public policy. In market-speak, this was termed the "Greenspan put". Implicitly, it increased the risk appetite of the markets and reduced investors' attention to downside risk. If things went wrong, the Fed would sort it out.

A Growing Trade Imbalance, a Savings Glut and Financial Innovation

During this same period, global trade continued to grow and new, structural imbalances emerged that changed the nature of the international financial system.

The imbalance was caused by Western economies importing ever more goods from Asia. Western consumers were borrowing to finance their consumption and Western governments were borrowing to finance budget deficits, while Asian consumers and governments were saving and investing. The global financial system facilitated this imbalance and enabled the transfer of Asian savings to Western borrowers. A "savings glut" emerged, which kept market interest rates low despite the higher financing needs of the West. Developing economies were "shifting from being net importers of financial capital to being net exporters, in some cases very large net exporters".[12]

This shift occurred at the turn of the century. According to official statistics,[13] the current account of industrialised countries had moved from a *surplus* in 1999 to an annual *deficit* of 1.5% of world GDP in 2006. Emerging markets and oil-producing countries were the mirror image, as the graph in Figure 2.1 shows. Poorer countries were lending money to richer countries to buy their exports.

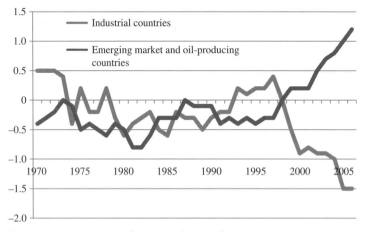

Figure 2.1   Current account surplus/deficit in % of world GDP

---

[11] Anna Schwartz blames Fed for sub-prime crisis, *The Telegraph*, 13 January 2008.
[12] The Global Saving Glut and the U.S. Current Account Deficit, Ben S. Bernanke, 10 March 2005.
[13] World Economic Outlook, IMF, April 2007.

These trends were accompanied by the introduction of the Euro at the turn of the century, which created a new, deep and liquid capital market. For the first time, European borrowers could borrow efficiently from bond investors in their own currency, as American companies had been able to for decades.

Technological advances spurred financial innovation. New techniques for transferring risk boosted the activity of the bond markets. The biggest innovations were securitisation, funding arbitrage vehicles and the "credit default swap" (CDS). These are described below; they grew rapidly in size and complexity, while offering a seemingly perfect way for risk to be spread to new investors and thus reduce the overall risk in the system.

To illustrate the rapid and exponential growth in new financial products, consider the growth of the CDS market. A CDS is a contract where the seller gives protection against the default of the reference entity in exchange for a fee. It is like an insurance policy against default. Buyers of protection could use CDS to reduce their exposures for tactical or strategic reasons. Sellers of protection could use CDS to generate risk-based revenues, without the hassle of making loans. Traders could use CDS to take positions in the market where they felt there was value to be earned. The total of all credit default swap transactions grew from next to nothing in 2001 to $60,000bn in 2007 – see Figure 2.2.

Financial engineering took on the aura of alchemy and its complexity outstripped the sophistication of investors and regulators. All areas of the financial industry – including its regulators, managements and even its customers – were filled with such confidence that they began to ignore the fundamentals of risk.

The head of the Federal Deposit Insurance Corporation in the USA noted that there had arisen a "prevailing belief that financial markets, through financial engineering, had created a system where risks were easily identified and transferred from parties who were risk averse to those who were willing, ready and capable to assume these risks. The collapse of these markets calls these beliefs into question."[14]

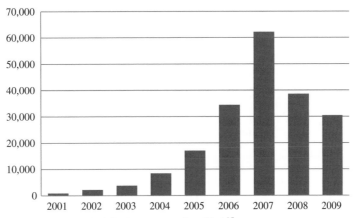

Figure 2.2   Growth in the credit default swaps market ($bn)[15]

---

[14] Managing the transition to a safer financial system, Sheila C. Bair, Chairman, Federal Deposit Insurance Corporation, September 2009.
[15] ISDA.

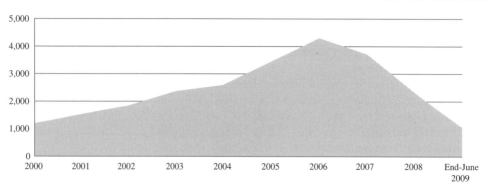

Figure 2.3   Growth of the securitisation market in the USA and Europe ($bn)[16]

Just as technology has transformed the fields of communications and transport, making things possible that were unthinkable a couple of decades prior, so did people assume that finance could also leap forward and give them the ultimate "Holy Grail" of risk-free reward. In this pursuit, banks and investors were happy to trust the risk assessment of specialised third-party agencies, who had devised tools to identify and measure the risk in the capital markets. The credit ratings agencies gave ratings to securitisation bonds (see Section 3.6.5), which were made up of portfolios of mortgage loans or similar assets. By splitting up the portfolio into slices, different investors could take different risk profiles on the same pool of mortgages, some with higher risk and a higher return and others with less risk and a lower return. Investors – including some of the most sophisticated banks in the world – trusted the expertise of the ratings agencies and their assessment of the riskiness of the mortgage portfolio and how the individual slices spread that risk. In a nutshell, securitisation appeared to be the perfect tool to provide a high-yield, low-risk product for investors and low-cost finance for borrowers. The securitisation market quadrupled in the run-up to the financial crisis, as shown in Figure 2.3.

At the same time, there was the rise of a new type of funding arbitrage vehicle in the wholesale market: the "conduit" and the "Specialised Investment Vehicle" (SIV). Although the names make them sound complex, in fact they did something very straightforward. They invested in (supposedly) high-quality, long-dated investments and borrowed at low rates on a short-term basis. The arbitrage created a profit stream that seemed risk free, for the risk of their funding sources evaporating was not seen as a worry. Again, clever technology appeared to offer a breakthrough and people loved it.

Faced with a wall of money seeking a decent yield in a low-interest rate environment, the new efficiency of the capital markets led to an odd situation: money became too cheap. This is illustrated in a chart from early 2007, which featured in the Bank of England's *Financial Stability Report*. The chart in Figure 2.4 breaks down the cost of borrowing into the cost a risk-free investment (the bottom layer), the risk of the borrower (middle two layers, both expected and unexpected loss, see Section 3.3) and the "residual" cost (the top slice in the chart). This slice can be thought of as the return that the lender gets by putting their money to work. It

---

[16] Global Financial Stability Report, IMF, October 2009.

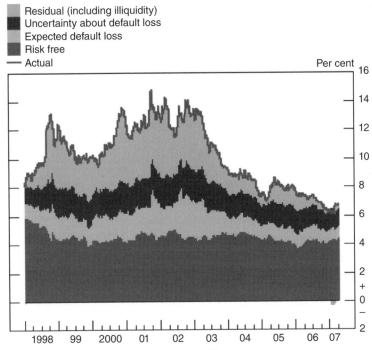

Figure 2.4   Decomposition of borrowing costs over time[17]
Note from the original source chart: Decomposition of borrowing costs for UK high-yield corporates.
The decomposition assumes a debt maturity of 20 years. For details, see Churm, R and Panigirtzoglou,
N (2005), 'Decomposing credit spreads', Bank of England Working Paper no. 253.

collapses to zero towards the end of 2006. Banks and bond investors were simply not being
compensated for the provision of funds. Clearly, the disciplines of *caveat emptor* and market-
based pricing were not being observed.

The factors set out above are the consequences of deeper imbalances in the global economy,
in which "the US financial sector bridged the gap between an overconsuming and overstimu-
lated United States and an underconsuming and understimulated rest of the world".[18]

Note that, unlike many commentators, we do not single out the banks' excessive leverage, lack of capital, scarcity of on-hand liquidity reserves or weak term funding structures
as causes of the crisis. Why? Because we see these as second-order factors, symptoms of the
underlying failure of risk management and over-confidence. Whilst it is true that banks would
have fared better during the crisis if they had had better financial resources, it must be stressed
that more capital, more liquidity and more funding are not themselves remedies for the weaknesses of the banking industry.

---

[17] Financial Stability Report, Bank of England, April 2007, sourced from Bloomberg, Merrill Lynch,
Thomson Datastream and Bank of England calculations.
[18] *Fault Lines*, R. Rajan, 2010.

Table 2.1   Factors contributing to the fragility of the financial system

Feature	Impact
Politics and society	Massive confidence and belief in free markets
	Poor oversight of the banking industry (by shareholders, management and supervisors)
	Risk management failures and loose underwriting standards
	Policy to increase levels of home ownership among the disadvantaged in the USA
Low interest rates	Policy-induced boom in asset prices and borrowing
	Recycling of trade balance surplus in Asia into Treasuries keeping rates low
Global imbalances	Asian savings lead to savings "glut" and a Western borrowing binge
	Widening of trade surplus in some countries
Introduction of the Euro	More liquidity, cheaper and greater levels of finance available
Abundant liquidity	No attention to liquidity risk: money is infinite and elastic
"Greenspan put"	Increased risk appetite due to limited downside
Financial innovation	More ways to manage risk but also easier ways for investors to misprice risk
Combination of the above	Decline of investor discipline and neglect of *caveat emptor* rule
Interconnectedness	Huge growth in the number and value of transactions between financial counterparties

2.3 "WHY DIDN'T ANYONE SEE THIS COMING?"

A much wider cast of characters share responsibility for the crisis: it includes domestic politicians, foreign governments, economists like me, people like you. Furthermore, what enveloped all of us was not some sort of collective hysteria or mania. Somewhat frighteningly, each one of us did what was sensible given the incentives we faced. Despite mounting evidence that things were going wrong, all of us clung to the hope that things would work out fine, for our interest lay in that outcome. Collectively, however, our actions took the world's economy to the brink of disaster, and they could do so again unless we recognize what went wrong and take the steps needed to correct it.[19]

This question, asked by many including Queen Elizabeth II at the London School of Economics in November 2008,[20] has one very clear answer: they did. But no-one paid too much attention: the warnings were not acted upon. "The threats to global financial stability that were bound to result from the build-up of severe macroeconomic financial imbalances were noticed and widely commented upon, but did not lead to any concrete policy action aimed at

---

[19] *Fault Lines*, R. Rajan, 2010.
[20] *Daily Mail*, 6 November 2008.

reducing these imbalances".[21] Perhaps the clearest indicators of tensions and risk were the excellent analyses in the April 2007 edition of the Bank of England's "Financial Stability Report" (FSR). As well as the chart referenced earlier (Figure 2.4), showing that borrowing costs were too low, the FSR gives very clear and accessible analyses that were, in aggregate, wholly supportive of the view that firm action of some sort was required. These analyses charted, amongst other items, the continuing rise in share prices, the declining risk premium demanded by investors, the increasing delinquency in American subprime home loans, the increasing indebtedness of UK corporates, and the rapid growth in the size of major international banks' balance sheets. The FSR concludes its risk assessment, observing in classic British understatement that:

> In practice, the vulnerabilities are unlikely to be exposed in isolation, since several are interdependent and a number could be triggered by common shocks. An increasingly likely stress scenario would be a sharp unwinding of low risk premia, which then triggered a pickup in corporate defaults as credit conditions tightened. The unwinding of leveraged positions in corporate credit markets could lower market liquidity, amplifying falls in asset prices. The sharp movements in some markets in late February and early March highlight the potential for a more marked adjustment in asset prices if underlying conditions were to change more fundamentally. If price falls led to a generalised retreat from risk-taking, and a rise in correlation across asset markets, the scope for diversification against such shocks would be reduced. In such a scenario, the sustainability of high revenues generated by "originate and distribute" business models could be called into question.[22]

In retrospect, the analyses are highly relevant, if not completely prescient. The FSR assumed that corporate credit defaults would be the major feature of any unwind, rather than the banking sector itself. But still, it is disappointing that such clear warnings from a leading authority had such little impact. At the time, several people observed that financial bubbles were like parties and "it is essential to take away the punchbowl when the party gets going".[23] But they all acknowledged the difficulty of such actions.

The fragility and risk of the monoline insurance industry was highlighted by Bill Ackmann at length well before the subprime collapse,[24] while clear warnings during the early stages of the over-heating of house prices internationally were well documented by such authoritative institutions as the IMF.[25]

Later chapters deal with proposals meant to ensure that early warning signals are acted upon and that risk management remains at the fore, even when confidence is at a peak.

Advocates of market-led regulation were disappointed by the fact that market indicators did not anticipate the scale of the risks that were building up in the banking industry. If we look at a diverse set of five blue-chip banks in Table 2.2, we can see how unpredictive these market measures[26] were:

---

[21] Reform of the global financial architecture: a new social contract between society and finance, Hugo Banziger, Chief Risk Officer, Deutsche Bank.

[22] Financial Stability Report, Bank of England, April 2007.

[23] Implementing the macroprudential approach to financial regulation and supervision, Claudio Borio, Head of Research and Policy Analysis, Bank for International Settlements.

[24] Is MBIA Triple A?: A Detailed Analysis of SPVs, CDOs, and Accounting and Reserving Policies at MBIA, Inc., Gotham Partners Management Co., LLC, 9 December 2002.

[25] World Economic Outlook: The Global Demographic Transition, IMF, September 2004.

[26] Bloomberg.

Table 2.2 Overview of rating, equity valuation and CDS levels of major banks between 2007 and 2013

	August 2007	August 2009	February 2013
Barclays Bank			
S&P Credit Rating	AA stable	AA– negative	A+ negative
Stock Price-to-Book Value Multiple	2.11	0.94	0.68
Credit Default Swap (5yr senior)	35	84	138
UBS			
S&P Credit Rating	AA+ stable	A+ stable	A stable
Stock Price-to-Book Value Multiple	2.50	1.51	1.29
Credit Default Swap (5yr senior)	28	102	104
Deutsche Bank			
S&P Credit Rating	AA stable	A+ stable	A+ negative
Stock Price-to-Book Value Multiple	1.36	0.84	0.65
Credit Default Swap (5yr senior)	42	94	105
Handelsbanken			
S&P Credit Rating	AA– stable	AA– stable	AA– negative
Stock Price-to-Book Value Multiple	1.79	1.45	1.56
Credit Default Swap (5yr senior)	–	75	64
Morgan Stanley Bank			
S&P Credit Rating	AA– stable	A+ negative	A negative
Stock Price-to-Book Value Multiple	1.76	1.07	0.74
Credit Default Swap (5yr senior) (USD)	82	140	139

The same information for banks that needed to be resolved in some manner or other makes for grim reading (Table 2.3).

On the eve of the onset of the financial crisis, popular perception was that banks were a safe bet and the source of perpetual growth with little downside. Their profits were seen as real and not the product of an increasing level of risk. Typical of this sentiment was an article in mid-2006 in *Fortune* magazine entitled: "Why bank stocks are cash machines: With their high yields and low P/Es, they offer the potential for solid long-term gains with little risk."[27] Quite simply, the mood was optimistic – naïvely so.

---

[27] *Fortune Magazine*, 19 May 2006.

Table 2.3 Overview of rating, equity valuation and CDS levels of selected troubled financial institutions (as of August 2007)

	August 2007
Northern Rock	
S&P Credit Rating	A+ negative
Stock Price-to-Book Value Multiple	1.46
Credit Default Swap (5yr senior)	93
Lehman Bros.	
S&P Credit Rating	AA− stable
Stock Price-to-Book Value Multiple	1.60
Credit Default Swap (5yr senior) (USD)	95
AIG Financial Products	
S&P Credit Rating	AA stable
Stock Price-to-Book Value Multiple (AIG)	1.33
Credit Default Swap (5yr senior) (USD)	66
HBOS	
S&P Credit Rating	AA− stable
Stock Price-to-Book Value Multiple	1.74
Credit Default Swap (5yr senior) (March 2008)	195
Hypo Real Estate	
S&P Credit Rating	A− watch positive
Stock Price-to-Book Value Multiple (31 Dec 2007)	1.20
Credit Default Swap (5yr senior)	–

2.4 THE BEGINNINGS OF A CRISIS

Although the tensions were building during 2006, the first ominous sign of an impending crisis was the profit warning from HSBC on 7 February 2007 (see Section 5.4). It was disturbing, to say the least, for such a major bank to be announcing such a marked deterioration in the performance of its American business. However, for most people, the start of the financial crisis was marked by the announcement by BNP Paribas, on 9 August 2007, that it was freezing valuations on some of the funds that it administered on behalf of clients:

> The complete evaporation of liquidity in certain market segments of the US securitisation market has made it impossible to value certain assets fairly regardless of their quality or credit rating. The situation is such that it is no longer possible to value fairly the underlying US ABS assets in the three above-mentioned funds. We are therefore unable to calculate a reliable net asset value ("NAV") for the funds. In order to protect the interests and ensure the equal treatment of our investors, during these exceptional times, BNP Paribas Investment Partners has decided to temporarily suspend the calculation of the net asset value as well as subscriptions/redemptions, in strict compliance with regulations.[28]

---

[28] BNP Paribas News & Press Room website, release dated 9 August 2007.

The first months of the crisis were dubbed a "subprime crisis" and the jargon word "subprime" is now well understood around the globe. Of course, it refers to the mortgages provided to people who were unable to put down a large deposit for a house and unable, by conventional metrics, to pay down the mortgage balance over time. In fact, they were only able to service the interest payments due to subsidised introductory rates and only keen to take on the debt in the first place in the hope of profiting from rising real estate prices. Many subprime loans were for properties other than the primary dwelling of the borrower: they were speculative. The word "subprime" originates in the USA and it was in the USA that the market for subprime mortgages flourished. Banks and mortgage brokers were able to originate mortgages, parcel them up into securitisation structures and sell them off into the capital markets. The ratings agencies ran their cursory analyses and assigned AAA ratings to the vast majority of the mortgage pools. As we have seen, the quest for yield had led to investor myopia – they were duped by the superlative ratings and mispriced the risk.

When house price increases cooled off, the rising levels of mortgage delinquency led to losses in the subprime world. Several small subprime specialists had gone bust in 2006, but it was the HSBC profit warning that initiated a more intense market focus on subprime exposures. Day after day, financial institutions around the world disclosed their exposure to subprime and their estimate of the losses they faced. Evidently, the problem was not confined to just the loans themselves. In addition to subprime loans which the banks had themselves extended, exposure to the problem could arise via:

- Pooled loans within securitisation bonds; for some banks, this included securitisations that they had been building up for selling on (so-called "warehouses" of loans).
- CDOs: investments that had bought bonds from different securitisation pools and wrapped them together to create a pool-of-pools.
- CDO-squareds, a kind of pool-of-pool-of-pools.
- SIVs (Special Investment Vehicles), which some banks had established to invest in long-term subprime-related assets via short-term funding: quite simply, they were used as a low-risk "carry trade" (see Glossary).
- Inventory held within trading operations.
- And for all of these, exposures that had been guaranteed by buying default insurance from a specialised financial guarantor or insurance company – the "monolines".

These new structures were not irrelevant. For example, SIVs may sound like an esoteric backwater of the banking industry, but in aggregate they were huge: total SIV assets were over $300bn. Examples of SIVs include those shown in Table 2.4.

And SIVs were specialised in holding bank paper and securitisation bonds (Table 2.5).

No-one could readily understand where the losses – which were clearly going to be enormous – would hit. The global nature of the financial markets and the complexity of the loans, which had been pooled and sliced multiple times and in myriad ways, made the question impossible to answer with any degree of certainty.

Banks started to disclose more details on their exposure profiles. Analysts and the media became familiar with the technical jargon and the pockets of subprime where losses were likely to be the greatest: which towns and cities, which year (or "vintage") of loan, which rating. But the fact that the subprime bonds were hardly being bought and sold in any volume in 2007 led to a situation where it was difficult to give a meaningful value to subprime securities

Table 2.4   Examples of SIVs making up 42% of total SIV holdings[29]

Name of the vehicle	Sponsor	Issued securities as of November 2007
Carrera Capital Finance	HSH Nordbank AG	$401m
Harrier Finance	West LB AG	$10.3bn
Kestrel Funding	West LB AG	$2.9bn
Asscher Finance Ltd	HSBC	$473m
Beta Finance Corporation	Citigroup	$16bn
Centauri Corporation	Citigroup	$16.9bn
Cheyne Finance	Cheyne Capital	$5.9bn
Cullinan Finance Ltd	HSBC Bank plc	$2.2bn
Dorada Coporation	Citigroup	$8.5bn
Five Finance Corporation	Citigroup	$10.3bn
Hudson-Thames Capital	MBIA	$495m
Links Finance Corporation	Bank of Montreal	$19.1bn
Nightingale Finance Ltd	AIG	$301m
Premier Asset Collateralised Entity	Société Générale	$4.3bn
Sedna Finance Coporation	Citigroup	$10.7bn
Tango Finance Ltd	Rabobank	$7.8bn
Victoria Finance Ltd	Ceres Capital Partners	$987m
Whistlejacket Capital	Standard Chartered	$4.9bn
White Pine Corporation Ltd	Standard Chartered	$4.3bn
Zela Finance Corporation	Citigroup	$2.5bn

Table 2.5   Breakdown of SIVs assets[30]

Financial	42.6%
RMBS	23.2%
CDO	11.4%
CMBS	6.1%
Credit card	5.0%
Student Loan	4.4%
Auto loan	1.1%
ABS	2.2%
Other	3.3%

---

[29] Moody's takes rating action on certain Structured Investment Vehicles following its latest review of the sector, November 2007.
[30] SIVs: An Oasis of Calm in the Subprime Maelstrom, Moody's, July 2007.

with a face value of trillions of dollars. The uncertainty itself became a source of risk that spread rapidly into the market through two major channels:

- Firstly and most obviously, it raised fears about the creditworthiness of the most exposed banks who might be facing the most severe losses.
- Secondly and less apparently, it increased the need for banks to have high quality assets to satisfy collateral posting obligations, in the case of derivatives and repos. Where the assets of banks had declined in value and quality, their derivatives counterparties required them not only to top up the amount of collateral but also to improve its quality: increasingly, subprime bonds were not acceptable as collateral for such arrangements.

2.5 THE CRISIS INTENSIFIES

The crisis intensified because of increasing fears about solvency, a continuing ebb of confidence away from all market participants and the drying up of liquidity across most dimensions. Systemic crises will tend to have these features: they are brought about by the interplay of solvency, confidence and liquidity.

Banks that enjoy high levels of *solvency* should be the ones that are able to meet their obligations and hence maintain stable operations – depositors and investors should have confidence in them and continue to trust them with their funds, ensuring liquidity and the availability of funds when and where they are needed. When markets are benign, confidence is strong and liquidity is ample: even banks pursuing high-risk strategies have little trouble attracting funds. Of course, the flipside of this is also true. As soon as confidence evaporates, for whatever reason, investors' fears can become a self-fulfilling prophecy, as funding dries up and the viability of the bank is placed in doubt.

The second half of 2007 witnessed a slow degradation of the confidence in the banking system. It became clear not only that subprime mortgage bonds were showing signs of significant deterioration but also that these bonds were held in major volume by banks. But which ones? Some capital markets banks had tens of billions of dollars worth of subprime bonds in various parts of their businesses and, unsurprisingly, confidence in these institutions started to take a hit. But it was by no means clear which banks were ultimately at risk, for subprime bonds had been distributed worldwide and packaged, repackaged and traded. Investors fretted about where the problems lay and how the crisis might unfold.

Market fears were for the solvency of the banks in question, yet they manifested themselves in a liquidity crunch, caused by the withdrawal of funding in the securitisation markets and term funding markets. Banks that were reliant upon securitisation markets (Northern Rock is an example, see Section 5.11) faced real challenges making payments to their customers as they fell due and were forced to sell some of their (not infinite) liquid asset buffers. Banks that could not obtain long-term funding took short-term funding, but this made the term structure of their balance sheets ever more fragile and increased the stress on the daily task of fund-raising from the market to stay operational. Credit Default Swap (CDS) is a proxy often used to measure the changes in credit risk perception by the market: the average CDS of 14 major international banks increased from 50bp to 300bp at the peak of the crisis – see Figure 2.5.

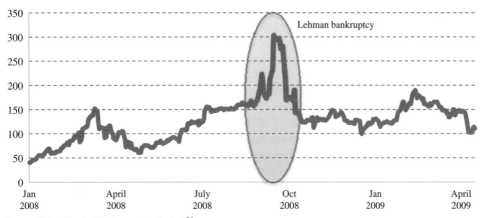

Figure 2.5   Bank CDS spreads (in bp)[31]

Famous names became victims. For example, Bear Stearns had built up massive subprime-related exposures in several areas of its business. It became increasingly clear to market participants that it would have difficulties facing its obligations. In early 2008, Bear Stearns was bailed out via a rescue package involving JP Morgan, which bought the firm, and the New York Federal Reserve, which provided a $30bn loan to enable the firm to avoid meltdown and the catastrophe of contagious market turmoil. At around the same time, AIG also came under threat when the level of risk in its balance sheet started to become apparent and counterparties started to demand collateral to be posted against their exposures.

The subprime crisis was seen as a resolvable crisis that would have episodic not systemic ramifications. Indeed, in the middle of 2008, a mild sense of optimism prevailed. The fundamental belief in the robustness of banks remained intact, based as it was on the faith that firstly, banks are low credit risk compared to corporates and secondly, banks have practically infinite and elastic access to cheap liquidity through the financial markets. This faith was tested to destruction by the default of Lehman in September 2008.

2.6 MELTDOWN: THE LEHMAN BANKRUPTCY

> "Smart risk management is never putting yourself in a position where you can't live to fight another day", says Mr Fuld.[32]

Lehman's bankruptcy was a turning point in the financial crisis for the whole banking industry, as it revealed the systemic impact of the bankruptcy of a large bank. Since Lehman, no other major bank has been allowed to go bankrupt.

---

[31] BIS.

[32] Fuld of experience: By learning from past mistakes, Dick Fuld has brought Lehman Brothers back from the brink, *The Economist*, 24 April 2008.

The days and weeks that followed the collapse of Lehman were uncharted territory for most market participants. At times, there was a sense of panic, at other times it was one of despondency. For the first time in a long time, people feared for the survival of the global economic system.

Is this an exaggeration? No. "The US financial system is finding the tectonic plates underneath its foundation are shifting like they have never shifted before. It's a new financial world on the verge of a complete reorganisation," noted Peter Kenny from Knight Equity Markets,[33] while Bill Gross, the highly respected Chief Investment Officer of PIMCO, compared the panic that was seizing dealers who were having to unwind their positions to an "imminent tsunami".[34] Around that time, Alan Greenspan, the former Chair of the US Federal Reserve, horrified by the fragility of the financial system and the risk of a systemic collapse, observed: "There's no question that this is in the process of outstripping anything I've seen and it still is not resolved and it still has a way to go."[35]

As banks attempted to rein in their exposures to other banks, there was a freeze in the interbanking market. Banks were simply unwilling to lend to each other. For years, banks had lent to each other at a rate that was essentially the same as the central bank's policy rate. In mid-September 2008, that arrangement broke down. The rate at which banks were prepared to lend to each other (represented by LIBOR) rose to as much as 350bp (3.5%) above the central bank's policy rate (represented by the "Overnight Index Swap" or OIS). Such a spike showed the extent of distrust in the banking industry towards other banks, as demonstrated by the graph in Figure 2.6.

A huge drop in market liquidity threatened to lead to forced selling of assets to meet payments and a subsequent downward spiral in the value of financial assets, which would put the solvency of all banks at risk. International trade, which relies on an efficient banking system, could have ground to a halt, with a major impact on global economic activity. The economic shock to the system could have been similar to events that unfolded in the Soviet Union when it collapsed. The shock to the world economy could have been of the order of 20% or so in a short timeframe – at those levels, social unrest is not out of the question.

Lehman's demise was followed by multiple bank failures, raising the threat of systemic crisis and destroying confidence even further:

- AIG had to be rescued by the Federal Reserve on 16 September 2008.
- Merrill Lynch had to be rescued by Bank of America during the same weekend that Lehman filed for bankruptcy.
- HBOS was purchased by Lloyds TSB on 18 September.
- Washington Mutual was purchased by JP Morgan on 26 September.
- In Belgium, Fortis was nationalised on 28 September, while the Franco-Belgian bank Dexia had to be recapitalised on 30 September.
- Bradford & Bingley in the UK was nationalised, with its branches and deposit business being sold to Santander, on 28 September.

---

[33] Bloody Sunday: Wall Street Is Hit by Financial Tsunami, CNBC.com, 14 September 2008.

[34] *The Guardian*, 15 September 2008.

[35] Greenspan to Stephanopoulos: This is "By Far" the Worst Economic Crisis He's Seen in His Career, ABC News, 14 September 2008.

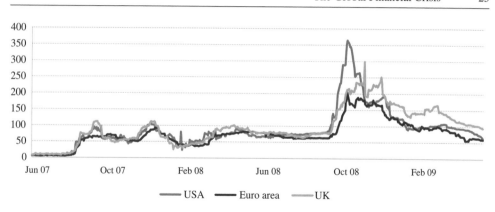

Figure 2.6   LIBOR-OIS spread (in bp)[36]

- Wachovia was bought by Wells Fargo on 3 October.
- Kaupthing, Glitnir and Landsbanki in Iceland had to be nationalised at the beginning of October 2008.

September and October 2008 were dark days in the banking industry and the world economy. Banks dominated the headlines of the TV news every night and few commentators were able to propose a fix.

2.7 MASSIVE INTERVENTION INTERNATIONALLY

Sensing the nature and scale of the danger, governments across the world responded with measures to keep the banking system alive.

Liquidity Support

Countries like the UK, France, Germany and Ireland put in place state guarantees to restore confidence in bank lending. Banks would issue under their own name but the investor would benefit from an unconditional guarantee from the home state. "Government Guaranteed Bonds" (GGBs) soon became a new asset class, bringing liquidity back to banks' funding profiles and restoring banks' ability to transform risk and access liquidity – Figure 2.7.

Central banks across all major economies (including the USA, Australia, Brazil, Canada, Switzerland, the Eurozone, the UK, Hong Kong, Japan, Korea) also played a crucial role by performing the role of "lender of last resort" and offering repo facilities to refinance illiquid assets in the balance sheet of banks. In the Eurozone, the ECB monetary operations, originally organised as a tender for a predefined amount of liquidity and for a limited period, soon turned into an unlimited offer of liquidity at a fixed rate and for a period extending up to one year. The Special Lending Scheme (SLS) in the UK allowed British banks to obtain funding. Coordination among central banks also allowed access to foreign currency funding, vital for the global dollar-denominated business of European banks.

---

[36] BIS Annual Report 2009.

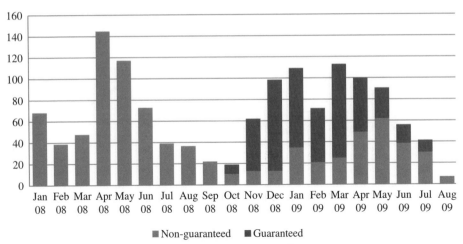

Figure 2.7   Issuance volumes of bonds by banks (global, $bn)[37]

The level of liquidity pumped into the economy between 2008 and 2009 was unprecedented. The balance sheet of the US Federal Reserve doubled in size.[38] ECB lending to banks also doubled, from €400bn on average before the crisis to more than €800bn (see Figure 2.8).

Solvency Support

As well as keeping money flowing, in many countries, governments put in place solvency support mechanisms to ease the fear of meltdown. As losses materialised, many struggling banks

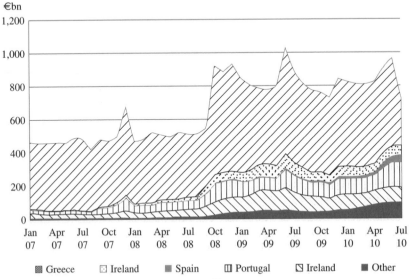

Figure 2.8   ECB lending to Eurozone banks (€bn)[39]

---

[37] IMF, Dealogic.
[38] US Federal Reserve.
[39] Annual Report 2010, IMF.

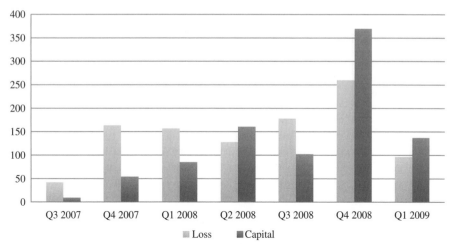

Figure 2.9   Bank losses and capital injections ($bn)[40]

were recapitalised by the state – see Figure 2.9. The aggregate value of these recapitalisations amounted to hundreds of billions of dollars.

In some cases, the state was forced to "sanitise" troubled banks by taking problematic assets from them or underwriting the value of such assets at a low level. The lessons of prior crises (in Sweden, for example, in the early 1990s) led some governments to set up separate "bad banks" for the problematic assets. This underwriting provided a valuable backstop to market fears, restoring some degree of confidence to the banks' balance sheet – see Table 2.6.

As the Lehman episode illustrates, state support is often seen as a preferable solution to bankruptcy. Authorities are working on better alternatives to state support (see Section 4.6 on resolution regimes, for example), but such alternatives were not available at the outset of the current crisis. In 2007, banks did not have high levels of capital or liquidity reserves; there were no "living wills" or resolution plans.

These actions, the magnitude of the commitment and the high level of coordination around the world soon produced dramatic effects: the financial system, though still fragile, recovered from its fears of meltdown. In the second half of 2009, confidence slowly returned, aided by some significant measures by the authorities to improve the strength and resilience of the banking industry. In particular, new "stress tests" and an industry-wide increase in capital level requirements amounted to a public declaration on the strength of banks.

The Stress Tests
Market fears about the strength of banks were based upon the fact that the accounting and regulatory numbers no longer meant anything: they did not quantify the ability to withstand a further deterioration in the economic situation. Everyone knew that the losses in the banks' portfolios could be greater than their capital reserves, but it was not possible to assess this using the information available. To meet this need, regulators required banks to run their financials through a scenario of deteriorating conditions and report on what their capital levels were likely to be.

---

[40] BIS Annual Report 2009.

Table 2.6   "Bad bank" and solvency backstop mechanisms (examples)

Country	Mechanism	Description
Ireland	NAMA (National Asset Management Agency)	NAMA was set up in December 2009 to cleanse the Irish banks of problem loans to property developers. Technically a private sector company (to keep the finances off the state's balance sheet), NAMA bought loans with a face value of €74bn from the Irish banks at an assessed "market value". In practice, this meant a discount of 58% from the nominal value. The loss on sale caused a severe solvency deficit at the Irish banks, but improved their clarity of purpose and removed uncertainties around their viability. NAMA is actively working on the resolution of problem loans and has generated in excess of €10bn since inception.[41]
Switzerland	StabFund	UBS was burdened with around $60bn worth of investments in subprime bonds and similar. At the end of 2008, the StabFund was set up so that UBS "caps future potential losses from these assets, secures their long-term funding, reduces its risk-weighted assets, and materially de-risks and reduces its balance sheet". The assets were transferred at independently appraised market prices as of 30 September 2008.
		The equity in the StabFund is at a level of around 10% and the rest of the financing is a loan from the Swiss National Bank. UBS issued convertible bonds to the Swiss Federation in order to finance the equity contribution and maintains an option to buy back the equity at a preferential price, should the assets perform well.[42] The value of this upside to UBS shareholders was $2.3bn at the end of 2012.[43]
United Kingdom	APS (Asset Protection Scheme)	In order to improve the viability of RBS, the UK government set up the APS to provide insurance on losses above a certain level on a varied portfolio of troubled loans. The insured portfolio had a nominal value of £282bn and RBS was left with the exposure to first losses up to £60bn, with the APS providing 90% insurance cover for losses beyond that and RBS retaining the exposure for 10% of losses (to keep RBS focused on minimising losses). The scheme terminated in late 2012. In total, RBS paid about £2.5bn for the insurance cover and, since losses were well within the "first loss" layer, the government did not have to pay out anything.[44]

---

[41] NAMA website (www.nama.ie).

[42] UBS further materially de-risks balance sheet through transaction with Swiss National Bank, UBS website, 16 October 2008.

[43] UBS Fourth Quarter Report 2012.

[44] RBS exits UK Government's Asset Protection Scheme, The Royal Bank of Scotland Group plc, 17 October 2012.

Country	Mechanism	Description
Netherlands	Illiquid assets back-up facility	ING had amassed a portfolio of €28bn worth of US subprime mortgage bonds, the potential risk of which was causing problems for the group. "Market prices for these securities have become depressed as liquidity dried up, which had an impact on ING's results and equity far in excess of reasonably expected credit losses."[45] It agreed an "Illiquid Assets Back-up Facility" with the Dutch state covering 80% of the exposure, in return for a fee. The assumed value of the bonds was a discount of 10% of the par value, which was quite generous, since the bonds were trading at discounts of around 35% at the time.[46] ING remained the legal owner of 100% of the securities and exposed to 20% of any results on the portfolio.
Belgium	Asset Protection Plan	KBC had invested €20bn in CDOs, most of which were guaranteed by the troubled monoline credit insurer MBIA. These positions were causing a lot of problems for KBC and they wanted to remove the uncertainty. The asset protection plan provided by the Belgian state was in three layers. The first layer of loss (€3.2bn) was all for KBC; the second layer (€2bn) was also down to KBC but with the state agreeing to buy KBC shares to cover 90% of the value of the loss; the third layer (€14.8bn) comprised coverage of 90% of credit losses by the state.[47]
Spain	SAREB	*"La Sociedad de Gestión de Activos procedentes de la Reestructuración Bancaria"* (Sareb) was set up in late 2012 to purchase troubled real estate loans from several Spanish banks. Its assets are set to rise from the initial €45bn to as much as €90bn. In most respects, it is similar to the Irish NAMA, though the transfer value of assets is curiously being described as "the real economic value of the assets", which presumably means at a premium to open market price levels. Despite this generosity, Sareb is promising 15% annual return on equity to its private sector investors.[48]
USA	TARP	Following the collapse of Lehman Brothers, the US Treasury created the Troubled Asset Relief Programme (TARP) as an exit strategy for financial institutions holding subprime assets. The fund is under the responsibility of the US Treasury and has a capacity of $700bn of which $415bn was utilised at the end of April 2013.[49] Assets are purchased against warrants from the seller and can be sold by the TARP to create capacity for more purchases. TARP has also been used to recapitalise banks directly through the Capital Purchase Programme.

---

[45] ING update on results and measures to reduce risk and costs, ING Group, 26 January 2009.

[46] NautaDutilh advises on innovative ING – Dutch State deal Illiquid assets back-up facility may lead the way, NautaDutilh, April 2009.

[47] Overview of capital-strengthening measures agreed with the Belgian State and the Flemish Region, KBC, 6 August 2009.

[48] Restructuring and Recapitalisation of the Banking Sector: the Asset Management Company (Sareb), FROB, 29 October 2012.

[49] TARP monthly report to US Congress, April 2013.

The Federal Reserve, alongside the other US regulators (the FDIC and the OCC) conducted a "Supervisory Capital Assessment Program" (SCAP) on 19 American banks and released the results on 7 May 2009. The positioning of the results was meant to boost confidence in the banking sector:

> These examinations were not tests of solvency; we knew already that all these institutions meet regulatory capital standards. Rather, the assessment program was a forward-looking, "what-if" exercise intended to help supervisors gauge the extent of the additional capital buffer necessary to keep these institutions strongly capitalized and lending, even if the economy performs worse than expected between now and the end of next year. The results released today should provide considerable comfort to investors and the public. The examiners found that nearly all the banks that were evaluated have enough Tier 1 capital.[50]

In fact, the SCAP found that the banks needed to increase their capital by $75bn in aggregate, including $34bn for Bank of America.[51] A series of capital increases ensued, mostly from the US government's TARP programme (described above).

A few weeks later, the EBA stress test of 2009 found that all was well with Europe's banks. Under a scenario that was worse than the central base case, European banks would lose €400bn, yet still maintain strong capital ratios: "the aggregate Tier 1 ratio for the banks in the sample would remain above 8% and no bank would see its Tier 1 ratio falling under 6% as a result of the adverse scenario."[52] Such a result was of little use. The markets knew that banks were vulnerable and wanted to see those vulnerabilities addressed. A clean bill of health did not assuage fears about European banks. Future stress test exercises in Europe would become a little more demanding.

The comforting message of the 2009 stress tests was intended to calm markets. In the US, this objective may have been met, with the aid of government capital injections, but the European stress tests were seen as a joke. The market was expecting a better elucidation of the weaknesses of the banks, not an excuse. Market observers reacted badly, pouring scorn and predicting a "Japanese-style future for Western banks, in which a thinly capitalised system staggers along, insisting on its rude health, while the state follows holding crutches an inch beneath its armpits. If that is the answer, then the stress tests were asking the wrong question."[53]

Basel III Proposal

A week before Christmas 2009, the Basel Committee released its response to the financial crisis, the proposals that were to become known as Basel III.[54] The markets warmed to the proposals, which were seen to require significant capital-raising and improvements in funding and liquidity structures. Over the coming weeks and months, analysts studied and interpreted the proposed rules, identifying those banks who would need to raise fresh equity in order to comply with the new, stronger standards. The efficacy of Basel III is discussed in Section 4.5, though of course a long-awaited set of proposals in the regulatory framework did nothing to avert the immediate crisis.

---

[50] Statement regarding the Supervisory Capital Assessment Program, Statement by Chairman Ben S. Bernanke, Federal Reserve, 7 May 2009.

[51] The Supervisory Capital Assessment Program: Overview of Results, Federal Reserve, 7 May 2009.

[52] CEBS's Press Release on the Results of the EU-Wide Stress Testing Exercise, EBA, 1 October 2009.

[53] Hospital pass, *The Economist*, 14 May 2009.

[54] Consultative proposals to strengthen the resilience of the banking sector announced by the Basel Committee, 17 December 2009.

2.8 SOVEREIGN CRISES

The subprime crisis caused the solvency of banks to be called into question. Confidence and liquidity dried up. The bankruptcy of a major international bank threw the entire banking system into disarray and panic. Government support measures brought much-needed stability and confidence back to the system and averted a disastrous meltdown. However, the "post-Lehman" period also carried a hangover.

It brought an abrupt end to the financial boom that some countries had been experiencing, as debt-fuelled investment and construction programmes slowed down. In most countries, house prices corrected sharply. Consumer and corporate confidence evaporated, causing domestic consumption and investment to shrink as discretionary spend was curtailed. People in all walks of life adopted a new-found – and, occasionally, rather fashionable – sense of austerity.

In a nutshell, there was a weakening in overall economic growth and a stretching of the finances of some governments that had been forced to bail out their domestic banking sector.

The attention of economists turned to the financial viability of governments and the capital markets started to fear the creditworthiness of the most distressed, whose borrowing needs were increasing. In general terms, there were two types of problems. Governments were forced to borrow more, primarily to bail out their banking industry. And the financial crisis brought into the foreground the issues of public sector profligacy, over-indebtedness and structural problems in the real economy. The fear of sovereign default – practically unheard of in developed economies in modern times – intensified. According to Eurostat, the overall impact of government support to the financial sector in Europe represented 5.2% of European GDP in 2012.[55]

The macro-economic statistics tell an ugly story. The current financial crisis has damaged the creditworthiness of many countries, pushing them massively into deficit and forcing them to add vast amounts of debt to their existing government borrowings. More disturbingly, economic growth has been knocked off-trend, resulting in a huge output loss of around a quarter of annual GDP or more (see Table 2.7). On an individual level, for many, there has been a permanent loss of wealth, security and happiness.

The health of the economy is key for healthy banks and so is the health of the government, for banks and their governments are heavily intertwined.

Banks play a key role in the national economy and are regulated by a government agency. If banking gets into trouble, the country can suffer and the state's financial position can be significantly weakened. On the other hand, banks pay income taxes and employ people: they are direct contributors to the economy and the public budget. In some countries, the financial services industry is a major sector of the economy.

Banks are also major buyers of the sovereign debt of their home country, or at least they traditionally have been. The concept of lending to the government is an odd one and most of the time, banks treat their "sovereign" entity as risk-free. After all, most governments have the ability to print money to repay their debts and the cost of sovereign borrowing is commonly used in finance as proxy for the "risk-free" rate as opposed to market return in models such as the CAPM. The natural asset for a bank to invest its liquidity portfolio may appear to be a risk-free government bond: indeed, liquidity regulation gives incentives for banks to hold sovereign debt as a liquidity buffer.

---

[55] Support for financial institutions increases government deficits in 2012, 2013, Eurostat.

Table 2.7 Selected macro-economic indicators

Country	S&P credit rating (April 2013)	2007 budget deficit[56]	2012 budget deficit[57]	2012 debt-to-GDP ratio[58] (%)	3-year output loss (as % trend GDP)[59]	Banking assets to GDP % (2012)[60]
USA	AA+ neg	−2.9%	−7.6%	107	31	90
UK	AAA neg	−2.7%	−7.7%	89	25	463
France	AA+ neg	−2.7%	−4.5%	90	23	420
Germany	AAA	−0.2%	+0.1%	83	11	326
Italy	BBB+ neg	−1.5%	−2.9%	126	32	257
Spain	BBB− neg	−1.9%	−7.4%	91	39	339
Greece	B−	−3.9%	−7.6%	170	na	220
Ireland	BBB+	+0.2%	−8.5%	118	106	839
Portugal	BB	−2.7%	−6.1%	119	37	300
Switzerland	AAA	+1.3%	+0.3%	47	0	469
Australia	AAA	+1.8%	−0.8%	27	na	202
Canada	AAA	+1.6%	−3.8%	88	na	336
Japan	AA− neg	−2.5%	−9.1%	237	na	196

The formidable convergence of sovereign yields following the creation of the Euro has hidden some fundamentally different economic realities in Greece, Portugal, Spain and Italy on the one hand and Germany on the other. As Figure 2.10 suggests, the widening that started in 2009 may have been interpreted as a sign of tension in the Eurozone, but looking at the situation in 1999, it appears more like a correction. The financial crisis and slower growth that ensued have put pressure on sovereign credit and the notion of a "risk-free" rate definitely counts as another victim of this crisis.

There is, however, no reason for banks to invest specifically in their own home country, they simply need liquid assets in their operating currency. The Euro creates a specific situation, in that the individual sovereigns are − for the time being at least − not mutually guaranteed and there is a discernible difference between the credit risk of different countries. Banks in Greece chose to buy Greek government bonds rather than lower-yielding German government bonds because it appeared profitable to do so. Nor is there a need for them to buy long-term government bonds as liquidity assets rather than short-term bonds or even cash. Again, banks that choose to buy longer-term instruments are generally seeking to increase their profitability and reduce the "drag" of holding low-yield assets in their liquidity portfolios.

---

[56] Comparing Public Spending and Priorities Across OECD Countries, Center for American Progress, October 2009.
[57] *World Factbook 2012*, CIA.
[58] World Economic Outlook Database 2013, IMF.
[59] IMF.
[60] Sources: EBF, RBA, FSB, SNB.

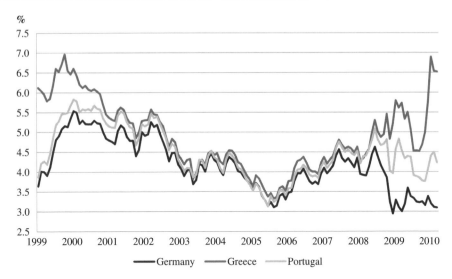

Figure 2.10   Relative Eurozone yields [61]

At any rate, for the countries currently under an IMF programme, it was the banks in Ireland that caused major problems for the sovereign (needing capital injections equivalent to 41% of GDP[62]), while in Greece and Portugal, it was the other way round: public sector weakness led to significant direct losses for the banks (€26bn for Greek banks during the recent sovereign debt restructurings[63] and €4bn for Portuguese banks as a "sovereign capital buffer" under the EU Capital Exercise of 2011[64]). Later on in this book, we consider ways to reduce the linkage between sovereign and banks by removing the costs of bank bail-outs from the government's responsibility and removing the need for banks to invest in the debt of their sovereign at all.

Sovereign weakness in the Eurozone has led to speculation that certain countries will be forced to leave the currency union. Corporations and consumers have gradually transferred large amounts of their money across borders within the Eurozone. This deposit flight, which has yet to develop into a full-blown run, along with the collective interest in keeping the Eurozone together, has resulted in the European Commission and the heads of governments moving forward with the project of a full Banking Union, structured around a European guarantee mechanism of deposits and European regulation of banks. This strategy seems an appropriate response for Europe, as the existence of a single currency makes no sense without other ancillary unions. It is patently a "double or quits" approach to a troubled situation: more Europe is the only way to save the Euro. We note the strange logic of a currency causing a political situation rather than supporting it: this seems odd to a dispassionate observer, if not to a European. The political solution of "more Europe" may not be appealing to all members of

---

[61] BNP Paribas.

[62] Ireland's report card, Department of Finance, October 2012.

[63] PSI costs domestic lenders dearly, ekathimerini.com, 20 April 2012.

[64] EU Capital Exercise – Final results, EBA, 8 December 2011.

the European Union. In any case, it may be too late to build a proper banking union, as macro events may overtake the initiative. The situation with Cyprus' currency controls, for example, shows us that the principles of currency union are precarious and open to compromise.

2.9 AFTERSHOCKS AND SKELETONS IN THE CUPBOARD

There is an insightful saying, widely attributed to the American investor, Warren Buffett: "It's only when the tide goes out that you learn who's been swimming naked." For the banking industry, this wisdom has meant that it has taken a violent financial crisis to flush out scandals and behaviours that are shocking and disturbing in the extreme. Though they are not directly related to the financial crisis, they are still symptoms of failures in risk management.

Recent examples include those shown in Table 2.8. Many examples of misconduct are in the UK, partly due to high levels of disclosure there: this does not imply the absence of problems elsewhere.

Table 2.8   Selected examples of recent scandals affecting banks reputation

Currency manipulation	In the middle of 2013, it emerged that regulators in Zurich, Hong Kong, Brussels and London were investigating the possibility that benchmark currency rates had been manipulated. Investigations are ongoing.
The LIBOR scandal	Several leading wholesale banks were found to have manipulated their reporting of the industry-standard interest rate, used to define the interest payable on millions of customer contracts. This was either to avoid owning up to the true cost of funding during the depths of the crisis (i.e. under-reporting) or to attempt to manipulate LIBOR to make trading gains (i.e. mis-reporting). The investigations have uncovered incriminatory call recordings and e-mail conversations and severe management lapses. Major fines have been issued and several prominent management teams (e.g. Barclays' CEO and COO) have been replaced.
Derivatives losses at Monte dei Paschi da Siena	In February 2013, the oldest bank in the world, Monte dei Paschi di Siena, reported an unexpected loss of €730m[65] in some structured transactions that it had undertaken to boost earnings. Reporting on the story, Bloomberg commented that it showed "how investment banks devised opaque products that years later are leaving companies and taxpayers with losses. From the Greek government to the Italian town of Cassino, borrowers have lost money on bets that were skewed in banks' favor."[66]
Mis-selling of derivative products to small businesses (UK)	The UK FSA is currently investigating instances where small businesses were provided with interest rate derivatives without the appropriate process being followed, resulting in a financial loss to the customer. "FSA found that over 90% of the sales of Interest Rate Hedging Products (IRHPs) to 'non-sophisticated' customers did not comply with one or more of our regulatory requirements."[67] In some cases, small businesses were pressured into contracts such as inverse floaters, where the interest rate on the loan falls when policy rates rise and rises when policy rates fall: these customers were left with unaffordably high rates on their loans when policy interest rates plummeted in 2008.

---

[65] Monte dei Paschi di Siena investor relations website, 7 February 2013.
[66] Deutsche Bank Derivative Helped Monte Paschi Mask Losses, Bloomberg, 17 January 2013.
[67] Interest Rate Hedging Products, Pilot Findings, FSA, January 2013.

Mis-selling of Payment Protection Insurance (PPI) to retail customers (UK)	During the last decade or so, UK retail banks got into the habit of pressuring retail customers who were taking out a loan into simultaneously taking out an insurance policy to cover the loan repayments in case of the borrower getting sick, becoming unemployed and other reasons. For many borrowers, this was a bad product, expensive and ineffective. For the banks, it appeared immensely profitable, with a profit margin of about 80–90% of the product cost: payouts on the policies were rare and low. Banks are now being forced to recompense customers and some £14bn[68] in redress provisions have already been taken, half of which is accounted for by Lloyds Banking Group[69] "Even as we have got used to the iniquity of the banks, the latest revelations still take the breath away. The scale of the payment protection insurance (PPI) misselling scandal is truly gigantic. [...] The banks sold 20 million PPI policies by 2006, and between 2001–10 amassed colossal sales of £34bn, equivalent to a quarter of the entire UK GDP [sic]."[70]
Losses at JP Morgan's "Chief Investment Office" unit	In early 2012, some derivatives trading positions in a specialised unit at JP Morgan went wrong and lost the bank $5.8bn. The "CIO" unit was positioned as a natural hedge to the core business of JP Morgan. But "flawed trading strategies, lapses in oversight, deficiencies in risk management"[71] led to the exposures getting out of control. (See Section 5.8.)
Trading fraud: Kweku Adoboli at UBS	In September 2011, UBS announced that it had lost $2.3bn as a result of unauthorised trading conducted by Kweku Adoboli, a London-based trader in UBS' synthetic equities team in London. The authorities concluded that the "rogue trader" fraud was not stopped because of of failures by UBS to adequately supervise the business and poor risk management processes. (See Section 5.10.)
Contravention of sanctions and money-laundering abuses	A set of serious compliance breaches has recently come to light involving major international banks in their US operations. These breaches have related to failures to follow the correct procedures for dealing with customers, intended to reduce the risk of money-laundering and breaking of American sanctions against certain countries (e.g. Iran, Libya, Burma, Sudan). The banks involved were HSBC (see Section 5.4) and Standard Chartered.
FSA mystery shopping exercise	Again in the UK, the FSA has recently published the disappointing results of its "mystery shopper" exercise. "The FSA found that only three-quarters of customers received good advice and had concerns with the quality of advice in the other quarter."[72] Clearly, an industry where one-quarter of clients are receiving bad advice is worrying.

Evidently, there have been many scandals, damaging both financially and reputationally. The ones above are mere highlights. It may be coincidence that these transgressions are coming to light at the present moment. But, more likely, it is because the banking industry suffered

---

[68] Price bar lowered for Lloyds resale, *Financial Times*, 1 March 2013.

[69] Annual Report and Accounts 2012, Lloyds Banking Group.

[70] LIBOR isn't half of it, Michael Meacher MP for Oldham West and Royton, 29 October 2012.

[71] Report of JP Morgan Chase & Co. Management Task Force Regarding 2012 CIO Losses, 16 January 2013.

[72] Assessing the quality of investment advice in the retail banking sector: A mystery shopping review, FSA, February 2013.

severe and systemic lapses of risk management during the bubble years preceding the current financial crisis. The environment will have contributed to bad behaviour, since undoubtedly "fiddles are more remunerative and easier to conceal during an asset bubble".[73] There are almost certainly many more shocking episodes to unfold as the industry continues to find "skeletons in the cupboard". Hopefully, these revelations and episodes have highlighted crucial areas for improvement and positive change will result.

2.10 WHO IS TO BLAME?

The chief punishment is this: that no guilty man is acquitted in his own judgement.[74]

The current financial crisis has had a major negative impact on the wealth and wellbeing of the global economy. Millions of people have had their lives transformed and tens of millions more have had their personal financial situation damaged. Quantified impact estimates relay the hard economic facts: in the European Union, for example:

> Public intervention cost taxpayers substantial sums of money and even put some Member States' public finances at risk. Between October 2008 and October 2011, the Commission approved €4.5 trillion (equivalent to 37% of EU GDP) in state aid measures to financial institutions, of which €1.6 trillion (equivalent to 13% of EU GDP) was used in 2008–2010. Guarantees and liquidity measures account for €1.2 trillion, or roughly 9.8% of EU GDP. The remainder went towards recapitalisation and impaired assets measures amounting to €409 billion (3.3% of EU GDP). Budgetary commitments and expenditure on this scale are not sustainable from a fiscal point of view, and impose a heavy burden on present and future generations. Moreover, the crisis, which started in the financial sector, pushed the EU economy into a severe recession, with the EU's GDP contracting by 4.2%, or €0.7 trillion, in 2009.[75]

Beyond the data, the impact is quite clear: the experience of a financial crisis is unpleasant, unfair and unacceptable.

Blame the Bankers

It would be convenient to find a single cause for the crisis, identify the appropriate remedies and thus resolve the problem. The popular media has tended to follow this approach and has fostered the view that there are specific parties to blame and that it is through their actions exclusively that the financial crisis was brought about. Naturally, since this is a financial crisis more than anything, there has been a desire to blame the banking industry – and bankers in particular – for the problems.

The specific aspect of banking that seems to draw popular ire is the asymmetry of gains and losses. This has been expressed several times as either "heads I win, tails you lose" or, to put it in more technical terms, "the privatisation of gains and the socialisation of losses". This perceived asymmetry of risk and reward is not a new aspect of banking: in

---

[73] An eternal chancer critiques RBS failures, Jonathan Guthrie, FT Lombard, 6 February 2013.
[74] *Satires*, Juvenal, c 100 AD.
[75] Staff Working Document 167, European Commission, 6 June 2012.

1837, the President of the United States reportedly expressed his anger at such a situation: "Gentlemen, I have had men watching you for a long time and I am convinced that you have used the funds of the bank to speculate in the breadstuffs of the country. When you won, you divided the profits amongst you, and when you lost, you charged it to the bank. You tell me that if I take the deposits from the bank and annul its charter, I shall ruin ten thousand families. That may be true, gentlemen, but that is your sin! Should I let you go on, you will ruin fifty thousand families, and that would be my sin! You are a den of vipers and thieves."[76]

The perception of intense unfairness is reinforced when people see how much bankers are paid, in good times and in bad. Mega-bonuses are paid to senior bankers who are supposed to be superstars, yet are often exposed as unethical and incompetent. Bankers are highly paid and have not been seen to suffer unduly as a result of the crisis. They continue to collect bonuses, hardly any previous bonuses have been "clawed back" and scandals based on egregious behaviours continue to emerge. The banking industry seems rotten: "From excessive levels of compensation, to shoddy treatment of customers, to a deceitful manipulation of one of the most important interest rates, and now this morning to news of yet another misselling scandal, we can see that we need a real change in the culture of the industry."[77]

Deeper Structural Issues

However, it would be wrong to assume that bankers' culture alone brought about a financial crisis of this proportion. This crisis may have reached its boiling point in the boardrooms and trading floors of banks around the world, but it has its roots in other, fundamental aspects of our economic and financial system:

- Major, structural imbalances in our global economy, savings patterns and trade flows.
- Excessive belief by all parties in the stability and sustainability of a loosely regulated, free-market system.
- Political inability to nip an asset bubble in the bud and rein in borrowing; indeed, the promotion of popular yet unsustainable policies based on increasing levels of governmental and personal indebtedness.
- Major failings in risk management at banks, including an over-reliance on statistical techniques and insufficient challenge of assumptions; in a word, over-confidence.
- Regulatory and supervisory failings on the part of several of the world's leading financial authorities.
- A crisis of governance in many of the world's leading banks, with unclear accountability for ruinous strategies and management processes.
- Ineffective shareholder governance and accountability of regulatory and supervisory authorities (or to put it dramatically, a crisis of capitalism and democracy).
- Difficulties in understanding how markets set asset prices: the recent decision to award the Nobel prize to Eugene Fama, Lars Peter Hansen and Robert Shiller highlights not only the importance of their contribution but also the remaining challenges.

---

[76] Attributed to Andrew Jackson, President of the United States.
[77] Financial Stability Report Press Conference Transcript, Bank of England, 29 June 2012.

Limiting the analysis of this crisis to the behavioural issues of bankers may satisfy a psycho-logical need for retribution and give the public at large the confirmation that they are innocent bystanders, but this will miss the point. Our ability to prevent further crises happening in the future will depend on our ability to understand clearly what brought us to the predicament in which we find ourselves. Hating bankers may have become a global sport, but it does not solve the structural issues in our economy and banking system: "The wide appeal of scapegoating banking is motivated by a sense of incomprehension towards the workings of the world. In contrast to previous times, there is a relative dearth of accounts that provide a convincing structural explanation for the global economic upheaval. In such circumstances the wider structural imbalances that have afflicted the different spheres of economic life are difficult to discern. That is one reason why the fantasy that Wall Street and greedy bankers have brought down an otherwise robust economy is so widely upheld."[78]

---

[78] Hating bankers a global sport, *The Australian*, 8 February 2012.

3

Methodologies and Foundations

This chapter is meant to set out some of the *very basic* ways of thinking about the key arguments in banking risk management. We have not attempted to give a full description of all the subjects, as this would require thousands of the technical underpinnings to be reiterated. Instead, we have set out the most important elements and described the bits where – in our experience of working with senior bank executives, regulators and industry observers – there is merit in going over the basics once more. We just don't think that people have a good enough grounding in the basics of risk, capital, liquidity, derivatives and accounting to be able to have a meaningful debate on how better to regulate and manage the modern banking industry.

To illustrate this view, here are some stylised statements we might hear from people whose views matter (this includes regulators, supervisors, customers, managers and bankers):

"Banks made lots of money in 2005 and lost a lot in 2008."

"When the accountants became sterner, the bank became insolvent."

"Hybrid capital doesn't absorb losses."

"It's amazing that XYZ bank went bust with such a good Basel ratio."

"We had a low-risk strategy, taking customers' deposits and investing them in AAA-rated bonds. It's not our fault that we went bust."

"If the regulators, ratings agencies and stock analysts couldn't spot it, then what can we do?"

We hear these types of statements all the time and it leads us to the view that the industry is not well enough informed on basic matters. This brief chapter serves as a humble – and, we hope, useful – contribution to bridging the understanding gap.

3.1 HOW DO BANKS MAKE OR LOSE MONEY?

In order to support a broad understanding of the banking industry and a constructive debate on how best to improve it, a recap on the ways that commercial banks make money is instructive. And, given recent experience, it is also worthwhile bearing in mind the ways in which banks can *lose* money too, causing pain to their owners and, should they fail, to their customers and to society.

A bank operates as both a service provider and a financial intermediary. As a service provider, it undertakes certain administrative activities (asset management, payments transmission and the like) for a fee. This aspect of their business can go wrong and cause problems, as customers know all too well from episodes where the ATM network shuts down.

However, most of the problems in the current financial crisis have been caused by the risks that banks took in their intermediation role. By borrowing funds from their depositors and creditors, then investing or lending those funds, banks run the risk that their investments or loans will turn sour and the bank will be unable to repay its own commitments. Any inability to repay can cause bank failure. If the value of the investments or loans falls below the value of the bank's borrowings, then the bank is *insolvent*; if the bank's creditors lose faith in the bank's ability to repay, they may withdraw their funds and the bank may fail due to *lack of liquidity*. So a bank's financial condition depends upon maintaining a position where the value of its loans and investments exceeds the value of the funds it has itself borrowed and ensuring that it can make repayments on its borrowed funds on a timely basis, to maintain confidence.

A solvent and liquid bank that has the confidence of its customers, creditors and regulators can then operate as a commercial concern and seek to make a commercial return for its owners. The business of banking – in fact, the credit intermediation role – is a business of *risk transformation*. Banks are able to make a commercial return from risk intermediation because they:

- Are *uniquely* able to gather deposits from the population, by dint of their regulated status.
- Can *generally* borrow from more cheaply than their customers are able to (though this is not always the case).
- Build such a large, granular and diversified portfolio of loans that the losses from customer defaults become predictable.
- Possess the underwriting capabilities for managing credit and risk in general.
- Can fund themselves from short-term sources, such as demand deposits, while lending on long maturities, such as 25-year mortgages. Their financial maturity profile is imbalanced and they are said to be undertaking "maturity transformation".
- Act as market-makers and/or brokers in the capital markets, with the ability to make a commission on customer trades.
- Trade in the capital markets to exploit market inefficiencies or even put their own capital to work in taking positions ("proprietary trading").

When banks' activities are recorded in the accounts, we can see the revenues and costs of their operations:

- Interest income (from loans and other interest-bearing assets).
- Interest expense (on deposits and market funding sources).
- Net interest income (the difference between the two items above).
- Fee income (from activities where the bank is a service provider).
- Trading income (from customer trades, market-making and proprietary trading).
- Operating expenses (staff, equipment and third-party expenses).
- Operating income (the net sum of the income and expense items above).
- Cost of bad and doubtful debt (provisions and write-offs, for cases where customers are unable to repay their loans or the investments have somehow turned sour).
- Pretax profit (operating income after bad debt).
- Tax.
- Net income or profit-after-tax.

Banks try to grow their revenues, while keeping costs and write-offs down. But it's a tricky balancing act, as revenue growth tends to be accompanied by risks of losses. The case studies in Chapter 5 give some good examples of situations where the push for revenue led to some banks taking excessive risk and ultimately making ruinous losses.

Table 3.1   Reported profit before tax of Anglo-Irish Bank[1]

Year	Profit before tax (€m)
2002	261
2003	347
2004	504
2005	615
2006	850
2007	1,243
2008	784
2009 (nationalised 21 January 2009)	−12,829
2010	−17,619
2011	−873

Risk does not feature in a bank's official accounts. In the income statement, we can see the impact of higher interest expense, provisions and write-offs, which are all the consequences of risk-taking. But there can be a lag of several years between risk being taken, revenues being generated and losses flowing through. So when the accounts indicate that a bank is making good levels of profit, it does not mean that it is growing the value of its owners' investment. In fact, it does not mean much at all. Banks can appear to be making money when in fact they are destroying value, making their owners and stakeholders poorer.

In a word, the accounting conventions do not measure value creation. In order to illustrate this, consider the reported accounting profits of Anglo-Irish Bank shown in Table 3.1.

As profits were peaking in 2007, Anglo-Irish's market value soared to some €12bn. Investors were lured by the high and increasing reported profits being generated by the bank, but did not appreciate the vast risks that the bank was running, so vast that the subsequent losses totalled more than €30bn. We now know that Anglo-Irish Bank was reporting accounting profits by taking huge amounts of risk. Anglo-Irish did not merely have bad years in 2009 and 2010: it had bad years in 2006, 2007 and 2008, only the accounts did not show that. If we had a measure of "risk-adjusted profit" and an ability to represent the risk being taken, it would clearly have been negative, as illustrated above.

The key thing, therefore, is for banks to measure their profits once a margin for risk has been taken into account. Not just *realised* risk that leads to losses today, but *unrealised* risk that leads to potential losses in the future. Some banks have developed "economic capital" methodologies (see Section 3.5.3) that attempt to show such risk-adjusted profitability. They do not use regulatory capital measures, which are a poor proxy for risk and do not capture accurately all the risks that a bank runs. The economic capital is meant to reflect management's view of risk and how it sees its profitability in terms of return-on-economic-capital or ROEC. In general terms, a bank with a higher ROEC is getting a better return-on-risk through being more efficient, more effective or more diversified. Analysts can also look at the profit generated by a bank, once it has met its cost-of-capital. In other words, the economic capital absorbed by the business in order to be creditworthy is "rented" at

---

[1] Anglo-Irish Bank Annual Report and Accounts.

Table 3.2   BBVA economic profit[2]

€m	2008	2009	2010
Profit (A)	1,779	4,789	1,743
Average economic risk capital (ERC) (B)	19,614	22,078	24,322
Risk-adjusted return on economic capital (RAROC) = (A)/(B)	9.1%	21.7%	7.2%
ERC × cost-of-capital (C)	2,053	2,476	2,981
Economic profit (EP) = (A) – (C)	(275)	2,313	(1,238)

the cost-of-capital and the surplus profit generated over and above the cost-of-capital is the value-added of the business or "economic profit" (EP). In theory, an economic profit of zero means that shareholders are getting the returns they require for the risks that are being run and no more; positive EP means that shareholders are getting more than they demand and are thus pleased with their investment; negative EP means that shareholders would rather disinvest in the business.

This concept is illustrated by looking at the economic profit analysis calculated by BBVA (see Table 3.2).

In this example, all three years were profitable on an accounting basis, but only 2009 was a good year for shareholders. Interestingly, 2010 looked similar to 2008 in terms of accounting profits, but due to the extra risk being taken by the business and the additional capital required to take that risk (about a quarter more), the charge for risk capital was nearly €1bn more and the economic profit nearly €1bn worse.

The risk-adjusted, economic profit of a large number of banks from around the world has been studied in a survey by Boston Consulting Group, with the consultants calculating that "the banks in our study generated a cumulative €295billion of economic profit from 2006 through 2010".[3]

The components of this shareholder value destruction are as shown in Table 3.3.

Clearly, for banks, getting risk and capital management right is the main driver of performance, since funding, provisions and capital charges make up 69% of revenues in aggregate. Note that in 2010 the cost of funding – driven by governments pumping cheap liquidity into the banking system – has dropped to only 30% of revenue, whilst the capital charge has risen to 25% of revenues. The economics of banking have shifted.

The important point is that, although banks can often appear highly profitable on a non-risk-adjusted basis, they often fail to meet their cost-of-capital.

Unfortunately, risk-adjusted methodologies are complex and subjective and so they are not widely employed or utilised. The stock market, for example, focuses on accounting metrics, such as earnings and net book value. Whereas we know that risk is a crucial consideration in measuring the success of a bank, few stock analysts pay sufficient attention to it. Their recommendations on which banks to buy and sell are based on an assessment of earnings power, rather than an in-depth, risk-based appraisal. In the last few years, the recapitalisation needs of banks have proven to be a major driver of poor share price performance as bank shareholders

---

[2] BBVA Annual Report 2010.
[3] Facing New Realities in Global Banking: Risk Report 2011, ©2011, The Boston Consulting Group, December 2011.

Table 3.3 Economic profit analysis of large banks

€bn	Income	Refinancing costs	Operating costs	Loan loss provisions	Capital charges	Economic profit
2006	2,039	973	606	67	207	186
2007	2,365	1,241	666	100	251	107
2008	2,243	1,203	708	232	308	−208
2009	2,073	724	773	369	423	−216
2010	2,016	632	805	242	501	−164
Total	10,736	4,773	3,558	1,010	1,690	−295
As % of income	100	44	33	9	16	−3

have seen the value of their investments diluted. The stock market was forced to find crude ways of estimating the risk levels and capital needs of banks. Now that banks appear by and large recapitalised, bank earnings can once more be seen as the source of dividends or growth and hence treated as "capital cash flows". Analysts are refining their earnings models and building valuations based on discounted dividend cash flows and/or assumed multiples on accounting book values. Once again, risk as a concept for stock valuation is receding from the fore. Most of the assumptions to get the discount rate and the multiples are very crude, barely capable of showing any insight into the risk profile of the bank in question at all.

Despite their losses on bank stocks over the last five years, investors are focusing once more on accounting metrics and neglecting risk assessments. This is disturbing. In order to understand exactly why, the following sections look at the key concepts of accounting and risk.

3.2 WHAT'S A BANK WORTH?
KEY ISSUES IN ACCOUNTING FOR BANKS

> Nowadays people know the price of everything and the value of nothing.[4]

When we consider the financial condition of a bank, the natural place to start is with its accounts. These are based on accounting conventions and give the basic financial information, from which an assessment of the bank's ability to honour its commitments and generate a commercial return for its shareholders can begin. But they do not give us much information on the risks that a bank is running or its ability to absorb the impact of any losses that result from those risks. So while it might be true that "clear, transparent and comprehensive accounting standards are indispensable preconditions for managers, investors and supervisors to be able to understand the actual risks to which a bank is subject",[5] it would be wrong to assume that today's accounting standards give us sufficient information to understand the risks of a bank.

---

[4] *The Picture of Dorian Gray*, Oscar Wilde.
[5] High-level expert group on reforming the structure of the EU banking sector, Erikki Liikanen, October 2012.

The basic objective of accounting is to provide clear and reliable information to various parties (including management, investors, tax authorities and regulators) to enable them to make business decisions. For a bank, like any other corporation, this information consists of a balance sheet at a given date and an income and cash flow statement over a given period.

But banks' accounts have specific features that are materially different to those of industrial corporations in many important ways.

- For a start, they are more highly leveraged, with debt-to-equity ratios of 20:1 or higher, versus 2:1 or lower for a typical industrial corporation.
- Secondly, a bank's core business is the transformation of money on a large-scale basis, so cash flow statements are less informative than for industrial corporates.
- Thirdly, the main driver of bank failure tends to be the deterioration in the value of its financial assets relative to its financial liabilities; corporates, on the other hand, tend to fail due to deterioration in profitability. To be fair, for both banks and corporates, these fundamental problems tend to lead to actual failure via cash flow problems.
- Fourthly, as noted in the previous section, the source of profit in a bank is largely risk-taking activity, the scale of which tends not to be recognised in the accounts. A major "cost" is invisible. The income statement (sometimes called the "Profit and Loss account" or P&L) is of limited importance.
- Lastly, the major difference is that banks are regulated and trusted transmission agents and depositories for the money supply: they trade on confidence and can fail if confidence evaporates. People want to place their money in an institution that will be able to pay it back to them. It must be solvent, meaning that it has assets worth more than its liabilities, and liquid, with the means at hand to pay deposits back when required.

Given these specifics of the banking sector, the most important aspect of accounting for banks is the balance sheet. The balance sheet gives an estimation of the net assets or capital of the bank, which is a key source of solvency, resilience, confidence, viability and commercial value. However, one of the most difficult issues in drawing up a bank's balance sheet is the basis on which to value financial assets and liabilities.

In essence, this comes down to a decision on whether to adopt an "historic cost" or a "fair value" basis and, if the latter, then how to determine fair value. This is no trivial matter and is one that continues to cause problems for all interested parties – in part because there is, in all probability, no way that is demonstrably "correct". The arguments in this debate are neatly summarised by Erkki Liikanen:

> Mark-to-market requirements in existing accounting rules can be a source of pro-cyclicality due to volatility in financial institutions' profitability and capital adequacy. Such issues are heightened in periods of limited market liquidity and depressed market prices. Particular challenges are also caused by the use of models-based estimates of market values, when market prices are not available. However, marking-to-market allows early detection of problems and transparent valuation of a firm's balance sheet. Historical cost accounting can lead to financial problems remaining undetected for a long period of time and can thus also cause lack of market confidence in a particular firm or entire sector of financial institutions.[6]

---

[6] High-level expert group on reforming the structure of the EU banking sector, Erikki Liikanen, October 2012.

Under old-fashioned "Generally Accepted Accounting Principles" (or GAAPs), banks used to report their financials almost exclusively on an historic cost basis. Loans were held at their full principal value until they happened to default on payments; securities and investments were held at the price paid for them until they were sold, at a profit or a loss.

Today, modern accounting standards – and particularly the International Financial Reporting Standards or IFRSs – attempt to place a fair or market value on securities and investments that are being held with a view to selling them in the near future. If the assets are traded on deep, liquid markets (such as major stock exchanges), then this poses few practical problems. But if there are few observable price inputs, then the estimation of a market or fair value is not straightforward. Either way, there are some philosophical challenges to market valuation, especially if the market pricing is perceived to be irrational or volatile. The spot price at any given time might not be the true value for a bank who is holding for a longer time period and is not therefore a "forced seller". A bank's management might think, for example, "Why should I write down the value of my bond portfolio just because everyone else is selling to meet their fund redemptions?" or "Why should I mark my entire equity holding at the price of the last stock exchange transaction? I could never transact my entire holding at that price, there would never be the capacity." Mark-to-market accounting based on "fair valuations" gives a liquidation value in today's market, which might be wholly unrealistic. On the other hand, holding an asset at its historic cost is merely a record of history: it gives no sound indication of the realisable value of that asset, merely what was paid for it.

Generally, securities and investments are only a minor part of banks' balance sheets. By far the greatest component of their assets is the loan book. Loan books are still accounted for using the historic cost accounting method. Quite simply, a loan is booked in the bank's accounts at the value of the principal outstanding, assuming it is performing and not delinquent. Accounting regimes do not require the bank to show in its accounts the riskiness of the borrowers and so the loan assets appear at their original "par" value. Nor do the accounts adjust for loans made at interest rates that are well above or below the prevailing rate. Let us be clear on what this means for the accounts of the bank. So long as the borrower doesn't miss a payment, the loan is held at the amount outstanding, no matter how risky the borrower is, no matter how the market views that borrower and no matter what rate the loan bears. Quite simply, the carrying value of a loan in the accounts need not bear any relation to its economic value at any point in time.

Of course, as maturity approaches, the true value of the loan should tend towards the amount outstanding, but in many cases it does not. This matters in situations where the borrower is unable to repay or refinance elsewhere when the loan matures. If the bank calls a default, it is likely to incur losses, depending on the value of security or collateral: this tends to be undesirable. So what we see is banks using the massive capacity for forbearance built in to the accounting standards: they can "extend and pretend", rolling the loan over for a further period, in the hope that the borrower's situation improves and the latent losses evaporate.

This mismatch between true value and accounting value is at the root of several issues in banking: why bank stocks can trade well below book value, why banks are often slow to deal with problem loans, why seemingly solvent banks go spectacularly bust.

Of course, there are strict policies to dictate how loan write-offs are accounted and how the financial reserves or "provisions" that precede the actual write-off need to be shown. But provisions are only made where there is clear evidence that a loss is likely to occur: even in a

Table 3.4   Arguments for and against a fair value approach to accounting

In favour of fair value approach	Against fair value approach
• Encourages early corrective action • Encourages risk transfer and diversification • Lower chance of "surprises", such as the "provisions cliff" • Better information reduces market uncertainty	• FV generates artificial income volatility • Loans are "lend and hold" and so spot valuations are irrelevant • Banks' role is to smooth intertemporal shocks • Fair valuation is unreliable and lacks comparability

poorly performing bank with a large number of risky loans, most loans will still be unlikely to default and more likely to perform and repay.

Is there scope to consider a "fair value" approach to the loan book, or indeed a comprehensive fair valuation of the bank's balance sheet? The debate rages in accounting circles, and the main arguments appear to be as shown in Table 3.4.[7]

As can be seen, there is no clear resolution of the issue. But recent experiences (for example, the loan book carrying values of Greek government bonds and Spanish real estate developer loans) have shown us that there can be major distrust in the traditional approach. Market analysts have been forced to estimate realistic values for assets being carried at unrealistic values. This uncertainty has increased distrust and reduced confidence in banks' solvency, hampering the workings of the banking system in some instances. Is this preferable to putting fair value information in the hands of investors and allowing them to make their own judgements?

The arguments against information volatility assume that volatility would be harmful. For example, we hear arguments about the subprime crisis that "the root of this crisis is bad mortgage loans, but probably 70% of the real crisis that we face today is caused by mark-to-market accounting in an illiquid market".[8] But the other side of the argument is more convincing: better information has to give a better outcome. Sophisticated markets can handle the truth.

> Increased volatility in accounting magnitudes is not necessarily a problem if investors correctly interpret the information disclosed [...] mature financial markets would be in a position to appropriately interpret this increased volatility.[9]

Adding to the tension between valuation approaches of balance sheet assets is the need to consider off-balance sheet assets and also the liability side of the balance sheet. At present, future profit streams or franchise value are barely recognized as assets of a bank, yet these are significant items of value, not just in a theoretical sense but also on a concrete disposal value basis. On the liability side, the introduction of fair valuation has introduced major confusion, even ridicule, as banks show major accounting profits when their market credit spreads increase, thus reducing the fair value of their own debt and producing an accounting profit and an increase in net worth, i.e. accounting equity.

---

[7] Based on arguments in Fair Value Accounting and Financial Stability, European Central Bank, April 2004.
[8] Mark-to-Market Mayhem, Brian S. Wesbury and Robert Stein, First Trust Advisors, 25 September 2008.
[9] Fair Value Accounting and Financial Stability, European Central Bank, April 2004.

Table 3.5 Fair value of own debt for
Société Générale

Period	€m
Q1 2010	102
Q2 2010	254
Q3 2010	−88
Q4 2010	160
Q1 2011	−362
Q2 2011	16
Q3 2011	822
Q4 2011	700
Q1 2012	−181
Q2 2012	206
Q3 2012	−594
Q4 2012	−686

To illustrate this last point, consider the revenues that appear in Société Générale's income statement[10] due to the fair valuation of own-debt instruments (see Table 3.5).

These numbers are substantial: for example, in Q3 2011, Société Générale reported net income of €691m which included the effects of an accounting "gain" of €822m on its own debt. This aspect of fair valuation is confusing. It is also overridden by all regulators and analysts who are trying to distil a meaningful and "realistic" view of a bank's solvency from the accounts. That said, the fair value of these liabilities can be considered "real" if the debt is being charged a lower-than-market rate or if the bank is able to buy it back from investors at a discount.

What is clear is that, should we move to a different (i.e. more "fair value") accounting approach for banks, the meaning of the accounting numbers will change. We may need to re-appraise the relevance of the net assets calculation, accept and tolerate greater volatility and develop more sophisticated views on the financial position of banks. For example, there may be scope for adopting so-called "confidence accounting", whereby a range of values is considered, bearing in mind uncertainty and differing perspectives (see Section 7.1.1).

In the world of accounting, national standards are converging into a set of international standards, the International Accounting Standards (IAS) or International Financial Reporting Standards (IFRS). These are already adopted in most major, international banks, with the notable exception of the USA, which retains usage of its national standard, US GAAP, controlled by the Financial Accounting Standards Board or FASB. Despite attempts at convergence, there are myriad differences between the two regimes.

---

[10] Société Générale investor relations website.

However, the most important and relevant differences between IAS/IFRS and US GAAP are as follows:

- Positions that are presented on a net basis under US GAAP but gross under IAS/IFRS (primarily derivatives subject to master netting agreements, repurchase and reverse repurchase agreements and pending settlement balances).
- Rules for consolidation of entities.
- How certain items appear in the income statement (e.g. loan origination costs, pension expenses, currency translation adjustments, share-based compensation).

The presentation of repo and derivatives businesses is the most important difference, since it needs to be understood in order to make comparisons between IFRS-reporters and GAAP-reporters for measures such as the leverage ratio, banking assets-to-GDP or return-on-assets. Sadly, many commentators still make comparisons between banks that use different accounting standards and fail to adjust for the differences; they sometimes subsequently draw the wrong conclusions.

Within IFRS, the most important change in the pipeline is IFRS 9. This is a change in the way in which banks account for their losses. Instead of the current, backward-looking, "incurred loss" approach, IFRS will use a forward-looking "expected loss" (EL) model – similar in many ways to the Basel notion of expected loss (see Sections 3.3 and 4.4.6). Such changes are controversial, raising a number of practical issues, for example:

- How to calculate EL? Basel models haven't been reliable.
- Why one-year EL not lifetime?
- Does the current standard not allow forward provisioning?

IFRS 9 is meant to be more meaningful and helpful to risk managers and investors:

> The International Accounting Standards Board (IASB) and Financial Accounting Standards Board (FASB) have been invited to reconsider the incurred loss model in order to recognise and measure loan losses that incorporate a broader range of available credit information. This would clearly narrow the gap with expected loss calculations, which incorporate past information that can be much richer than in the current, narrow, incurred loss approach.[11]

However, some see it as superfluous. Accounting information should not seek to measure or manage forward risk, since other means exist for this aim:

> The problems that led to the crisis did not lie in the accounting standards. Banks assumed boom and bust had gone, so they did not retain sufficient capital. They gave it all away in dividends, buybacks and pay. They were down to 2 per cent equity compared with total assets. The financial statements reflected this: were the regulators sound asleep? Banks mispriced risk and then did not see how bad the problem was. Balance sheets have to be strong enough to accommodate potential losses. [...] So you do not need prudence in the sense of nebulous conservative accounting to ensure that banks have sufficient capital to weather the bad times. But you do need that quality on bank boards and among the "prudential" regulators, and transparent, neutral accounts for the investor.[12]

---

[11] Minimising the impact of future financial crises: six key elements of regulatory reform we have to get right, Jaime Caruana, General Manager, Bank for International Settlements.
[12] Report the Reality, Sir David Tweedie, *Financial World*, March 2013.

The fact that the accounting balance sheet is not a strong guide to true economic value gives rise to the need for market participants – notably regulators, ratings agencies and market analysts – to make adjustments to the reported accounting numbers. Almost everyone removes accounting goodwill (the asset created when something is bought for a price above its accounting "value") and intangible assets (such as software) from the net asset calculation, focusing instead on tangible net assets. Other key adjustments include deduction of "fake" equity, such as own shares, and the accounting "gains" derived from the fair valuation of own debt instruments, described above. One does often wonder why these items appear in the accounts in the first place, if they are universally overridden by the people who actually use the numbers for practical purposes.

Accounting standards give us a comparable method of looking at banks' financial position, but they do not portray the likely economic or risk-adjusted value of the bank. Worse, in stressed situations, the net assets of the bank can be vastly different on an economic or realised basis than on an accounting basis. Yet still, investors remain focused on the accounting numbers. This drives companies, including banks, to conduct transactions to improve reported financial metrics, say boosting accounting equity or profitability, or reducing the volatility of accounting numbers. For example, banks can seek to switch assets between the trading book (fair valued) and the banking book (not fair valued). Such transactions frequently have little or no economic basis. The Proteum transaction, described in Section 5.9 in the case study on Barclays, is an example of a large and controversial transaction designed to have significant accounting benefits.

In conclusion, it seems that when assessing the quality, value and creditworthiness of a bank, the accounts of a bank are a good place to start but a highly unsatisfactory place to stop. The accounting valuation of each asset – and indeed of each liability – is debatable. The regulator or investor who is attempting to look at the financial strength of the bank using the accounting net assets as a point of departure is faced with a huge problem. Despite this, the frameworks used by regulators and investors assume that accounting numbers are somehow meaningful and suitably reliable.

3.3 WHAT IS RISK?

> Fortune is a fickle courtesan.[13]

Risk is the potential for bad things to happen unexpectedly and risk management is the art of dealing with that potential. In theory, risk is also the potential for good things to happen, but the word is generally applied to the *downside* rather than the *upside*. So, we often hear statements like "There is a risk I will get a pay cut next year" and rarely statements like "There is a risk I will get a pay rise next year".

Banks are in the business of taking and managing risk. Risk is at the heart of banks' business, of banking regulation and, ultimately, of banking crises. Clearly, the concept of risk merits some fundamental consideration.

---

[13] Napoleon on the eve of Borodino.

Table 3.6   The main types of risk in banking

Type of risk	Bank loses money if:
Credit risk	The borrower fails to repay their loan
Collateral risk	The collateral or security pledged against a loan proves insufficient to cover the repayment of the loan
Interest rate risk	The interest rate payable on deposits or other sources of the bank's funds rises to more than the rate being charged on the bank's loans
Currency risk	Exchange rates move, in such a way that the bank's liabilities grow in value more than the banks assets
Investment risk	Investments that the bank has made (e.g. in a marketing campaign) do not produce the necessary payback
Trading risk	The bank's holdings of trading assets decrease in value
Operational risk	Something goes wrong in the bank's business operations, due to fraud, systems errors, bad management practices or even plain old industrial accidents such as fire
Liquidity risk	The bank is unable to repay its depositors and investors on a timely basis
Funding risk	The bank's cost of funds rises more than the income generated on its assets

Society needs risk-takers. All forms of human activity carry risk – there is no such thing as "risk-free". If society shunned risk, there would be no investment and no exploration; it's hard to see how there could even be any consumption. Next year's crop wouldn't be planted because of the risk of bad weather or low grain prices. No-one would ever cross the road. In fact, the pillars of modern society would crumble. Is it too dramatic to point out that the human race would end, due to lack of desire to accept the risks of childbirth? On the other hand, we know only too well the consequences of taking too much risk: asset bubbles, financial crises and, ultimately, economic stagnation.

So, as the providers of risk capital for the real economy, banks need to take risk and "manage" it so that it is not ruinous in either extreme. Getting it wrong would damage not only the owners of and investors in the bank, but society as a whole.

Some of the main types of risk taken by a bank takes include those listed in Table 3.6.

Since banks take these risks, they need to manage them. In effect, a bank is a business that has the people and the infrastructure to manage risk. Specifically, this means banks can:

- measure risk;
- price risk (based on expected outcomes but also taking into account surprises);
- decide which risks to take (and which to avoid);
- monitor risk;
- mitigate risk; and …
- ultimately, absorb the losses that are the inevitable by-product of a risk-taking enterprise.

A few basic concepts help to illustrate this topic and allow an understanding of the key concepts in risk management for banks.

The first step in risk management is a *probability assessment*. Banks need to find ways to estimate the chances of losses at the level of an individual customer loan and also at a portfolio level. To do this, they collect historic data and trawl it for explanatory variables. For example, a bank may find that on average each year, 5% of its loans default at a cost to the bank, once collateral is taken into account, of 3% of the loan balances. Therefore, the cost-of-risk is seen to be 3% pa. In theory, customers need to be charged 3% pa for the bank's cost-of-risk to be covered. On further analysis, the bank finds that the default rate is mostly due to customers in the west of its region of operations, owing to tougher economic conditions in the west. The cost-of-risk is 4% pa in the west and only 2% in the east. It only seems right to price the loans in the west at a more expensive rate than those in the east. As the bank gets better and better at using the information that it collects and holds, the probability calculation gets better and better too. The bank will have developed the ability to calculate the average cost-of-risk for different types of borrowers.

This average cost-of-risk is also known as the "*expected loss*". But some years will be worse than average and some will be better. If the expected loss is 3% pa, it's quite feasible that one year, the cost-of-risk will be 4% or 5%. It could be 10%: we don't know and all we have is the historic time series of actual outcomes in previous years. These losses in excess of expected loss are known as "*unexpected loss*".

The next step is very important. Banks attempt to estimate the size of the unexpected loss. They do this in three steps.

1. *Data Mapping*: The bank maps all historic losses to understand the distribution of actual losses and how they vary around the average – the result of this is called a "*loss curve*". The picture in Figure 3.1 shows how this might look for a made-up example: in this case, for example, the block on its own shows that the bank has had a bad loss experience in 2008, losing between 6% and 7% of the value of its loan book, as against only 3–4% in 2007.

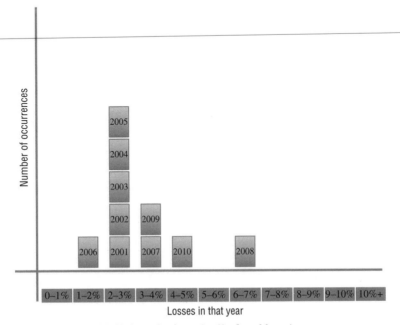

Figure 3.1   Losses in Bank ABC's loans business (as % of total loans)

2. *Loss Curve Formula*: The losses are unlikely to be completely random. Nor will there be an equal frequency of losses at various levels. In fact, most years will see losses that are close to average. The number of years when the losses are significantly worse than average will be few and far between. The bank knows the median average or *expected loss* (in this case, 2–3% is the expected loss) and the way in which the actual losses tend to distribute around the median (in this case, a statistical measure of volatility – or "standard deviation" of 1.42%). The risk profile of the business has been measured. See Figure 3.2.

3. *Using the Loss Curve to Model Risk*: Now that the formula for the loss curve is "known", the bank can effectively assume that unexpected loss is "known". Not all of the loss levels need to have occurred in the data set. The curve can be interpolated to fill gaps and extrapolated to extend its reach. It can interpolate and extrapolate from the known examples to give an estimate of the unknown. To use the immortal words of Donald Rumsfeld, the size of potential losses has become a "known unknown". Each point on the loss curve has a probability and a value: the bank has modelled risk and has derived the statistical probability of losses at various given levels. See Figure 3.3.

Section 4.4.6 deals with the notions of "expected loss" and "unexpected loss" in more detail, in particular as regards their treatment under the Basel regulatory regimes, for this statistical approach is baked into the Basel frameworks.

The statistical tools used in the steps above are not excessively complicated. Modern IT systems can calculate loss curves with ease, allowing banks to crunch the data millions of times to try to find *predictive variables* that will help them improve their understanding of risk and make better risk management decisions.

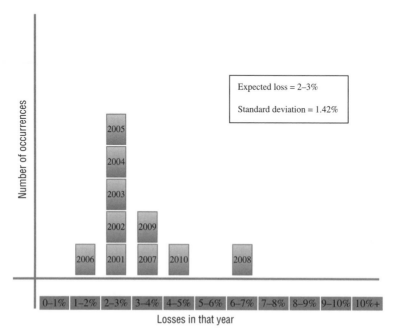

Figure 3.2   Quantifying the risk profile of the business

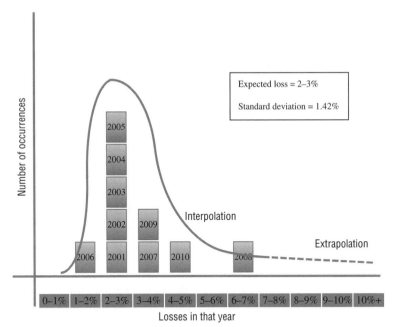

Figure 3.3   Interpolation and extrapolation of data

Using the loss curve as a tool, risk modellers can quantify the probability of losing a certain amount of money in a given year. In fact, the way this is represented is the probability of losing less than that amount and is termed a *"confidence level"* around unexpected loss. So, a bank might say: "Our expected loss is $4m and our unexpected loss at a 99.5% confidence level is $7m." What this means is that the bank's calculations indicate that the average year will see losses of $4m but one year in 200, losses could reach $11m.

The same approach is used for other types of risk – trading risk, operational risk and so on. The most common trading risk methodology is the "Value at Risk" or "VaR" method. This was pioneered by JP Morgan in the 1990s and widely applied by the banking industry. Historic outcomes are used to derive loss curves that are then used to assess remote scenarios using an assumed distribution. As we have learned in the last five years, risk modelling of this sort has its limitations.

In August 2007, the Goldman Sachs CFO David Viniar famously noted that "we are seeing things that were 25-standard deviation moves, several days in a row".[14]

Apparently, the probability of Goldman Sachs' trading losses is about the same as winning the UK Lottery (odds of about 1 in 2,500,000) not just once or twice but 21 times in a row.[15] Put another way, one would only expect to see such variances once in a period of time that is much, much longer than the entire history of the universe. The probability is mind-numbingly low. One can safely assume that the models and the methodologies were wrong.

The last five years have shown us that we have not tamed risk. Indeed, we can't even adequately measure it.

---

[14] *Financial Times*, 13 August 2007.
[15] How Unlucky is 25-Sigma?, Kevin Dowd, John Cotter, Chris Humphrey and Margaret Woods, 24 March 2008.

Part of the problem is the human mind. Humans have trouble contemplating probabilities that are outside our normal experience base, either very high or very low. We can sometimes assume that highly probable events will definitely happen and highly improbable events will never happen. In real life, however, highly improbable events happen all the time. There are so many things that are highly improbable that one or other of them is bound to happen. We just don't know which.

Improbable events happen all the time. Let's take an illustration.

We all know that it is improbable for two people to share the same birthday. Similarly, on the face of it, it might seem surprising if, in a school class of 30 kids, there were two who shared a birthday. In fact, it's 70% likely. The reason is that we are assessing the probability of *any* of the kids having a birthday matching *any* of the others – not a particular date. If it were one given date, then the probabilities are lower: the chances of another kid in my class of 30 sharing *my* birthday is low – it's 29-in-365 or about 9%. What does this have to do with risk in the banking system? It simply illustrates that unlikely events do happen, potentially more frequently than we realise.

This illustration is based on a situation where we understand the probabilities quite well. There are 365 days in the year and a roughly equal likelihood of a person being born on each of them (let's ignore 29 February and the prevalence of induced births prior to Christmas Day). But for some situations, the probabilities are so small they are virtually unmeasurable; or, there simply isn't any reliable track record. Will this plane crash? Will this oil rig blow up? Still others could be viewed as "unknown unknowns". Will this start-up investment make me money? Will the space shuttle successfully complete its mission? Will I make it home on time? Probability statistics don't help us much in these considerations, or at least they are hugely unreliable. We are sailing towards the edge of our understanding, away from the "known unknowns" and towards the "terra incognita" at the edge of the map.

This concept has been usefully explored by Nassim Nicholas Taleb, most notably in his book "*The Black Swan*".[16] Taleb's main thrust is that we cannot rely upon probabilities and the known world; we have to live in a world in which improbable events occur. His motif is the black swans that European explorers found in Australia when they arrived in the eighteenth century. Until that point, the definition of a swan would have been a particular type of white bird; the notion that swans could be black would have been seen as preposterous. Our minds assume that we have seen all possible permutations and we try to construct a world-view based on that data, whereas in fact we should remain open-minded to alternative outcomes and ready to deal with whatever situation develops.

In the banking industry, much of the science of risk management is based on deterministic logic. It is not common for banks to incorporate the potential for "Black Swans" into their risk processes. For example, the risk models used by most banks are based on tidy statistical distributions (such as the so-called Gaussian curve), which tempt the management of the bank – and regulators and investors too – to think that risk can be determined from the historic data sets. The risk management thinking proceeds along the lines of:

- We have data.
- The data shows patterns and distributions.
- We can calculate an average, expected loss for the business.

---

[16] *The Black Swan: The Impact of the Highly Improbable*, Nassim Nicholas Taleb, 2008.

- We can run a stress test to improve resilience in extreme situations.
- AAA ratings or sovereign debt can be seen as practically risk-free.
- We know – from our formula – how much capital is needed for a given bank.
- History proves the assumptions; counter-arguments are proved wrong.

As you can see, the logic breaks down at a certain point, but the risk management approaches can drift into an assumption that risk has been defined and tamed. Of course, along with the conquest of risk comes a confidence that leads to the proclamation of the end to boom and bust and also to sloppiness, as important details are overlooked (for example, in the subprime crisis, ratings agencies and investors did not take into account the deteriorating underwriting standards in the years 2006 and 2007). Confidence is procyclical, with the absence of losses tending to indicate the absence of risk. Indeed, "financial risk models are least reliable when they are needed the most. Because they are conditional on the sample used in the estimation, they generally build in momentum type effects into the forecasts."[17] Moreover, confidence generally also leads to a great deal of leverage.

In a nutshell, it is vital to acknowledge that you can *model* risk but you cannot *know* risk.

But if we cannot *know* risk, is there any point in *modelling* risk? Are the efforts of the statisticians in the banks and ratings agencies a waste of time? Well, there is a point and they are not wasting time. This is because risk modelling:

- ensures that information is collected and standard risk questions are considered (*"Plans are worthless, but planning is everything"*[18]);
- gives the institution a "best guess" of how its risk portfolio behaves under normal conditions;
- creates a foundation for scenario analysis – what would happen in unlikely situations?

We should not become nostalgic for the crude tools of yesteryear. Modern approaches backed up by information technology give us new capabilities in managing risk:

> In engineering, medicine, science, finance, business, and even in government, decisions that touch everyone's life are now made in accordance with disciplined procedures that far outperform the seat-of-the-pants methods of the past. Many catastrophic errors of judgement are thus either avoided, or else their consequences are muted.[19]

Many observers believe that the banking industry needs to go back to its roots, particularly in the area of risk assessment. Undoubtedly, the local knowledge and on-the-ground presence of the traditional bank manager represents an invaluable source of risk information. It also ensures that the relationship between bank and client is intimate and based on trust. But we also need to take into account the lessons learned during the bad debt problems of the early nineties, which led to the introduction of computer-based scoring and modelling systems. Risk capabilities can be strengthened through the standardisation and centralisation of certain activities; automation can harness the power of modern IT systems to enable a more in-depth assessment of individual risk decisions and a better portfolio-level understanding. These modern approaches do not eradicate the need for an appropriately expert front-line interface with

---

[17] On the efficacy of financial regulations, Jón Daníelsson, London School of Economics.

[18] Remarks at the National Defense Executive Reserve Conference, Dwight Eisenhower, 14 November 1957.

[19] *Against the Odds: The Remarkable Story of Risk*, Peter Bernstein, 1996.

the customer and the transaction. But a return to decentralised processes based on human gut-feel would be disastrous.

Importance of Diversification

In risk management, one of the key lessons from past failures is that diversification is one of the most powerful ways of reducing risk. Intuitively, we know that it is wrong to "put all your eggs in one basket". If one thing goes wrong, all is lost. As Shakespeare's Antonio observes in *The Merchant of Venice*, diversification reduces overall risk levels and the chances of losing everything:

> My ventures are not in one bottom trusted,
> Nor to one place; nor is my whole estate
> Upon the fortune of this present year:
> Therefore my merchandise makes me not sad.[20]

By diversifying risks, we can reduce the risk of losing everything. Somewhat counter-intuitively, a more diversified risk portfolio has a *higher* chance of *something* going wrong than a less diversified portfolio – but a *lower* chance of *everything* going wrong. In other words, the unexpected loss is smaller for a diversified institution, while the expected loss is higher. This is true if the risks aren't strongly linked to each other, aren't likely to happen at the same time. In risk jargon, diversification is increased if the risks aren't *correlated*. And, of course, expected losses are not a source of risk, because we have defined risk as bad things happening unexpectedly. If bad things (such as losses) happen as they are expected to happen, then that is simply the cost of doing business. A low-risk bank does not have zero losses, it has a low level of surprise losses.

If diversification reduces the chance of disastrous outcomes, it generally also smooths the investment returns of a portfolio. Individual investment assets will behave in different ways and, to a greater or lesser extent, cancel each other out. The return profile is smoothed and more predictable. Aside from a greater expected loss, the by-product of a smoother profile, diversification has only one other cost: reduced potential for *upside* surprises. We often see retail investors shunning diversified investments as they hunt for outsized returns or "the next big thing". Not so professionals. They hate volatility and fear lack of diversification, in particular because there is on average no gain to be had in undiversified approaches. An undiversified strategy will on average have the same return as a diversified strategy but will be more risky. There is no reward for the additional risk of a non-diversified investment, or to put it differently: "the lack of diversification across alpha sources can be a remarkably painful source of unrewarded risk."[21]

Diversification was studied extensively in the 1950s with the development of "portfolio theory" by Harry Markowitz.[22] Diversification was seen to help define an "efficient frontier" of maximum return for a given risk level, or lower risk for a given return target. The idea of diversification is still present in the risk management of banks, although the difficulty is to identify whether assets which seem to behave differently are not in fact correlated in times of stress.

A good example of diversification is HSBC, see Section 5.4. HSBC had subprime-related losses in the USA of some $50bn through its Household Finance operation there. But these

---

[20] *The Merchant of Venice*, William Shakespeare.
[21] Rob Brown, Benchmark Plus Management, LLC.
[22] *Portfolio Selection: Efficient Diversification of Investments*, Harry Markowitz, 1959.

losses were manageable, as they were mitigated to a large extent by the strong profits of HSBC units in relatively trouble-free markets in other geographies.

Other banks fared worse, by having "all their eggs in one basket". HBOS, for example, was diversified by business line but concentrated in property: when the financial crisis struck, it lost money on US Alt-A bonds, UK commercial property lending, Australian commercial property lending, UK buy-to-let mortgages, equity stakes in property companies, Irish property lending ... Clearly, diversification into non-correlated businesses is more important than mere geographic or asset class diversification.

Above, we have stated that "diversification is one of the most powerful ways of reducing risk" and this is our firm belief. Of course, at the lowest level, negative outcomes – the failed crop, the sunken ship, the shift in currency rates – will still occur. But diversification of risk will improve the resilience of a bank and reduce risk at the *institutional* level. If the entire banking industry improves its level of risk diversification, then aggregate risk at the *systemic* level reduces: aggregate losses are the same but their impact is reduced. Enhancing genuine risk diversification, or at least stopping ridiculous over-concentrations building up, must be at the heart of any sound risk management strategy.

3.4 WHAT IS AN RWA?

RWA is the acronym for Risk-Weighted Asset – an asset that has a weighting applied to it according to its perceived riskiness. The primary use for RWAs is to determine regulatory capital requirements. Chapter 4 describes some of the key regulatory developments in this area.

RWAs are hugely important to the banking industry: it is vital to understand what they *really* represent, in order to have a meaningful debate on how to achieve "better banking". Some – including the global regulatory standard that is Basel III – consider that a bank's level of RWAs is an indicator of the amount of risk that the bank carries. For example, using this perspective, Deutsche Bank has RWAs of €334bn[23] whereas Intesa San Paolo has €299bn,[24] so Deutsche Bank has more risk than Intesa San Paolo and hence should carry more capital in order to achieve the same level of solvency. The RWA number is assumed to have quantified the risks of a given bank – quite an achievement! Many people, however, including some of the world's most senior regulators, consider that RWA methodologies do not give us an effective summary of the risks of a bank and would rather scrap risk-weightings altogether.

The notion of RWAs was introduced by Basel I in 1988 (see Section 4.3). Banks' exposures were allocated to buckets and each bucket was "weighted". For example, a $100,000 mortgage received a 50% risk-weighting and thus contributed $50,000 to the total RWAs of the bank in question. The aggregate amount of RWAs of the bank is the denominator of the regulatory solvency ratio. It sums up the risk of an institution, from a regulator's capital adequacy perspective, in a single number. Banks are required by the regulator to operate with an amount of regulatory capital of at least 8% of the total RWAs. The solvency ratio is also used by market analysts as a key performance measure. The approach to RWAs under Basel II (and Basel III) Standardised approach is much the same as Basel I, but has more buckets and uses credit

---

[23] 4Q2012 Financial Data Supplement, Deutsche Bank.
[24] Basel 2 Pillar 3 Disclosure as at 31 December 2012, Intesa San Paolo.

ratings to differentiate within asset classes. Most big banks used the "Internal Ratings Based" (IRB) approaches of Basel II (and Basel III) and hence model their own RWAs, under supervision by the regulator (see Section 4.4).

Note that minimum capital amounts are often converted into RWAs and vice versa. They are seen as the same thing in different units. Banks often quote their minimum capital requirements by showing the number that is 8% of their RWAs, so that a capital requirement of €100m would be seen as the same thing as €1,250m of RWAs. Conversely, when regulation stipulates a minimum level of capital (for example, for operational risk and market risk under Basel II), it is often "converted" into an RWA equivalent by multiplying it by 12.5, which is the inverse of 8%. So a capital requirement of $100m for operational risk could be expressed as equivalent to RWAs of $1,250m. Strictly speaking, the notion of an RWA should have been dismissed with the advent of Basel II and we should be concerned uniquely with minimum capital requirements. This seemed to be the case, with one bank noting that "under the Basel II capital regime we are required to hold a specific amount of capital, and do not have a specific capital ratio target as under Basel I".[25] But the inherited traditions of Basel I anchored people to the notion of an RWA and the magic 8% figure and so they remain.

To illustrate what an RWA is and how it relates to capital requirements, let us look at a simple mortgage loan of €100,000 and what its risk-weighting might be under the advanced internal ratings based (AIRB) approach of Basel II and Basel III (see Table 3.7).

The bank has calculated, using a statistical analysis of historic data in its files, that the mortgage in question has a 1-in-200 chance of defaulting in a typical year and, should it default, the bank will recover only 80% of the money owed and lose the remaining 20% or €20,000. Across the portfolio of mortgages, the probable level of loss (i.e. the expected loss) amounts to an average of only €100 per €100,000 mortgage. The illustration assumes that this typical or expected loss can be extrapolated into an unexpected loss level of €800 more, using statistical means, at a confidence level of 99.9%. In other words, the bank has calculated that only 1 in every 1,000 mortgages of this kind will result in losses of more than €900 in a given year. Or we could say that the mortgage will lose *on average* €100 and maybe another €800 *if things go terribly*. Of course, these potential loss calculations only make sense across a large and varied portfolio of mortgages.

The capital requirement of the mortgage is set at €800, which can be expressed (by multiplying through by 12.5) as risk-weighted assets of €10,000. The mortgage is said to have a risk-weighting of 10%, since the RWAs are 10% of the exposure. Likewise, every other risk asset on a bank's books is assigned a risk-weighting and the overall risk exposure of the bank is expressed in terms of total RWAs. Note that, under the Standardised Approach of Basel regulations, the mortgage would simply have been given a 35% risk-weighting, irrespective of its perceived or modeled riskiness.

Just as the notion of risk is complex, so the notion of risk-weighted assets is problematic and has recently become hotly debated. If we cannot "know" risk, how then can we "know" the capital required by any given bank? Can we distil the risk of an institution into a single number? And even assuming that the notion of RWAs has some validity, then who should define the appropriate risk-weightings?

---

[25] Alliance & Leicester 2007 Annual Report.

Table 3.7   Worked illustration of an RWA calculation

Balance of loan	€100,000
Maximum exposure at default	€100,000
Probability of default p.a.	0.5% (1-in-200)
Loss given default	20%
Expected loss p.a.	€100
Unexpected loss (99.9% confidence)	€800
Capital requirement	€800 (i.e. 0.8% of exposure)
RWA equivalent	€10,000
Risk-weighting of mortgage	10%

Maybe no-one should define any risk-weightings and we should have only unweighted risk measures that just use the accounting values of risk exposures. This is the view of proponents of the leverage ratio, such as Sheila Bair, who ran the FDIC until recently:

> Given the obvious flaws in the way banks risk-weight assets under Basel II, regulators' primary focus should be on constraining absolute leverage through an international leverage ratio.[26]

Some of the biggest investors in banks are also sceptical about the continuing usage of complex RWA calculations:

> The Basel 2-IRB approach to risk-weighting has become too complex and susceptible to individual bank interpretation, which distorts any inter-bank comparison by investors. A return to a simpler risk based measurement system, or improved disclosure of the "bridge" from gross assets to RWA, should be considered.[27]

One key consideration is whether we want to have "standardized", flat risk measures. Basing regulatory capital requirements on a risk-weighting that is set by the regulator can steer banks to seek out areas where the regulator has "got it wrong" and build high-yielding and highly-leveraged exposures to seemingly low-risk assets that carry large potential tail risk. Many of the problems of the current financial crisis have been caused by banks piling into AAA-rated subprime bonds and certain government bonds, for example, due to their low regulatory risk-weight under the prevailing regulations.

The balancing concern is that the weighting of risk assets using the banks' own risk models could be seen as amenable to manipulation by the banks, if they use the complexity and subjectivity of the rules to arbitrage the system. This argument is currently topical and, as evidence, looks at the disparity of risk-weightings between countries, methodologies and institutions as evidence that RWAs calculated by banks under the IRB approach are not to be trusted. Proponents of this argument see the following benchmarking data, for example, as unsettling (Figure 3.4 and Table 3.8).

---

[26] Testimony of Sheila C. Bair before the Senate Committee on Banking, 7 December 2011.
[27] Written Evidence in response to call for evidence made on 15 October 2012: Submission from The Association of British Insurers, Parliamentary Commission on Banking Standards.

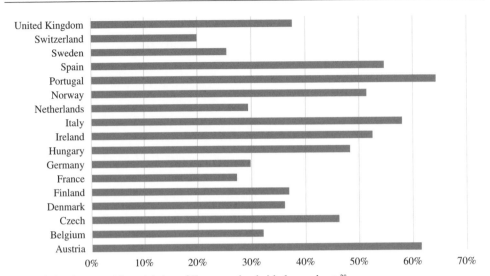

Figure 3.4 Average risk-weighting of European banks' balance sheets[28]

The fundamental question is whether risk-weights for the same asset classes and the same borrowers should be similar. One of the earliest studies into the topic was conducted by the UK FSA in 2009. They expected some degree of differences and yet also some consistency:

> We do not intend that the IRB process generate identical PDs for the same obligors across firms. Were this to occur, it might cause systemic risk. Nonetheless, we would expect some overall comparability of PDs across firms and between firms' PDs and the long-run default rates corresponding to the credit ratings of external agencies.[29]

On that occasion, the FSA's conclusion was that there were differences between banks, but nothing to cause concern. Overall consistency was satisfactory.

More recently, the IMF published a comprehensive paper on the RWA issue. The authors highlight some of the worrying trends in market perception of the RWA measure, including the observation that "higher RWA density is now considered as an indication of more prudent risk measurement".[30] In other words, the market is becoming suspicious of banks with low risk-weightings on their assets, since this may be indicative of under-reporting of risk levels. Of course, it could be that certain banks with high risk-weightings are under-reporting their risk levels too: a higher average risk-weighting does not imply conservatism.

There are undeniably differences between and within regions in the risk-weightings of banks' balance sheets. There are many potential explanations for this: different business mix,

---

[28] Study on Internal Ratings Based (IRB) Models for Residential Mortgages in Europe, European Banking Federation, 5 July 2012.

[29] Results Of 2009 Hypothetical Portfolio Exercise For Sovereigns, Banks And Large Corporations, UK FSA, 1 March 2010.

[30] Why Do RWAs Differ Across Countries and What Can Be Done About It?, Vanessa Le Leslé and Sofiya Avramova, IMF, March 2012.

Table 3.8 Risk weights for corporates and residential mortgages for a sample of European banks (2011)[31]

	Corporates	Residential mortgages
UBS	33.9%	7.9%
Rabobank	32.2%	9.0%
Barclays	38.2%	15.9%
Nationwide BS	–	4.8%
HSBC	54.1%	51.2%
DNB	54.0%	12.3%
Swedbank	63.5%	7.1%
BBVA	49.1%	27.7%

legal systems, macro-economic conditions, product designs, and so on. Within a given country and asset class, one would expect significant differences between institutions, given different risk appetites and competitive positioning. Use of different Basel II methodologies will give rise to different risk-weightings, as the progress towards the Advanced IRB Approach gives a "reward" in allowing modelled risk-weightings to be applied, which are generally lower than those under the Standardised Approach. When looking at risk-weightings that are often *declining* as the economic environment deteriorates, the authors point out that this could be due to purposeful changes in business mix towards lower risk exposures, improvement of collateral arrangements, smoothing of risk-weights due to through-the-cycle methodologies that will understate risk in an economic stress, improved risk information due to ongoing data cleansing and migration to Basel II AIRB approved models. There is also undoubtedly an element of removal of conservatism, which was generally built into initial Basel II models five or ten years ago. The IMF authors conclude that:

> RWAs calculated by individual banks' internal models (IRB) can be significantly different for similar risks. Supervisors are currently working on this issue. The Group encourages them to take strong and coordinated action to improve the consistency of internal models across banks. The treatment of risks should be more harmonised in order to produce greater confidence in the adequacy and consistency of the IRB-based capital requirements.[32]

Their paper advocates neither the scrapping of model-based risk-weights nor the standardisation of risk-weightings, instead favouring a hybrid approach, with multiple measures and less reliance upon solvency ratios *per se*:

> Neither moving back to Basel I or the Basel II Standardized Approach, nor allowing banks to use their models unchecked for RWAs carries much appeal [...] In the ultimate analysis, it should be recognized that capital adequacy is but one, albeit key, part of a holistic approach to assessing banks' financial strength.[33]

---

[31] From the banks' 2011 Pillar 3 reports.
[32] High-level expert group on reforming the structure of the EU banking sector, Erikki Liikanen, October 2012.
[33] Why Do RWAs Differ Across Countries and What Can Be Done About It?, Vanessa Le Leslé and Sofiya Avramova, IMF, March 2012.

Other critics of the banking industry seem undecided in their preference for risk-weights set by the regulator or by the banks themselves:

> The Basel system of weighting loans and investment according to their supposed riskiness, those poisonous incentives to game and cheat the rules, remains intact. Banks will continue to devote their resources to those loans and investments deemed by the regulators to be least risky, rather than making their own proper commercial judgements about how and where to extend credit. And thus banks will still be able to pull the wool over the eyes of owners, creditors and regulators about how strong or weak they really are.[34]

Clearly, there is a dilemma. Should risk measures be comparable or heterogenous? Should banks be free to make their own "proper commercial judgements" or should they be told how much risk they are carrying? The answer seems to be that regulators and analysts would like to have both: "From a financial stability perspective, it is desirable to have some diversity in risk management practices so as to avoid that all banks act in a similar way. When banks would have identical response functions, economic cyclicality would increase, potentially creating additional instability. At the same time, excessive variation in risk measurement is clearly undesirable. Finding the right balance is the key."[35]

These views represent the current preferences and objectives of the authorities and they do seem somewhat contradictory. Diversity, subjectivity and complexity appear to be in conflict with harmonisation, comparability and simplicity. Recently, however, there has been a strong shift towards towards the harmonisation objective:

- The Swiss authorities now require Swiss banks using the internal-ratings based approach to report solvency metrics in parallel under the Basel Standardised Approach.[36]
- The UK FSA applied "slotting" rules to override banks' risk models for commercial real estate loans and apply standardised risk-weights instead.[37] Unsurprisingly, the standardised risk-weights were higher than the banks' own modelled risk-weights. The FSA estimated the impact of the change to be equivalent to £1bn–£3bn of additional capital requirement for UK banks.[38]
- Wayne Byres, the chairman of the Basel Committee, stated that he thought it would be a good idea for investors to be able to see what would be a bank's RWAs under the Standardised Approach, to see how much capital their internal models had "saved" them.[39]
- In the USA, the Collins amendment means that banks' RWAs under the IRB approaches cannot be any lower than they would be under the US Standardised Approach.[40]
- In the EU, the EBA is pushing for capital requirements for banks using IRB to have a minimum "floor" linked to the Standardised Approach: "at a time when concerns about the quality of bank assets cast doubt on the calculation of risk-weighted assets, a reliable,

---

[34] *How Do We Fix This Mess?*, Robert Peston, 2012.
[35] From ideas to implementation, Stefan Ingves, Chairman of the Basel Committee, 24 January 2013.
[36] Financial Stability Report, Swiss National Bank, 2012.
[37] BIPRU 4 Annex 1 Supervisory Slotting Criteria for Specialised Lending, UK PRA Website.
[38] Internal ratings-based probability of default models for income-producing real estate portfolios–Guidance Consultation, UK FSA, October 2010.
[39] Banks annoy supervisors with whitewash, *FT Deutschland*, 11 July 2012.
[40] Basel III regulatory consistency assessment (Level 2) Preliminary report: United States of America, Basel Committee, October 2012.

harmonized backstop in the form of a capital floor would be beneficial in reassuring market participants regarding the reliability of the regulatory benchmarks."[41]
- Scorn is being poured on the notion of IRB by senior UK regulators: "Grade inflation is the result of banks marking their own exams. This is a problem for regulators, who cannot really police this complex beast. Increasingly it is a problem for investors in banks, too, who cannot make any sense of the published capital and regulatory ratios."[42]
- The Swedish regulator has set a floor of 15% on mortgage risk-weights, as compared to the average IRB risk-weights that are around 5% in Sweden; the impact of the floor is estimated to be an incremental capital requirement of SEK 20bn for the Swedish banks.[43]
- In Norway, the regulator is considering the introduction of a 35% risk-weight floor for mortgages, up from today's 10–16%.[44]

These developments indicate that many of the advances of Basel II are being scrapped and the notion of an RWA is returning to what it was under Basel I: the accounting value of the exposure multiplied by a risk-weight set by the regulator. Whilst convenient, this retrogressive trend does involve a trade-off, which carries the risks of arbitrage, under-reporting of risk and herd-like behaviour. It is not clear how the authorities intend to deal with these risks.

3.5 WHAT IS CAPITAL?

> There is no objective basis for ex-cathedra statements about levels of capital. There can be no certainty, no dogma about capital adequacy.[45]

Bank capital is an important yet elusive concept. It is the driver of solvency and resilience; of profitability and value; of confidence and confusion. Crucially, capital is at the heart of the regimes of bank regulation. It certainly merits a fuller assessment and a better understanding.

In common parlance, the word "capital" can be synonymous with "money" but it can also mean "wealth". In the banking industry, it is often used in a way that is close to the notion of "equity", the value of the shareholder's investment. Contrary to popular perception, capital is not a set of obligatory reserves that can be called upon. It is not a pile of cash set aside for a rainy day. A bank's capital is an accounting concept – not a cash concept. This point is important and is not widely understood, as has recently been noted in the book *The Banker's New Clothes*: "The confusion about the term 'bank capital' is pervasive. Numerous media reports say that banks must 'set aside' capital to satisfy new regulations. References to capital reserves suggest that the regulation forces banks to hold cash that sits idly in the bank's tills

[41] Letter reference EBA/Op/2012/04 from Andrea Enria (EBA) to Michel Barnier (EC), 21 November 2012.
[42] Oral Evidence Taken Before The Parliamentary Commission on Banking Standards, Andy Haldane, 21 January 2013.
[43] Risk weight floor for Swedish mortgages, Finansinspektionen, 21 May 2013.
[44] Norwegian Fixed Income, SEB, 17 December 2012.
[45] Banking Regulation, Profits and Capital Generation, W.P. Cooke, *The Banker*, August 1981.

without being put to work in the economy. A bank lobbyist is quoted as saying, 'A dollar in capital is one less dollar working in the economy.'"[46]

The people who own the bank have set it up with some initial funds: they have "capitalised" it. The bank then takes deposits from customers and issues bonds to investors – these amounts owed to creditors are the bank's main liabilities. With these borrowed funds, the bank makes loans and investments – these are its assets. The capital of the bank is the difference between the two sides of the business. It could be seen as what would be left if the loans were repaid, the investments sold and the funds borrowed from creditors repaid. Capital is – in essence – the net accounting assets or "equity" of the bank. The greater the amount of capital, the bigger the available cushion to be able to repay creditors, should the realisation value of the assets turn out to be worse than anticipated. So in theory, more capital means less risk for creditors.

Immediately, we have an issue to resolve. If the capital is equivalent to the net assets, then the accuracy of its value relies upon the accurate valuation of the assets and liabilities of the bank. As we have seen in Section 3.2 above, most assets and most liabilities are calculated on a basis that, while not arbitrary, often bears little resemblance to economic reality. Given these limitations, is there any hope for the capital number to be meaningful? Can we honestly say that a bank with a large amount of accounting capital is, indeed, strong and solvent?

Unfortunately, for much of the time, banks are insolvent on a snapshot basis, even if the accounting value of their assets appears to exceed the value of their liabilities. In other words, if they were required to repay all of the funds they had borrowed from creditors, including the deposits taken from private individuals, they would be forced to liquidate some of their assets, comprising mostly long-term loans, at a loss; losses would probably exceed the accounting capital and the bank would be unable to repay all of their creditors in full. This "fire sale" approach envisages the immediate closure and wind-down of the bank as a "gone concern". As a "going concern", however, banks are able to wait for their loans to repay at more or less the value at which they are carried in the accounts: on a "going concern" basis, most banks are definitely solvent. In a clearly circular fashion, they rely upon "going concern" status to maintain the confidence required to wait for loans to mature. If that confidence were to dissipate, a seemingly solvent bank could be rendered insolvent.

In order to maintain going concern status, therefore, banks make sure that they have sufficient capital sourced from their shareholders rather than creditors. Creditors know that there is a cushion of financial resources to absorb unexpected losses in the business operations of the bank and insulate them from the risk of such losses. The shareholders know that they are "on the hook" for losses during tough times and accept this situation because they also gain from the profit generated by the bank during good times. The capital may not be enough to protect creditors and depositors during a sudden collapse of the bank, but it should be sufficient to preserve confidence in the bank and allow it to retain the crucial "going concern" status.

In a nutshell, capital is the shock absorber that smooths the ride for the creditors and keeps them on board.

Different stakeholders want different things from banks; they will use different agents to manage their situation; and the agents will use different tools and capital measures to pursue their objectives. See Table 3.9.

Because of this difference in perspectives, there are subtly different views on capital, which reflect the different objectives and perspectives on risk from the various parties. The following sections delve deeper into the notion of capital and take into account these differing perspectives.

---

[46] *The Banker's New Clothes*, Anat Admati and Martin Hellwig, 2013.

Table 3.9 Use of agents and measures in banking

Stakeholder	Agent	Measure	Objective
Everyone	Auditor	Accounting capital	Objective information
Society	Regulator	Regulatory capital	Service and stability
Bondholder	Ratings agency	Ratings capital	Return-of-capital
Shareholder	Management	Economic capital	Return-on-capital (i.e. profit)

3.5.1 Regulatory Capital

To maintain a solid and stable banking industry, the regulator aims to ensure that banks have enough capital to be able to ride through the lumps and bumps inherent in their businesses without losing confidence or failing. Regulation of the capital base of banks ensures that banks do not over-extend themselves in terms of financial resources:

> It is no wonder that bank capital is regulated. When borrowing and lending is profitable, it is tempting for banks to scale up their operations and to borrow and lend too much in relation to their capital, in effect reducing the effectiveness of the potential capital cushion.[47]

For regulators, the role of capital is crucial. They understandably want the banking industry to have high capital levels, relative to the risks that the banks run. In recent times, they have over-emphasised this component of their job, focusing on the intense detail of capital requirements, while neglecting certain aspects of risk management. It is all very well having big shock absorbers, but a few driving lessons to avoid more of the potholes would not go amiss! In turn, banks have focused too much on the regulatory capital requirements of their business as a proxy for risk management:

> The Basel Committee on Banking Supervision (BCBS) has put too much emphasis on its Capital Adequacy Requirement. [...] We find more reasonable to interpret regulatory capital requirements as defining, together with other indicators, thresholds for supervisory intervention rather than recommendations for risk management policies of banks.[48]

Later sections of this book develop this theme – the need for better risk management more than simply "more capital" – further and drive towards some proposals on risk management as well as regulatory capital requirements.

In defining capital requirements, regulators acknowledge that capital will never cover extreme catastrophes, such as the inability of all the bank's borrowers to repay any of their loans to the bank. There is no "zero failure" mindset, nor is there a "zero leverage" requirement that would limit banks to financing their customers solely with their shareholders' equity capital:

> Banking is all about risk taking and leverage, so it must be recognised that banks will always be exposed to some potential losses that will exceed their capital.[49]

---

[47] Is it a good time to nationalise the banks?, Evan Davis, BBC, 17 March 2008.
[48] The Treatment of Distressed Banks, Dewatripont and Rochet, 2009.
[49] Meeting the Challenges of the Implementation of Basel II, Bernie Egan, APRA, 13 March 2007.

Instead, the notion of "risk appetite" is used (a measure of the tolerance towards bank failures): under Basel rules, for example, the regulatory requirement for capital is supposed to equate to a confidence level of 99.9% that the bank will not become insolvent in a given year. Regulators also acknowledge that accounting equity does not represent a realistic view of the economic solvency of the bank. Whereas the accountant aims to represent the financial situation of the firm using a "true and fair" approach,[50] the prudential authorities are primarily concerned with preserving financial stability and protecting depositors from losses in the case of problems. In theory, the regulator is trying to ensure that, should the bank fail, the capital of the bank is a sufficient buffer and depositors and creditors can get their money back in full.

Regulatory capital measures, therefore, apply several prudential deductions or filters to the accounting numbers, removing accounting items that are of dubious or uncertain value upon a rapid liquidation. The main filters are goodwill and intangible assets, such as software or brands. Regulators also deduct "fake" capital, such as any shares that have been issued but are held temporarily by the bank's own Treasury department, as well as provision shortfalls, in cases where provisions are less than the bank's expected annual loss on the risk assets. The new Basel III rules introduced some new regulatory deductions from capital, such as the value of tax credits due to prior tax losses that are carried forward and can reduce a future tax bill ("deferred tax assets").

Subordinated liabilities, which are sometimes accounted for as debt and sometimes as capital, are included in the regulatory capital measures, but are seen as lower quality capital and are subject to strict design criteria (see below).

The validity of these deductions and adjustments to the accounting capital is debatable. Many of the deducted items do have a real economic value in case of a sudden need to wind up the bank: goodwill, for example, often relates to subsidiaries that have a potential sale value that is in excess of the value at which they are carried in the accounts. But then, the logic of realisable value is not used for the loan book, whose size will far exceed the items deducted above and whose "mark-to-market" variance could well dwarf the scale of the official deductions during a period of stress. During such periods, the bank might well be economically insolvent, though this does not appear in the accounting figures. We are reminded that regulatory forbearance – ignoring economic reality and focusing on accounting metrics – can be the biggest source of capital available to a bank.

Whatever it signifies, the point to note is that regulatory or prudential equity is materially different to accounting equity and does not necessarily represent a realistic or economic view of the capital resources available.

Due to the lack of precision around the assumed timeframe of disposal used in the valuation of assets, regulators have grown used to the notion of capital being divided into two types: "going concern" and "gone concern". *Going concern* capital generally relates to the regulatory equity of the bank, the adjusted net assets figure described above. If the bank makes a loss, the loss depletes reserves and reduces the accounting equity of the bank; the prudential equity capital is also reduced. Assuming the losses are modest, the bank remains a going concern, even though its prudential equity is lower. Should the losses be more severe, the prudential equity is depleted to such a point that regulatory triggers are breached and certain resolution processes kick in (see Section 4.6).

---

[50] Statement of Principles for Financial Reporting, Accounting Standards Board, 1999.

Gone concern capital, on the other hand, is more than just the equity capital of the bank. It also includes subordinated debt instruments. Should the bank fail and enter resolution or bankruptcy, the holders of the subordinated debt capital instruments are liable to see the value of their claim written down in the case of resolution or limited by the recovery value from the bankruptcy proceedings. This means that the chance of depositors and senior creditors losing money is lessened.

3.5.2 Hybrid Capital

Hybrid capital is a general term that refers to capital instruments that have a combination of equity-like and debt-like features. Hybrids insulate depositors and senior creditors from the potential negative impacts of bank failure, since their claim is subordinated to the claims of depositors. High quality hybrids bear coupons that are discretionary or deferrable in times of stress, so they can be seen to improve the solvency position of the bank on a going concern basis. But, in a normal situation in a healthy bank, they behave very much like debt, with a fixed income coupon and principal amount.

Hybrid capital has been used by corporations, including banks, for hundreds of years. Since the legal system differs by country, the exact form of the instruments has varied, but there have generally been "preference shares", which are non-voting shares with fixed dividend payment, and "subordinated loans", which rank behind senior loans during the bankruptcy process. Increasing use of hybrid capital by banks led to attempts by the Basel Committee in 1988 to propose an international standard for hybrid capital definitions and the amount of hybrid capital that banks could include in their capital base in lieu of shareholder's equity.

More recently, Basel III has introduced the requirement for all regulatory capital instruments to be loss-absorbing in advance of legal insolvency. This is in response to a perceived failure of some traditional hybrid instruments, many of which were contractually obliged to continue paying coupons to investors even as their issuing banks were facing capital shortfalls.

Regulators are also trying to promote contingently convertible capital instruments or "CoCos". These start life as bonds and, at a pre-determined trigger point, convert into equity either through conversion into shares or through a write-down of the principal value of the CoCo. However, neither of these conversion routes adds any new financial resources to the bank or increases its resilience; they merely reshuffle the claims of capital providers to the residual value of the bank.

Hybrids are important for ensuring an efficient and effective capital base for banks. Theory (in particular, the Modigliani–Miller theorem) often serves as an argument in favour of more equity in the capital structure of banks,[51] but there are practical limitations: "while an all-equity bank might well exist in principle, no such banks exist in practice."[52] Due to their fixed-income or bond-like qualities, there is a broader pool of investors looking to invest in them than in stocks and shares. Hybrids provide the basis for these fixed-income investors to invest in banks, providing loss-absorbing capital at a lower cost than would be the case for equity.

---

[51] Optimal bank capital, David Miles, Jing Yang and Gilberto Marcheggiano, Bank of England, April 2011.
[52] *Merton Miller on Derivatives*, Merton Miller, 1997.

3.5.3 Economic Capital and Ratings Capital

Auditors and regulators are not responsible for designing the value-creating strategies of a bank and making the day-to-day risk decisions regarding business opportunities: these are the responsibilities of bank management. For management to make the right decisions, it needs a risk and capital methodology that is more of a real, economic assessment than the methodologies used to inform the accounting and regulatory perspectives. Such internal risk and capital methodologies are seen as realistic or "economic": they are often labelled as "economic capital" methodologies.

Likewise, ratings agencies have found regulatory capital measures to be unsuitable for their own assessment of a bank's solvency. For example, Standard & Poor's (S&P) has determined that it needs a view of a bank's solvency that is free from the subjectivity and non-comparability of the Basel II and Basel III modelled RWA approaches, while also incorporating S&P's sceptical views on the definition of regulatory capital. This proprietary "risk-adjusted capital" (RAC) methodology is described in Section 3.10.2. S&P's RAC ratios for banks can often be materially different from the regulatory capital ratios and they are meant to be globally comparable between banks in the same country and across differing regulatory regimes.

3.5.4 Cost-of-Capital and Return-on-Capital

For shareholders in a bank, it is important that their investment gives them an attractive commercial return. The accounting measure of return-on-equity (ROE) is the most commonly used measure of profitability, though it is plagued with the same challenges that afflict all accounting-based measures, given its reliance on debatable accounting valuations and the fact that it does not necessarily factor in the risks that a bank is running. In the period 2000–2006, the accounting ROE of large banks varied between 15 and 20%. The top performers achieved ROEs in excess of 25%.[53] Needless to say, returns since then have been poor and unpredictable.

For a shareholder to want to invest, or continue to invest, in a bank, the returns must be "attractive", which in this sense means greater than a notional hurdle rate (the cost-of equity or COE). Few banks disclose what they think that hurdle rate is. One example of a bank that does is Barclays, which currently believes its cost-of-equity is 11.5% pa.[54] If a bank's profitability is below its COE, shareholders should rightfully seek to disinvest, putting the bank into run-off, stripping operating costs and surplus capital out of the business and maximising the value of their investment.

The task of bank management is generally seen as ensuring growth in profitability by building strong revenue streams and keeping costs and provisions low. However, the notion of risk and capital needs to be introduced and risk-adjusted performance targeted. Management needs to manage the risk profile of the bank and pursue capital efficiency. By capital efficiency, we mean that the revenues are commensurate with the risks involved. This is not just the regulatory capital consumed by an activity, for regulatory capital is not an accurate reflection of the real riskiness of that activity for that bank. Instead, banks should be managed according to risk-adjusted measures such as return on economic capital.

---

[53] Banking 2012: Revenue Growth and Innovation, Accenture, 2012.
[54] Barclays PLC Strategic Review, 12 February, 2013.

More recently, stock markets have focused on the availability of distributable profits, since much of the profitability of banks over the past five years has been absorbed by the need to build up greater regulatory capital buffers. That "capital gap" represents lost value for the bank's owners. Only once the correct capital levels have been built up is the bank in the situation to distribute profits to its shareholders in the form of a dividend, share buyback, acquisition, or simply organic business growth. Thus, for the time being, capital cash flow is a key metric. Unfortunately, investors are assuming that surplus capital generation is driven by regulatory capital levels, rather than economic capital levels. Risk is still being neglected.

3.5.5 Capital in a Stress Scenario

One feature of capital that has received little attention is the behaviour of capital in a stress scenario. This can mean, on the positive side, the ability of a bank's management to proactively manage the bank's regulatory and economic solvency during a period of stress. Examples of such management actions include: slowing down origination, selling risk assets into the market while it is still open, tapping investors who have been pre-marketed, executing pre-underwritten stock issues. Recent history has shown us that the ability to *manage* solvency can be just as powerful as simply having a great stock of capital. Good capital management makes the solvency of the bank more dynamic and liquid – and hence more powerful. This neglected feature of capital is picked up as a part of our proposals in Chapter 7.

The other aspect of capital in a stress scenario is how quickly it can evaporate. Several banks have failed with apparently healthy solvency ratios. SNS Reaal in Holland, for example, passed the EBA stress test in July 2011, had a core Tier 1 ratio of 8.8% at September 2012,[55] and collapsed on 31 January 2013. Yet, on 2 February, Jan Sijbrand, the head of regulatory operations at the Dutch Central Bank, was reported as saying that "there was no capital left in SNS Bank".[56] In this case, the failing was that of the metric: SNS was economically insolvent all along and it was only the removal of forbearance that brought about the collapse.

3.5.6 Bail-in Capital

Recent developments on resolution regimes have introduced the notion of "bail-in", namely that banks should be allowed to fail without going into formal bankruptcy procedures (see Section 4.7). Under a bail-in regime, the subordinated debt is clearly designated as loss-absorbing capital, as was always the intention. In addition, an element of debt beyond the regulatory capital element is also subject to write-down or conversion into shares, should the losses prove greater than that which can be absorbed by the regulatory capital base. Of course, in the ultimate scenario, all funds entrusted to a bank might be seen as having the potential to absorb losses – that is certainly the case for corporates. The obvious exemptions are secured debt, such as securitisations, since those investors have property rights over the assets on which their claim is secured, and guaranteed depositors, whose funds are guaranteed by the government or the state deposit guarantee fund. All other creditors rely upon the health of the bank to be able to repay them their money. In effect, bail-in rules make it clear that lenders to banks

---

[55] Trading update third quarter 2012: SNS REAAL posts third quarter net profit of € 34 million, SNS, 6 November 2012.
[56] Bloomberg, 2 February 2013.

are at risk – they are de facto capital providers. They always were, but the legal procedures were so awkward that there may have been an implicit assumption of state bail-out: the state was assumed to have provided a contingent and implicit capital line. Removing this ambiguity should make orderly bank resolution more feasible. It shifts risk from the state to the senior bond investors. But it should also avoid the disastrous effect of a bankruptcy procedure which, in the case of Lehman Brothers, appears to have resulted in heavier losses for senior creditors than were strictly necessary: "in effect, the company's bankruptcy acted as a loss amplifier, multiplying the scale of the problem by a factor of six."[57]

Now that bail-in is becoming a reality, the question arises of what the real distinction is between regulatory capital resources and bail-inable capital resources. More and more, banks resemble entities with a tranched capital structure where the regulatory treatment may be just describing the waterfall of losses. The notion of regulatory capital may now be obsolete.

3.6 WHAT ARE LIQUIDITY AND FUNDING?

> Imagination equals nostalgia for the past, the absent; it is the liquid solution in which art develops the snapshot of reality.[58]

3.6.1 Concepts

The concept of "liquidity" is for banks what cash flow is for industrial corporations. And just as "cash is king" for corporates, with many otherwise superb businesses failing solely due to cash flow issues, so is liquidity the ultimate test for a bank. No matter how profitable or solvent the bank might appear, its success or failure will ultimately depend upon its ability to keep the cash flowing and honour its obligations towards depositors and creditors: in a word, to retain market confidence and avoid a "run".

Liquidity is the ability to meet payments when they come due or withdrawals as demanded; liquidity risk is the risk that the bank might not be able to make those payments on a timely basis. Being liquid is a good and necessary thing for a bank, but a perfectly "liquid" bank with zero liquidity risk would need to have perfectly matched assets and liabilities. This could be done in two ways:
1. Deposits are committed to the bank on a short-term basis and this is always likely to be the case "because people do not like to let their money out of their sight";[59] in some languages, the phrase for demand deposits is "a vista" or "on sight". A perfectly matched bank that was funded entirely by depositors could do nothing with those funds except deposit them with the central bank (the "owner" of the currency) as a deposit. Such a bank would be of dubious social, economic and commercial value.
2. Alternatively, a bank lending money that could only be repaid over the long term, such as bridge-building or buying a house, could fund itself by borrowing from the bond markets on a matched, long-term basis. This is conceivable, but would be very expensive, since creditors would demand a significant premium for the fact that their funds were tied up for so long.

---

[57] From bail-out to bail-in, *The Economist*, 28 January 2010.
[58] Cyril Connolly.
[59] *Lombard Street: A Description of the Money Market*, W. Bagehot, 1910.

In reality, neither of these matched situations is plausible for a typical commercial bank. Banks need to undertake some degree of "maturity transformation"; they need to be "illiquid" to a certain extent. If every depositor demanded their money back on the same day, the bank would not be able to cope: it would not have the necessary funds on hand to pay up. This is not a problem due simply to lack of banknotes, i.e. physical cash. It is a problem due to lack of money in the broadest sense, not just physical banknotes: if it wired the money to customers, the payments could not all be honoured by the payments system.

3.6.2 Liquidity Management and Liquidity Risk

So a bank is an institution that takes liquidity risk and matches up the needs of depositors, who want their money available for withdrawal at all times, and borrowers, who are not able to repay the credit extended to them on demand and need some term repayment agreement. One of the roles of a bank is to conduct a certain degree of "maturity transformation" or "liquidity transformation". The repayment terms of the bank's assets and of their liabilities do not match precisely, but the mismatch – or liquidity risk – is tolerated and managed according to the risk management policy set by the bank's owners and regulators.

Liquidity management has to cover both the asset and the liability side of the balance sheet:

- Stability of funding on the liability side of the balance sheet is achieved by having the appropriate mix of short- and long-term funding.
- On the asset side, the ability to generate cash at short notice is achieved by having a stock of assets that can readily be sold.

In a modern bank, the maturity mismatch can be huge. For example, a mortgage bank such as HBOS has most of its assets maturing in the long term (£255bn in over 5 years) and most of its liabilities maturing in the very short term (£225bn in under 1 month) (see Figure 3.5).

Nevertheless, a major contractual maturity gap does not necessarily mean huge liquidity risk. In the example above, the short-term liabilities are largely demand deposits, which are *technically* repayable on demand but *in practice and in aggregate* are left with the bank for a very long period of time. This difference between contractual (what could happen) and behavioural (what is expected to happen under various scenarios) maturity is behind the notion of "sticky" deposits. Retail deposits are considered to carry little systemic liquidity risk, since their behavioural "stickiness" is reliable and retail investors tend to react late in a crisis, well after professional, sophisticated, wholesale creditors have withdrawn their funds. That said, the panic of retail depositors is sometimes the cause of a "run".

Bank runs are well-known to the public, for example forming the backdrop to the famous movies "It's a Wonderful Life" and "Mary Poppins". A retail bank run is highly visible and graphic: rumours start, depositors worry and rush to withdraw their savings, denials abound, withdrawals continue and eventually the withdrawals themselves cause a collapse, even if the initial rumours proved to be unfounded. A bank run could also happen out of the public view, with major wholesale providers of funds pulling the plug; online banking offers another source of rapid cash outflow, with the "refresh" button taking the place of the round-the-block queue. Yet the decades running up to the current financial crisis had very few bank runs in the more developed banking markets. Indeed, to many western bankers in 2006 and 2007, the concept of a bank run seemed remote and to mention such a risk seemed insulting. Bank runs

	Up to 1 month £m	1 to 3 months £m	3 to 12 months £m	1 year to 5 years £m	Over 5 years £m	Policyholder funds* £m	2005 Total £m
Assets							
Cash and balances at central banks	1,670		8				1,678
Items in course of collection	753						753
Financial assets held for trading	14,992	10,251	6,504	1,826	8,193		41,766
Derivative assets	444	580	816	2,336	6,239	84	10,499
Loans and advances to banks	8,161	5,225	1,868	272	380	1,450	17,356
Loans and advances to customers	27,566	50,604	14,885	47,363	203,350		343,768
Investment securities	3,370	302	2,209	8,438	37,242	52,773	104,334
Total financial assets	**56,956**	**66,962**	**26,290**	**60,235**	**255,404**	**54,307**	**520,154**
Liabilities							
Deposits by banks	16,904	11,072	3,810	187	68	2	32,041
Customer accounts	174,659	11,037	9,052	3,198	3,002		200,948
Financial liabilities held for trading	13,727	5,106	6,021	153			26,007
Derivative liabilities	323	821	735	2,319	4,378		8,576
Insurance contract liabilities	84	166	805	892	2,072	17,951	21,970
Investment contract liabilities	8	22	2,310	462		39,357	42,157
Unallocated surplus						974	974
Debt securities in issue	19,265	38,851	23,200	37,909	38,736		157,961
Other borrowed funds	93	49	587	1,195	18,330		20,254
Total financial liabilities	**225,061**	**67,124**	**46,520**	**46,315**	**66,584**	**58,284**	**509,888**

*Assets and liabilities associated with policyholder funds have been excluded from the maturity profits in the above table. This is on the basis that the underlying liquidity risks are for the account of the policyholders and have no direct impact on the Group results. The expected maturities of these assets and liabilities are shown on the following pages.

Figure 3.5   Contractual maturity analysis of assets and liabilities (example)[60]

were seen as belonging to a less sophisticated, naïve day and could only be imagined in the modern era in quirky emerging markets. The collapse of Northern Rock, the so-called "Run on the Rock",[61] reminded us that even the most developed and sophisticated banking system in the modern era can have a bank run.

Liquidity transformation is one of the core functions of a bank and, in normal conditions, it generates a positive "carry", since short-term funds pay a lower rate than long-term loans. A bank with a lower level of liquidity risk would have to pay more for longer-term funding and would have a lower net interest income as a result.

Likewise, asset-side liquidity is generally a costly affair and a greater degree of risk in running lower levels of asset liquidity will generally result in greater revenues. The more liquid assets are generally better known, traded in size and widely held. Investors should always prefer an asset that is easier to sell rapidly and without a large discount to one that takes a while to find a buyer and/or needs a steep discount to dispose successfully. Therefore, investors who can rely upon having funds available for the long term should take the extra revenue from investing in illiquid assets. Investors who cannot rely upon such stability of funding should hold highly liquid assets in their asset-side liquidity portfolios. The most liquid asset is cash; many banks choose to hold substantial cash balances at the central bank to cover short-term liquidity fluctuations with certainty. There is a "carry" cost to asset-side liquidity and, as with the liability-side funding approach, the bank needs to carefully consider the right degree of liquidity risk and the revenue and profitability implications.

Derivatives can be a major drain on liquidity, since the market requires banks to post collateral with their counterparties to cover the market value of their derivatives transactions.

---

[60] HBOS Annual Report, 2005.
[61] The Run on the Rock, House of Commons Treasury Committee, 24 January 2008.

Table 3.10   Changes in liquidity due to the current financial crisis

	2006	2013
Banks as borrowers	• Banks were considered far less risky than corporates • Banks could count on a deep interbanking market	• Banks scrutinised as much as corporates • Interbank market has episodes of unreliability
Cross-border flows	• Global currencies fungible through currency swaps	• Currency swap market unreliable
Liquidity cost	• Liquidity cost was predictable	• Volatility in funding cost and investor appetite
Asset liquidity	• Various assets were considered liquid reserves	• Even government bonds have periods of illiquidity. Asset liquidity is driven by central bank

Securitisation vehicles can behave in a similar manner. The collateral requirement increases in the event of a ratings downgrade, as a consequence of the higher credit risk. Banks with large derivatives portfolios or heavy users of securitisations are thus highly vulnerable to credit ratings downgrades.

During the run-up to the current financial crisis, banks were highly confident in their liquidity positions. Some had built up significant exposure to subprime bonds in their liquidity portfolios. They assumed that their assets could be sold rapidly if needed and with little, if any, financial loss on disposal. After all, they were highly rated and had been traded in volume for years. Some banks in the Eurozone held (and continue to hold) a large portion of their asset liquidity buffers in highly risky and high yielding domestic government bonds, since regulations prefer such assets. On the funding side, banks assumed that funding markets were infinite, elastic and cheap and would remain so. They shortened the funding maturities of their balance sheets. This increased net interest revenues and profitability. Indeed, there was a trend, starting in the mid-1990s, to treat banks' Treasury functions as businesses in their own right – "profit centres" rather than simply support functions or "cost centres". Many banks came to rely upon the revenues flowing from their Treasury operations to bolster lacklustre performance in the customer-facing businesses. Some banks showed these separately: at Alliance & Leicester, for example, Treasury made up nearly 10% of the overall profitability of the bank.[62] Most others chose to mix the Treasury profits in with the other divisions' profits in the reported accounts.

The resulting increase in liquidity risk was increasingly overlooked in the run-up to the current financial crisis due to the focus on profitability: "The practical reality in most banks is that daily funding and profit maximisation engage almost all of the time and attention devoted to liquidity risk management."[63] Recent market developments have resulted in a renewed focus on liquidity management and the need for banks and regulators to adapt to a new environment, in which a number of assumptions have changed fundamentally (see Table 3.10).

Liquidity risk management has moved from a neglected, mundane, obscure element of a bank's operations to a highly strategic process.

---

[62] Annual Report & Accounts 2007, Alliance & Leicester plc.
[63] *Liquidity Risk Measurement and Management*, Leonard Matz and Peter Neu, 2007.

3.6.3 Interbank Funding, the Money Markets and Central Bank Support

The interbank market provides a place for banks to place any excess funds they may have in the short term – or draw upon funds if they need to. The sums involved can be enormous, even though they are part of the routine activity of the banking sector. As a result of excessive leverage and over-reliance on short-term funding, the interbank market concentrated a lot of the imbalances that contributed to the current financial crisis.

Growing tensions and loss of confidence within the banking system during 2008 had a severe impact on the amount of interbank lending: volumes collapsed by 40% between March 2008 and December 2008, leaving banks with huge pressure to find alternatives for their funding needs (see Figure 3.6). Solvency was, of course, in doubt, but the most pressing need for banks was to pay their liabilities as they fell due. Quite simply, an inability to pay would mean that the bank in question was bust.

There is a direct link between the decreasing value of assets and the increase in liquidity requirements. Assets which could previously be used to raise, say, $100 on the repo market might only allow, say, $70 to be raised if they become perceived as more risky and thus command a higher "haircut" for collateral purposes: the borrowing bank will be forced to find alternatives to fund the shortfall. A similar mechanism is at play when a mark-to-market loss on a derivative contract required the counterparty to post more collateral to the bank on the other sides of the trade. Even before the bank realises any loss by either unwinding the derivative or selling the assets, the change in the mark-to-market accounting value has an immediate impact on liquidity. The loss of confidence in 2008, which culminated with the collapse of Lehman, led to a freeze of two major sources of bank refinancing: the interbank repo market and the US money market funds.

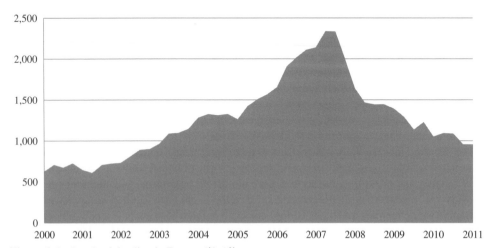

Figure 3.6   Interbank lending in Europe ($bn)[64]

---

[64] BIS.

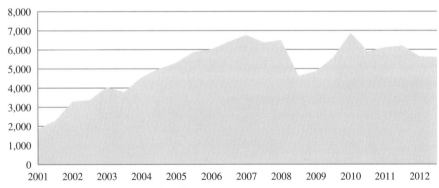

Figure 3.7   Size of the repo market ($bn)[65]

The Repo Market

A repurchase agreement, or "repo" in the jargon, is a popular form of secured funding in which a bank lends a security against cash for a given period of time. The guarantee provided by the collateral reduces the credit exposure to the lender and allows the borrower to access financing for a longer maturity and at more attractive rates than the unsecured market. For the borrower of the security, it is an efficient way to invest its cash in exchange for a return. As capital markets developed and a larger amount of high-grade securities were issued (namely, AAA tranches of CDOs and ABS), the repo market grew rapidly over the years to around $5,000–$7,000bn (see Figure 3.7).

The amount of financing available through the repo market shrunk as the collateral quality of subprime assets deteriorated. Loss of confidence caused knock-on problems during the subprime crisis, when banks who were repo lenders questioned the real value of subprime bonds as collateral, cutting access to refinancing to those banks who were already facing difficulties and were often heavily reliant upon access to repo.

US Money Market Funds

The US money market funds are large investors in bank "Commercial Paper" (short-term borrowings) and, for this reason, an important provider of liquidity to American banks as well as foreign banks with dollar-denominated assets to refinance. Tensions rose in this market, also affecting the Asset-Backed Commercial Paper (ABCP) market, which was one of the main markets used to refinance the assets of SIVs (see Section 2.6). Cost became prohibitive, jumping from a few basis points to 500bp and more in November 2008 (see Figure 3.8).

Central Banks as Providers of Liquidity

This massive potential funding shortfall threatened the whole banking system with collapse. If banks cannot fund themselves overnight, they will fail; the contagion in 2008 would have been systemic. Central banks were forced to step in and provide large amounts of liquidity. In all currencies, the central bank is the ultimate provider of liquidity, since it owns and operates the currency. The extraordinary provision of short-term funding by central banks kept banks funded when the private funding markets had almost completely shut down. See Table 3.11.

---

[65] European repo market survey, ICMA.

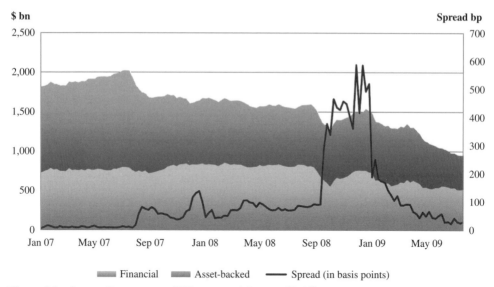

Figure 3.8   Outstanding amount of US commercial paper ($bn)[66]

Table 3.11   Examples of Central Bank funding facilities

Central Bank	Facility	Amount used (June 2009, $bn)[67]
Federal Reserve	Term auction facility	282
Federal Reserve	Commercial paper funding facility	114
Federal Reserve	Term asset-backed securities loan facility	25
Federal Reserve	Outright purchases of assets Agency MBS Agency debt Treasury securities	 462 97 184
ECB	Long-term refinancing operations (LTRO)	1,019
ECB	Covered bond purchases	(programme started in July 2009)
Bank of England	Asset purchase facility	173
Bank of Japan	ST liquidity provision	777
Bank of Japan	Outright purchase of assets Commercial paper Corporate bonds	 21 18

---

[66] Global Financial Stability report, IMF, October 2009.
[67] Federal Reserve, ECB, Bank of England, IMF.

Table 3.12 List of long-term refinancing operations by the ECB[68]

Date	Maturity (years)	Alloted amount (€bn)	Bid amount (€bn)	Number of banks
24 June 2009	1	442	442	1,121
30 Sept 2009	1	75	75	589
16 Dec 2009	1	97	97	224
26 Oct 2011	1	57	57	181
21 Dec 2011	3	489	489	523
29 Feb 2012	3	530	530	800

The provision of huge amounts of liquidity caused the balance sheets of the central banks to balloon. The balance sheet of the Bank of England, the Federal Reserve and the ECB grew respectively by 188, 127 and 65% after implementing their various measures. In normal market conditions, these emergency liquidity facilities would not have been used for two reasons. Firstly, they can be relatively expensive and secondly, they can carry a stigma: no-one wants to be seen needing to use the emergency funding lines.

Prior to 2008, the ECB's liquidity operations had a pre-set amount and were allotted on a competitive basis for a period ranging from 1 week to 3 months. To address the need for longer-term funding, the ECB conducted a 1-year liquidity operation in June 2009, which had a low fixed rate (1%), no size limits and a flexible definition of eligible collateral. This "Long Term Refinancing Operation" (LTRO) had clearly lost its stigma: it was used by more than 1,000 institutions, who took €442bn of funding in total (see Table 3.12). The LTRO was later extended to a 3-year maturity.

Of course, the central banks are providing *liquidity* to the system, not *funding*. The huge amount of money being lent in the liquidity operations of central banks eventually finds its way back into the central bank as a deposit from a cash-rich bank. Instead of recycling their excess deposits in the interbanking markets, cash-rich banks choose to deposit their excess liquidity at the ECB. In effect, the central bank is, because of the heightened perception of credit risk of banks, acting as a liquidity hub for the entire system – see Figure 3.9.

Unintended Consequences

There is no doubt that central bank intervention prevented a collapse of the financial system. Nevertheless, the exceptional measures give rise to additional risks: an increase in central banks' exposure to credit and a distorting effect on asset prices. This provision of liquidity, combined with other anti-recessionary measures such as quantitative easing and a prolonged period of low interest rates, have impacted the apparent liquidity and price of assets. "Current policies come with a cost even as they act to magically float asset prices higher, making many of them to appear 'as good as money.'"[69]

The yield on troubled Eurozone sovereigns can serve as a case in point. Taking Spanish government bonds as an example, the direct purchases by the ECB and increased holdings by Spanish banks (Spanish banks' holdings of domestic government bonds grew from

---

[68] European Central Bank.
[69] There will be haircuts, Bill Gross, PIMCO Investment Outlook, May 2013.

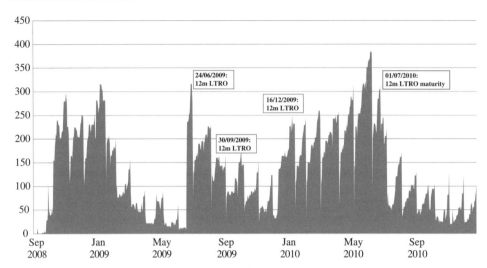

Figure 3.9   Funds deposited by banks at the ECB (€bn) [70]

€147bn in April 2010 to €230bn in January 2012[71]) have been major factors in driving down the yield.

This non-conventional approach has worked in bringing confidence back in the Eurozone and has dramatically reduced the cost of funding and liquidity for financials. But, like the "Greenspan put" in the USA (see Section 2.2), these measures have contributed to the build-up of risk in the financial system. The "exit strategy" is unclear and will certainly be challenging. "The easy monetary policies in advanced countries have been essential, in my view, to support the economy, and they remain essential to support the economy. But, their use over a prolonged period of time may cause side effects such as excessive risk-taking, leverage, and asset bubbles. So, the question is, are we seeing evidence that those risks are growing? And the answer is 'yes'. We're seeing some evidence in the United States as well as in emerging markets."[72]

3.6.4 Deposit Guarantee Schemes

In order to reduce the chances of a bank run, where retail depositors panic and withdraw their funds from a troubled bank, most countries run a deposit guarantee scheme (DGS). These protect the value of a bank deposit up to a certain amount, either through a government promise or guarantee, or through access to a fund that is built up over time by the banks.

The schemes are generally meant to cover only retail deposits, not corporate, wholesale or institutional funds. The amount of coverage per institution and per depositor can vary. For example, in the EU, deposits up to €100,000 are covered, in the USA the limit is $250,000, while in Australia deposits up to A$1m are covered.[73]

---

[70] Ibid.

[71] Spanish Treasury.

[72] Transcript of the Press Briefing on the Global Financial Stability Report, José Viñals, IMF, 17 April 2013.

[73] Thematic Review on Deposit Insurance Systems: Peer Review Report, Financial Stability Board, 8 February 2012.

DGSs charge the banks in their universe a premium for the depositor protection they provide. These premiums are sometimes risk-adjusted (as in the USA, Argentina, Canada and Turkey[74]) with an assessment of the riskiness of the bank driving the premiums paid per unit of coverage. In many other countries, the premiums are flat-rate, with no adjustment for the riskiness of the bank covered.

Those non-risk-adjusted DGSs highlight the problem of moral hazard in the DGS concept. If the public perceives that their deposit is 100% safe, no matter into which institution it is deposited, then they will not pay any attention to the riskiness of their bank. Risky banks will be able to attract retail deposits at low cost to finance their risky lending. The existence of the DGS will reduce the incentive for banks to be prudent and creditworthy. Well-run, low-risk banks have campaigned against flat-rate DGS premiums,[75] high DGS limits and even the existence of DGSs in principle.[76]

The other limitation of DGSs is that they do not cover institutional clients, whose deposits are "lumpier" and the withdrawal of which can have more severe consequences than a retail run. On certain occasions (e.g. Dexia), governments have been forced to give blanket guarantees on all the liabilities of a bank, as an emergency response to the beginning of a run.

Text of the press release issued to counter a run on Dexia on the morning of 4 october 2011[77]

François Baroin, Minister of the Economy, Finance and Industry and Didier Reynders, Belgian Minister of Finance commit to support Dexia.

As part of the restructuring of Dexia, the Belgian and French States, in liaison with the central banks, will take every necessary measure to ensure safety of depositors and creditors. To this end, they commit to provide their guarantee to the financings raised by Dexia.

3.6.5 Securitisation

Securitisation was a new financing technique that emerged in the 1970s whereby loans were turned into bonds. A bank assigns a number of loans to a portfolio or "pool" and sells them to a subsidiary called a Special Purpose Vehicle (SPV). The SPV then borrows money from investors by issuing bonds. The income from the loans is used to pay the interest coupon on the bonds and also to amortise or repay them. If the loans turn sour, the investors take the hit from the credit losses, not the bank. The bank is off the hook and the investors have assumed the risk. The reason that it is necessary for bonds to be issued is that the risk of the loan pool is sliced up or "tranched", with some some investors preferring safer tranches and others preferring riskier tranches.

Securitisation issuance peaked at nearly $5,000bn in 2006 (see Figure 3.10).[78]

---

[74] Ibid.
[75] Annual Report and Accounts, Nationwide Building Society, 2009.
[76] Deposit Guarantee Schemes are recipe for trouble, Dr Wim Boostra, Rabobank, 25 February 2011.
[77] Minister of the Economy, Finance and Industry, 4 October 2011.
[78] Global Financial Stability Report, IMF, October 2009.

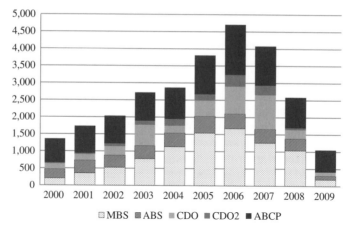

Figure 3.10   Global private-label securitisation issuance by type ($bn)

Types of Loan

All sorts of loans can be securitised. Most securitisations contain only one type of loan – prime residential mortgages, say, or auto loans, but never a mix of mortgages and auto loans – so that investors can understand what they are buying into. In order to manage concentration risk, however, most of them are quite diversified within the asset class, for example containing mortgages to thousands of borrowers across several regions. Residential mortgages are by far the most common type of loan to be securitised, but examples of other loan types include commercial mortgages, auto loans, consumer loans and credit cards. The technology has even been applied to other types of cash flows that resemble loans, for example streams of royalties. By way of illustration, in 1997, David Bowie securitised the royalty streams of 10 years' worth of certain of his tracks (including "Let's Dance" and "China Girl") raising $55m from the sale of these "Bowie bonds". Other artists, such as James Brown, Iron Maiden and Rod Stewart, subsequently entered into similar arrangements.[79]

Tranching

Securitisations tend to be quite large (say, $500m or more) and are subdivided into separate layers or tranches. Certain investors might choose to buy the low-risk tranches, which will always repay unless the number of customer defaults extends beyond a very high and highly improbable level. Some might choose to invest in the riskier tranches, which are more likely to bear losses but pay a higher coupon. So, different scenarios of customer defaults on their loans will lead to different outcomes for the various tranches of bond investors in the securitisation transaction. In theory, the interest coupon on the bonds reflects their place in the securitisation hierarchy and the expected losses and risks of that tranche.

   The theory of tranching relies upon the diversification within the pool. In other words, how likely are the defaults of some loans to coincide with the defaults of others? If diversification is high, correlation is low: the risk is contained within the lower tranches of the securitisation and there is little risk in the higher ("senior") tranches. Conversely, if diversification is low

---

[79] Comments on Music Royalty Securitizations, Duff & Phelps Credit Rating, September 1999.

and correlation is high, then the risk in the senior tranches is not much lower than in the junior tranches. Assumptions on the correlation of loans are key to getting the right tranching and the right risk assessment of the tranches. Many subprime securitisations were too optimistic on the assumed lack of correlation. They received credit ratings that were too good and suffered losses that were higher than the risk models indicated. The impact of different correlation assumptions can be illustrated in this example:

> When the default correlations are zero, 20% of the [securitization] get the highest rating Aaa, with the mezzanine tranches taking half. Simply by increasing the default correlations to 10% the Aaa tranche vanishes. By increasing the correlations to 30% the best we can do is Ba.[80]

The mis-estimation of correlation assumptions is one of the reasons that there were large losses on US subprime bonds rated AAA. The loans were much more correlated than had been supposed.

Role of Credit Ratings

In a securitisation, investors need to appraise the risk of their tranche of a large pool of bank loans. Many relied upon the judgement of the credit ratings agencies, for whom the designation of ratings to securitisation deals became a major business line.[81] The agencies developed statistical models that showed how the tranched transactions would behave in a stressed scenario based on historical precedent. The statistically computed probability of losses was summarised in the credit rating. Ratings became central to the securitisation industry: transactions were structured to optimise the ratings of the various tranches, so that investors would be attracted. New techniques, such as the creation of securitisations-of-securitisations or CDO, were developed in order to squeeze out extra amounts of highly-rated paper that would be gobbled up by investors.

Banks were keen users of securitisation for five main reasons, explained in Table 3.13.

The problems in the securitisation model became apparent with the many securitisations of US subprime mortgages. The fundamental problem was that money had been lent to people who were unlikely to be able to service and repay the loan, and the value of the underlying collateral (i.e. the house against which the mortgage had been lent) was less than the amount of the mortgage. The subsequent steps in the securitisation chain involved negligent investors over-paying for low-quality securities, in part guided by excessive reliance upon inappropriate credit ratings.

> At the core of it all is poor underwriting standards. This point can not be emphasised enough. Everything else down the securitisation chain is affected by this initial shortcoming. This crisis is no different from others in that weakness in many banks' fundamental underwriting principles was, among other factors, a key contributor to the asset quality problems that have arisen. In addition, poor risk management at a number of firms resulted in a massive build-up of risk concentrations within and across institutions that further compounded already weak asset quality.[82]

---

[80] On the efficacy of financial regulations, Jón Daníelsson, London School of Economics.
[81] Investor Presentation 1Q 2013, Moody's.
[82] Beyond the crisis: the Basel Committee's strategic response, Nout Wellink, Chairman, Basel Committee.

Table 3.13   Main reasons for banks to use securitisation

Overall cheaper source of financing	Since securitisation notes could achieve ratings far higher than that of the originating bank, with the vast bulk being rated AAA, the yield on a securitisation bond was generally cheaper than raising conventional funding based on the bank's own credit rating.
Availability of funding	Securitisation was sometimes the only form of refinancing available for lower rated issuers to access long-term liquidity. Securitisation notes were also able to be used as collateral for central bank refinancing operations such as the the ECB LTRO.
Diversification of investor base	ABS investors are a distinct class of credit investors. The vast volumes of AAA-rated notes and the historical performance and stability attracted more risk-averse investors. This is an important opportunity for banks, who can then access long-term funding as a fall-back position when other forms of funding dry up.
Regulatory capital arbitrage	Under Basel I, securitisation was used to reduce the regulatory capital requirements of the bank. For example, a $100 portfolio of mortgages would require at least $4 of regulatory capital if it were financed on the bank's balance sheet in the traditional way ($100 × 50% risk-weighting × 8% minimum regulatory capital requirement = $4). If securitised, the regulatory capital requirement could be reduced drastically, often to under 1% of the total balance, requiring several times less than previously. This was because banks could sell around 97% of the exposure to investors and "retain" the riskiest tranche of "first loss", which only required a tiny amount of capital. The scope of regulatory arbitrage was reduced drastically when the more intelligent Basel II rules came into force.
De-risking/Risk transfer	Since securitisation gives non-bank investors the opportunity to invest in bank loans, it is a tool for risk transfer across the boundaries of the banking industry. Securitisation notes are held by all kinds of asset managers: insurance companies, pension funds, mutual funds, central banks and so on. In theory, this dissipates the risks of the banking industry in a good way. In practice, there were new risks introduced by the securitisation process: lax underwriting, poor governance of the origination process (which often became "pump and dump"), increased opacity, over-reliance on credit ratings and circularity (as banks ended up with securitisation exposures in their warehouses, SIVs and Treasury portfolios). *Caveat emptor* was not heeded.

What was the actual default experience of investors in securitisation bonds? The answer is totally different for each of the two main markets: "From mid-2007 to the end of 2010, only 0.95% of all European structured-finance issues defaulted, compared to 7.7% of all US structured-finance issues, and 6.3% among the universe of global corporate bonds."[83] It would be fair to say that the European default experience is approximately what the bonds would have been expected to suffer, whereas the US default rates are somewhat higher than expectations, yet better than people's worst fears at the low ebbs of the market during 2008 and 2009.

Many people are sceptical of the desire of a bank to sell a portfolio of loans it has originated. There is now a common, though by no means self-evident, assumption that the bank

---

[83] Outlook for the Securitisation Market, *OECD Journal*, 2011.

that lent the money in the first place should retain some sort of risk involvement all the way through to repayment of the loan. There is a fear that banks will originate poor-quality loans if they have no interest in them beyond point of origination and sell-on; they will "pump and dump". In other industries and markets, companies sell on assets to willing investors, without this fear. It seems to have arisen purely as a reaction to the subprime debacle, even though it does not appear to be a cause.

To put it technically, the bad experience of the subprime debacle has *reversed the disintegration of the value chain of bank lending*. New regulations on securitisation require the originating bank to retain "skin in the game" in order to preserve some kind of alignment of interest between the originator and the buyer of the securitisation notes. The new regulations also make it quite inefficient for banks to invest in securitisation notes. Unfortunately, the securitisation label has such a stigma that it is – for the time being – effectively hobbled as a tool for banks to broaden and diversify their financial investor base.

3.6.6 Covered Bonds

Covered bonds are a particularly low-risk form of bank debt, as their repayment is doubly secured, firstly on the covenant of the issuer and secondly on high quality pools of prime residential mortgage loans or public sector loans. The investor only fails to get repaid in the event that the issuer defaults *and* the pool of assets is worthless. Such a safe investment enables banks to benefit from a refinancing in the market at an attractive cost. Naturally, covered bonds have tended to receive superlative credit ratings: the right structure from a good bank will generally be given the top rating of AAA by the ratings agencies.

Covered bonds were invented in Germany in the eighteenth century. Covered bonds now exist in many different jurisdictions and in various forms. The common characteristics are:

1. Issued by a bank, they are liabilities of the bank and stay on its balance sheet.
2. Backed on a *dual recourse basis* by high quality assets (such as public sector loans or prime residential mortgages meeting strict criteria): in other words, covered bonds are quality, secured funding. In the case of failure of the issuing bank, investors have a preferential claim on the cover pool assets, which are not included in insolvency proceedings.
3. The pool is not fixed but is dynamic, with its composition changing over time; the quality of the pool is validated by an independent third party.
4. The pool is over-collateralised: the investor gets paid in full even if the cover pool assets fall in value by a certain amount.

Table 3.14 gives an overview of the major covered bond frameworks in activity by jurisdictions as well as the outstanding volume of bonds issued.[84]

Because of their superlative credit quality, covered bonds have been an important part of the funding strategy of banks during the current financial crisis. They have exhibited a strong resilience to market volatility and during many periods have been the only access for banks to long-term funding. Plus, covered bonds are generally treated as eligible assets for the lending operations of central banks. Unsurprisingly, banks have reacted with a larger amount of covered bonds assets either sold to investors for refinancing or kept on their balance sheet as a contingent source of access to funding.

---

[84] BNP Paribas.

Table 3.14   Covered bonds by country (examples)

	Implementation of legal framework	Outstanding volume end 2011 (€bn)
Germany	• Current Act came into effect in 19 July 2005 • Previous legal framework dates back to 1899	586
France	• 1999	366
Spain	• 1981 • Actual benchmark issuance started in September 1999	402
Italy	• May 2007	64
Netherlands	• First structured CB was issued in 2005 • Regulatory framework was introduced in summer of 2008	54
UK	• First structured CB was issued in July 2003 • Regulatory framework was introduced in March 2008	198
Sweden	• July 2004 (outstanding mortgage bonds were converted into covered bonds when the law came into place)	209
Denmark	• Current framework was amended in 2007 • Previous framework dates back to 1850	351
Canada	• First structured CB was issued in October 2007 • Regulatory framework was introduced in April 2012	39
Belgium	• 2012	4

Going forward, covered bonds should remain a solid and dependable source of funding for banks to refinance their loan book on the best terms. They are the best credit instrument a bank can offer to investors, since they have dual recourse and are over-collateralised. In case of bank failure, the losses to covered bond investors should be low, as they are exempt from bail-in provisions. They tend to be highly rated and highly liquid, both of which features investors love. New types of covered bonds could be considered, for example expanding to other asset classes such as SME loans.

Of course, the safer the covered bond, the riskier the rest of the funding structure. If assets are available to covered bond investors in the event of bank failure, then they are not available to regular, unsecured investors: they are *encumbered*. Regulators, investors and ratings agencies are paying attention to levels of encumbrance and can set a cap to the percentage of the balance sheet eligible for covered bond refinancing.

As the graph in Figure 3.11 shows clearly, the crisis has put secured funding and covered bond issuance at the forefront. Covered bond issuance increased from under €100bn in 2000 to more than €500bn in 2011. The use of covered bonds to access central bank funding has been a driver behind this success, but covered bonds have also become the most stable and efficient form of long-term *market-based* funding for banks originating mortgages.

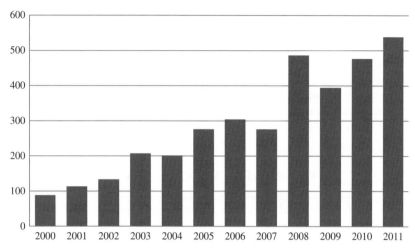

Figure 3.11   Total covered bonds outstanding (backed by mortgages) (€bn)[85]

3.6.7 Liquidity Stress Tests

The recent and intense focus on improving banks' funding and liquidity structures has led to a broader use of stress tests in the banking industry. Stress tests allow a simulation of liquidity needs under various scenarios. Of course, stress tests are deterministic. The outputs of the stress tests are a direct reflection of the assumptions taken. Consequently, they are seen either as useless if the assumptions are not harsh enough or punitive if the assumptions relate to extreme conditions, remote from reality. There seems to be little agreement on how severe a stress banks should realistically plan around and be tested against. The scenarios for idiosyncratic stress (single institution in problems) are far easier to deal with than for a systemic stress (where the entire industry is in trouble).

At present, there are few satisfactory role models for a liquidity stress test. The US Federal Reserve is extending its solvency stress tests to include a deeper assessment of liquidity risk, but this is unlikely to give much insight, as it will be based on a limited set of scenarios.

Multiple scenario analysis (or "wargaming", see Section 7.7.2) is a good way to assess liquidity risk and trigger a better understanding of the impact various events affecting access to liquidity can have on the environment and ability to fund the balance sheet.

Measures that can be Taken during a Liquidity Stress
As well as keeping liquidity risk under control, banks can actively manage a deteriorating liquidity position, for example:

- Ensuring information flow on key liquidity metrics, within the bank, with key counterparties and with the central bank.
- Slowing down growth (in most banks, the origination function is not very reactive to feedback from the Treasury on funding problems).

---

[85] European Mortgage Federation, Hypostat 2011.

- Repricing products.
- Relationship meetings with key big-ticket depositors.
- Selling, securitising or syndicating loans.
- Boosting public confidence (restocking ATMs, directors making large personal deposits etc.).

These actions have been used by several banks during the last few years and are likely to form the backbone of the liquidity management contingency plans of all banks.

3.7 WHAT IS A DERIVATIVE?

Derivatives are innovations in risk sharing, not in risk itself.[86]

The "D" word … Derivatives are financial products that seem to draw criticism from many angles. The public perception of derivatives is that they are unnatural monstrosities: opaque, complex, difficult to comprehend, enormously risky and – like Dr Frankenstein's monster – beyond the control of their creators. Warren Buffett, the Chairman of Berkshire Hathaway, famously observed that he considered that "derivatives are financial weapons of mass destruction, carrying dangers that, while now latent, are potentially lethal".[87] As described elsewhere, the exposure to or risk management of derivatives has played a major role in the troubles of a number of financial institutions in recent times (for example, JP Morgan, AIG, Bear Stearns, Lehman, Dexia). That they are risky is clear. But they also have an important utility that means they should be managed not shunned. "Derivatives are something like electricity: dangerous if mishandled, but bearing the potential to do good."[88]

Derivatives are contracts, where the amount paid by each side of the contract varies according to a reference measure. The value of the derivative is *derived* from the value of the reference measure.

There are three basic sorts of derivative contract, as described in Table 3.15.

Financial derivatives have seen vast amounts of innovation and creativity, most of it useful and good but some of it dubious.

> The range of derivatives contracts is limited only by the imagination of man (or sometimes, so it seems, madmen). At Enron, for example, newsprint and broadband derivatives, due to be settled many years in the future, were put on the books. Or say you want to write a contract speculating on the number of twins to be born in Nebraska in 2020. No problem – at a price, you will easily find an obliging counterparty.[89]

One type of innovation relates to the development of credit derivatives such as the credit default swap (CDS). The CDS is protection against default, similar in many ways to an insurance policy. It played an important role in the development of the subprime crisis and was the product at the heart of the huge exposures and losses carried by AIG and the other monoline credit insurers.

---

[86] *Big Bets Gone Bad: Big Bets Gone Bad: Derivatives and Bankruptcy in Orange County. The Largest Municipal Failure in U.S. History*, Philippe Jorion, 1995.
[87] To the Shareholders of Berkshire Hathaway Inc., Warren Buffet, February 2003.
[88] Arthur Levitt, chairman SEC, Congress Testimony, 5 January 1995.
[89] To the Shareholders of Berkshire Hathaway Inc., Warren Buffet, February 2003.

Table 3.15   Three basic derivatives types

Futures	Contracts with a counterparty to purchase a product at a given price on a certain date in the future. Futures are normally standard agreements traded in exchanges, such as futures on US Treasuries. This form of derivatives developed initially in ancient civilisations as a way for farmers to lock in a price for their crop.
Swaps	Contracts where two counterparties exchange payment streams, for example a variable-interest-rate ("floating-rate") stream for a fixed-rate stream; or a stream in US Dollars for a stream in Canadian Dollars.
Options	An option contract gives the buyer the right but not the obligation to buy a given asset at a given price (the "strike price") on a given date. Or, to sell a given asset at a given price (the "strike price") on a given date. The option to buy is a call option and the option to sell is a put option.

DERIVATIVES: A WORKED EXAMPLE

Suppose a Swedish company has the opportunity to borrow some money in US dollars at an attractive rate: let's assume it would cost them a lot more to borrow the funds in Swedish kroner, or the sum they need to borrow is so huge that the kroner market would not be big enough. The company will exchange the dollars into kroner on the day it gets the loan – that much is straightforward. But during the life of the loan, it faces the risk of a fluctuation in the foreign exchange rate, which will impact the repayments it has to make. Those repayments are denominated in dollars. An appreciation of the dollar will increase the kroner amount of debt to be repaid, potentially causing financial problems.

The Swedish company could manage this risk through a derivative. The derivative would function as follows:

1. The Swedish company agrees a cross-currency swap with its bank. This fixes the schedule of kroner payments that the company must make and the dollar amounts it will receive.
2. At each date when interest and principal are due, the company receives a dollar amount and pays a kroner amount, as per the agreed derivative schedule.
3. When the loan is finally due for repayment, the final amount of dollars and kroner changes hands and the transaction terminates naturally.

The derivative (this one is known as a "cross-currency swap") has transformed the dollar borrowing into kroner borrowing. For the company, the end result is as if they had borrowed in the local currency all along. They are not exposed to fluctuations in the exchange rate at all.

That risk has been entirely transferred to the bank that has provided the derivative. They themselves will have the job of hedging their own exposure to changes in market rates – this can be done by finding a counterparty that has the "mirror image" needs of the Swedish company, needing to pay in dollars but wanting to receive kroner. Perhaps this "mirror image" is an American company that has to pay some Swedish employees and doesn't want the amount to vary when expressed in dollars. The market mechanisms that banks use to balance their exposures are rarely as simple as merely finding a mirror image, but it illustrates well the concept of derivatives risk management.

At this level of detail, derivatives can be fairly simple to understand and should not be too daunting. However, the risks of derivatives should also be apparent. One of these risks is *counterparty risk*. Since derivatives contracts are generally long-term contracts struck at market levels on the day of agreement, if the market moves in one's favour, they can become a significantly valuable asset. If this happens, they are said to be "*in the money*". Conversely, if the market moves in the opposite direction, the derivative would become "*out of the money*". When a derivative is an asset – when it is "in the money" – the value of that asset relies upon the ability of the derivatives counterparty to keep their side of the deal. To mitigate against this risk, most derivatives counterparties have arrangements in place to secure their future receipts by posting collateral, such as cash or high quality bonds. In the case of default the collateral will be seized by the counterparty to make up for the amount of the "in the money" asset that they have now lost due to the contract terminating early. In most derivatives transactions between professional counterparties, collateral is calculated every day and the collateral management process is codified in an industry standard agreement, the Collateral Standard Agreement (CSA).

Increasingly, derivatives are being managed centrally by clearing houses, which are specialised institutions that manage the valuation and collateral process at arm's length and on a bigger scale. In principle, this is meant to reduce the risks of derivatives settlement in a crisis situation.

Development of Derivatives
Derivatives are very much related to the real economy. As noted above, the first futures were used in the agricultural sector. A farmer is exposed to a large number of risks and has to be able to plan his production and pay for his input costs such as seed, fuel and wages. Securing the future sale price for his crop enables him to avoid financial problems when market rates shift and so he is more stable and productive as a farmer, making the broader economy better off.

In the last fifty years, since the collapse of the Bretton Woods agreement on currency rates, the risks of currency fluctuations to participants in international trade have increased. Financial markets have responded to this risk management need by providing future contracts on foreign exchange. In May 1972, futures contracts on various major currencies started to trade on the Chicago Mercantile Exchange. Option contracts followed later in the 1980s as options pricing methodologies were developed.

Information technology has also played a major role in the development of derivatives. Since derivatives involve the computation of future cash flows for pricing and risk management purposes, powerful IT has played a key role in the increasing sophistication of derivatives.

Standard derivatives are traded on exchanges, but many tailored derivatives are managed on a bilateral basis between the bank and its counterparty. These trades are known as over-the-counter (OTC) and are difficult to measure precisely but surveys conducted by the BIS have given an estimated size of nearly $700,000bn.

Criticism #1: Derivatives are a source of losses
Most people struggle to understand anything beyond the basics of mathematics, science and technology. If these areas bring complexity into their everyday lives, they are tolerated, if they are proven to be failsafe. If problems occur with complex things – and persistently occur – then people are justified in blaming the complexity.

Prima facie, this *appears* to be the case with derivatives. However, truly complex derivatives in actual fact account only for a small fraction of the entire universe being traded. Furthermore, the most spectacular losses involving derivatives (for example, Orange County,

Metallgesellschaft, Barings, Société Générale) did not involve complex products, but were rather about risk management failures on simple and standard contracts that were highly visible and traded on exchanges. This should be no surprise: truly complex derivatives are rarely transacted in large size, whereas the simpler, standard contracts traded on exchanges have strong liquidity and so allow for risk-takers to build large positions. When markets shift unexpectedly, the risk management failings are exposed.

> For all the horror stories about derivatives, it is worth emphasizing that the world's banks have blown away vastly more in bad real estate deals than they'll ever lose on their derivatives portfolio.[90]

Criticism #2: Derivatives are speculative

When it comes to entering into derivative contracts, the distinction between speculating and hedging is a fine one. Economic agents use derivatives to modify the cash flows on their assets (or liabilities) and cover themselves against certain events or market configurations. As such, entering into a derivative involves taking a view on the direction of the market.

We all do it. Anyone who has a mortgage or a savings account has had to make the decision to consider, say, a fixed rate deal or a long-term deal. Choosing the *right* structure depends on one's view of the market as much as on one's true risk management needs. Few people are willing to pay the extra risk premium required to de-risk their own personal finances, for example by locking in their mortgage payments to a long-term fixed rate that is quite high.

One potentially disturbing aspect of derivatives is their ability to contain a high degree of embedded leverage. Customers wishing to build a credit exposure on Volkswagen, for example, can decide to buy a Volkswagen bond for cash. Alternatively, they can sell a Credit Default Swap (CDS) on Volkswagen with minimal cash outlay. The credit exposure will be similar and the customer who has sold the CDS will only need to post collateral for as much as the value of the contract is negative. The CDS customer will collect the associated CDS premium in a similar way as it would receive the coupon if it had purchased the bond.

The unfunded nature of derivatives is very often what explains the disconnect between the implied level of risk in cash instruments (bonds) and derivatives (CDS).

The volume of CDS on a given credit is not related to the outstanding amount of securities from this same credit and it is very often much larger. Also, the CDS levels and the credit spreads on cash bonds are very often disconnected and there are a number of reasons for this:

- Unlike cash bonds, CDS are non-funded instruments, which means that they are easier to access, especially in times when liquidity is expensive and scarce.
- CDS are usually more liquid and standardised instruments than outstanding bonds, which may not always be available when dealers have reduced inventories and are often more complex to use (duration can vary with the coupon level, the issue size and initial placement can weigh on the liquidity etc.).
- CDS are also used as a "proxy" instrument for a trading position when another instrument is not readily available. This is, for example, what happened after the ban on "naked" CDS protections on sovereign (in which a trader buys protection on a sovereign without owning the underlying credit exposure) decided by the European Union in November 2012 and which has led to a surge in buying of protection on European financials, seen as well correlated with sovereign risk (see Table 3.16).

---

[90] *Merton Miller on Derivatives*, Merton Miller, 1997.

Table 3.16   Changes in CDS volume traded ($bn)[91]

	Q4 2012	Q1 2013
EU sovereign CDS	228	168
iTraxx senior financials	252	400

It is also one of the reasons behind the growth of the derivatives markets to, in many cases, multiples of the underlying securities these derivatives were supposed to hedge.

As Figure 3.12 shows, the secondary credit spread on the "cash bonds" (in this case the 5Y senior unsecured issued by ING in May 2011 and January 2012) are well correlated with one another. The secondary credit spread represents the risk premium asked by the market for holding these bonds and bizarrely this spread differs widely from the cost of credit protection on these bonds for a period of 5 years. In theory, an investor should be indifferent between holding the bond or selling CDS protection on the credit. In fact, the CDS is wider, reflecting the stronger demand for protection on these bonds, especially in the months that followed the peak of the crisis in the Eurozone.

The relative size of the derivatives market and the strategies involving the use of derivative instruments to hedge market moves has been criticised as the "*tail wagging the dog*".[92] It has also been identified as one of the causes of the 1987 stock market crash, during which the derivatives-based strategies of portfolio insurance using stock index futures, combined with the automated response of certain programme trading strategies, exacerbated the fall in the stock market.

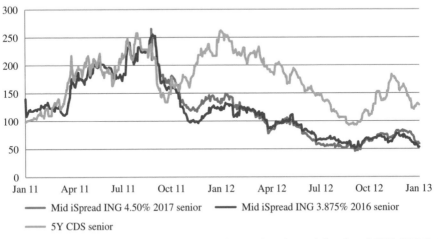

Figure 3.12   Difference in the risk premium implied by ING senior cash bonds and ING CDS (bp)[93]

---

[91] *Financial Times*, DTCC.
[92] John Shad, former Chairman SEC (1981–1987).
[93] Bloomberg.

On balance, it would seem that derivatives can be a tool for risk management or risk exposure, for hedging or speculating, for stability or volatility. But they are only a tool. In the same way that "guns don't kill people, people do", it can be argued that any problems involving derivatives are generally indicative of broader risk management failings.

> Contrary to the widely held perception, derivatives have made the world a safer place, not a more dangerous one. They have made it possible for firms and institutions to deal efficiently and cost effectively with risks and hazards that have plagued them for decades, if not for centuries. True, some firms and some financial institutions have managed to lose substantial sums on derivatives, but some firms and institutions will always find ways to lose money. Good judgement and good luck cannot be taken for granted.[94]

Criticism #3: Derivatives spread risk in the financial system in an uncontrolled way

Some people have criticised the way that derivatives have been used to allow the accumulation of risks in certain corners of the financial system, thus harming its overall stability. Clearly, derivatives cannot make risk disappear, but merely transfer it. "A bank's use of futures to hedge its own inventory does not, of course, eliminate the price risk of the underlying bond; it merely transfers that risk to someone else who does want to bear the risk."[95] Certain areas of the derivatives market have become a source of trading profits and losses rather than a protection market. It appears to provide a new source of risk, rather than merely shifting existing risk into a different location. The vast notional amounts in question are concentrated in a fragile system:

> At 1st May 2009 nearly 40% of gross outstandings in single-name CDS concerned reference entities in the financial sector. Instead of redistributing credit risks, CDS have actually contributed to intensifying systemic risk by concentrating exposure on a handful of highly interconnected players that are simultaneously buyers, sellers and underliers. This has spawned a new type of risk, "too interconnected to fail", which has superseded "too big to fail" risk.[96]

Derivatives can provide the illusion that the risk has disappeared from a certain segment or product in the market, when it has simply been transferred into another part, where it may or may not be the source of weaknesses affecting the entire the financial system.

Criticism #4: The derivatives market is too big in size

Between June 2006 and December 2011, the derivatives market doubled in size. Interest rate products represent the largest component, with nearly $500,000bn of notional exposure. That's seven times more than global GDP, which is around $70,000bn. The size of the derivatives market has reduced only as a result of the current financial crisis – see Figure 3.13.

---

[94] *Merton Miller on Derivatives*, Merton Miller, 1997.
[95] Ibid.
[96] Credit default swaps and financial stability: risks and regulatory issues, Banque de France.

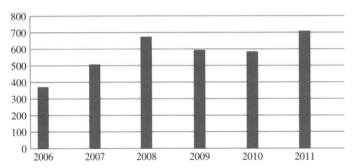

Figure 3.13   Global OTC derivatives notional amounts outstanding ($trn)[97]

3.8 MARK-TO-MARKET AND PROCYCLICALITY

> The pro-cyclical behavior of asset values is an economic reality. No good policy purpose would be served by attempting to hide the fact by corrupting accounting standards.[98]

The banking industry is notoriously cyclical; it relies upon confidence; it provides leverage to the economy; and it is massively leveraged itself. Each of these features introduces volatility and they combine to make the issue of managing cyclicality highly important.

Is Risk (Pro-)Cyclical?

In good times, people feel better. Their confidence rises and the price they are willing to pay for an asset increases. The increase in price makes the owner feel good and improves their confidence. Retail investors look to their professional advisors to produce good investment returns and so the professionals follow the trend, buying the assets that are in vogue and rising in price. Banks join in, lending money to finance asset purchases. As the good times roll, asset prices keep rising, the leveraged investor makes more money than the unleveraged investor and no-one loses money. Confidence keeps growing and turns into exuberance. As asset bubbles develop, the price that is being paid for the asset in question rises far above any fundamental value. Even if professional investors are sceptical about the true value of the asset, their customers demand investment performance that is at least in line with the market as a whole: a contrarian asset manager often loses custom in an upswing. Banks find themselves under pressure to lend to the "sure thing" investments and experience strong growth and accounting profits. When investment bubbles collapse or general macro-economic conditions turn sour, conditions reverse. Quite simply, banks lose money in busts. Defaults are cyclical. To exacerbate the situation, it is not only the probability of default that increases with deteriorating economic conditions. Risk mitigants often fall apart too: undrawn facilities get drawn down, increasing exposure; correlation increases; levels of recovery on defaulted assets decrease. Bank losses are not just cyclical, they are highly cyclical.

---

[97] BIS.

[98] Mark to Market Accounting—What Are the Issues?, Warren Coats, Cato Institute, Cato.org, 29 October 2008.

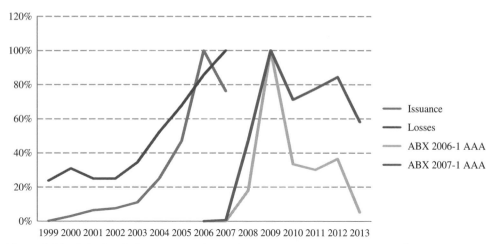

Figure 3.14   Subprime indicators as % of peak (issuance and losses on ABS CDOs,[99] loss of value according to subprime ABS indices[100])

The question of risk, however, is a little more complex. If we look at the source of banks' losses during difficult situations, they relate overwhelmingly to risk exposures taken during periods of rising asset prices, low credit losses and falling credit spreads. Banks are assimilating risk during booms. Risk *losses* appear cyclical, but in fact, risk *origination* tends to lead the realisation of losses by around a quarter of a cycle.

To prove this empirically is challenging, but a set of recent data may help at least to illustrate the point. For subprime mortgage-backed securities, *confidence* (as proxied by issuance volumes) peaked at the end of 2006, *actual risk* (as proxied by eventual losses) peaked during 2007, while the *market perception* of risk peaked in the middle of 2009 (see Figure 3.14). These data are not conclusive, but they hopefully demonstrate a two-year gap between the origination of the mortgages and the market realisation of the losses.

In other words, the point of lowest risk-return payoff is immediately before the peak of a "boom" period and the point of highest risk-return is immediately before the trough of the "bust". Ironically, the risks on which banks lose the most money are the ones that are priced the lowest. The fundamental problem is that our perception of risk tends to be clouded during upswings. Cycles always overshoot reality. We only know the exact timing of peaks and troughs in retrospect and, indeed, there are often "mini-peaks" and "false troughs".

> Market prices behave more like thermometers of financial distress, measuring its temperature once it rises, than as barometers of distress, providing signals of its future materialisation (Borio and Drehmann, 2008). Hence the paradox of financial instability: the system appears strongest precisely when it is most vulnerable. This can easily contaminate the point-in-time measures of system-wide risk and also those of individual institutions' contributions to it.[101]

---

[99] Collateral Damage: Sizing and Assessing the Subprime CDO Crisis, Federal Reserve Bank of Philadelphia, May 2012.

[100] Markit ABX series.

[101] Implementing the macroprudential approach to financial regulation and supervision, Claudio Borio, Head of Research and Policy Analysis, Bank for International Settlements.

The Bank for International Settlements agrees with this viewpoint and was, indeed, aware of it well before the current financial crisis:

> It is better to think of risk as increasing in booms, not recessions, and that the increase in defaults in recessions simply reflects the materialisation of risk built up in the boom.[102]

Unfortunately, this view on risk is not universally held. Some observers and experts seem to think that banks become more risky during downturns and do not see losses as the realisation of risk that is already in the system: "Since the value of collateral is likely to be procyclical, asymmetric information will be relatively high in business cycle downturns and relatively low in booms."[103] We disagree with this latter viewpoint, preferring instead to believe that risk and losses are cyclical but not synchronised, owing to the difficulties in perception and measurement of risk.

Cyclical elements, such as risk, can become "procyclical" if they themselves feed back and cause cyclicality. In other words, the perception of high risk can cause fear of losses, which leads to a "credit crunch" where losses are caused by the lack of credit availability. Conversely, the perception of low risk can lead to exuberance and excessive supply of credit, leading to poor risk decisions and, ultimately, greater losses than would otherwise have occurred.

Should Information and Methodologies Reflect or Suppress Cyclicality?

Regulatory authorities appear to see certain methodologies as procyclical, in that they could amplify volatility and reduce financial stability. Examples of this include fair valuation, upfront recognition of profit and use of ratings-based triggers. These methodologies may have led banks to increase risk exposure when risk was not apparent (encouraging high volumes of structured transactions, for example); equally, they may have precipitated a downward spiral at times when losses became apparent and market risk appetite diminished.

Given the confidence link between perceived and actual performance, it is tempting to assume that suppressing risk information can, in itself, diminish risk. The opposing view is that the market does not like to be fed inaccurate or incomplete information, is not fooled by optimistic information and ascribes a risk premium to situations where lack of reliable information leads to uncertainty.

Policy options being considered seek to temper the irrational exuberance of a boom and soothe the rush for the exits as the bust approaches (see Table 3.17).

Current accounting standards do not look forward; prudential standards partially do, through the notion of "expected loss": the estimate of the average loss for the next year is deducted from regulatory capital. In future, through IFRS 9, accounting measures may incorporate a similar forward loss projection.

> If loan loss reserves are set to equal expected losses, in a forward-looking predictive manner, rather than equal to ex post realized losses, then the procyclical tendencies of banking can be mitigated somewhat. That is, as economic conditions are forecast to deteriorate, the bank would be required to reserve higher levels against the higher loan losses expected to occur because of the cyclical sensitivity of both PD and LGD, thereby reducing lending activity (EAD) at capital constrained banks in preparation for a cyclical downturn.[104]

---

[102] Procyclicality of the financial system and financial stability: issues and policy options, BIS, March 2001.
[103] Bank Risk Strategies and Cyclical Variation in Bank Stock Returns, Baele, Vennet and Van Landschoot, May 2005.
[104] A survey of cyclical effects in credit risk measurement models, BIS Working Papers No 126, January 2003.

Table 3.17 Anticyclical measures (examples)

Tools to dampen risk-taking during upswings	• Forward-looking risk-measures (e.g. stress tests or momentum-based measures) • Minimum risk capital requirements (or margin for derivatives transactions) • Increasing level of counter-cyclical buffers
Tools to calm markets during downturns	• Forbearance • Relaxation in minimum standards • Decreasing level of counter-cyclical buffers

Having said that, the one-year time horizon is somewhat arbitrary and disappointing. The level of dampening that it can provide is limited. Already, there is some support for the lifetime loss approach, whereby banks set aside an expected loss (EL) provision not just for one year's EL but for the EL for the entire life of the loan:

> More forward-looking measures of expected losses deviate substantially from incurred loss provisions. [Consider if] banks are assumed to hold provisions for lifetime loan losses based on the assumption that write-off rates gradually return to their long-run rate. Expected loss provisions exceed the actual stock of provisions because they incorporate both backward and forward-looking elements. This simple experiment would have resulted in UK banks holding around £50 billion of extra provisions leading into the crisis and needing to increase provisions by less as the crisis broke.[105]

In fact, this approach is being partially used already: the Bank of England's "Financial Policy Committee" is currently using a definition of capital for stress test purposes that incorporates a three-year EL on real estate lending.[106]

Basel II attempted to address the issue of procyclicality and allowed the choice of risk-weightings that were based on economic conditions and risk perceptions that were either (a) prevailing ("point in time" or PIT) or (b) average ("through the cycle" or TTC). A third broad alternative was considered: the "downturn" version, where banks assume that risks and default levels will be as bad as their models' data history allows. In essence, the PIT approach leads to more volatile risk appraisals and risk-weightings, whereas the TTC is smoothed. Neither approach is satisfactory: the PIT model is more procyclical and the TTC model less reliable, understating risk in a downturn. Few observers have questioned why average risk-weights have remained remarkably stable as economic conditions have deteriorated: TTC risk-weights are a major component of the technical answer.

Like regulators, credit ratings agencies also want to reduce the volatility in their assessments. The agencies' credit ratings are meant to be a *relative, medium-term* measure of creditworthiness rather than a volatile or absolute measure:

> Ratings will, on average, relate to subsequent default frequency, although they typically are not defined as precise default rate estimates. Moody's ratings are therefore intended to convey opinions of the relative creditworthiness of issuers and obligations [...] Moody's ratings process also involves forming views about the likelihood of plausible scenarios, or outcomes—not forecasting them [...]. Normal fluctuations in economic activity are generally included in these scenarios, and by incorporating our views about the likelihood of such scenarios, we give our ratings relative stability over economic cycles and a sense of horizon.[107]

---

[105] Bank of England Financial Stability Report, November 2012.

[106] News Release – Financial Policy Committee statement from its policy meeting, 19 March 2013, Bank of England, 27 March 2013.

[107] Understanding Moody's Corporate Bond Ratings and Rating Process, Moody's Investor Services, May 2002.

Are Buffers and/or Forbearance the Right Tools to Combat Deleveraging in a Downturn?

One of the challenges in managing cyclicality is the simple fact that buffers tend to become de facto minima. We call this the "two spare wheels" mentality: if you need to carry one spare wheel, then you may choose also to carry a "spare spare". Off-road drivers will understand the notion of "two spare wheels", especially if they have ever been caught out a long way from home with a second puncture! Similarly, the banking industry often treats mandatory buffers as minima. The true buffers are the banks' own voluntary buffers (which are therefore genuine surpluses) over and above a regulator-prescribed buffer. This was the case in the UK in 2012 with the banks' liquidity holdings, which were seen by the Bank of England as hindering the provision of credit to the real economy:

> Market contacts had suggested that investors' expectations of banks' liquidity holdings were, in part, framed by regulatory minima. And even if regulatory guidance was not a constraint at present, it could become so in periods of severe stress. For these reasons, the Committee agreed that it should reinforce the previous messages from the FSA that ILG ratios were not hard floors and liquid asset holdings were useable in times of market strain for the duration of the stress.[108]

Sometimes, to use a back-up carries a stigma: if you're using it, then you might be in trouble. There are examples where standby resources have been stigmatised initially and successfully de-stigmatised through universal utilisation – the use of ECB repo funding in 2007 and in 2009 is a good example.

We are left with a dilemma: can buffers ever be used in practice, or are they actually just increased minima? Having a high buffer and a clear policy on its utilisation could help to mitigate the risk of buffers becoming minima:

> There are ways in which this risk can be reduced. One is having buffers and minima that are sufficiently high, underpinned by a credible framework, so that the solvency of the institutions does not come into serious doubt. Another is communicating the rules of the game clearly, so that their application is not seen as a departure from standard practice, which could signal serious concern with the condition of the banks. Even so, it is hard to judge at this stage whether these steps would be sufficient to allow an effective operation of the buffers.[109]

Perhaps forbearance is the answer? The authorities have the power to "destroy" or "create" capital merely by changing the measurement methodologies. We have seen forbearance used in this way several times recently, with mixed results (see Table 3.18).

In summary, neither buffers not forbearance can solve the procyclicality problem. The market tends to see through them in times of stress. The only credible way to handle procyclicality appears to be to run *voluntarily* with high levels of surplus capital and liquidity in good times, with careful utilisation of the surplus during difficult times and clear communication of the realistic value of risk assets, rather than obfuscatory forbearance. Of course, the best way to handle procyclicality is to manage risk in an anticyclical way, avoiding the busts altogether.

---

[108] The Record of the Bank of England Financial Policy Committee Meeting, 22 June 2012.
[109] Implementing the macroprudential approach to financial regulation and supervision, Claudio Borio, Head of Research and Policy Analysis, Bank for International Settlements.

Table 3.18 Examples of forbearance tactics used by the authorities in response to the financial crisis

Transfer of assets to banking book in 2008	At a time when market trading was not a reliable indicator of value, due to extreme volatility and poor liquidity, the International Accounting Standards Board (IASB) issued amendments to the key accounting standards IAS 39 (Financial Instruments: Recognition and Measurement) and IFRS 7 (Financial Instruments: Disclosures) allowing the reclassification of certain financial instruments from trading book to banking book.
	In this respect, the IASB was reacting to criticism that the accounting rules were creating problems: "In addressing the rare circumstances of the current credit crisis, the IASB is committed to taking urgent action to ensure that transparency and confidence are restored to financial markets."[110]
	Of course, the part-suspension of fair value approaches results in carrying values that are above market values. This can have unintended consequences, according to believers in fair valuation approaches:
	"In the short-run, the amendment has served to provide relief to most troubled banks avoiding fair value losses and ultimately regulatory costs from supervisory interventions. However, analyses of longterm effects on capital market show that the suspension of fair value measurement leads to a significant increase in information asymmetry, supporting claims that fair value measurement of financial assets provides useful information for capital markets."[111]
Carrying government bonds of troubled Eurozone sovereigns at inflated value	Many countries apply a prudential filter to bonds held in the "available for sale" (AFS) portfolio. In other words, changes in market values are shown in the accounts but the regulator neutralises the effect of the mark-to-market on these assets. Effectively, AFS bonds are carried at full face value in the regulatory balance sheet, no matter what the market price. In all countries, bonds held in the "held to maturity" (HTM) portfolio are carried at face value: even in the accounts, there is no mark-to-market.
	During 2010 and 2011, the markets were concerned about the solvency of certain banks who had a lot of troubled sovereign debt. The regulatory solvency was not trusted.
	The valuation practice for government bonds was reversed in the EBA stress test of 2011. Banks were required to build a "sovereign buffer" of capital to cover the negative mark-to-market of any government bonds of troubled Eurozone nations they were carrying. This treatment applied no matter the accounting treatment. In total, there was €40bn of buffer required.[112]
Zero risk-weighting of Eurozone government bonds, as enshrined in Europe's CRD IV	Under EU capital rules, there is a "mutual and unqualified exemption of certain sovereign risks from capital charges, an exemption inconsistent with Basel II's risk-sensitive framework".[113] This has drawn criticism from the Basel Committee and from countries outside the EU. No change appears to be forthcoming.

---

[110] IASB amendments permit reclassification of financial instruments, IASB, 13 October 2008.

[111] Relaxation of Fair Value Rules in Times of Crisis: An Analysis of Economic Benefits and Costs of the Amendment to IAS 39, Jannis Bischof, Ulf Brüggemann, Holger Daske, May 2010.

[112] Results of bank recapitalisation plan, Andrea Enria, Chairperson of the European Banking Authority, 8 December 2011.

[113] Sovereign risk in bank regulation and supervision: Where do we stand?, Hervé Hannoun, BIS, 26 October 2011.

3.9 ROLE OF REGULATION, SUPERVISION AND SUPPORT

Banks are risky yet necessary. The combination of their importance to our economy and society and the awful calamities that can occur during financial crises means that banks have to be monitored, controlled and supported. All sectors of the economy are regulated by the general commercial laws of the land, to ensure fair business practices and consumer protection, for example. Utility sectors such as electricity companies and water companies are regulated in order to prevent monopolistic exploitation and to preserve systemic stability. Similarly, banks need regulation, supervision and support.

- *Regulation*: A set of rules and requirements used to dictate the practices of banks and improve the chances of fairness, market stability and institutional resilience.
- *Supervision:* Monitoring adherence to regulation and applying subjective and qualitative judgements where required.
- *Support:* Provision of backstop financial support and resolution procedures, to minimise the social and contagion impact of breakdowns in the private markets or, at worst, of bank failures.

Most of the time, people use the word "regulation" when they in fact mean the combination of regulation, supervision and support. Throughout this book, we have used the word in this loose sense.

These regulatory functions are orchestrated by the public authorities, such as the central bank, Treasury and/or the specialised financial services supervisory authority in each jurisdiction. This can mean that there are layers of regulation, at state and federal levels for example, with some duplication at each level. The exact organisation of the authorities who regulate and supervise the banking industry is a fascinating question for central bankers and regulators themselves, but is not treated as an important variable in this book.

Some of the leading banking regulators in the world include those listed in Table 3.19.

Internationally, there is international coordination by bodies like the Bank of International Settlements and, within that, the Basel Committee for Banking Supervision. Note that the Basel Committee is just a "club" with no legal or supervisory authority. So, for example, when we say "what is the impact of Basel III?" we really mean "what is the impact of the specific national variant of Basel III", for there is no pure, global banking regulation. As described in Section 4.5.9, different countries have implemented Basel regulations in different ways.

The regulatory challenge is to take international regulatory principles and translate them into a workable, national regulatory framework.

Performance of Regulation during the Current Financial Crisis

Fortunately, there has been a lot of soul-searching debate among regulators about their failure to spot and prevent the current financial crisis. One leading diagnosis concludes that:

> there seems to be general acceptance that ineffective financial regulation and supervision in several countries has been an important contributing factor to the current financial crisis. Financial supervisors in many instances did not understand the business models of the institutions they were supervising and the nature and extent of risk-taking that was occurring. As a consequence, they failed to take appropriate remedial actions, such as forcing institutions to curb risky practices and increase capital requirements and loss provisions.[114]

---

[114] Is there a need to rethink the supervisory process?, John Palmer and Caroline Cerruti, IMF, 15 June 2009.

Table 3.19   Who are the regulators of banks?

Country	Regulator
USA	Federal Reserve
	SEC
	OCC
	FDIC
UK	PRA (succeeds the FSA)
	FCA (ditto)
Singapore	MAS
Australia	APRA
EU	EBA and ECB
Germany	BaFin
France	ACP
Switzerland	FINMA
Canada	OSFI
Hong Kong	HKMA
China	CBRC
Russia	Bank of Russia
Spain	Bank of Spain

Regulators were swept away with the bubble mentality of the pre-crisis years, especially in the prevalent belief that free-market forces would act as a natural form of supervision that would reduce the reliance upon the authorities; this belief was at the heart of Basel II and especially the philosophy behind Pillar 3, "Market Discipline".

In addition to this misplaced reliance on market dynamics, regulators had (in general, but not all) developed a hands-off approach to regulating. Most of their efforts to preserve financial stability were focused on drafting complex and detailed prescriptive rules, instead of knowing what was happening at the coalface of the industry. This approach has been described as:

> a concept of regulation and supervision that is outdated and ineffective – a concept that places greater reliance on rules such as capital requirements and high level monitoring of compliance with those rules, than on proactive, interventionist supervision with a strong on-site component, in order to understand the risks institutions are taking and to take appropriate actions when the risks are not properly managed.[115]

More disturbingly, regulatory authorities were slow in acting on clear signs that the financial industry was under increasing stress. The early warning signs that started appearing in late 2006 tended to be misinterpreted or ignored. When regulators did act, it was in the manner of the bureaucrat not the risk manager:

> Questions were being raised, but for the most part, they were being raised in muted tones, without a ringing call to action. And when occasional calls to action did ring out, they were sometimes met with intolerance and a reluctance to recognise evidence that challenged conventional wisdom.[116]

All the evidence points to a monumental failure of regulation. Many of the world's leading regulators had settled themselves into a risk management job without displaying any

---

[115] Ibid.
[116] Ibid.

competence in risk management. The excuses offered, the lack of dismissals at senior levels within the regulators (indeed, accolades and knighthoods for some) and the mild restructurings that have followed this failure all point to the worrying conclusion that the underlying regulatory problems persist. This theme is picked up in the "blueprint" section on regulation in Chapter 6.

The objective diagnostic is somewhat damning and indicates that much work needs to be done to fix the regulatory structures. The IMF's diagnostic is that there were at least ten failings:[117]

Different policy choices in balancing innovation and soundness

The "madness of crowds"

Political and market pressure on supervisors

A "race to the bottom" among supervisors to create institution-friendly regimes

Weak supervisory governance models and inadequate mandates

Weak supervisory cultures, along with inappropriate incentives within supervisory bodies

An inadequate understanding within supervisory agencies of financial institutions and what drives their behaviours

Inadequate supervisory/central bank mandates and "tripartite" arrangements

Sub-optimal cooperation among supervisory bodies and ineffective consolidated supervision of large financial groups

Absence of real, on-site supervision in some supervisory agencies.

What Does Good Regulation and Supervision Look Like?

The work by the authorities is allowing a consensus to develop on the point that effective regulation or supervision should be:

intrusive, adaptive, proactive, comprehensive, and conclusive. For this to happen, the policy and institutional environment must support both the supervisory will and ability to act. A clear and credible mandate, which is free of conflicts; a legal and governance structure that promotes operational independence; adequate budgets that provide sufficient numbers of experienced supervisors; a framework of laws that allows for the effective discharge of supervisory actions; and tools commensurate with market sophistication are all essential elements of the will and ability to act. However, making all this come together is the more intangible and difficult part.[118]

In other words, a supervisor needs to have more common sense and more teeth. It is true that fulfilling these functions is no small task, given the rising complexity of international finance and the capital markets, combined with an overall increase in the level of individual and corporate indebtedness in the economy. Acknowledged experts have highlighted this point:

A greater focus on intensive bank supervision and decisive early intervention actions, underpinned by effective powers for competent authorities are equally important to ensure banks' risks and their management are supervised effectively. At the same time, this presents considerable challenges in day-to-day supervision, in particular in relation to complex banks and to business lines where risk profiles can change significantly in very short time periods and thereby risk outpacing supervisory control.[119]

---

[117] Is there a need to rethink the supervisory process?, John Palmer and Caroline Cerruti, IMF, 15 June 2009.
[118] The Making of Good Supervision: Learning to Say "No", IMF, May 2010.
[119] High-level expert group on reforming the structure of the EU banking sector, Erikki Liikanen, October 2012.

Resource Gaps

For example, one point is the lack of sufficient skill, resource and remit to effectively manage the banks, for which they were responsible. Data on this point is hard to come by, but the UK seems to have around 4,000 people in the FSA costing £578m per annum[120] and a further 1,600 in the Bank of England policy functions costing £134m per annum.[121]

Clearly, some of these resources need to deal with the thousands of smaller companies and the mundane administrative aspects of financial supervision, such as ensuring all staff are properly accredited. But is it possible that regulators have loaded up on large numbers of talented but relatively inexpensive administrators to ensure compliance with the big, fat rule book, at the expense of staff with front office skills and deep technical product expertise, who can engage effectively with the senior management of the banks? If a more intimate style of regulation and supervision is required, are the regulatory resources up to it? This is not just a matter of money – the regulator needs to have access to similar resources to those of the banks they are regulating. At present, it does not appear that this is the case, though it is impossible to prove empirically. Chapter 7 looks at the challenge of creating a "supervisory elite" that is capable of working with the banks in a hands-on way, in order to improve the effectiveness of bank supervision.

Anecdotal evidence indicates that senior people in the regulatory authorities can often have a weak understanding of financial institutions, what drives behaviours and the way that bankers respond to regulatory and supervisory initiative.[122] Data suggests that few have worked in financial institutions and the ones that have were employed by banks as lawyers or economists rather than traders, risk managers or salespeople.[123] The political nature of bank regulation can also cause the leaders of our regulators to become intensely aware of the need to fit with other civil service departments and professional bodies. Senior regulators, therefore, can often pursue a purist or academic approach, to act as standard-setters rather than hands-on risk managers.

Lack of Vision

Many of the issues raised by the authorities and experts can actually be addressed by existing regulations and supervisory standards and codes. They do not explain adequately why financial regulators in a number of countries failed to do a better job in their handling of the financial crisis. Nor do they inspire confidence that the fundamental failings are being addressed. Some of the failings are down to incompetence, people failing to do their job adequately due to a lack of perspective or "vision". Drifting into crisis along with the popular sentiment is just not good enough:

> Supervisors are expected to stand out from the rest of society and not be affected by the collective myopia and consequent underestimation of risks associated with the good times.[124]

---

[120] FSA website and Bloomberg.
[121] Bank of England Annual Report 2012, policy functions only.
[122] Is there a need to rethink the supervisory process?, John Palmer and Caroline Cerruti, IMF, 15 June 2009.
[123] Ibid.
[124] The Making of Good Supervision: Learning to Say "No", IMF, May 2010.

It was not the job of regulators to sit on the sidelines. Their job was to monitor and steer the financial industry. The recent investigation into the manipulation of the LIBOR interest rate by banks shows us that the regulators were asleep at the wheel:

> Although the financial authorities, including London's FSA, can congratulate themselves on the draconian punishment, the bigger question is how they managed not to identify a scam that seems to have been common knowledge for years before anything was done. The FSA report says "manipulation was discussed in internal open chat forums and group emails and was widely known". But not, apparently, by the regulators. Nor did it appear to have registered with the bank's own compliance department, which ran five separate internal audits during the period. This raises questions about the efficacy of compliance and whether the people whom banks employ to monitor behaviour are anything like as alert as the individuals they are meant to be monitoring.[125]

Sometimes, supervisors and regulators have failed to grasp the importance of global economic and financial imbalances, despite having identified many of the incumbent risks. RBS's acquisition of ABN AMRO is a case in point that underscores this issue. The acquisition of ABN AMRO by a consortium led by RBS greatly increased RBS's vulnerability. The decision to fund the acquisition primarily with short-term debt rather than equity eroded RBS's capital adequacy and increased its reliance on short-term wholesale funding, which left it highly vulnerable to the credit crunch. In addition, the acquisition significantly increased RBS's exposure to structured credit and other asset classes on which large losses were subsequently taken. The FSA failed to undertake a fundamental analysis of the underlying assets. Moreover, according to the FSA report on the failure of RBS, the Basel II rules applied by the FSA and other regulatory authorities across the world, were, in hindsight, "*severely deficient*" and "*dangerously inadequate*", allowing RBS to operate with inadequate capital and excessively high leverage. Moreover, the FSA placed too much reliance on the firm's senior management, which led to insufficient challenge of key business areas.[126] This shows that there was not only a lack of focus on macro-systemic issues but also plenty of scope for gaps in accountability to develop.

What is particularly distressing about the current financial crisis is that we thought we were better prepared to prevent, mitigate and/or manage such a crisis than ever before.[127] In the aftermath of the Asian financial crisis, international financial institutions and academia devoted a great deal of energy to improving the quality of the regulatory and supervisory framework. It was hoped that a combination of stronger regulatory frameworks and more effective supervision would help to avoid, or at least mitigate the effects of, a possible next crisis. However, financial innovation in the last century produced new banking products and strategies whose risk characteristics were not well understood. As a result existing supervisory tools and methods were not refined and enhanced to remain relevant in the changing risk environment. This in turn greatly increased the time between risk identification and supervisory response, thereby precipitating the crisis.

At the start of the current financial crisis, the overall mindset of the regulators and supervisors may have been focused on the narrow administration of procedures and documentation rather than thinking and acting. Unfortunately, the focus on compliance with prescriptive rules may have resulted in a negligent lack of oversight and a lack of flexibility in approach. "As

---

[125] *Evening Standard*, 19 December 2012.
[126] The Failure of the Royal Bank of Scotland, UK FSA, December 2011.
[127] Is there a need to rethink the supervisory process?, John Palmer and Caroline Cerruti, IMF, 15 June 2009.

the prudential supervisor, we need to make sure that we do not have a Maginôt Line, but flexible defences that address the different types of risk that can accompany a strongly growing economy – risks of over-confidence, of poor strategic decision-making, of eyes 'off the ball' on credit standards and risk management generally."[128]

Indeed, the regulatory/supervisory models that appear to have been most effective (see Sections 5.13 and 5.14 for some brief case studies on the experiences of Canada and Australia) were those where the regulator and the supervisor proved able to keep in touch with the industry *on the ground*, identify risks as they emerged and deal with matters in a practical, no-nonsense way. There is not sufficient evidence to determine whether there is a role model regulator, which the rest of the world could emulate. But the relative intimacy with the industry and effectiveness of supervision in certain countries gives us some ingredients to carry forward into the proposals for a better regulatory and supervisory model outlined in Chapter 7.

3.10 RATINGS AGENCIES AND CREDIT RATINGS

> Alpha children wear grey. They work much harder than we do, because they're so frightfully clever. I'm awfully glad I'm a Beta, because I don't work so hard. And then we are much better than the Gammas and Deltas. Gammas are stupid. They all wear green, and Delta children wear khaki. Oh no, I don't want to play with Delta children. And Epsilons are still worse. They're too stupid to be able to read or write. Besides they wear black, which is such a beastly color. I'm so glad I'm a Beta.[129]

No discussion or diagnostic of the current financial crisis is complete without considering the role of the credit ratings agencies, their services and how their credit ratings are used.

Credit ratings agencies provide important information and judgements for their customers, who are professional investors. The most famous of their products is the credit rating itself. Indeed, it is front-page news when an important change in the credit rating of a company, bank or government occurs. For example:

> Standard & Poor's removed the United States government from its list of risk-free borrowers for the first time on Friday night, a downgrade that is freighted with symbolic significance but carries few clear financial implications.[130]

The credit ratings agencies were born in the USA in the middle of the nineteenth century, providing investors with information on the booming railroad sector. In the early part of the twentieth century, the agencies moved on from mere information provision and started giving their judgements on the corporations they analysed.

These credit opinions, summarised in a shorthand credit rating such as "AAA", are generally based on public information and the ratings agencies' formal methodologies, combined with their subjective judgement. They are opinions on creditworthiness. "Standard & Poor's credit ratings are designed primarily to be forward-looking assessments of creditworthiness of

---

[128] Supervisory Lessons From The Global Financial Crisis, John F. Laker, Chairman, Australian Prudential Regulation Authority, December 2010.
[129] *Brave New World*, Aldous Huxley.
[130] *The New York Times*, 5 August 2011.

Table 3.20   Credit ratings scales

S&P rating	Moody's rating	Fitch rating	Average credit loss[131]
AAA	Aaa	AAA	0.03%
AA+	Aa1	AA+	
AA	Aa2	AA	0.11%
AA−	Aa3	AA−	
A+	A1	A+	
A	A2	A	0.26%
A−	A3	A−	
BBB+	Baa1	BBB+	
BBB	Baa2	BBB	1.10%
BBB−	Baa3	BBB−	
BB+	Ba1	BB+	
BB	Ba2	BB	6.31%
BB−	Ba3	BB−	
B+	B1	B+	
B	B2	B	13.27%
B−	B3	B−	
CCC+	Caa1	CCC+	
CCC	Caa2	CCC	
CCC−	Caa3	CCC−	
CC	Ca	CC	
C	C	C	
D	D	D	

issuers and obligations. The ratings are not measures of absolute default probability. Credit-worthiness can encompass not only likelihood of default, but also payment priority, recovery, and credit stability."[132]

There are three main credit ratings agencies that are relevant to the banking sector: Standard & Poor's, Moody's and Fitch. The ratings they publish range from "AAA", meant to represent the most creditworthy borrower and the least likely to default on its debt, to default grades (see Table 3.20).

---

[131] Average five year cumulative credit loss rates, 1982–2007, which would need to be divided by five to give annual equivalent. Sourced from Corporate Default and Recovery Rates, 1920–2007, Moody's, February 2008.

[132] Default, Transition, and Recovery: A Global Cross-Asset Report Card of Ratings Performance in Times of Stress, Mark Adelson, Standard & Poor's Ratings Services, 8 June 2010; reproduced with permission of Standard & Poor's, a division of The McGraw-Hill Companies, Inc.

Table 3.21   Mapping of long-term to short-term ratings

Long-term S&P rating	Long-term Moody's rating	Short-term S&P rating	Short-term Moody's rating
AAA to AA−	Aaa to Aa3	A–1+	P–1+
A+ to A	A1 to A2	A–1	P–1
A− to BBB	A3 to Baa2	A–2	P–2
BBB to BB+	Baa2 to Ba1	A–3	P–3
Below	Below	B	Non-prime

Each rating also has an "outlook", which is either "positive", "stable" or "negative". This is meant to indicate the likely direction of a rating and is especially useful in a dynamic situation, for example a bank that is growing in profitability and franchise.

The credit ratings referred to above are long-term issuer credit ratings. But ratings agencies also give a short-term rating, meant to represent the chances of a default in the near term (under one year). For banks, there tends to be a direct mapping of the long-term rating to the short-term rating, as listed in Table 3.21.

The important thing to note about the short-term rating is that it is used extensively by investors in the short-term money markets, a crucial source of finance for most major international banks. Maintaining a short-term rating of at least A-1 or P-1 is essential for banks with significant wholesale operations. The loss of an A-1/P-1 rating can result in the need to alter the entire business model.

How do agencies arrive at a credit opinion and a rating for a bank? The credit rating agency assigns an analyst to each bank. The job of the analyst is to apply the agency's methodology to the bank, using publicly available financial information, supplemented where necessary by additional data provided to the agency on a private, confidential basis. The analyst then presents their conclusions and rationale to a rating committee, which decides on matters of opinion and the ultimate credit ratings assigned to the bank, in order to ensure rigour and consistency across the universe of rated banks.

Credit ratings used to be assigned in a fairly judgemental and subjective way and there are lots of arguments to support such an approach. There is no algorithm for credit analysis. Agencies even avoided legal liability for the consequences of their credit opinions by issuing them under the First Amendment of the United States constitution, namely the right of free speech. This approach has since been challenged, especially in cases where "the Ratings Agencies' ratings were not mere opinions but rather actionable misrepresentations".[133]

Recently, the agencies have been pressured to adopt more rigorous, standardised, harmonious and transparent methodologies. Consequently, we have seen the publication of the bank ratings methodologies of Moody's ("Moody's Consolidated Global Bank Rating Methodology", 29 June 2012) and S&P ("Banks: Rating Methodology and Assumptions", 9 November 2011).

The methodologies of both Moody's and S&P isolate the bank's own creditworthiness on a *standalone* basis before assessing whether there is potential for external support that will

---

[133] Recommendations on the Regulation of Credit Rating Agencies, Task Force on Regulatory Reform Banking Law Committee, American Bar Association, 5 November 2010.

boost the credit quality. For banks, the role of external support is significant: "External support has improved ratings by three notches on average most recently, from about two in 2007."[134] These two agencies have ratings methodologies that are similar in structure but different in emphasis – the following sections give a brief overview of them.

3.10.1 Moody's Bank Methodology

Moody's labels its bank rating methodology as "transparent, predictive and consistent".[135] It starts with a scorecard-based assessment, using a combination of hard and soft factors. Each of the factors carries a weight in the scorecard and there is no adjustment to account for the fact that several of them appear to double-count the same fundamental credit drivers. The output is an intrinsic, standalone rating called a Bank Financial Strength Rating (BFSR) on a scale of A to E. This is also expressed in the ratings scale where Aaa is the highest: using this scale, it is termed a Baseline Credit Assessment (BCA). The BFSR/BCA is meant to be a measure of the likelihood that a bank will require assistance in order to avoid a default. Moody's then considers whether the bank is likely to receive assistance from a parent or government in case of problems, and uses another scorecard-based methodology to combine the probability of support with the credit quality of the entity providing the support to give the bank's overall issuer credit rating. An example of this complicated but fairly mechanical procedure is shown below. In this case, Svenska Handelsbanken is given a BFSR of C, which maps to a BCA of a3. Once three notches of support from the Swedish state are factored in, the issuer credit rating ends up at Aa3 (see Table 3.22).

In general, Moody's ratings for banks are higher than the other agencies', though the difference is shrinking: "The all-in ratings assigned by Moody's in mid-2007 were roughly 1.5 notches higher on average than those assigned by Standard & Poor's and Fitch. This difference has recently declined, and stood at around one notch in April 2011."[136] This could be due to a broadly more bullish view on the banking sector's prospects and/or a more confident view on the likelihood of provision of public sector support.

3.10.2 S&P's Bank Methodology

S&P's methodology starts with an assessment of the riskiness of the banking industry in each country, based on its structural strength and the strength of the economy. This gives a starting point, or "anchor", for assessing the banks in that country. S&P then looks at four bank-specific factors (business position, capital and earnings, risk position, funding and liquidity), awarding the bank positive or negative notches, depending on whether it is better or worse than average. The result of this exercise is the standalone credit profile (SACP). S&P then takes additional direct support from the bank's parent group or sovereign government into account, in order to calculate support notches and the overall issuer credit rating (ICR). This is illustrated for Svenska Handelsbanken in Figure 3.15.

Interestingly, S&P has devised its own capital ratio to assess the relative solvency of banks. Since Basel II and Basel III risk measures and capital definitions are different in different

---

[134] Rating methodologies for banks, Frank Packer and Nikola Tarashev, *BIS Quarterly Review*, June 2011.
[135] Global Bank Rating Methodology: An Introduction, Moody's Investor Services.
[136] Rating methodologies for banks, Frank Packer and Nikola Tarashev, *BIS Quarterly Review*, June 2011.

Table 3.22   Example of the Moody's methodology: Svenska Handelsbanken AB[137]

Qualitative factors	(50% weighting)	C+
	Franchise value	C+
	Risk positioning	C–
	Operating environment	B+
Financial factors	(50% weighting)	C+
	Profitability	C
	Liquidity	C–
	Capital adequacy	B+
	Efficiency	B
	Asset quality	A
Bank financial strength rating (BFSR)		C
Baseline credit assessment (BCA)		a3
Notches for support		3
Issuer credit rating		Aa3

countries – indeed, each bank has a different internal risk model that calculates regulatory risk-weighted assets in a subjective way – S&P feels that they are not comparable and hence it is unable to use them. Instead, it has developed a measure of capital that is roughly similar to the definition of Tier 1 under Basel III and a proprietary risk-weighted assets methodology. Under the S&P methodology, banks' risk assets are each allocated to one of several buckets and all assets in the bucket are then given a flat risk-weight according to the country of risk. Currently, all Italian corporate loans, for example, are weighted at 136%. The S&P ratio is quite often different from the regulatory capital ratio and may, in some instances, be more insightful, especially where the regulatory rule is generous (e.g. threshold deductions under Basel III or treatment of bancassurance operations under the Financial Conglomerates Directive in the EU).

S&P's view on capital adequacy serves as a good illustration that there are alternatives to regulatory capital measures. The S&P measure can, in many instances, prove more insightful and meaningful than the regulatory measure. In Section 7.5, we consider other alternative ways of looking at capital.

3.10.3 Structured Finance Ratings

In addition to assigning a rating to companies, the ratings agencies also assign a rating to the securities that those companies issue. This includes straightforward senior debt issues, subordinated debt and hybrid capital instruments (see Section 3.5) as well as specialised asset-backed securities (see Section 3.6.5 on securitisation). In securitisation, bundles of loans are pooled and sold off into a standalone legal entity that is distinct from the

---

[137] Credit Opinion: Svenska Handelsbanken AB, Moody's, 17 April 2013.

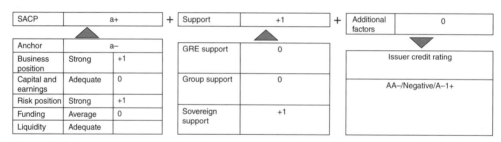

Figure 3.15   Example of the S&P methodology: Svenska Handelsbanken AB[138]

bank who initially lent the money. This securitisation vehicle owns the loans; there is no "recourse" to the originating bank. The vehicle then issues bonds in tranches, with the junior tranches taking the risk of "first loss" and the senior tranches at risk for losses that are beyond the capacity of the junior tranches. By dint of diversification, the risk of losses occurring in the senior tranches can be estimated to be fairly slim. In fact, with a thick enough junior tranche, the senior tranches can be seen as close to risk-free and assigned a rating of AAA.

The ratings agencies set up dedicated teams and specialised statistical models to assign ratings to securitisation bonds. The statistical models were able to calculate the theoretical probabilities of default of the securitisation bonds, based on the nature of the underlying loans and the size and structure of the tranches of bonds. They then gave ratings to each tranche of a securitisation pool. The agencies helped issuers structure transactions with a maximum amount of highly-rated tranches, and particularly the superlatively-rated AAA-rated tranches, which were seen as risk-free funding tranches. On average, a mortgage pool of $100m could be tranched such that $75m–$85m of AAA-rated bonds could be issued to fund it and the remainder of the tranches would receive lower credit ratings.[139]

Market exuberance led to the creation of CDOs that bought up the lower tranches of securitisation bonds and packaged them up into a pool. These pools were, in turn, tranched into layers of bonds. For example, a further set of AAA-rated bonds could be issued out of a CDO that contained only BBB-rated bonds, for the ratings models assumed a low level of correlation. The degree of re-securitisation was repeated again, when CDOs bought tranches in other CDOs and became CDO-squareds. The CDO-cubed also appeared[140] and there was widespread concern about the risk that securitisation technology was allowing incompetent investors to expose themselves to risks they did not understand.[141]

---

[138] Svenska Handelsbanken AB, Sean Cotton and Alexander Ekbom, Standard & Poor's Ratings Services, 27 February 2013; reproduced with permission of Standard & Poor's, a division of The McGraw-Hill Companies, Inc.

[139] Credit Ratings and the Securitization of Subprime Mortgages, John Hull, University of Toronto, 11 May 2010.

[140] CDOs cubed: The first-ever triple derivative, Russ Ray, University of Louisville, in "Derivatives Use, Trading & Regulation", 2006.

[141] Clouds sighted off CDO asset pool, *Financial Times*, 18 April 2005.

The subprime crisis has exposed several severe failings in this approach:

- The ratings agencies assumed that loans that were being originated were similar to loans that had been made in the past; in fact, the nature and profile of the loans changed substantially over time (for example, mortgages were being originated with low introductory interest rates that would be impossible to service in the future, once the "teaser" rate expired).
- In addition to the above, fraudulent practices in some areas were prevalent and were not detected or factored in by the ratings agencies.
- Correlation assumptions were too optimistic. Historic assumptions based on "normal" market conditions proved invalid.
- Some investors had become totally reliant upon the credit rating as an estimate of the risk in the bond. The notion of *caveat emptor* had been lost.
- Resecuritisations (the creation of CDOs from securitisation bonds) went too far for investors to remain aware of the underlying risks they were running.
- On the other hand, to be fair, not all investors were duped by the superlative ratings: "Some tranches that were labelled AAA by the rating agencies carried spreads of 200 basis points above the risk-free rate, indicating that some investors were aware that not all AAA-ratings were equal, but many investors did not consider the risks beyond those captured by the ratings."[142]
- Since the ratings agencies were paid by the issuer of the securitisation bonds, it was in their interest to give their client the desired ratings. Whether this conflict of interest actually contributed to the "wrong" ratings being assigned is not clear.

One would think that structured finance ratings would be more reliable than the ratings of corporations, which have many more variable factors to take into account. Yet, in reality, the structured finance ratings in the USA (but not in Europe, interestingly) did not prove to be reliable as indicators of the risk in those products.

3.10.4 Use of Ratings in Regulation and Investment Policy

At some point, someone somewhere has to take a credit decision. Whose decision counts? Clearly, for the owners of the bank, the decision of the management they have appointed is the one that matters. But whose credit opinion should be counted on for regulation and supervision of banks and for the investment decision of the investor in bonds? If the views of bank management are not to be relied upon, and the regulator does not have the resources or the mandate to opine on relative credit strengths, beyond certain crude groupings (e.g. different rules for loans to governments, industrial corporations and regulated financial institutions), then the natural approach is to use the credit ratings assigned by one or other of the recognised and accredited ratings agencies.

Investors have long relied upon credit ratings to frame their investment mandate:

> Historically, banks were only allowed to invest in bonds in the four highest categories (hence the term "investment grade") while the companies with the bottom six ratings were generally considered too risky and speculative for financial institutions.[143]

---

[142] Beyond the crisis: the Basel Committee's strategic response, Nout Wellink, Chairman, Basel Committee.
[143] Pimco website, March 2012.

As well as the "investment-grade" distinction (bonds with a rating of BBB- and above) that forces many investors to avoid bonds with a sub-investment-grade or "junk" rating, several investors have mandates that limit their concentrations at various ratings levels, that require a certain return according to the ratings levels, or that require investments to be in the AAA ratings band. In the world of derivatives, collateral arrangements often stipulate the credit rating of the collateral to be posted and also have ratings covenants, whereby banks have to post extra collateral in the event that their own credit rating deteriorates. Lloyds Banking Group offers an illustration of the impact on collateral needs of a hypothetical ratings downgrade:

> A hypothetical simultaneous two notch downgrade of the group's long-term debt rating from all major rating agencies, after initial actions within management's control, could result in an outflow of £11 billion of cash, £4 billion of collateral posting related to customer financial contracts and £24 billion of collateral posting associated with secured funding.[144]

So in other words, rightly or wrongly, credit ratings do drive investment behaviour in a real way.

Many people think that the revenue model of the credit ratings agencies is flawed. Most of the revenues that are generated by the agencies are from issuers of bonds: this is called the "issuer pays" model. Analysts and investors pay for access to the research and databases of the agencies, but the fees make up only about one-third of the ratings agencies revenues.[145] With around two-thirds of the revenue base dependent upon issuer fees, some have suggested that the agencies were naturally inclined to give ratings that were overly generous to the issuer. These suggestions have been strongest in the area of securitisation bonds, which was the major area of growth for the agencies in the run-up to the current financial crisis and made up around half of their issuer fees.[146] Irrespective of the behaviours of the agencies, it is quite clear that an objective opinion is hard to form if one is also trying to generate fees on the basis of that opinion.

Regulators also make use of the credit ratings assigned by ratings agencies. Ratings are baked into many parts of Basel III for example. As an illustration, under the Standardised Approach, the risk-weighting of a loan to a corporate is set out in Table 3.23.

The question is, can regulators and investors entrust or outsource risk assessment to the ratings agencies? In the USA, the answer has clearly been "no". Section 939 of the Dodd–Frank Act, which is coming into effect at present, requires the removal of any regulatory references to credit ratings. Investors are instead encouraged to conduct their own analyses and form their own opinions.[147] The risk-weightings of bank loans in the USA under the Standardised Approach will be determined by the type of the loan and the type of the borrower. The system is clearly not risk-sensitive towards the creditworthiness of the borrower, beyond assigning them to a certain bucket based on their legal type. For example, all corporate loans will be weighted at 100%. For exposures to foreign governments and banks, the weightings are in part driven by the OECD country risk classification, previously only used for international standards on export credit risk. Some would call this a credit ratings agency of a sort, though

---

[144] Lloyds Banking Group Annual Report and Accounts 2011.
[145] Investor Presentation 1Q 2013, Moody's.
[146] Ibid.
[147] U.S. Implementation of the Basel Capital Regulatory Framework, Darryl E. Getter, Congressional Research Service, 14 November 2012.

Table 3.23   Risk-weightings of corporate loans (Standardised Approach)

Credit rating	Risk-weight
AAA to AA−	20%
A+ to A−	50%
BBB+ to BB−	100%
Below BB−	150%
Unrated	100%

it is not a private sector agency with a conflict of interest due to the "issuer pays" fee model. Use of the OECD ratings will throw up some interesting anomalies – for example, the ratings of Greece and Germany are the same and government bonds from those countries will have a 0% risk-weighting under the Standardised Approach.[148]

3.11 ANALYSTS, INVESTORS AND FINANCIAL COMMUNICATION

With such colossal stakes at risk, it is vital that the people who are on the hook – the "stakeholders" – are doing a good job in scrutinising and influencing the banks, as well as allocating their investment capital to the most appropriate destination.

Some banks are owned by wealthy individuals, by families, by customers (e.g. mutuals and cooperatives), by national and regional governments or by charitable trusts. But the majority of banks are owned by shareholders and the shares are listed on exchanges. Whatever the ownership model, all banks have a management that is accountable to their owners, though the level of direct and continuous feedback tends to be highest for those with share listings. Since all banks need funding to survive, they are all subject to the continuous judgement of providers of funding, whether that is the retail depositor, the corporate depositor or the wholesale debt capital markets.

Owners and shareholders get to make executive management accountable by voting on corporate and strategic matters via the usual shareholder governance processes, such as the Annual General Meeting and the day-to-day work of the Chairman of the Board. They can also (except for mutuals and cooperatives) manage their investment in the bank by divesting: selling the shares. Depositors and debt-holders have no votes in Board matters and thus exercise their influence ultimately by voting with their feet, i.e. by withdrawing their funding. The third main constituent is "society", in that society has an interest in the stable existence of each bank and the preservation of a functioning financial industry. Let us assume that employees of the bank fit broadly within this segment too.

Each of these constituents or "stakeholders" employs a set of professionals to look after their interests. These professionals scrutinise what the executive management of the bank is

---

[148] Country Risk Classifications of the Participants to the Arrangement on Officially Supported Export Credits Valid as of 25 January 2013, OECD website.

Table 3.24   Stakeholder structure

Main stakeholders	Motivation	Mechanism	Agent
Shareholders	Growth in the value of their investment *"Return on capital"*	Voting on strategic matters Appointment of the Board	Stock analyst (for listed banks only)
Depositors and debt-holders	Getting interest paid and principal repaid *"Return of capital"*	Provision or withdrawal of funds	Credit analysts and ratings agencies
Society	Stable, functioning financial industry	Regulation and supervision	Regulatory and supervisory bodies

doing and generate what they hope is a positive feedback loop, influencing the bank's operations to suits the stakeholders' interests.

The stakeholder structure can be summarised as in Table 3.24.

The mechanisms of governance are considered in greater detail in subsequent chapters. In this section, we will consider the information component alone.

The supervisor will have access to large amounts of detailed, confidential information and the power to request additional information or even to have the bank conduct specific analyses on request (such as a stress test).

The tools available to shareholders and debt-holders, on the other hand, are more limited:

- Periodic financial information (mostly quarterly, half-yearly and/or annual).
- Investor presentations by management.
- Occasionally, in-depth "Capital Markets Days" (for example, the Swiss bank UBS had an "Investor Day" on 17 November 2011).
- Intelligence provided to them by sources other than management (such as some independent market research or investigative journalism).

Immediately, a bottleneck is apparent: none of the stakeholders or their professional delegates – the analysts – has sufficient resource to adequately assess each bank in great detail on a dynamic basis. This is due to four fundamental problems:

- Firstly, investment portfolios are fragmented across hundreds of different banks and so analysts will struggle to achieve a meaningful level of "deep dive" on each name. Anecdotal evidence suggests that each investor analyses each name for only 2 to 3 hours per year on average. A typical equity research team for the banking sector is no more than a dozen strong and follows fifty or so names; credit research teams tend to be even smaller. The credit ratings agencies would typically have twenty or so banks covered by each analyst.
- Secondly, the banking industry is complex and ever-changing. "An investor in a CDO-squared would need to read in excess of 1 billion pages to understand fully the ingredients. With a PhD in mathematics under one arm and a Diploma in speed-reading under the other, this task would have tried the patience of even the most diligent investor. With

no time to read the small-print, the instruments were instead devoured whole."[149] Having said that, other aspects of modern life are complicated. Should an investor in an airline be expected to understand the details of jet propulsion and the geological drivers of the oil price?

- Thirdly, there is a woefully low level of standardisation and automation of information provided to analysts by banks (even today, amazingly, text form i.e. PDF is the most common file format, spreadsheet form is rare and template-driven XML almost unheard of). So, as banks are producing more and more information, with quarterly reports running to hundreds of pages and numerous cross-cuts of data being provided in Pillar 3 disclosures, unfortunately the information is seldom being used. Much of the detail is not relevant to the analysts' specific interests and the cost of assembling the data on an industry-wide basis is too high. When relevant information is provided on a standard basis in electronic format, analysts jump for joy – and manage to derive good insights (a good example of this is the publication of comprehensive information on sovereign debt exposures for the first time in the 2010 EBA stress test).
- Fourthly, the very nature of banking risk means that analysts struggle to generate much valuable insight into the quality of banking stocks or credits, a problem which is exacerbated by an often superficial, perfunctory or historical approach to risk assessment by the analysts. A look at analyst reports from 2007 shows that there was little predictive content of any use. Analysts did not dig into the front-line business activities of what the banks were doing and form market-shaping conclusions on the risks that were accumulating. Instead, equity analysts focused on refining their earnings models, which were – and remain – better suited to assessing business growth prospects than risk outcomes. It is painful – and potentially libellous – to select illustrations from historic research reports and conference call transcripts, but the studious reader is invited to explore this topic further to remind themselves about the nature of industry understanding during the initial stages of the current financial crisis.

Some commentators – and most banks – see dangers in high levels of disclosure and too much financial communication. As well as the large amount of work required, they fear that granular details may be misinterpreted and shine a light on areas of the business that do not warrant scrutiny. More frequent disclosure may lead to increased volatility in financial measures, which may spook investors. Hence, the potential for moving towards more detailed, real-time information provision is resisted. These concerns are real and not without foundation but the converse is also true: financial communication can lower the perceived risk and hence the cost of a bank's equity.[150] In other words, if shareholders understand the bank's risk profile better, they will not be assumed to "fear the worst" and will be satisfied with a lower return than otherwise.

Shareholder governance is also an important issue. Increasing levels of passive and international shareholdings have led to a decline in shareholder activism across all sectors, not just banking. This has been diagnosed quite clearly in the UK in the recent "Kay Report". The public stock markets and asset management industry have evolved to give a situation that "favours

---

[149] Rethinking The Financial Network, speech by Andrew G. Haldane, Bank of England, April 2009.
[150] Accounting Information, Disclosure, and the Cost of Capital, Richard Lambert, Christian Leuz, Robert E. Verrecchi, The Wharton School, University of Pennsylvania, March 2006.

exit over voice and gives minimal incentives to analysis and engagement".[151] One particular example of governance failings is the fact that problems in the structured finance markets were often blamed upon the ratings agencies, despite the fact that the agencies are merely the agents of the debt investors, who did not apply the maxim of *caveat emptor* sufficiently. Overlooked by many, this failure of governance is recognised by some central bankers:

> Notwithstanding rating agencies' shortcomings, many institutional investors had adequate instruments and resources to perform their own due diligence but failed to do so and appeared blind-sided in their quest for yield. The boards of these institutions overlooked the build-up of risk in their portfolios, highlighting that more remains to be done to further strengthen governance in this sector as well.[152]

Later chapters explore some ways to mitigate these serious problems. For the time being, the status quo continues and investors have a low level of understanding of a bank's risk profile and quality. The many casualties of the current financial crisis include banks where investors failed to act on clear signals of increasing risk levels and impending problems. What else can explain the absurd acquiescence to ruinous acquisitions proposed by management, illustrated by the shareholder votes in favour of RBS buying ABN Amro (94.5% of shareholders in favour, August 2007[153]) and Lloyds TSB buying HBOS (96% in favour, November 2008[154])?

In summary, the scope for effective market feedback to banks on their strategic risk decisions is severely limited by deficiencies in information, analysis and governance. It is unlikely that we will be able to significantly improve the banking industry without addressing these shortfalls.

---

[151] The Kay Review of UK Equity Markets and Long-Term Decision Making, John Kay, July 2012.
[152] Minimising the impact of future financial crises: six key elements of regulatory reform we have to get right, Jaime Caruana, General Manager, Bank for International Settlements.
[153] The FSA's report into the failure of RBS, House of Commons Treasury Committee, 16 October 2012.
[154] Lloyds TSB approves HBOS takeover, BBC, 19 November 2008.

4

Regulation of the Banking Industry

4.1 THE RELEVANCE OF BANK REGULATION AND SUPERVISION

This chapter sets out the key aspects of international regulation and supervision of the banking industry. This topic is important for a number of reasons: banking is a regulated industry; regulatory structures are arguably to blame – at least in part – for the current financial crisis; and great hope has been placed on the impact of the latest version of international financial regulations, the so-called "Basel III" regime. Indeed, the fact that the shortcomings of the banking industry are now a mainstream issue means that there is a broad need to understand at least the basic elements of banking regulation, so that the debate and its conclusions can be as informed as possible. There is no need for mind-numbing details and technical intricacies, but there is value in presenting the Basel regime and its variants in a clear and accessible way. Hopefully, the arcane world of banking regulation and supervision can then be critically appraised and – in subsequent chapters – a constructive proposal set out.

The explanations below will only skim the surface of what has become a sub-industry in itself. The literature on Basel, for example, is vast and complex. This may mean that this modest chapter is a little too simplistic for the subject matter and is open to criticism for being an inadequate guide to a technical subject. We consider a summary approach to be valid: after all, one of the problems with current and proposed banking regulations is that they have become *too* technical, removed from reality, inaccessible and, consequently, ineffective. Of course, a more comprehensive coverage is readily obtainable from the regulators' source documents and the many dedicated synopses that have been compiled by various advisory firms. Our focus in this book is to give a reasonable understanding of the scope, nature and limitations of current regulations, so as to inform and contextualise the proposals in Chapter 7.

4.2 REGULATION AND SUPERVISION OF THE BANKING INDUSTRY PRIOR TO "BASEL I"

Money is ancient, with early forms of bartering rapidly being replaced with systems that used tokens of exchange such as coins, which had a monetary value based on convention. The most common forms of early money were precious metals, which retained their value due to their rarity and the inability of anyone to reproduce them cheaply and easily. In this way, gold and silver became common units of currency for our societies, though other tokens have been used, and continue to be used, in other contexts: for example, rum was a common currency in New South Wales at the end of the eighteenth century due to a deficit of metal currency.[1]

---

[1] *Foundations of the Australian Monetary System, 1788–1851*, S. J. Butlin, University of Sydney Library, 2002.

As soon as money had come into existence as an abstract yet powerful way of transferring value "on the spot" between two parties that are trading goods, so did the concept of credit, in which the value paid by the "borrower" is deferred to a later point in time. Of course, credit was only possible when the borrower's promise was sufficiently credible to the "lender", who accepted the risk of non-payment, generally in expectation of a decent return, the interest on the debt in question. The provision of credit allowed international trade to flourish. Trade was further encouraged by price contracts – an early form of financial derivatives – that allowed both sides to agree terms on a forward-looking rather than a "spot" basis.

Providers of credit and derivatives developed into a formal banking system of sorts, with the entire system based on risk and its antidote – trust.

> Trust is the root of all money. The soundness of any currency – whether comprised of metal disks, paper rectangles, or some other medium of exchange – depends on the extent to which each of its users trusts that others will view it as valuable.[2]

The lesson of history is that trust can be misplaced, leading to situations where the risk-takers build up excessive positions in credit and financial exposure, losing large amounts when the "bubble pops". These financial collapses tend to be extreme in their development and violent in their impact. Yet, financial crises keep on occurring, because we do not learn from past mistakes. Periods of financial over-confidence and misplaced trust are based on a rejection of the lessons of yesteryear and a feeling that "this time it's different". Asset bubbles are never *exactly* the same, but they are rarely different in character: as famously observed by Mark Twain, "History does not repeat itself, but it often rhymes".

The most infamous financial crises occurred during the heyday of European expansion into far-flung colonies. Fortunes were made by taking large risks in exploration, colonisation and development. Inevitably, bubbles developed.

The Mississippi Scheme of 1719 in France and the South Sea Bubble in England at around the same time were examples of national investment programmes that became so popular that the price of investments rose far above what they were rationally worth, before collapsing. The promise of huge riches from the exploitation of the colonies was backed up with a healthy dividend, paid for by new entrants to the pyramid scheme. The prospects of the underlying companies failed to materialise and investors, many of whom had literally fought to be able to buy their shares, lost everything.

"Tulipomania" in the 1630s in Holland, on the other hand, was not provoked to boost the public coffers, but arose discretely and organically. Tulip bulbs, which were then quite rare, began to change hands for higher and higher prices. There are records of sales of single bulbs at a price equivalent to the value of twelve acres of land.[3] A sophisticated trading infrastructure developed and seemed to distract the nation from other means of generating wealth. People bought the bulbs in the expectation that the rising price trend would continue and a profit could be made on subsequent sale of the tulip bulb, despite its obviously limited utility. When the bubble collapsed, prices tumbled and many Dutch people were dismayed to find that they

---

[2] George Eliot and the Precious Mettle of Trust, Richard D. Mallen, *Victorian Studies*, 2001.
[3] *Extraordinary Popular Delusions and the Madness of Crowds*, Charles Mackay, 1841.

had exchanged a large portion of their wealth for a mere few bulbs. The social impact of these major financial crises was profound:

> Many who, for a brief season, had emerged from the humbler walks of life, were cast back into their original obscurity. Substantial merchants were reduced almost to beggary, and many a representative of a noble line saw the fortunes of his house ruined beyond redemption.[4]

Twentieth-century financial crises have also led to major social shifts, with the Wall Street Crash of 1929 leading to economic depression and contributing to the rise of nationalism and even to the Second World War.

The susceptibility of finance to excess and the awful consequences of financial crashes have led to attempts to regulate the industry, forcing a degree of financial discipline onto the banking industry.

In ancient history, regulation was often based on religious principles, with money-lending frowned upon and left to outsiders. Usury was often a crime with harsh punishments. Banks were subject to normal commercial principles and had unlimited liability: if a bank failed, its owners lost their wealth, were bankrupted and often went to debtors' prison. In essence, there was no distinction between a deposit and an investment. Regulation began to limit the ability to issue banknotes and thereafter to require a minimum backing of banknotes issued, via a compulsory reserve. For example, the 1893 Banking Law in Italy required that 40% of notes issued had to be covered by gold reserves.[5] In England, banks were prohibited from issuing banknotes altogether by the Bank Charter Act of 1844. Liquidity remained the major concern of the regulatory authorities, even though deposits were not common or sizeable. In fact, "as joint stock banks operated without any other type of legal constraint apart from restrictions placed on note issues, a crucial issue was how secure were their deposit liabilities. As contemporaries fully realised, the security of deposits, in large part, depended on bank-owners' personal wealth."[6] The demise of unlimited liability during the investment boom of the mid-nineteenth century led to closer regulation of the capital of banks.

Of course, banks have often been constrained in their business activities by regulations concerning product pricing (such as centrally mandated standard interest rates for deposits or loans), restrictions on business mix, and restrictions on the entry of foreign banks into local markets and foreign exchange controls. But the focal regulations for this book tend to be around solvency and liquidity.

Until the 1980s, the use of regulatory ratios for prudential regulation was explicitly rejected: the regulatory framework was mainly based on a case-by-case review of banks. Regulatory ratios were considered inadequate to capture the risk level of each financial institution. Subjective assessments were preferred.[7] There had been periods when benchmark ratios had been used, such as in the 1930s and 1940s, when state and federal regulators in the USA began to

---

[4] Ibid.
[5] The Bank of Italy from its inception to the 1936 Banking Law, Banca d'Italia website.
[6] The Trading Of Unlimited Liability Bank Shares: The Bagehot Hypothesis, Charles Hickson and John Turner, Queen's University of Belfast, September 2002.
[7] *From Basel 1 to Basel 3: The Integration of State-of-the-Art Risk Modeling in Banking Regulation*, Laurent Balthazar, 2006.

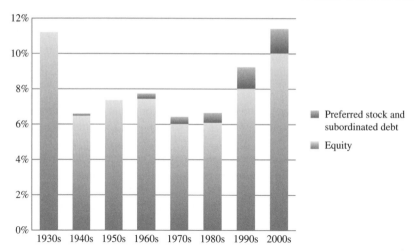

Figure 4.1   Capital as a proportion of the balance sheet for FDIC-insured commercial banks[8]

look at the ratios of capital-to-total deposits and capital-to-total assets, but both were "dismissed as ineffective tests of true capital adequacy".[9]

In 1978 the FDIC Manual of Examination Policies instructed examiners that "...capital ratios ... are but a first approximation of a bank's ability to withstand adversity. A low capital ratio by itself is no more conclusive of a bank's weakness than a high ratio is of its invulnerability."[10]

In the late 1970s and early 1980s, the number of bank failures began to increase, often due to thin capital levels, which had eroded over time (see Figure 4.1).

In 1981, the federal banking agencies in the USA introduced explicit numerical requirements for regulatory capital. In this instance, the standards were based on a ratio of accounting leverage: the amount of capital relative to the bank's total assets. Definitions of capital differed slightly, depending on the regulatory agency involved, and the minimum required levels ranged from 5 to 6%. But the American regulators also "stressed the importance of a comprehensive risk assessment, including off-balance-sheet risks, in identifying whether additional capital is needed to supplement the regulatory minimum capital ratios, and emphasized the need for international convergence of capital standards in maintaining a level playing field".[11] The American authorities looked at European practices and observed that European regulators had also introduced risk-based capital standards in the early 1980s.[12]

These regulatory trends formed the backdrop for the development of "Basel I".

---

[8] FDIC historical bank statistics.

[9] Basel and the Evolution of Capital Regulation: Moving Forward, Looking Back, FDIC, 14 January 2003.

[10] Ibid.

[11] Ibid.

[12] Ibid.

4.3 THE BASEL CAPITAL ACCORD AKA "BASEL I"

In 1930, a group of national central banks set up the "Bank for International Settlements" (BIS) to deal with the issue of reparation payments that had been imposed on Germany by the Treaty of Versailles following the First World War. The BIS is often referred to as the "central banker's central bank" or, since it is headquartered in Basel (Switzerland), it is also commonly referred to as "Basel", in the same way that the European Commission is referred to as "Brussels" or the US Federal Government is referred to as "Washington". The current stated objective of the BIS is to "serve central banks in their pursuit of monetary and financial stability, to foster international cooperation in those areas and to act as a bank for central banks".[13]

Within the BIS organisation, the "Basel Committee on Banking Supervision" (BCBS) deals with issues related to bank regulation and supervision. It is not a regulator itself and has no legal authority. Instead, it acts merely as a club, providing a "forum for regular cooperation on banking supervisory matters"[14] and developing guidelines and standards, which are then voluntarily applied in international jurisdictions, in full or in part. At present, there are 27 members of Basel (Argentina, Australia, Belgium, Brazil, Canada, China, France, Germany, Hong Kong SAR, India, Indonesia, Italy, Japan, Korea, Luxembourg, Mexico, the Netherlands, Russia, Saudi Arabia, Singapore, South Africa, Spain, Sweden, Switzerland, Turkey, the United Kingdom and the United States). The staff of Basel is seconded from the regulatory authorities of Members. The present Chairman of the Committee is Mr Stefan Ingves, Governor of Sveriges Riksbank, the Swedish central bank.

During the 1970s various international financial crises, such as the oil price shocks of 1973 and 1979, as well as an increase in competition between international banks, "brought the issue of regulatory supervision of internationally active banks to the fore".[15] Work began on developing a common international framework for banking regulation. In July 1988, Basel issued the 30-page document entitled "International Convergence of Capital Measurement and Capital Standards", now commonly known as the Basel Capital Accord or Basel I.

The 1988 version of Basel I was quite modest in its aims and simple in its structure. Basel sought a reasonable degree of regulatory convergence, with the twin objectives of (a) strengthening the "soundness and stability of the international banking system"; and (b) providing an internationally consistent level playing field "with a view to diminishing an existing source of competitive inequality among international banks". The second aim was, in part, a response to worries that aggressive foreign lenders in the USA were able to offer loans to American customers on better terms because they were regulated on a different basis. Basel I was focused on credit risk, i.e. the risk of losses from loans that are not repaid, rather than investment risk or other types of risk; it prescribed capital as a source of stability. It was purposefully simple, in order to be pragmatic. It proposed a minimum standard for internationally active banks and was therefore not intended to define risk management practices nor target operating levels of capital for major banks. Most importantly, the accord had a sober humility, noting that supervisors had to take a broad range of risks into account, that there were areas of the regulation that needed further work, and that capital was not necessarily the panacea to cure all ills: "capital ratios, judged in isolation, may provide a misleading guide to relative strength".

---

[13] BIS website.
[14] Ibid.
[15] Ibid.

There were four key components of Basel I:

- A *definition of capital*, which required a minimum of one-half of the bank's capital to be equity capital and reserves ("Tier 1"), with the remainder allowed to include debt instruments with equity-like features ("Tier 2").
- A *deductions regime* that adjusted for differences between the accounting and the prudential approach, removing, for example, accounting goodwill from the equity measure.
- A *risk-weighting approach* to defining the need for capital, whereby risk exposures are assigned to one of five risk-weighting buckets (0, 10, 20, 50 and 100%). This was deemed fairer and more rational than a simple gearing approach, since certain types of assets were clearly less risky than others. Basel was keen to point out, however, that "the weightings should not be regarded as a substitute for commercial judgement for purposes of market pricing of the different instruments".
- A solvency *ratio of capital to weighted risk assets* (dubbed the "Cooke ratio" after the then Chairman of the Basel Committee) with a minimum standard set at 8%.

4.3.1 Definition of Capital

Basel I set out a definition of regulatory capital that became the standard for many years. The notions of "core" capital and "supplementary" capital were introduced (see Table 4.1).

In principle, a bank could finance a capital requirement of £100 with a capital structure containing only £25 of shareholder equity (see Table 4.2).

In practice, no bank built a capital structure that pushed the rules to the limit, but capital leverage was employed extensively by banks in some sophisticated countries, as they tried to boost their shareholder returns by keeping equity levels low. The non-equity regulatory capital

Table 4.1   Elements of regulatory capital (Basel I)

Core capital ("Tier 1")	Equity (comprising shares and reserves and also including, by the way, the minority interests in the equity of subsidiaries not wholly owned)	**At least half** of the total regulatory capital amount had to comprise Tier 1 capital	Ordinary shares plus reserves and minority interests to be **at least half** of the Tier 1 capital Remainder could be preference shares and similar instruments
Supplementary capital ("Tier 2")	High-quality, long-term subordinated debt instruments	**No more than half** could comprise Tier 2 capital	Within Tier 2 capital, dated instruments (the so-called Lower Tier 2) could only be used up to a limit of half of the Tier 1 levels Undated, perpetual instruments (Upper Tier 2) would count in full towards regulatory capital levels, so long as total Tier 2 was less than Tier 1

Table 4.2   Theoretical geared capital structure (Basel I)

Tier 1	Equity: ordinary shares, reserves, minorities	£25
	Preference shares or similar	£25
Tier 2	Upper Tier 2 (perpetual)	£25
	Lower Tier 2 (dated)	£25
	Total regulatory capital	**£100**

securities were attractive to fixed income investors and could (unlike equity) be denominated in foreign currency, thus helping to finance the multi-currency risks in the banks' international operations. Good examples include the use of preference shares in the UK and "*bons de participation*" in Switzerland.

Moreover, some banks started to issue bonds that were high quality Tier 1 capital in their nature (being perpetual, subordinated and having a coupon that could be forgone in certain circumstances without leading to bankruptcy) but contained additional, investor-friendly features, such as coupons that increased over time. These so-called "innovative" instruments were limited under Basel rules to a maximum 15% of Tier 1 capital.[16]

4.3.2 Deductions Regime

Regulators could not simply use the accounting equity of the bank as the measure of capital. Instead, they defined a number of adjustments that could be applied to the accounting balance sheet, to give a more meaningful measure of regulatory capital:

- The most obvious and largest of these was the deduction from regulatory capital of accounting goodwill. This item was seen to be of dubious value from a solvency perspective, since it merely indicated the premium over net book value paid for an acquisition.
- Investments in other regulated financial institutions, such as other banks, asset managers and insurance companies, were recommended for deduction, but in practice a variety of national treatments was used, ranging from full deduction to no deduction at all, treating the investment instead as a normal corporate risk.
- Certain accounting items were deducted from equity but then treated as lower quality Tier 2 capital: for example, general provisions held for yet-to-be-identified losses and revaluation reserves.
- Lastly, Basel I also treated the value of latent revaluation reserves of holdings of equity instruments as Tier 2 capital, but only once a 55% discount – or "haircut" – had been applied, to allow for fluctuations in value.

For most banks, the deductions made little difference to the overall amount of capital they had: for them, gross regulatory capital was broadly similar to net regulatory capital. But for some, such as those who had made large acquisitions that generated goodwill on the balance sheet, the gross/net difference was substantial.

---

[16] Instruments eligible for inclusion in Tier 1 capital, Basel Committee, 27 October 1998.

Table 4.3 Basel I risk-weights summary

Risk-weight	Loans and investments
0%	Cash and OECD sovereign debt Short-term or rolling unfunded commitments
10%	Some public sector entities
20%	Banks in the OECD and short-term loans to non-OECD banks
50%	Residential mortgages Long-term unfunded commitments
100%	Most other assets, including corporate and retail lending; non-OECD governments and long-term loans to non-OECD banks; real estate and equity exposures

4.3.3 Risk-Weighting Approach

Having designed a relevant definition of net solvency capital, the Basel authorities then considered what the most appropriate measure would be for assessing the overall level of risk in a bank. Simplistic accounting amounts were not seen as suitable for prudential purposes, as they did not differentiate between the starkly different risk profiles of different asset classes. Basel I, therefore, introduced a risk-weighting approach, which assigned assets to buckets that then had a weighting factor applied, to come up with a total figure of risk-weighted assets, upon which capital requirements would then be set. The standard risk-weighting buckets were broadly as shown in Table 4.3.

The simplicity of the bucket approach has some attractions, but it also left the RWA measure wide open to blatant manipulation and arbitrage. Two examples stand out:

- Banks set up a series of "specialised investment vehicles" (SIVs) and "conduits", which borrowed money from the wholesale markets on short terms and at low rates and used that money to buy supposedly low-risk assets. The SIV/conduit made a profit that was the difference between the high return on its assets and the low cost of its funding. Since the back-up funding facility had a maturity of less than one year, the commitment to the SIV/conduit carried a 0% risk-weighting and thus did not add to the bank's regulatory capital requirements. Return-on-regulatory-capital was huge. As a consequence of this arbitrage, the SIV industry had reached an estimated $400bn in assets by July 2007.[17]
- Assets could be repackaged and restructured using securitisation techniques, in order to reduce the Basel RWAs. Mortgage securitisation was used for regulatory capital "relief" in this way. The way that the rule worked was that a pool of mortgages that required, say, $800 of risk capital ($20,000 mortgages × 50% risk-weighting × 8% capital requirement) could be transformed using securitisation techniques into a structure that used only $300 or so of risk capital (assuming that the bank retains 1.5% of the mortgages = $300 and this is deducted from regulatory capital).

Of course, these arbitrages result in lower regulatory capital requirements, relative to the real or economic risk in the actual risk assets. In some ways, the simplicity of Basel I encouraged banks to devise ways to use the rules to hide risk.

---

[17] *Risk*, 7 July 2009, quoting research by Fitch.

4.3.4 Ratio of Capital to Risk Weighted Assets

Basel set out a minimum capital requirement of 8%. Surprisingly, this number was not the subject of intense analytical study, as one would expect of an august body such as the Basel Committee. Little time was spent on the theoretical derivation of the minimum – nor was it just plucked out of the air, however. Instead, the 8% was calibrated with a view to the actual average capital levels in the system at the time and a desire for banks to be highly resilient to financial stress. Subsequent quantitative research[18] has found that the level was roughly correct, given the policy objectives and the tolerance at that time for bank failure.

At the time of the introduction of Basel I, most well-known large banks had a Cooke ratio only slightly above the 8% minimum. For example, in 1990, Barclays reported a Tier 1 of 5.8% of RWAs and a total capital ratio of 8.3%.[19] Banks in America had a Tier 1 ratio of 6.5% on average and a total capital ratio of 9.5%.[20] By setting the new minimum at the previous average, Basel I had the desired effect of encouraging banks to increase capital levels. Internationally, the average Cooke ratio "of major banks in the G-10 rose from 9.3% in 1988 to 11.2% in 1996".[21]

4.3.5 Modifications to Basel I

As noted above, the original 1988 version of Basel I focused on credit risk, which is by far the most important type of risk in a classic, commercial banking business model based around loans. Basel I did not incorporate any capital requirements for the banks' securities trading activities, which were growing in size and relevance at that time. So, in 1996, Basel I was enlarged to include the capital charges for market risk.

Market risk is the risk that arises when a bank's trading assets (such as bonds, equities, foreign exchange and commodities or in the related derivative markets, including interest rate and credit derivatives) change in value. The 56-page "Market Risk Amendment" required banks to value their trading assets at current market values, even if that was not the case in their accounts. Then, banks had the choice of applying either the formula-based "standardised measurement" method or the "internal models" approach to risk measurement. The latter was based on internal (i.e. bank-designed) statistical models, which were fed with historic data covering a period of at least a year, thus allowing the potential changes in value of the trading book assets to be estimated. The potential losses, termed "value-at-risk" or "VaR", were calibrated on a 99% confidence level, meaning that those losses would only have been exceeded once in every 100 scenarios. Banks were also told to make the assumption that assets would be held for 10 trading days, which increases the risk significantly. The technical requirements for these internal VaR models were set out in the Basel document. Banks were also required to use their models to assess the impact of an extreme market event and review the results, though this did not drive any capital requirement.

The use of VaR models for regulatory capital measurement was a precursor to the models-based approach for credit and operational risk that came in with Basel II. In fact, it was only

---

[18] What We Know, Don't Know and Can't Know About Bank Risk: A View From the Trenches, Kuritkes and Schuermann, 2008 paper.
[19] Barclays plc Annual Report, 1990.
[20] FRBNY Quarterly Review, Autumn 1992.
[21] Capital Requirements And Bank Behaviour: The Impact Of The Basle Accord, BIS, 1999.

three years later, in June 1999, that Basel issued its first consultation paper on "A New Capital Adequacy Framework". The development of the Basel II mindset had well and truly begun. "With hindsight, a regulatory rubicon had been crossed."[22]

4.3.6 Impact of Basel I

In retrospect, Basel I was an extremely elegant regulatory regime for capital adequacy. In this respect, it probably did achieve the modest objectives of the Basel Committee:

> The two principal purposes of the Accord were to ensure an adequate level of capital in the international banking system and to create a "more level playing field" in competitive terms so that banks could no longer build business volume without adequate capital backing. These two objectives have been achieved. The merits of the Accord were widely recognized and during the 1990s the Accord became an accepted world standard, with well over 100 countries applying the Basel framework to their banking system.[23]

But Basel I became obsolete as the industry to which it applied became more sophisticated. It was undoubtedly clear and uniform, reliable and accessible. But at the same time it was incomplete, excessively crude and open to arbitrage.

> The regulatory capital requirement has been in conflict with increasingly sophisticated internal measures of economic capital. The simple bucket approach with a flat 8% charge for claims on the private sector has given banks an incentive to move high quality assets off the balance sheet, thus reducing the average quality of bank loan portfolios.[24]

Not only did Basel I fail to ensure that risk in the banking industry was adequately backed by loss-absorbing capital resources, it may well have permitted – or even promoted – some of the risk-arbitrage structures that grew to become a serious hazard to the financial system.

4.4 BASEL II

> Increasingly, the new supervisory techniques and requirements try to harness both the new technologies and market incentives to improve oversight while reducing regulatory burden, burdens that are becoming progressively obsolescent and counterproductive. This is becoming especially true in evaluating the capital adequacy of banks.[25]

In the early 1990s, certain large banks suffered heavy losses, due to exposures to emerging markets and property bubbles. Risk management capabilities remained old-fashioned and error-prone. At the same time, information technology was advancing rapidly, giving banks

---

[22] The Dog and the Frisbee, speech by Andrew G. Haldane, Bank of England, August 2012.

[23] The New Basel Capital Accord: an explanatory note, Basel Committee, January 2001.

[24] Ibid.

[25] Remarks by Chairman Alan Greenspan at the Federation of Bankers Associations of Japan, Tokyo, Japan, 18 November 1996.

vast new information processing and storage opportunities. In this environment, leading banks decided to invest heavily in IT systems and modern, information-based risk management methodologies. In capital markets business lines, the VaR methodology became widely accepted as a form of trading risk management. In the classic lending business, banks began to use powerful, "expert" information technology models to identify exactly where they suffered losses in the past and therefore which type of lending would give them what level of losses in the future, across a range of likely and less likely scenarios. Risk was being modelled based on known features of the borrower. Irrespective of the risk-weighting defined by Basel I, banks were forming their own views on the relative economic risk of lending to different types of borrowers and different types of loans. The world's largest banks had become a lot more sophisticated than the regulators.

4.4.1 Objectives of Basel II

As a result, national regulators and the Basel Committee began the development of a more sophisticated regime for international bank regulation. The work began in earnest in 1997, with a discussion draft in 1999 and a firm proposal in 2001 for "a more risk-sensitive framework".[26]

Whereas the objectives of Basel I were around fairness and harmonisation, the objectives of Basel II were to improve the risk management and resilience of the banking industry:

- Make capital requirements more risk-sensitive and therefore relevant (but not, in aggregate, higher: "The intention is to leave the total capital requirement for an average risk portfolio broadly unchanged"[27]).
- Utilise the information, resources and judgements of the banks themselves, since they are better placed than a central regulator.
- Broaden the coverage of risk assessments and capital models, to take into account risks that were omitted under Basel I.
- Reduce the scope for blatant arbitrage that simplistic risk measures created.
- Increase the importance of the role of supervisors and, crucially, the capital markets in determining where risk was being accumulated and where capital should flow.
- Make smaller or less sophisticated banks improve their risk management practices, emphasising recent progress in process (e.g. centralisation) and IT innovation (e.g. risk modelling and database development).

4.4.2 The Three-Pillar Approach

In order to meet these objectives, the Basel Committee designed a multi-prong approach: "the new framework [Basel II] intends to improve safety and soundness in the financial system by placing more emphasis on banks' own internal control and management, the supervisory review process, and market discipline."[28]

---

[26] The New Basel Capital Accord: an explanatory note, Basel Committee, January 2001.
[27] Ibid.
[28] Ibid.

To understand how Basel II was supposed to work, it is important to understand this "three-pillar" framework:

- Pillar 1: minimum capital standards;
- Pillar 2: supervisory review; and
- Pillar 3: market discipline.

In essence, Basel sought to reduce reliance upon mechanistic, bottom-up calculations. One of the key innovations of Basel II was "to supplement the current quantitative standard with two additional 'Pillars' dealing with supervisory review and market discipline. These were intended to reduce the stress on the quantitative Pillar 1 by providing a more balanced approach to the capital assessment process."[29]

All three pillars were seen to be mutually dependent. In other words, any one of the three pillars doesn't work without the other two:

> The new Accord consists of three mutually reinforcing pillars, which together should contribute to safety and soundness in the financial system. The Committee stresses the need for rigorous application of all three pillars and plans to work actively with fellow supervisors to achieve the effective implementation of all aspects of the Accord.[30]

As we shall see in later chapters, unfortunately Basel II in practice has been interpreted as primarily the Pillar 1 element, a more sophisticated version of the Basel I capital ratio.

4.4.3 Pillar 1: Minimum Capital Requirements

Pillar 1 is the part of Basel II's integrated framework of pillars that will be most familiar to observers of the banking industry. Pillar 1 assesses a bank's risks on a bottom-up basis and converts that into a minimum capital requirement. In this respect, it is quite similar to Basel I, just more sophisticated and complex.

Like Basel I, the first pillar of Basel II looks at credit risk and market risk. In addition, it also provides a measure for operational risk. The capital requirement under Pillar 1 is the sum of these three components: credit, market and operational risk.

Credit Risk
Basel II provides banks with alternative ways of calculating their credit risk capital requirements for their loan books.

The most sophisticated (called "Advanced Internal Ratings Based" or AIRB for short) requires a bank to determine its own assessment of the probable loss for an exposure. The bank has to give five key inputs to determine this probability-adjusted loss (see Table 4.4).

These inputs are fed into a formula that calculates the risk-weighting for that exposure. Each asset will have its own risk-weight. As in Basel I, the capital requirement is 8% of the risk-weighted exposure amount. Only banks that can show they have the right depth of historic data and reliable risk models are allowed to use the AIRB approach; if they cannot demonstrate such capabilities, they need to apply one of the alternative approaches.

---

[29] Ibid.
[30] Ibid.

Table 4.4 Elements of the expected loss calculation

Default probability:	The chance of a borrower failing to repay the bank. This is estimated by identifying key features of the exposure – such as the industry for a corporate loan or the loan-to-value ratio for a mortgage – and assigning a grade or rating to the exposure, which then maps into a default probability percentage (hence the term "Internal Ratings Based")
Exposure at default:	For undrawn or partially drawn facilities, the expected amount of drawdown that will have occurred by the time a default happens
Loss given default:	The financial loss to the bank, net of loss recoveries from security or collateral arrangements (such as the sale of the house in case of a mortgage foreclosure)
Maturity of the exposure:	How long the bank has to maintain its exposure
Type of lending:	For example, residential mortgage, credit card or corporate loan

The "Foundation Internal Ratings Based" (FIRB) approach uses the bank's own assessment of default probability but all other inputs to the risk-weighting calculation are provided on a flat basis by the regulator: for example, all loans are assumed to have a 2.5-year maturity.

Both of these "IRB" approaches are radical departures from the philosophy of Basel I. They base capital requirements upon the institution's own judgement and experience. Of course, banks were not free merely to assign a low default probability to exposures as they saw fit – all models had to be rigorously validated by the supervisory authorities and regularly back-tested. But the period of implementation of Basel models also happened to be relatively benign in terms of economic environment and credit losses. Quite simply, loan books didn't look very risky on a look-back basis. The Basel Committee noted this in its impact study in 2006, but wasn't able to give an indication of the scale of this issue.[31]

The mathematics behind the IRB models are a statistical "black box" to most. Those interested should refer to the description of the basic mathematics produced by Basel.[32] Nevertheless, there are two mechanical areas of great general relevance, as they underpin some of the problems that risk-weighting approaches face.

Firstly, Basel II models purportedly measure the "expected" loss related to an exposure: the probability-adjusted amount that bank would expect to lose in an average year. If the bank calculates that there is a 1% chance of losing $200, then the expected loss is $2. The bank then applies a given correlation assumption to give a measure of "unexpected" loss: what the bank estimates its losses to be in an extreme stress scenario. Mathematics are being used to attempt to measure the potential impact of remote future potential scenarios. This can be highly unreliable, as the recent higher-than-modelled losses on several asset classes have reminded us.

Secondly, Basel II left open the important question of what risk the models are trying to gauge: the current perception ("point-in-time", which will be volatile and almost certainly

---

[31] Results of the fifth quantitative impact study (QIS 5), Basel Committee, 16 June 2006.
[32] An Explanatory Note on the Basel II IRB Risk Weight Functions, Basel Committee, June 2005.

Table 4.5   Risk-weighting of corporate loans (Standardised Approach)

Credit rating of corporate	Risk-weight of exposure (under Basel II Standardised Approach)
AAA to AA−	20%
A+ to A−	50%
BBB+ to BB−	100%
Below BB−	150%
Unrated	100%

out-of-date) or a more long-term view ("through-the-cycle", which will be equally wrong, under-estimating risk during the build-up to stress and over-estimating it during benign times). This problem of perspective leads to situations where RWAs clearly do not reflect the actual risks being faced, for example where banks in recessionary Greece or Spain do not have high risk-weightings on some of their loan books. In theory, risk-weightings (and hence regulatory capital requirements) should be forward-looking; in practice, they tend to suppress the impact of rising risk levels.

The "Standardised Approach" (sometimes referred to as SA) does not require any subjective or modelled inputs from the bank itself. The approach is similar to Basel I. Exposures are assigned to buckets of risk and a risk-weight is given per bucket. For example, there is a 35% risk-weight applied to residential mortgages that are below 80% of the property's value. The Standardised Approach has many more risk buckets than Basel I and, for several asset classes, relies upon the credit ratings assigned by ratings agencies. A corporate loan, weighted at 100% under Basel I, would be rated 20, 50, 100 or 150% under Basel II Standardised Approach, depending upon the credit rating of the corporate (see Table 4.5).[33]

Most large banks decided to use the IRB approach to credit risk, whereas smaller banks (those with less than €3bn in Tier 1 capital) tended to choose to operate the Standardised Approach (see Table 4.6).[34]

Table 4.6   Approach to determining regulatory capital requirements (Basel II Credit Risk)

	Standardised	Foundation IRB	Advanced IRB	Total
Large banks	2	29	65	82
Small banks	160	112	14	286
Total	162	141	79	368

---

[33] International Convergence of Capital Measurement and Capital Standards, A Revised Framework, Comprehensive Version, Basel Committee, June 2006.
[34] Results of the fifth quantitative impact study (QIS 5), Basel Committee, 16 June 2006.

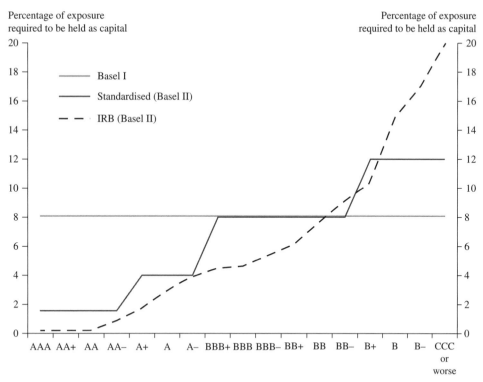

Figure 4.2   Regulatory capital requirements under different approaches

Of course, by design, different approaches to measuring credit risk give different risk-weightings for the same risk exposure and hence different regulatory capital requirements. Figure 4.2 illustrates how much capital a corporate loan exposure would need, depending upon its risk rating and the approach used. Note that the Basel I capital requirement is flat at 8%, irrespective of the riskiness of the asset; the Basel II Standardised Approach gives a "step function" capital requirement; and the Basel II Advanced IRB Approach gives a smooth increase in regulatory capital requirements as the assessed riskiness of the borrower rises.[35]

As noted above, the different correlation assumptions for different types of loans lead to risk-weights that differ, even where the default probabilities are the same. In short, the more granular portfolios attract a lower risk-weight, while larger, lumpier portfolios have a higher risk-weight. The Basel Committee has demonstrated some illustrative outputs (see Figure 4.3).[36]

---

[35] Basel II: A new capital framework, Reserve Bank of New Zealand: Bulletin, Vol. 68, No. 3.
[36] Basel II: International Convergence of Capital Measurement and Capital Standards: a Revised Framework, Basel Committee Publications No. 107 – June 2004, p. 197.

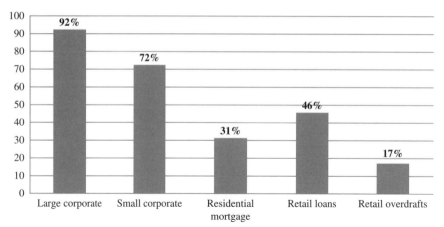

Figure 4.3 Risk-weightings of different types of loan under Basel II
Note: Data are for loans with a 1% default probability and 45% loss given default (except for residential mortgage, where 25% has been used)

To see whether the Basel illustration matches what a *real* bank has, it is useful to look at what a commercial bank reports as its risk-weighted assets in practice. Taking ABN Amro in the Netherlands as an example (see Figure 4.4), we can see that – unsurprisingly – the risk-weightings vary considerably across different products and client segments, due to the different risk profiles of those businesses.[37]

Market Risk
Basel II did not change the regulatory requirements for market risk from the 1996 rules. These continued to be based on a simple weighting approach per class of traded assets (the standardised approach) or, as adopted at all the major banks who had capital markets trading activities, the use of proprietary value-at-risk (VaR) models. Such models had been developed in the 1980s and 1990s and most were similar to the model that was developed and distributed by JP Morgan under the brand name "RiskMetrics".

VaR models were a significant improvement on previous, crude measures of market risk. But they had significant drawbacks. They were only reliable in "normal" market conditions. Their statistical power was insufficient to gauge the riskiness of a trading portfolio under more extreme stress scenarios. For managing risk on a day-to-day basis, they were a useful tool, but to define the regulatory capital required to deal with extreme situations, they were next to useless. What is more, their outputs translated into absurdly low levels of regulatory capital requirements. The industry confirmed that their own risk assessment of their trading activities was quite different from the Basel capital requirements. Deutsche Bank, for example, pointed out that they held "for Market Risks around 4-5x more Economic Capital than regulatory capital".[38] In 2007, out of a total of €13.3bn economic capital usage, Deutsche Bank reported that €3.5bn was used for market risk (26%). Yet from a regulatory perspective, market risk RWAs of €14bn made up only 4% of the total RWA base of Deutsche Bank of €315bn.[39]

---

[37] Pillar 3 Disclosure 2011, ABN Amro Group N.V.
[38] Reform of the global financial architecture: a new social contract between society and finance, Hugo Banziger, Chief Risk Officer and Member of the Management Board, Deutsche Bank.
[39] Deutsche Bank AG Annual Report, 2007.

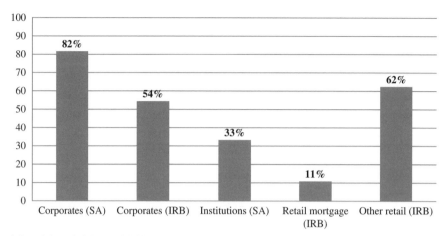

Figure 4.4   Risk-weightings of different types of loans under Basel II: ABN Amro 2011

Operational Risk

The Basel II framework rightly highlighted the many risks to which a bank is exposed that are operational in nature: fraud, systems failure, fire and so on. Basel defined these operational risks as the "risk of loss resulting from inadequate or failed internal processes, people and systems or from external events. This definition includes legal risk, but excludes strategic and reputational risk."[40] Despite a lot of work and consideration, there was little progress in finding a way adequately to measure these or capitalise a bank to be resilient to them. Since operational risk tends to increase in proportion to the size of the bank, Basel settled upon the crude metric of 15% of annual revenues as the capital requirement in the most basic form (*"Basic Indicator Approach"*). Other more advanced methods were also allowed, including the *"Standardised Approach"*, whereby the metric is based on slightly different percentages according to business line, and the *"Advanced Measurement Approach"*, in which banks could use their own experience of losses due to operational risk in order to determine capital requirements.

Most banks opted to use the most basic form of measurement for operational risk, although larger banks tended to favour the more sophisticated approaches (see Table 4.7).[41]

In practice, the capital requirement for operational risk works as a scaler, making up around 15% of a bank's Pillar 1 capital requirements. The calibration of the operational risk capital requirement appears to have been driven by the prevalent practices of sophisticated banks: "Many major banks now allocate 20% or more of their internal capital to operational risk"[42]

Operational risk is a difficult concept. The catch-all definition results in a category of risk that is undoubtedly important and still neglected. It seems fair to say that "operating risk is the least understood and least researched contributor to financial institution risk".[43] Banks

---

[40] International Convergence of Capital Measurement and Capital Standards: A Revised Framework, Basel Committee, June 2006.

[41] Results of the fifth quantitative impact study (QIS 5), Basel Committee, 16 June 2006.

[42] The New Basel Capital Accord: an explanatory note, BCBS, January 2001.

[43] Report on Consolidation in the Financial Sector, Group of Ten, January 2001.

Table 4.7 Approach to determining regulatory capital requirements (Basel II Operational Risk)

	Basic Indicator Approach	Standardised Approach	Advanced Measurement Approach	Total
Large banks	2	32	22	56
Small banks	81	65	0	146
Total	83	97	22	202

undoubtedly need to focus on the risks that they face, beyond credit and market risk. They need to assess and manage those risks. Basel II introduced an explicit regulatory requirement for operational risk for the first time and encouraged banks to improve their risk management in this area. But translating operational risk into a quantified, Pillar 1 capital requirement proved, and continues to prove, problematic.

4.4.4 Pillar 2: Supervisory Review

Recognising the limitations of Pillar 1, Basel introduced a supervisory review requirement that

> requires supervisors to ensure that each bank has sound internal processes in place to assess the adequacy of its capital based on a thorough evaluation of its risks. The new framework stresses the importance of bank management developing an internal capital assessment process and setting targets for capital that are commensurate with the bank's particular risk profile and control environment. Supervisors would be responsible for evaluating how well banks are assessing their capital adequacy needs relative to their risks. This internal process would then be subject to supervisory review and intervention, where appropriate.[44]

The supervisory review was intended to cover areas not addressed in Pillar 1 risks. In this way, Pillar 2 is a "catch all". The types of risk it seeks to address are listed in Table 4.8.

In the industry jargon, Pillar 2 is made up of an internal capital adequacy assessment programme (ICAAP), which incorporates a statement of risk appetite, outline of business strategy, identification of the material risks, capital plans and stress/scenario tests; these are then subject to the supervisory review (SREP).

The application of Pillar 2 was largely left to national discretion and, on the whole, neglected. This led the Basel Committee constantly to reiterate the importance of Pillar 2:

> This is not a compliance exercise! Senior management and boards of directors need to lead the process and ensure that their institutions establish robust internal systems that capture all material risks for their institution in a rigorous manner. The better banks measure and manage their risks, the more comfortable supervisors and the market will become with respect to their Pillar 1 processes, as well as the amount of overall capital that Pillar 2 indicates is appropriate.[45]

In some countries (e.g. Denmark), there was an explicit Pillar 2 add-on to RWAs or capital requirements; in others (e.g. UK), the Pillar 2 results were kept private; in others (e.g. France, Germany), there was no capital add-on at all.

---

[44] The New Basel Capital Accord: an explanatory note, BCBS, January 2001.

[45] Basel II and financial institution resiliency, Nout Wellink, Basel Committee, 27 June 2007.

Table 4.8   Pillar 2 risk types

Type of risk	Description of Pillar 2 risks
Concentration risk	The bank's risk profile contains exposures that are more highly correlated than Pillar 1 measures indicate. This could apply, for example, to banks that operate in only one country or specialise in a small number of businesses.
Residual value risk	The assumed future value of an asset turns out to be too optimistic. It generally applies to fixed assets. The best example is in car leasing, when it is hard for the bank to estimate the value of the car at the end of the lease.
Interest rate risk/ ALM risk	Interest rate risk in traded assets should be captured by the market risk component of Pillar 1. The risk that shifting interest rates damage the bank's income and solvency ("interest rate risk in the banking book" or IRRBB) concerns the way that deposits and loans adjust in different ways, due to different maturities and market dynamics. Note that in Australia, IRRBB is a Pillar 1 measure.[46]
Liquidity risk	The bank has trouble refinancing itself, due to funding market turbulence, poor planning or other reasons.
Insurance risk	The bank's insurance arm loses money, to an extent that is not already covered by Pillar 1 RWAs or capital deductions.
Pension risk	The bank's pension obligations to staff increase, requiring additional funding from the bank.
Business/strategy risk	The bank's chosen strategy fails to perform, resulting in lower revenues and profits.

Certain countries adopted a system of "capital planning buffers" and a bank-specific "individual capital guidance". In the UK, for example, banks were required to hold much more than the Basel capital minimum:

> The FSA under this authority sets individual capital guidance levels (ICG) for each bank based on the FSA assessment of the firm's Pillar 2 system. Breaching ICG, or capital deteriorating in a way that might be expected to breach the ICG, is a trigger for FSA actions. For the eight very high-impact banks, the ICG target ranges from 110 percent to 198 percent of their Pillar 1 minimum capital requirement.[47]

This approach to setting minimum capital requirements has allowed local regulators, in this case the UK FSA, to demand that banks increase their capital levels to be better prepared for potential future losses, in other words

> to apply judgement in overlaying the Pillar 1 modelled capital requirements with Pillar 2 capital buffers. Since 2008, required Pillar 1 capital in the major UK banks has increased from £151bn to £186bn. Pillar 2 capital buffers set by the FSA, in all, have increased during the same period from just under £20bn to £150bn. Put simply, in the regime up to 2008, there was no judgemental overlay of capital buffers, now there is such a buffer. This is a product of good judgemental supervision.[48]

---

[46] Implementation of the Basel II Capital Framework, Supervisory Review Process, APRA, 21 December 2007.

[47] United Kingdom: Basel Core Principles for Effective Banking Supervision Detailed Assessment of Compliance, IMF, July 2011.

[48] The challenges in assessing capital requirements for banks, Speech by Andrew Bailey, FSA, 6 November 2012.

4.4.5 Pillar 3: Market Discipline

During the development of Basel II, the authorities recognised that the capital markets were a key judge of the risk management and capital disciplines of a bank: "Market discipline can contribute to a safe and sound banking environment."[49] The markets had the resources, agility, self-interest and ability to act, which were simply not available to the supervisors. Acting on a belief that efficient markets were the best means for the banking industry to be regulated, they put in place the beginnings of a disclosure regime, to put into the public domain key risk data that were not available in normal accounting disclosures.

> The Committee aims to encourage market discipline by developing a set of disclosure requirements which will allow market participants to assess key pieces of information on the scope of application, capital, risk exposures, risk assessment processes, and hence the capital adequacy of the institution. The Committee believes that such disclosures have particular relevance under the Framework, where reliance on internal methodologies gives banks more discretion in assessing capital requirements. In principle, banks' disclosures should be consistent with how senior management and the board of directors assess and manage the risks of the bank. Under Pillar 1, banks use specified approaches/methodologies for measuring the various risks they face and the resulting capital requirements. The Committee believes that providing disclosures that are based on this common framework is an effective means of informing the market about a bank's exposure to those risks and provides a consistent and understandable disclosure framework that enhances comparability.[50]

Pillar 3 rules took up only 16 pages of the source Basel II documents, which ran to 251 pages in the draft June 2004 version and 347 pages in the final June 2006 version. They are essentially a list of information requirements, covering a qualitative (textual) description of risk management objectives, policies and techniques, as well as quantitative details on

- Scope of application.
- Capital structure (elements and instruments).
- Capital adequacy.
- Pillar 1 risks (credit, market and operational), including equities and securitisation holdings.
- Interest rate risk in the banking book.

In practice, Pillar 3 has proven to be a challenge, both for those who compile the information and those who are supposed to use it. None of the parties is satisfied with the arrangement. On the one side, Pillar 3 disclosure requires a lot of work by the bank; on the other side, investors are faced with reams of documentation that gives them lots of data but seldom provide the key information that they would like. These challenges and potential solutions are further considered later in the book.

---

[49] International Convergence of Capital Measurement and Capital Standards: A Revised Framework, Comprehensive Version, Basel Committee, June 2006.
[50] Basel II: International Convergence of Capital Measurement and Capital Standards: a Revised Framework, Basel Committee, June 2004.

4.4.6 Capital Calibration

As noted already, Basel II was not intended to change the aggregate amount of capital in the banking system. The Basel Committee was comfortable with the aggregate levels of capital in the system. There was no diagnostic of capital deficiency, nor any messaging to the banking industry that additional capital levels would be desirable.

> The Committee's goal remains as in the June 1999 paper, namely to neither raise nor lower the aggregate regulatory capital, inclusive of operational risk, for internationally active banks using the standardised approach.[51]

Instead, there was a clear goal to incentivise banks to adopt the more sophisticated approaches (namely, IRB for credit risk and AMA for operational risk) and thus achieve a reduction in minimum regulatory capital requirements. Basel was effectively bullying banks into adopting sophisticated risk management techniques:

> With regard to the IRB approach, the Committee's ultimate goal is to ensure that the regulatory capital requirement is sufficient to address underlying risks and contains incentives for banks to migrate from the standardised approach to this IRB approach.[52]

In order to be sure that the introduction of the new regulations would not cause a flight of capital from the industry, between 2001 and 2006 the Basel Committee conducted several "Quantitative Impact Studies" into how RWAs and minimum capital levels would be affected by the adoption of Basel II methodologies. The third of these, results of which were published in May 2003, found that banks using the AIRB methodology would have, on average, a minimum capital requirement that was 6% lower than under Basel I. Basel decided to introduce a scaler of 1.06, in order to keep the average requirement flat to Basel I.

> The Committee applies a scaling factor in order to broadly maintain the aggregate level of minimum capital requirements, while also providing incentives to adopt the more advanced risk-sensitive approaches of the Framework. The scaling factor is applied to the risk-weighted asset amounts for credit risk assessed under the IRB approach. The current best estimate of the scaling factor is 1.06.[53]

This crude scaler, applied to the outputs of sophisticated, in-depth statistical modelling, is one of the more ludicrous features of Basel II. Since the impact study results came relatively late in the preparation for implementation, and the Basel Committee had stated clearly its objective of flat capital levels, it was perhaps a necessary plug. On the other hand, given the sophistication of IRB approaches, the presence of a crude and inaccurate scaling factor of dubious import is remarkable. It demonstrates the misguided attachment that the Basel Committee gave to defined and deterministic solvency measures that did not, in actual fact, reflect the true risks either of the individual institutions or of the industry in aggregate.

---

[51] The New Basel Capital Accord: an explanatory note, Basel Committee, January 2001.

[52] Ibid.

[53] Basel II: International Convergence of Capital Measurement and Capital Standards: a Revised Framework, Basel Committee, June 2004.

The fifth impact study, published in June 2006, found that the minimum capital requirements under Basel II could well be substantially (6.8%) lower than for Basel I, even with the scaler in place, but nonetheless decided to keep the scaler at 1.06, noting that the calculations were subject to benign economic conditions and data uncertainties.[54] Perhaps the introduction of an adjusted scaler would have attracted negative attention.

Under the IRB approach, banks use their historic experience to determine an expected (or average) loss for a portfolio of exposures, then combine these data with the given levels of confidence and correlation to determine the unexpected loss levels and hence the capital requirement and the risk-weighted asset amount. In the underlying calibration of Basel II IRB risk models, therefore, the key supervisory inputs are *confidence level* and *correlation*.

The Basel Committee set the confidence level "at 99.9%, i.e. an institution is expected to suffer losses that exceed its level of Tier 1 and Tier 2 capital on average once in a thousand years. This confidence level might seem rather high. However, Tier 2 does not have the loss absorbing capacity of Tier 1. The high confidence level was also chosen to protect against estimation errors that might inevitably occur from banks' internal PD, LGD and EAD estimation, as well as other model uncertainties."[55]

What does this confidence level mean? Well, as the quote from Basel indicates, the level of capital set should be the amount that is burned through only once in a thousand years for a given bank or by one bank per 1,000 in a given year. Unfortunately, such remote probabilities are at the edge of our reasoning (as will be discussed in later sections) but that at least is the intention of the parameter.

There has been a fair amount of questioning of the appropriateness of this confidence calibration, given the many bank failures in recent years. The key observations to make at this stage are:

- Risk models are not good at measuring tail risk. To pretend that we can calibrate them with precision is misguided.
- We should not misinterpret the "1-in-1,000 years" calibration as implying that we will never see a bank failure in our lifetimes. There are thousands of banks in the world and only a very small percentage managed to burn through their entire capital base during the last five years. Strictly speaking, the Basel calibration may well be statistically accurate.
- In practice, in the current financial crisis, banks were forced to seek state aid because their capital positions fell below the minima required by the market and the regulator to continue to operate, not because they had exhausted their capital reserves. Basel II was unrealistic on capital adequacy, because it failed to recognise the need for banks to maintain confidence rather than simply have a positive level of regulatory capital after a shock event.

The Basel rules on correlation define the level of surprise (or, technically, unexpected loss) we can expect from given asset portfolios. This is important to recognise, as the risk assessment and capital requirements all stem from the estimates of "surprise". Even though these factors are buried within the Basel mathematical formulae, they are real drivers of what the capital metrics actually mean.

The Basel Committee set the correlation calibrations, with different calibrations for different asset classes – see Table 4.9.

---

[54] Basel Committee maintains calibration of Basel II Framework, Basel Committee, 24 May 2006.

[55] An Explanatory Note on the Basel II IRB Risk Weight Functions, Basel Committee, June 2005.

Table 4.9 Correlation calibrations by asset class (Basel II)

Asset class	Correlation calibration
Large corporate, Bank or Sovereign	Between 12% (for high PD assets) and 24% (for low PD assets)
Small corporate	Between 8% (for high PD assets) and 20% (for low PD assets)
Mortgages	15%
Retail overdrafts	4%
Retail loans	Between 3% (for high PD assets) and 16% (for low PD assets)

What do these correlation calibrations mean? In essence they define the relationship between expected loss and unexpected loss. For a given set of IRB parameters (PD, LGD, EAD), the expected loss (EL) is the same. But different correlation assumptions will drive different levels of unexpected loss (UL).

In simplistic terms, Table 4.10 shows how it works.

The higher the correlation number, the greater the UL relative to the EL. For example, a book of high PD retail loans (such as credit cards) might be expected to lose £100 in an average year and £200 in a really bad year, while a book of mortgages might be expected to lose £50 in an average year but £500 in a really bad year. The mortgages are more sensitive to the economic environment and are said to be more correlated. They will have a lower expected loss but a higher unexpected loss (and thus risk-weighting and capital requirement) than the credit cards.

In order to illustrate this, Barclays' credit card business had an EL of £1,100m in 2005 and £20bn of RWAs, while the investment banking business had an EL of only £85m but RWAs of £96bn.[56] Investment banking is good in an average year but awful in a bad year. It has more risk (UL) than credit card lending.

Table 4.10 Calculation steps for credit risk capital requirements (Basel II IRB)

Inputs	Modelling	Outputs
PD	Complex formula	Expected loss
LGD		
EAD		

Inputs	Modelling	Outputs
Expected loss	Complex formula	Unexpected loss ("risk")
Correlation		Capital requirements

4.4.7 Capital Supply and Mix

Basel II did not change many aspects of the Basel I definition of capital. The main points of refinement or clarification that it codified are shown in Table 4.11.

In several countries, some of these changes had already been adopted in advance of official Basel II adoption.

---

[56] Barclays plc Annual Report 2005.

Table 4.11   Key elements of Basel II definition of capital

Capital mix	• Limits on Tier 2 capital
	• 15% limit for so-called "*innovative*" Tier 1 instruments that had been introduced in 1998[57] (see Section 4.3.1)
	• The largely irrelevant "Tier 3" capital class
Deductions from regulatory capital (50% from Tier 1 and 50% from Tier 2)	• Investments in other regulated financial institutions (although the actual treatment was left open to national choice)
	• Any deficit in provisions relative to expected loss
	• Retained tranches of securitisations

4.4.8 Implementation of Basel II

Basel II required many banks to build modern risk management capabilities from scratch. This involved new processes, new systems, new methodologies and new staff. The organisational effort is not to be underestimated.

> The banking industry is only now acquiring the technical ability to measure credit and operational risk in the manner envisaged in the new proposal. Considerable efforts will be needed in the coming two years by banks and supervisors to acquire the necessary skills to implement the new Accord.[58]

Despite the challenges, Basel II was adopted by most signatory countries during 2007 and 2008 (see Table 4.12).

Table 4.12   Date of adoption of Basel II framework (examples)[59]

2007	Singapore
	Japan
	Hong Kong
	Taiwan
2008	Australia
	Canada
	European Union (CRD)
	India
	New Zealand
	South Korea
Stayed with Basel I	USA
	Russia

---

[57] Instruments eligible for inclusion in Tier 1 capital, Basel Committee, 27 October 1998.
[58] The New Basel Capital Accord: an explanatory note, Basel Committee, January 2001.
[59] Status of Basel II, Basel 2.5 and Basel III adoption: links to domestic implementation documents, Basel Committee, April 2012.

Some large countries decided to stay out of the Basel II regime. Most notably, the world's largest economy and banking regime, the USA, is a Basel Committee member yet has not yet implemented Basel II in full. In this case, the non-adoption was a case of severe foot-dragging caused by a scepticism towards the methodologies. Reportedly, the US authorities were not happy with the results of the impact studies conducted by the American banks. These indicated that internal models would reduce the capital requirements significantly:

> The Fed and other regulators looked at the results and thought something didn't smell right, and consequently dragged their feet over Basel II. In my view, the US was in a better position than most European authorities because we didn't reduce capital requirements.[60]

Even among those signatories that adopted Basel II, there were many differences in implementation. Some were more stringent than the global standard, due to conservatism. For example, the minimum capital requirement in Qatar was set at 10% rather than 8%; in Australia, banks were told to assume at least 20% losses on a defaulted mortgage, rather than the global standard of 10%. On the other hand, some national authorities sought to weaken the requirements of Basel II in their country, to reflect the specific nature of their banking industry. For example, in many countries the treatment of insurance subsidiaries required no Tier 1 capital at all to back insurance risks: this was sometimes a temporary measure to smooth implementation, though in other cases it reflected a belief that the standard Basel treatment was overly conservative or "harsh".

4.4.9 Critique of Basel II

Basel II was a giant leap forward for bank solvency regulation. It effectively mandated the adoption of modern risk management techniques, which were not being widely adopted by the majority of banks. These techniques promised a better understanding of risk and a more economic pricing of risk, which should result in a more efficient allocation of capital in the economy. Its coverage of risk went beyond just credit risk and covered new market developments, such as securitisation. And it highlighted the subjective nature of risk and the necessary involvement of bank management, supervisors and investors in the risk management process, through the three pillar framework.

> Above all, Basel II has helped to spread and hard-wire best risk management practice within the banking industry.[61]

However, it was by no means complete and by no means perfect. Indeed, its fundamental structures exposed several constraints and areas of weakness in the banking industry, as well as some profound conflicts that the concept of risk management raises. The ten key issues are as follows:

1. Complexity
Basel II was complex, because risk is complex. But complexity serves a purpose only up to a point, and the excruciating detail of Basel II goes far beyond the point at which our understanding of the risks of the business improves. This is a central thesis of this work and

---

[60] "Basel II was a big mistake": Larry Meyer exclusive interview, CentralBanking.Com, 14 July 2010.
[61] Implementing the macroprudential approach to financial regulation and supervision, Claudio Borio, Bank for International Settlements.

is converted into a concrete counter-proposal in Chapter 7. At its heart, the argument here is that of Occam's Razor, namely that the simplest explanation is the one to be favoured in the face of a problem. And since we struggle with many basic aspects concerning a bank's solvency (such as the true value of an asset, the future probability of losses and so on), we are frankly kidding ourselves if we ascribe objective truth to increasingly complex accounting and risk models.

Inevitably, measures are going to be either simple and easy-to-use or thorough and insightful. The goal of having measures that are both simple and insightful is probably impossible. The criticism of Basel II is that its complexity may have given us a framework that is neither simple nor insightful.

The architects of Basel, however, thought that the complexity did improve our understanding of risk and that the new regime would help to avoid a costly misalignment of capital resources and sources of risk. In the eyes of the Basel Committee, the cost:benefit analysis felt like a net positive:

> The new framework is less prescriptive than the original Accord. At its simplest, the framework is somewhat more complex than the old, but it offers a range of approaches for banks capable of using more risk-sensitive analytical methodologies. These inevitably require more detail in their application and hence a thicker rule book. The Committee believes the benefits of a regime in which capital is aligned more closely to risk significantly exceed the costs, with the result that the banking system should be safer, sounder, and more efficient.[62]

As Basel II got more complex and became Basel III (see next chapter), the challenge of complexity was seen as a pure benefit, with little consideration for the point at which the complexity hinders the objectives of risk management:

> Complexity is a byproduct of the desire, among regulators and banks, for risk sensitivity. Risk measurement will never be perfect. Simplicity, however, can sometimes come at a cost. Ignoring risk does not make it disappear. Without measuring risk properly, we may allow it to build up undetected.[63]

That said, the Luddite view, that modelling risk at all is fruitless and we should proceed with very basic, non-risk-adjusted information, is also dangerous. Some analysts and regulators like to believe that modern banks can be assessed using a minimum of technical analyses and bemoan the increase in the processing required in looking at, say, a bank's solvency, not recognising that modern IT systems make detailed analyses quite practical: "the number of calculations has risen from single figures to over 200 million. The quant and the computer have displaced the clerk and the envelope."[64]

The point is, a balance has to be struck, and it is not clear that Basel II found the right balance.

2. Liquidity
Basel II did not include new, international regulations on funding and liquidity. The Basel Committee acknowledged that liquidity and funding were major challenges and areas

---

[62] The New Basel Capital Accord: an explanatory note, BCBS January 2001.

[63] "Basel III is simpler and stronger", Stefan Ingves, Chairman of the Basel Committee, 15 October 2012.

[64] Capital discipline, speech by Andrew Haldane, Bank of England, 9 January 2011.

where better regulatory standards were required. Just as the current financial crisis was brewing, in December 2006, it established the Working Group on Liquidity to review the existing Basel guidance, which dated from 2000 and was very high level and principles-based rather than prescriptive.[65] As recent experience has shown us, the aspects of funding and liquidity are fundamental to the resilience and stability of the banking industry. The absence of effective approaches towards regulating and supervising liquidity practices proved to be damaging.

3. Procyclicality

By introducing risk-adjusted measures into the regulatory regime, Basel II rightly acknowledged that risk can be dynamic rather than static. In other words, the riskiness of a bank increases when the economy worsens and this should be reflected in the risk measures used for bank regulation.

However, there is potential for the dynamic assessment of risk to cause banks to behave in a way that is *procyclical*. By reducing their risk exposures during a period of economic stress, banks will cause further economic stress, since they will be forcing borrowers to repay when they are least able or making access to loans harder at that point when people and businesses need to borrow the most (a so-called "credit crunch").

Basel II did not consider ways in which this potential for procyclicality could be addressed. Nor did it deal with the fact that risk actually precedes losses and is thus peaking at the same time as confidence and then actually falling as losses emerge. This anti-phasing could actually be the source of useful anticyclical tools to smooth the impact of economic cycles. Instead, it could be argued that over-reliance on the cyclical, risk-adjusted measures introduced by Basel II increased the incentive for banks to load up on supposedly low-risk assets in the years 2005 and 2006, assets which were to prove ruinous. What is less clear is whether Basel II is, in fact, entirely relevant to this point of cyclicality, since bank decision-making in those relevant years was often still based on Basel I methodologies.

4. Incomplete Implementation

We cannot truly judge the effectiveness of Basel II because it was never fully implemented. Basel II took the best part of a decade to conceive, design and calibrate. Its implementation has been partial and slow. Of course, introducing new, sophisticated risk management practices into a large, global industry was never going to be trivial. But the "three pillar" concept never really caught on as intended and the mindset changes implied within Pillars 2 and 3 may well take a generation to implement – unless they are scrapped before then. So this element of critique is not of the Basel II framework but of the way it has been realised.

5. Challenges to Models

Basel II became over-reliant on statistical models purporting to turn risk into a defined quantity, to remove the uncertainty from risk. This supposed vanquishing of risk by an army of advanced statisticians, in turn, led to a massive rise in confidence to levels that were beyond prudence.

---

[65] Sound Practices for Managing Liquidity in Banking Organisations, Basel Committee, February 2000.

At the very mechanical level, building a Basel II risk model requires large volumes of historic data across multiple asset classes. Sometimes, data gaps need to be addressed – for example, loss histories for low-default portfolios.[66] Key methodology decisions need to be addressed, such as how to deal with the difference between regulatory capital and economic capital. But the key issue on risk modelling is how to deal with extreme events, the so-called "tail risk". Basel II models do not tell us where unexpected losses will come in the extreme scenario, and so the 99.9% confidence claims lack credibility.

Models can help us understand risk profiles but they cannot know risk, nor can they tame risk. More humility in this area is essential, along with some of the proposals set out later in this book.

6. Subjectivity, or Lack of Objectivity

Risk is subjective and fortunately the architects of Basel II recognised this fact. But Basel II failed during implementation to ram this point home. In many ways, little changed. Banks continued to express their solvency in terms of the ratio of capital to risk-weighted assets; the 8% minimum stayed in place; Pillar 2 reviews were kept behind closed doors. It seems that many of the most influential stakeholders in the banking industry were under the impression that a risk-weighted asset had an objective definition and meaning – and was comparable across institutions. Some regulators and banks may have crossed the rubicon, but they left many in the industry behind.

As the current financial crisis unfolded, it is clear that many influential people in the authorities and in the financial analyst community had not bought in to the concept of subjectivity and the consequent lack of objectivity. They seem genuinely appalled that banks are allowed to generate their own risk-weightings, albeit under supervisory scrutiny. Meanwhile, many regulators neglected the challenges of supervision that Basel II entailed, in some cases failing to implement solid Pillar 2 assessments, in other cases focusing on process compliance rather than institutional and sectoral risk management.

As a result of this incomplete buy-in, the subjective elements of Basel II are under attack from many sides, especially the risk-weights that are attached to the Internal Ratings Based (IRB) approach. *Vox populi* wants objective information to ensure trustworthiness and comparability.

It is not clear how to resolve this apparent conflict between subjectivity and objectivity, though some ideas are floated in Chapter 7. The criticism here, therefore, is simply that Basel II represented sloppy implementation of a sound concept.

7. Role of Diversification

Diversification is a key tool in risk management, potentially the only cost-free hedge that there is. Everyone knows not to "put all their eggs in one basket" and the same is true for a bank. Other than a vague assessment under Pillar 2, Basel II does not address the diversification issue. When it was implemented in 2007, some people expected the issue of concentration and diversification to be part of the "next steps" leading to Basel III. Like liquidity, it was too important to be left out of a rigorous, formal framework and is thus a major failing of Basel II.

8. Need for Heterogeneity

One of the reasons for recommending the IRB approach was to encourage heterogeneity in the banking industry, to avoid a "rush for the doors" in the case of market turmoil or

---

[66] Validation of low-default portfolios in the Basel II Framework, Basel Committee Newsletter No. 6 (September 2005).

macro-economic stress. In fact, banks tend to operate in the same markets with the same clients and counterparties. They also bought their Basel II models from a small number of IT vendors and are thus using very similar risk management frameworks and data sets. In the market context or in risk management approaches, therefore, most banks do see things in similar ways and so the tendency for herd behaviour is strong.

Basel II should have been firm on sponsoring heterogeneity. It may seem strange to suggest it from today's standpoint, but regulation should have encouraged and fostered different approaches to banking, including some of the "shorting" activities that were left instead to the hedge fund industry. An industry with a more balanced perspective and diverse views might have been able to mitigate some of the procyclical exuberance evident in the run-up to the current financial crisis.

9. Over-reliance on Credit Ratings Agencies

Basel II promoted the use of banks' own risk assessments and internal ratings methodologies. But it also created large areas where the risk assessments and capital requirements were effectively delegated or outsourced to credit ratings agencies. Many banks came to rely upon these external ratings absolutely, making horrendous errors in, for example, assuming that a bond rated AAA had effectively zero credit risk. As a way of grouping bundles of assets into convenient sub-groups (for example, segregating high-PD corporates from low-PD corporates), the use of agencies is convenient. The use of ratings to define regulatory treatment of securitisations, however, went too far and the whole process became a ridiculous arbitrage.

10. Market Risk Module not Fit for Purpose

The methodologies for market risk were inappropriate for regulatory capital purposes and the actual outputs of the market risk element of Pillar 1 did not make sense. Banks' own internal economic risk models gave risk assessments and capital requirements that were a multiple of the Basel II regulatory requirement (see the example of Deutsche Bank from Section 4.4.3). This lax regulatory treatment incentivised banks to build up huge, superficially profitable trading businesses that would not have occurred with a more rational approach. The illusion of low risk led to excessive risk-taking and the largely invisible build-up of risk contributed to the current financial crisis, amplifying its ultimate impact.

4.5 BASEL III

The bad experiences during 2007, 2008 and 2009 caused consternation among regulators internationally. The Basel Committee reached a consensus on the causes of the crisis: excessive leverage, weak capital bases, poor funding profiles and insufficient liquidity buffers. As a result of these weaknesses, the market lost confidence in the solvency and liquidity of many banks, with a direct impact on the real economy, which left no other option than "unprecedented injections of liquidity, capital, support and guarantees, exposing taxpayers to large losses".[67]

---

[67] Basel III: A global regulatory framework for more resilient banks and banking system, Basel Committee, June 2011.

As well as ad-hoc, local measures to remedy some of the imperfections of bank regulation (such as the 2009 stress tests), regulators were able to develop a globally coordinated regulatory response within a timeframe that, relative to the usual glacial pace of regulatory reforms, was quite rapid. On 17 December 2009, the Basel Committee published its "consultative proposals to strengthen the resilience of the banking sector". These proposals have since been fleshed out and have been given the nickname "Basel III".

The Basel Committee views gaps in banking regulation as a primary driver of the financial crisis and proposes more regulation as the solution. This should come as no surprise. Moreover, the rapid drafting of the Basel III regulatory framework was nevertheless a grand compromise between regulators from various jurisdictions faced with different challenges. There was simply no time to rethink the guiding philosophies of Basel II and develop *ab initio* a new, balanced, elegant regulatory framework.

Basel III is not a revolution in bank regulation:

- It does not reject the fundamental tenets of Basel II, such as the self-measurement of risk.
- It remains focused on capital as the main source of resilience.
- It tweaks some of the weaker points of the previous regime (such as the definition of capital) and plugs some of the gaps in regulation (such as liquidity risk management).
- It is incremental in nature, even though the scale of those changes might be seen by some as large.

As described earlier, the move from Basel I to Basel II had kept the definition of capital broadly stable but made the calculation of capital requirements and RWAs more sophisticated. This time, the changes had the opposite emphasis: Basel III leaves the Basel II RWA framework largely intact while making major changes to the definition of capital. By introducing a global standard on funding and liquidity for the first time, the regime acknowledges the important role of these elements. In summary, Basel III sets out to ensure that banks have more and better financial resources with which to operate, to "improve the banking's sector ability to absorb shocks arising from financial and economic stress, whatever the source, thus reducing the risk of spillover from the financial sector to the real economy".[68]

4.5.1 Definition of Capital

Basel III increases the emphasis on equity capital as the primary shock-absorber for banks during periods of stress, since this is the accounting item that is depleted by losses during normal operations. The new regulations give a strict definition of what comprises "Common Equity Tier 1" (or CET1) capital – common shares and retained earnings – though some leeway is given for mutually owned and cooperative banks, who may not have these elements in the strictest legal sense.

Hybrid capital is tolerated, but the terms of permissible instruments are tightened to ensure that hybrids can absorb losses *in an accounting and legal sense* – through a write-down of principal or a conversion into common stock – if solvency breaches threshold levels or a

---

[68] Basel III: A global regulatory framework for more resilient banks and banking system, Basel Committee, June 2011.

"point of non-viability", as judged and declared by the regulator, is reached. In other words, hybrids can absorb losses without the bank being put into formal liquidation. Needless to say, the exact working of this loss absorption is not entirely clear or universally standard.

Non-compliant legacy capital instruments are phased out via a multi-year "grandfathering" process. The notion of Tier 3 capital, hardly used by anyone, was abolished and the distinction of "upper" and "lower" Tier 2 capital was removed.

Basel III introduced the concept of "contingent capital" but left it open for the time being. Several national authorities (e.g. UK, Denmark, Switzerland, Belgium) have introduced contingent capital into their range of permitted capital instruments, but only to fulfil capital requirements that are nationally discretionary and "super-equivalent": buffers that are in addition to the Basel requirements and Pillar 2 capital requirements, for example. Basel has noted that contingent capital appears an interesting concept due to the high quality of capital (loss-absorbing at an early stage, pre-underwritten and pre-funded, improved shareholder discipline) but that there are some major design challenges inherent in contingent capital structures (trigger unreliability, complexity, negative signalling and "the death spiral" that could occur as conversion approaches[69]).

4.5.2 Deductions

Certain financial items have always been excluded from the calculation of regulatory capital, since they are deemed to be unreliable sources of loss-absorption capacity. Goodwill – the excess over accounting book value paid for an acquisition – is a good example. But international capital deductions had diverged over time and several accounting items that were counted as "capital" had come under scrutiny as to their effectiveness.

Basel III tightened up and standardised the deductions regime. It also specified that deductible items should come out of the CET1 element of regulatory capital.

The main items to be deducted from CET1 under Basel III are as shown in Table 4.13.

In addition, Basel III has a set of deductions that apply only if the items are a major part of the bank's CET1 base. The types of asset that are deducted in this way are described in Table 4.14.

If these lines each add up to more than 10% of the bank's CET1, then the excess over 10% for each is a deduction. Anything under 10% of the bank's CET1 is treated as a risk-weighted asset. And if the three last ones add up to more than 15% in total of the bank's CET1, then the amount beyond that 15% is fully deducted.

The logic for these thresholds is unclear and the way of calculating them is arcane. Clearly, a complex mind has been at work in Basel! Note that the threshold approach is not used in Australia, where deductions are taken from CET1 no matter how large they are in relation to the bank's CET1. This is probably a more logical and clear approach, but it is not the Basel standard.

These deductions make a big difference to the capital base of certain banks under Basel III, as compared with Basel II. They can reduce the official level of CET1 by up to a third. See Table 4.15.

---

[69] Global systemically important banks: Assessment methodology and the additional loss absorbency requirement, Basel Committee, November 2011.

Table 4.13   Basel III deductions from Common Equity Tier 1

Item	Description	Prior (Basel II) treatment
Goodwill	The excess of the acquisition price of an asset over its accounting net book value	Deducted from Tier 1
Intangible assets	Software is the most common intangible asset in a bank's accounts	Deducted from Tier 1 (generally)
Fair value of own debt	Accounting item that generates a profit when the bank's own creditworthiness deteriorates	Deducted from equity Tier 1
Deferred tax assets due to tax loss carry forwards	When a bank makes a loss, it generates a tax credit that reduces the amount of tax it has to pay on future profits. This is booked as an asset. If the future profits fail to materialise, this asset is worthless	Not deducted from regulatory capital
Shortfall in provisions to expected losses	Since IRB risk-weights do not cover the probabilistic *expected losses*, this amount needs to be deducted from regulatory capital	Generally, was deducted 50% from Tier 1 and 50% from Tier 2
Pension fund assets	If a bank-sponsored pension fund is in surplus, then this shows as an asset on the accounting balance sheet. However, it is generally inaccessible. If the fund is in deficit, then this shows as a negative asset	Various treatments
AFS reserve	An accounting reserve caused by changes in the value of investments (debt, equity)	In some countries (e.g. UK), negative AFS reserves on debt instruments were reversed, on the assumption that any negative change in the value of debt instruments will tend to be temporary

Table 4.14   Basel III threshold deductions

Item	Description	Prior treatment
Minor (<10%) holdings of other financial institutions	Holdings of the equity of other financial institutions that are not significant	Treated as a normal exposure and RWA calculated
Significant (>10%) holdings of other financial institutions	Holdings of the equity of other financial institutions that are significant, i.e. the bank has a 10% stake or greater in them OR the individual stake is bigger than 10% of the bank's CET1	Tier 2 deduction or 50/50 from Tier 1 and Tier 2
Mortgage servicing rights	Accounted for as a capital item, this is actually a future revenue stream from fees paid for the servicing of mortgages that have been sold on or securitised	Not deducted
Deferred tax assets due to timing differences	Tax assets that arise from the timing difference between taking provisions and taking the tax-deductible write-down; not dependent on profit to realise the value	Not deducted

Table 4.15   Examples of impact of Basel III capital deductions

Bank	Basel II core Tier 1	Basel III deductions	Basel III core Tier 1	Comments
HSBC[70]	$139bn	$24bn	$115bn	Largest deductions ($15bn) are holdings in the CET1 of other financial institutions
Credit Suisse[71]	CHF34.8bn	CHF12.1bn	CHF22.7bn	Includes an estimated CHF5.2bn of deferred tax assets relating to tax loss carry-forwards
Lloyds Banking Group[72]	£37.2bn	£11.3bn	£25.9bn	Deductions include £5.7bn of deferred tax assets relating to tax loss carry-forwards and £5.1bn relating to the insurance subsidiary

Showing what a bank's capital amount is under Basel III is not yet universally possible. Some banks have been disclosing high-level numbers, but these are not detailed and the approach is not consistent between banks. In the UK, however, banks have been asked by their regulator to show in detail the impact of the new deductions on their regulatory capital. HSBC is a good illustration of what this looks like – see Table 4.16.

The deductions regime will also change the way that banks manage their businesses. For areas where the deduction is new, the incremental "consumption" of regulatory capital resources may make a business appear less capital-efficient: its return-on-regulatory-capital may have deteriorated below management's objectives. Already, there have been instances of banks selling businesses due to the new Basel III deductions regime. In the case of HSBC, for example, their holding in Ping An was sold at the end of 2012 for $9.4bn, generating a profit of $3.0bn and removing the future Basel III deduction for this stake.[73] It appears that the regulatory treatment of the Ping An stake was a key driver for HSBC's decision to sell.

4.5.3 Risk-Weighted Assets

Though Basel III did not introduce a rethink on the RWA approaches for credit risk or operational risk, it did shake up the regime for the market risk in their trading operations. There was simply too little regulatory capital assigned to the trading operations of big banks. If we take Deutsche Bank as an example, their regulatory capital requirement for market risk, based on 2009 market risk RWAs of €24.9bn, was a mere €2bn, even though the bank's own "economic capital" methodologies indicated a capital need of €4.6bn.[74]

---

[70] Annual Report and Accounts, HSBC, 2012.
[71] Annual Report 2012, Credit Suisse Group AG.
[72] Lloyds Banking Group Pillar 3 Disclosures, 31 December 2012.
[73] Annual Report and Accounts, HSBC, 2012.
[74] Financial Report 2009, Deutsche Bank.

Table 4.16   Estimated effect of Basel III rules on HSBC's regulatory capital position as at end 2012[75]

Item	Value $bn
Basel II core Tier 1 capital	138.8
Indirect investments in own shares	(1.3)
Surplus capital in minority interest stakes	(2.3)
Unrealised losses on available-for-sale debt securities	(1.2)
Unrealised gains on available-for-sale equities	+2.1
Property revaluation reserves	+1.2
Pension fund liabilities	(1.6)
Excess of expected losses over provisions	(3.2)
Transfer of securitisation positions from deduction to RWA treatment	+1.8
Profit-contingent deferred tax assets	(0.5)
Prudential valuation adjustment	(1.7)
Debit valuation adjustment	(0.4)
Immaterial holdings of CET1 of other financial institutions	(6.0)
Significant holdings of CET1 of other financial institutions beyond allowed thresholds	(9.0)
Deferred tax asset due to timing differences	(1.5)
Miscellaneous	+0.3
Total impact of deductions	(23.3)
Estimated Basel III CET1 capital	115.5

The market risk changes were introduced by Basel in 2009[76] and have become known by the nickname "Basel II.5", even though they are a bolt-on to Basel II. In most countries, they were implemented rapidly and with no lengthy transition.

The methodologies used to compute market risk RWAs are too technical to be covered in detail this book. However, there are some key points to be understood:

- Basel II.5 added to the "Value at Risk" (VaR) methodologies the notion of a "stressed VaR", which is the level of the VaR during a period of troubled (i.e. stressed) markets.
- It also added an "Incremental Risk Charge" (IRC) on the trading of bonds, CDS and equities, meant to cover the risks of default and the credit deterioration (or "migration") in those positions.
- Market risk RWAs more than tripled, the impact of stressed VaR and the IRC each being responsible for about half of the increase.[77]
- In this way, the quantum of regulatory capital for market risk became closer to banks' own calculations in their economic capital frameworks.

---

[75] Annual Report and Accounts, HSBC, 2012.
[76] Revisions to the Basel II market risk framework, Basel Committee, July 2009.
[77] Analysis of the trading book quantitative impact study, Basel Committee, October 2009.

Even though Basel II.5 achieved its primary objective, that of increasing the regulatory capital requirements for trading operations, it has made the RWA methodologies for market risk into a patchwork quilt of cumbersome, overlapping and often contradictory calculations. Its inelegance is not driven by the complexity of the underlying risks: it reflects not an actual risk methodology, more an arbitrary charging mechanism. "Risk managers say they are unlikely to use the framework decided by the Basel Committee for actual risk management."[78] Basel is currently designing a replacement that makes more sense, in its "fundamental review of the trading book". Instead of the highly unsatisfactory VaR methodology, which is bad at capturing tail risk, Basel is considering adopting an "Expected Shortfall" approach, which uses a broader set of scenarios and considers "both the size and the likelihood of losses above a certain threshold (e.g. the 99th percentile). In this way, ES accounts for tail risk in a more comprehensive manner."[79]

In addition to the measures introduced by Basel II.5, Basel III introduces a new capital charge for trading operations, based on the credit risk of trading counterparties. Counterparty risk is covered by a "Credit Valuation Adjustment" (CVA), which is a measure of expected loss, as well as a capital charge for the volatility risk of the CVA, a measure of unexpected loss. This CVA risk charge adds about 5% to the RWAs of a typical large bank,[80] though of course it will be significantly more for banks with large trading operations.

By way of illustration, HSBC's RWAs under Basel III will include an estimated $60bn related to CVA risk, which is indeed about 5% of HSBC's total RWAs. To give an idea of the relative scale of these new RWA amounts, at the end of 2012, its market risk RWAs under Basel II.5 were $55bn and its counterparty credit risk RWA amount was $48bn.[81] They are significant increases in the regulatory RWA base of banks with trading operations.

Lastly, banks will see their RWAs change under Basel III as certain items move from a deductions approach to a risk-weighted assets approach. In other words, the risk will be expressed not as a negative on the numerator of the solvency ratio but as a positive on the denominator of the ratio.

4.5.4 Minimum Capital Levels

It is a commonly accepted view that banks did not have enough capital, relative to the risks they were running, in the run-up to the current financial crisis. Basel III aims to remedy that in three ways:

1. by changing the methodology for the ratio;
2. by toughening the requirements on capital mix towards higher quality sources; and
3. by raising the minimum ratio requirements.

Methodology changes as regards deductions and risk-weighted assets calculations have caused a change in the CET1 solvency ratio of around 2.5 percentage points on average for large banks and slightly less for smaller banks. The actual impact on individual banks depends upon the business mix and national regulatory regime. Disallowance of newly non-eligible hybrid capital instruments has caused the total capital levels to be lower than Basel II levels to an even greater extent – see Table 4.17.

---

[78] *Risk* magazine, 3 September 2010.
[79] Fundamental review of the trading book, Basel Committee, May 2012.
[80] Results of the Basel III monitoring exercise as of 30 June 2012, Basel Committee, March 2013.
[81] HSBC Annual Report and Accounts 2012.

Table 4.17   Capital ratios under Basel II and Basel III at end 2011[82] and June 2012[83]

	Basel II		Basel III		Difference	
	December 2011	June 2012	December 2011	June 2012	December 2011	June 2012
Large banks						
CET1	10.4%	10.8%	7.7%	8.5%	2.7%	2.3%
Tier 1	11.7%	12.0%	8.0%	8.7%	3.7%	3.3%
Total capital	14.2%	14.4%	9.2%	9.9%	5.0%	4.5%
Smaller banks						
CET1	10.4%	10.9%	8.8%	9.0%	1.6%	1.9%
Tier 1	11.0%	11.4%	9.2%	9.5%	1.8%	1.9%
Total capital	14.3%	14.7%	11.0%	11.3%	3.3%	3.4%

Historical comparisons of regulatory capital ratios will now be difficult to make, given that the new Basel III methodologies produce ratios that are lower than historic measures. Therefore, it is important to remember that regulatory capital ratios under Basel III will be more exacting and that banks will be more solvent in an economic sense, even if reported ratios are the same as before.

As well as changing the units of measurement, Basel III has also introduced a more challenging capital mix. There is more emphasis on shareholder's equity. As well as insisting that all deductions are made from CET1, the net CET1 ratio after deductions must be at least 4.5%. This compares with the Basel II minimum, theoretically 2% CET1 and with far fewer CET1 deductions. Under Basel III, the Tier 1 minimum capital level is set at 6% (Basel II: 4%) and total capital at 8% (Basel II was also 8%) (see Table 4.18).

Table 4.18   Minimum capital levels

	Basel II	Basel III
Deductions	Largely from Tier 1 and total capital	All deductions from CET1
Denominator	Basel II RWAs	Basel III RWAs
CET1	2%	4.5%
Tier 1	4%	6%
Total capital	8%	8%

---

[82] Results of the Basel III monitoring exercise as of 31 December 2011, Basel Committee, September 2012.
[83] Results of the Basel III monitoring exercise as of 30 June 2012, Basel Committee, March 2013.

So, the 8% figure is preserved as a total capital minimum. But Basel III also introduces several new layers of capital requirements or "buffers", designed to:

- Encourage banks to maintain capital discipline if they are short of capital.
- Find a way to stop the cyclicality of risk becoming damagingly procyclical.
- Make banks who are seen as "too big to fail" even more resilient.

The first buffer is called the "capital conservation buffer". It effectively raises the minimum capital ratios for banks by 2.5%, even though Basel states that it "does not wish to impose constraints for entering the range that would be so restrictive as to result in the range being viewed as establishing a new minimum capital requirement".[84] Clearly, no bank is going to be willing to operate inside the capital conservation buffer. As well as regulatory sanctions curtailing discretionary distributions of dividends and bonuses, the bank in question would face severe market pressure and loss of confidence.

The second buffer represents an attempt to combat the cyclical nature of risk that can lead to excessive growth in indebtedness during a boom and force damaging contraction in credit supply by banks during a downturn. Basel III introduces a counter-cyclical buffer, meant to be imposed by national regulators during periods of high growth in credit and relaxed in times of low growth and/or stress. The level of this buffer can be as high as 2.5% of risk-weighted assets. It has already been utilised on a sectoral basis: in February 2013, Switzerland implemented a counter-cyclical buffer on mortgages, based on "the view that the real estate market is showing signs of overheating in certain segments and regions".[85] Raising minimum capital levels is an understandable action by regulators, but it is not clear how willing they will be to lower them in times of stress, nor how banks will behave when minima are dropped: in all likelihood, market pressures will force them to maintain high levels as a show of strength.

The third buffer is the buffer for large, systemically important, "too big to fail" banks. It is meant to be up to 3.5%. The list of 28 banks that are deemed systemically important on a global basis has been defined by the Financial Stability Board (see Table 4.19). In addition to these banks, national regulators have the option to designate banks as *domestically* systemically important. It remains to be seen whether smaller banks – who, incidentally, have always tended to run higher levels of capital than their larger peers, due to their lower levels of business diversification – end up anyway having capital levels that are similar to their bigger, blue-chip peers.

Lastly, there are emerging a series of national super-equivalent "buffers" that are additional to those in the Basel framework. For example, Denmark requires large banks to maintain a "crisis management buffer" equivalent to 5% of RWAs, though the capital covering this requirement can comprise lower-quality regulatory capital instruments, such as Tier 2 capital. This means that in Denmark, the current proposal could mean that the largest bank has a minimum regulatory capital requirement of around 17%, once bank-specific "Pillar 2" capital requirements are also taken into account.[86]

All in all, the *effective* solvency capital requirements for banks are several times higher under Basel III than under Basel II.

---

[84] Countercyclical capital buffer proposal, Basel Committee, July 2010.

[85] FINMA to oversee sector-specific counter-cyclical capital buffer, FINMA Press Release, 13 February 2013.

[86] Final Report, Committee on Systemically Important Financial institutions in Denmark, 14 March 2013.

Table 4.19 Global systemically important banks, November 2012[87]

Bucket	Banks
2.5%	Citigroup Deutsche Bank HSBC JP Morgan Chase
2.0%	Barclays BNP Paribas
1.5%	Bank of America Bank of New York Mellon Credit Suisse Goldman Sachs Mitsubishi UFJ FG Morgan Stanley Royal Bank of Scotland UBS
1.0%	Bank of China BBVA Groupe BPCE Group Crédit Agricole ING Bank Mizuho FG Nordea Santander Société Générale Standard Chartered State Street Sumitomo Mitsui FG Unicredit Group Wells Fargo

4.5.5 Leverage Ratio

For some, determining the solvency of a bank applying a risk-weighting to exposures seems questionable or at least error-prone. *Unweighted* solvency measures based on the accounting values of exposures have been used effectively in many countries over the years, including in the USA by the FDIC. But they were not adopted internationally. Basel II had identified the possibility of introducing a "leverage ratio" that compared a bank's capital resources to its unweighted bank's risk exposures, but decided against using such a measure. The experience of the current financial crisis is that there have been, in some cases, huge losses incurred on exposures to risk assets that carried low risk-weightings (such as AAA-rated subprime bonds or government bonds). Consequently, the Basel Committee decided to go

---

[87] Update of group of global systemically important banks (G-SIBs), Financial Stability Board, 1 November 2012.

ahead and include the leverage ratio in the Basel III package, as a "backstop" in case the assumptions behind the risk-weighted approaches failed. A calibration of this ratio at 3% was proposed, with the promise of conducting a full assessment and monitoring before finalising the calibration. At any rate, Basel proposed a slow implementation timeline, with disclosure of the actual ratio by banks in 2015 and having the leverage ratio as a binding requirement only in 2018.

The leverage ratio will only be a material consideration for banks that have huge leverage of a low-risk balance sheet. There are few of these – most commercial banks have a leverage ratio above 3% at present. Recent benchmarking by the Basel Committee shows that large international banks are currently running with an average leverage ratio of 3.7% on a Basel III basis, with only a quarter of those banks not yet meeting the mooted 3% requirement.[88] Most of these banks appear to be in Europe: data from the EBA indicates that nearly half of large European banks do not yet meet the 3% leverage ratio minimum.[89]

As a result of the scepticism towards risk-weighted measures, the leverage ratio has been gaining in popularity. Basel has published a clarificatory paper[90] and there have been moves in the USA to increase the leverage ratios of US banks.[91] It is hard to know what the leverage ratios of individual banks are, since the definition is debatable and banks have no duty to disclose, yet. Nevertheless, based on bank reporting for the year 2012, the following, listed in Table 4.20, would appear to be reasonable estimates of the leverage ratio.

Note that, in June 2013, Barclays was required by the UK authorities to raise capital to address the low level of its leverage ratio (see Section 5.9).

Table 4.20   Examples of actual leverage ratios

Bank	Leverage ratio	Comments
Barclays[92]	2.8%	~~Fully-loaded Basel III capital definition~~
RBS[93]	3.1%	Fully-loaded Basel III capital definition
HSBC[94]	4.2%	Fully-loaded Basel III capital definition
BNP Paribas[95]	5.1%	Capital definition is Basel II not Basel III
Bank of America[96]	6.1%	Estimate based on disclosed data

[88] Results of the Basel III monitoring exercise as of 30 June 2012, Basel Committee, March 2013.

[89] Basel III monitoring exercise – Results based on data as of 30 June 2012, EBA, 19 March 2013.

[90] Consultative Document: Revised Basel III leverage ratio framework and disclosure requirements, Basel Committee, June 2013.

[91] Safe banks do not mean slow economic growth, Thomas Hoenig, FDIC, *Financial Times*, 20 August 2013.

[92] Implementation of Basel 3 – leverage impacts, Annual Report 2012, Barclays.

[93] Pillar 3 Report 2012, RBS Group.

[94] Capital and Risk Management Pillar 3 Disclosures at 31 December 2012, HSBC.

[95] Fourth Quarter 2012 Results, BNP Paribas, 14 February 2013.

[96] Bank of America Corporation 2012 Annual Report.

Table 4.21 Leverage ratio of specialised banks

Bank	Description	S&P credit rating	Leverage ratio[97]
KfW	Kreditanstalt für Wiederaufbau is a development bank owned by the German state. Originally set up in 1948 to help finance the reconstruction of Germany following the Second World War, it now has a broader role	AAA	3.5%
BNG	Bank Nederlandse Gemeenten is a specialised financial institution that finances the Dutch public sector. It is owned 50% by the Dutch state and the other 50% by municipal authorities, provincial authorities and a water board	AAA	1.8%
NWB	Nederlandse Waterschapsbank is also a bank specialised in financing the Dutch public sector. It is owned 81% by the water boards, 17% by the Dutch state and 2% by the provinces	AAA	1.8%

In a surprise move, the UK authorities required their banks to comply with a relatively harsh version of the leverage ratio in the near term. Their metric uses "fully loaded" rather than phased Basel III rules for capital definition, does not take existing hybrid capital into account and applies extra deductions for impending fines and value adjustments. The move prompted the hasty formulation and negotiation of major recapitalisation plans by Barclays and by the Nationwide Building Society.[98]

There are some banks specialised in public sector lending who have very low leverage ratios, yet are deemed supremely creditworthy by the credit ratings agencies, as well as by the capital markets (see Table 4.21).

These banks will need to increase the size of their capital base by a significant multiple, in order to comply with the Basel III leverage ratio, unless they change their business model or seek some kind of waiver.

4.5.6 Liquidity and Funding

It may be somewhat surprising, but due to the focus on capital, Basel II did not include any prescriptions on banks' funding and liquidity profiles. This omission was acknowledged as a major issue by Basel. In retrospect, it was a major failing. As the financial crisis progressed, it became clear that the lack of a liquidity standard had resulted in fragile financial profiles for many banks and so liquidity and funding became key focuses for Basel III.

Citing the brutal change from normal conditions in which "asset markets were buoyant and funding was readily available at low cost"[99] to a complete and prolonged closure of financial markets, requiring massive central bank intervention, the Basel Committee has developed two new minimum standards: the *Liquidity Coverage Ratio* and the *Net Stable Funding Ratio*.

---

[97] From 2012 Annual Reports of the banks.

[98] PRA statements on bank capital and leverage ratios released in 2013, PRA, 30 July 2013.

[99] Principles for Sound Liquidity Risk Management and Supervision, Basel Committee, September 2008.

(a) Liquidity Coverage Ratio (LCR)

The LCR aims to ensure that banks are adequately resilient by holding a large enough stock of readily sellable ("liquid") assets to cover all their cash needs for a period of 30 days. The LCR is computed using the assumption of a stressed environment that mimics some of the conditions experienced during the current financial crisis:

- downgrade of credit ratings (by three notches);
- withdrawal of deposits by customers;
- access to wholesale markets restricted;
- increase in collateral requirements and "haircuts" for secured funding;
- increase in need for collateral for derivatives positions;
- drawdown of customers' committed credit lines and liquidity facilities.

The bank's stock of high quality liquid assets (HQLAs in the jargon) must be greater than the estimate of its net cash outflow over a 30-calendar-day period. In other words, the LCR must be more than 100%.

What counts as HQLA? Whilst cash reserves are an obvious source of liquidity, the Basel Committee also allows assets that have not already been pledged elsewhere and are "liquid in markets during a time of stress and, ideally, central bank eligible".[100] Their definition of this is that the HQLA must be at least 60% composed of cash and government securities, while the remaining 40% can include high grade corporate bonds (rated at least AA-) and covered bonds and even – up to a limit of 15% of total HQLA – riskier securities such as RMBS, investment-grade corporates with a rating below AA- and highly liquid equities. For banks in lucky countries where the government debt market is small (such as Australia), Basel proposes alternatives to HQLA, such as the provision of an overdraft – technically, a committed liquidity facility – from the central bank, for which the bank pays a commitment fee.

The irony of the HQLA definition is that, as the crisis in the Eurozone has shown, government bonds are not always liquid and are far from risk-free. In this way, the LCR may contribute to increased risk in the banking industry, as the fortunes of banks are more closely tied to the creditworthiness of their sovereign. Since the Basel III regulations on liquidity were drafted prior to the full onset of the sovereign crisis in the Eurozone, the HQLA definitions now seem ironic or even plain wrong. An alternative is proposed in subsequent chapters.

How are cash outflows calculated? Basel sets out assumptions for each type of banking product. For example, 3% of retail deposits are assumed to be withdrawn, 5% of small business deposits and 40% of large corporate deposits. All maturing *unsecured* debt is assumed to be repaid as it falls due during the period and payments on derivatives are also assumed to be paid on time, though *secured* debt is assumed to be extended by a factor, depending on the underlying collateral (the logic being that financing on good collateral will be refinanced more easily than on weak collateral or unsecured). Undrawn facilities are assumed to be drawn down by customers, if they are committed facilities, by 5% for retail and small business and 10% for large corporates (or 30% if the corporate's facility is a "liquidity facility", i.e. one designed to refinance that corporate if they themselves are unable to refinance their maturing debt). Cash inflows (e.g. customers repaying their debt due on time) are also taken into account, although new lending is assumed to continue during the stress period and soak up half of these inflows.

---

[100] Basel III: The Liquidity Coverage Ratio and liquidity risk monitoring tools, Basel Committee, January 2013.

Are these liquidity assumptions realistic? Experience from Greece indicates that deposit outflows can run at around 5% or so of a bank's deposit base per month in a stress scenario. In Greece, this has led to around one-quarter of the deposit base being withdrawn from local banks.[101] In the UK, Northern Rock reportedly lost 5% of its deposits in a single day.[102] More recent experience in Cyprus shows that the only way to stop massive outflows in a stress scenario is to take the draconian step of imposing capital controls.[103] The Basel III outflow assumptions may not prove robust enough for the rules to act as a decent barrier to a true liquidity crunch.

This definition of the LCR, published in January 2013, was a little less stringent than the initial proposals set out by the Basel Committee.[104] Whilst the modifications were seen by some as a climbdown in response to lobbying by the banking industry, in reality the outcome is a definition and a calibration that makes good sense overall – apart from the reliance on sovereign debt and the fact that, of course, superior resilience comes at a cost to bank profitability and/or customer product costs. The Basel Committee indicated that banks' LCRs were in the region of 125% under the latest definition of the LCR.[105]

(b) Net Stable Funding Ratio (NSFR)

Banks tend to have short-term deposits and long-term loans. The maturity transformation function of banks is important and, normally, few observers worry about the maturity risk posed by funding long-term loans with short-term deposits. However, in the run-up to the current crisis, banks increased the amount of funding they took from the capital markets and the short-term element of this proved to be unreliable, with liquidity drying up as markets seized. In other words, the transformation risk had become excessive: it needs to be regulated more closely and Basel has sought to define a standard measure. The main tool under Basel III is the NSFR, which is meant to be an improvement on the traditional loan-to-deposit ratio (LDR) and has the stated aim of promoting "resilience over a longer time horizon by creating additional incentives for a bank to fund its activities with more stable sources of funding on an ongoing structural basis".[106]

The NSFR is the ratio between long-term (or "sticky") funding sources and long-term (or illiquid) assets. For this ratio, the Basel Committee has adopted one year as the time horizon: wholesale funding over one year is seen as high quality and loans to customers for less than one year are seen as not requiring long-term funding. The behavioural realities of retail customers are taken into account. For example, retail deposits are seen as reliable and and given a 90% weighting; conversely, retail lending that is short-term is given an 85% weighting, since it will inevitably need to be extended during a stressed situation.

---

[101] Greek Bank Deposit Outflows Said to Rise Before Elections, Bloomberg, 13 June 2012.

[102] Rush on Northern Rock continues, BBC News, 15 September 2007.

[103] Restrictive Measures on Transactions, Central Bank of Cyprus website.

[104] International framework for liquidity risk measurement, standards and monitoring, Basel Committee, December 2009 and updated December 2010.

[105] Audio file of the introductory remarks from GHOS Chairman Mervyn King and the Basel Committee on Banking Supervision's Chairman Stefan Ingves as well as the question and answer session which followed, Basel Committee website, 6 January 2013.

[106] International framework for liquidity risk measurement, standards and monitoring, Basel Committee, December 2010.

Such a measure poses quite a challenge. The Basel Committee reports that the average NSFR is around 100%,[107] while the EBA reports that, for large European banks, the average NSFR is 94%.[108] These data imply that a substantial minority of banks are below the currently proposed regulatory minimum. Globally, 10% of banks are below 75% of the requirement; in Europe, 20% of banks are below 85% of the requirement. These inadequate funding structures point to the need to raise large amounts of term funding (€2,400bn in aggregate, of which half in Europe).

Focus on Liquidity Management
In addition to the new metrics, Basel III also focuses on the "soft" areas of liquidity management. These include the degree of funding diversification, the availability of unencumbered assets as a contingency for access to central bank funding, the liquidity risk by currency to consider potential inability to fund in a foreign currency due to closure of international bond or swap markets (as occurred in 2008/2009) and an overall assessment of the bank's funding market access under stressed conditions.

4.5.7 Derivatives Risk Management

The growth of the derivatives part of the banking industry (see Table 4.22) and the deficiencies of Basel II in this regard have necessitated improved regulation, which Basel III seeks to deliver. Derivatives will be subject to higher capital requirements for counterparty risks and there will be tighter rules on collateral management and margining.

Table 4.22   Global OTC derivatives market[109]

| DATE | Notional amounts outstanding, in $trn | | | | | |
	Foreign exchange	Interest rate	Equity	Commodities	CDS	Other
Mid 2006	38.1	262.5	6.8	6.4	20.4	38.3
End 2006	40.3	291.6	7.5	7.1	28.7	43.0
Mid 2007	48.6	347.3	8.6	7.6	42.6	53.2
End 2007	56.2	393.1	8.5	8.5	58.2	61.4
Mid 2008	63.0	458.3	10.2	13.2	57.4	70.5
End 2008	50.0	432.7	6.5	4.4	41.9	62.7
Mid 2009	48.7	437.2	6.6	3.6	36.1	62.3
End 2009	49.2	449.9	5.9	2.9	32.7	63.3
Mid 2010	53.2	451.8	6.3	2.9	30.3	38.3
End 2010	57.8	465.3	5.6	2.9	29.9	39.5
Mid 2011	64.7	553.2	6.8	3.2	32.4	46.5
End 2011	63.3	504.1	6.0	3.1	28.6	42.6

[107] Results of the Basel III monitoring exercise as of 30 June 2012, Basel Committee, March 2013.
[108] Basel III monitoring exercise – Results based on data as of 30 June 2012, EBA, 19 March 2013.
[109] BIS statistics.

Since derivatives are not loans, the regulatory capital rules for counterparty credit risk are more complex and something of a "black box" to an uninformed observer. Like a loan, a derivative that is "in-the-money" represents a credit exposure to the counterparty involved. If the credit standing of the counterparty deteriorates, the value of that credit exposure reduces and a notional loss is incurred. This Credit Value Adjustment (CVA) for derivatives is similar to a provision. Basel III introduces a capital requirement for potential changes in this CVA under a stressed scenario.

These improvements to the regulatory regime mean that counterparty credit risk is now much more onerous from a regulatory capital perspective than before. Numerous studies have shown how the capital requirement for a given trade increases by a factor of 3, 5 or 10, depending on the study. However, this is largely due to the inadequate capital requirements for derivatives under Basel II and fails to note the huge profitability of derivatives to banks based on return-on-regulatory-capital metrics. Derivatives should remain profitable for banks on the whole, though undoubtedly customer margins will increase and banks' behaviours and business models will need to adapt to the new regulatory reality.

One of these changes is the incentives to move a large portion of the derivative portfolio from a bilateral transaction between the bank and its customer – the over-the-counter (OTC) model – to clearing through central counterparties (CCPs) such as the LCH.clearnet, the Chicago Board of Trade and the New York Mercantile Exchange (CME Group). The sheer size of the OTC derivatives market is a cause of concern for regulators, and they worry about the failure of a counterparty, even if the experience of the Lehman default was not calamitous:

> Initial media estimates suggested that total gross insurance claims would amount to $400 billion, much higher than Lehman's bond debt of $150 billion or less. But preliminary estimates from ISDA, based on the auction, give a net figure of $7 billion only. According to DTCC, $72 billion in CDS was settled normally through the automatic settlement procedure on 21 October 2008, without incident. This made it possible to calculate the funds transferred from net protection sellers to net protection buyers at just $5.2 billion, or 7% of the notional amount. As a result, fears of serial default among protection sellers unable to settle their claims proved baseless.[110]

In theory, encouraging banks to move towards central clearing of standardised derivative products should reduce the risks in the system. Every bank wishing to enter into a derivative transaction will transact directly with the CCP and be required to post a specified amount of collateral. The bank's exposure will shift from its portfolio of thousands of counterparties to the CCPs. Of course, this makes the robustness and resilience of the CCPs themselves a major cause for concern and regulatory attention. There are also concerns about the massive absorption of systemic liquidity that the CCP margining will bring about.

4.5.8 Implementation and Transition

The goal of the Basel Committee was to achieve international implementation of the phased Basel III rules starting on 1 January 2013. This goal has been missed, for a variety of reasons:

- Insufficient political acceptance of the Basel III framework.
- The political process of lobbying and haggling over the exact nature of the rules to be adopted.
- The sheer volume and complexity of regulation, which has to be translated into a compatible, legal version in each jurisdiction.

---

[110] Credit default swaps and financial stability: risks and regulatory issues, Banque de France.

The Basel Committee does not appear worried by the delays in adoption and implementation.

> The delays are not critical at this point, for two reasons. First, the Basel III capital rules contain a lengthy phase-in period, meaning that in 2013 the new requirements should not be particularly burdensome for banks (eg none of the new deductions from capital are applied this year). Second, many regulators who have been unable to implement the new standards by the beginning of this year are still measuring and monitoring their banks' capacity to meet the new requirements. And, of course, markets are applying similar pressure. In other words, the "force" of the new capital regime is much broader than just those countries that have implemented their domestic regulations.[111]

The Basel Committee estimates that one-third of global banking assets were officially subject to the Basel III requirements as of 1 January 2013. This does not include the two largest economies in the world: the European Union and the USA. In fact, China, India, Singapore and Switzerland are the only major economies and banking systems that have adopted Basel III on time.

As well as adoption, the other element of the Basel III rules is a lengthy transition timeframe. This comprises four key components:

- A steadily changing definition of capital, as deductions are phased in over a five-year time period.
- So-called "grandfathering" of certain non-compliant regulatory capital instruments, over a ten-year period.
- A gradual rise in the minimum capital standards, over a ten-year period.
- Phased introduction of other measures, e.g. liquidity requirements, often accompanied by a parallel monitoring approach, which is meant to allow changes to the rules as their impact is observed more closely.

The market is, by and large, ignoring the methodological phase-in and assessing the solvency of institutions on a "fully loaded" basis, in other words, using the eventual rules rather than the prevalent rules. Increasingly, regulators are taking the same approach, for example during stress tests. The complexity of having a shifting definition of capital has proven to be too much for market analysts to process: a static definition is much easier to comprehend. And market confidence can only be achieved once a bank is fully compliant with the *future* rules, no matter whether it is compliant on the more forgiving current rules.

4.5.9 National Versions of Basel III

Just as different countries have struggled to adopt Basel III on time, so have they also failed to adopt Basel III in an harmonious fashion. On the face of it, this should be alarming, for regulators consider harmonisation to be essential:

> Due to the ongoing process of globalisation and the emergence of internationally active banks, international harmonisation of regulation has become essential in safeguarding the stability of the financial system.[112]

---

[111] From ideas to implementation, Stefan Ingves, Chairman of the Basel Committee, 24 January 2013.
[112] Banking regulation, Speech by Axel Weber, President of the Deutsche Bundesbank, 30 April 2010.

This global desire for harmonisation is even more intense when applied to the European Union. As with other matters outside the banking industry, the EU has adopted the mantra of "maximum harmonisation":

> Maximum harmonisation is thus necessary to achieve a single rule book aimed at further developing a truly harmonised European market by ensuring equal treatment, low costs of compliance and the removal of regulatory arbitrage.[113]

For this reason, Basel III has been implemented in the EU largely as a "regulation", which applies to all banks in the EU as a single rule book, rather than a "directive", which would need to be transposed into national legislation within each of the 27 member states of the EU and could be tweaked or augmented in the process.

Despite these noble statements, in practice, harmonisation is not essential globally and maximum harmonisation is not necessary in the EU. Such statements are, frankly, hyperbole. It would have been much more honest to state that harmonisation is important and should be pursued as much as possible, to such an extent that individual countries should set out the rationale for any departures from Basel III. Instead, the Basel Committee has developed a monitoring workstream that reports on global implementation and deviation from standards.

Harmonisation is not happening. Signatories to Basel III and members of the Basel Committee have chosen to apply provisions in their countries that are materially different from Basel III and not justified by specific macro-economic or structural features of the local economy. They are simply different because the local politicians and regulators do not agree with the Basel methodology. For example, in the USA and in Europe, bonds issued by the sovereign have been given a fixed risk-weighting in the solvency capital requirements of 0%, whereas under Basel III they should have been risk-weighted like any other asset. The Basel monitoring exercise is only concerned where national implementation results in weaker capital standards than under Basel III. In other words, regulators are concerned more with quality of rules than harmonisation.

The key divergences from Basel III are shown in Table 4.23.

4.5.10 Major Achievements of Basel III: Top Five

Whilst not perfect, Basel III is having several important impacts. The regulatory response to the financial crisis has delivered the following key elements:

1. Introduction of International Liquidity Standards for the First Time
In the eyes of regulators and bank management teams, liquidity was a neglected aspect of financial risk management. The introduction of international standards for funding and liquidity may not be the "final word", but it represents a good starting point from which to proceed. In particular, the revised definition and calibration of the LCR shows that the authorities are keen to improve the measures they use.

2. Positive Cost: Benefit (According to the Authorities)
Various parties have attempted to consider the costs to the economy of implementing the proposed regulatory reforms – and the benefits that they would confer upon society. Common

---

[113] Report to be submitted to the EBCI Full Forum, European Bank Coordination Vienna Initiative, Working Group on Basel III implementation in Emerging Europe, 12–13 March 2012.

Table 4.23   Key national divergences from Basel III

Country	Divergences from Basel III
USA	*Basel III will be implemented in the USA by regulations, which also implement changes required by the Dodd–Frank Act*
	• Requirements based on external credit ratings are not allowed. This particularly impacts securitisations, where the approach is completely different from the Basel approach, which is based on external credit ratings.
	• Permanent capital floor based on 100% of the US Standardised Approach (Collins amendment), whereas the Basel rule is 80% of Basel I.[114]
	• Tier 1 capital-to-assets leverage ratio already in place, whereas still being designed by Basel.
	• 3-year phase out of hybrid capital, versus 10-year in Basel.
	• Mandatory deduction from capital of investments in hedge funds and private equity funds as per the Volcker Rule.[115]
	• No rules implementing Basel III liquidity proposals.
Japan	No significant divergences noted by Basel Committee.[116]
European Union	In the EU, Basel III is implemented through "CRD IV", comprising a new Capital Requirements Regulation (the "CRR") and Capital Requirements Directive (the "CRD")
	• More generous treatment of minority interests for inclusion in the parent's capital.
	• Differences result in regulatory capital ratios being overstated under European rules relative to Basel III rules by more than 1% for a quarter of banks surveyed by Basel.
	• Application of a factor of 0.7619 to SME lending, introduced in Article 501 of the CRR, presumably for political purposes, to reduce the impact of a credit crunch on this sector.
	• Use of the Financial Conglomerates Directive in Article 46 of the CRR (the so-called "Danish Compromise) allows for various divergent approaches for bancassurers that will be less exacting than Basel III (which requires methods to be "at least as conservative as that applicable under deduction"). This flatters some EU bancassurers with large insurance operations by 1–2% on the regulatory capital ratio.
	• EU provided for a "permanent partial exemption" under which an IRB bank may continue to risk-weight certain exposures based on the standardised approach.[117]

(continued)

---

[114] Basel III regulatory consistency assessment (Level 2) Preliminary report: United States of America, Basel Committee, October 2012.

[115] Implementation of the Basel III Framework: Comparison of US and EU Proposals, Shearman & Sterling LLP, October 18, 2012.

[116] Basel III regulatory consistency assessment (Level 2): Japan, Basel Committee, October 2012.

[117] Basel III regulatory consistency assessment (Level 2) Preliminary report: European Union, Basel Committee, October 2012.

Table 4.23   *(Continued)*

	The finer details of the EU version of Basel III were finalised and the directive and regulation published in June 2013.[118] And the Eurozone continued to move towards so-called "banking union" with the further development of the "Single Supervisory Mechanism", whereby large and/or significant banks in the Eurozone will be supervised by the European Central Bank, rather than a national regulator. This will have political ramifications (e.g. it represents a further step towards political union) as well as some practical implications, such as the undertaking of a major Europe-wide "asset quality review" in the first half of 2014. This review is meant to give a better understanding of the financial health of those 150 banks and will be conducted by a number of consulting firms, since the ECB does not have the resources.
Intra-EU	Examples only: • Differences in adjusting bank capital for insurance holdings. • Swedish super-equivalence: floor on mortgage risk-weights. • UK super-equivalence: role of Pillar 2 and Individual Capital Guidance. • Danish super-equivalence: introduction of a "crisis management buffer".
Australia	• Full deductions regime for equity stakes and all DTAs: no "thresholds" approach. • Continuing use of 20% LGD floor on residential mortgages, versus Basel standard of 10%. • Continuing use of Pillar 1 RWAs for interest rate risk in the banking book. • Accelerated implementation, no transition period.
All countries	Major differences in accounting standards not addressed by Basel III.

sense indicates that the cost:benefit is positive, because the negative impacts of a banking crisis are just so terrible and leave an indelible scar on the economy. The Australian regulator summarises this viewpoint well:

> An Australia with a sounder banking banking system, which is internationally recognised for this soundness, but faces a 10 basis points increase in its overall capital and funding costs, would be pretty clearly superior to an Australia in which the banks are less sound, through lack of reform.[119]

For the more quantitative mind, the IMF has estimated that the impact of recent regulatory reforms would be an additional 0.18% added to customer lending rates in Japan, 0.31% in Europe and 0.48% in the USA and that banks could take mitigating actions and make cuts in operating expenses to reduce this impact to 0.08% in Japan, 0.18% in Europe and 0.28% in the USA.[120] The incremental financing costs passed on to customers cause economic output and wealth to be lost. In a separate analysis, the Bank for International Settlements sets out a full cost:benefit analysis. Under most assumptions, the benefits far outweigh the costs. Using a middle-of-the-road set of assumptions, the IMF study indicates benefits of around 2% of

---

[118] *Official Journal of the European Union*, 27 June 2013.

[119] APRA's Basel III Implementation Rationale and Impacts, Charles Littrell, Australian Prudential Regulation Authority, 23 November 2011.

[120] Estimating the Costs of Financial Regulation, IMF Staff Discussion Note, 11 September 2012.

economic output per year versus costs of around 0.3%.[121] These estimates are highly uncertain, largely due to a debate amongst economists as to whether the economic effects of a banking crisis are temporary (growth declines in the short term but reverts to a long-term trend over time) or permanent (growth is hit during the crisis and recovers but at a level that is permanently below its previous trajectory). The limitations of such estimation exercises are huge, the artificial assumptions that the authors make are numerous and the caveats and sensitivities with which the results are published are far-reaching. Nevertheless, they form the basis of the debate on the efficacy of higher capital levels and better funding structures.

3. Major Improvements in the Capital Regime for Capital Markets Trading activities ("Basel II.5")

The regulatory capital regime for capital markets trading businesses was inadequate. Fortunately, many banks used more realistic measures to run their businesses. As we have already noted, Deutsche Bank used to allocate "for Market Risks around 4–5x more Economic Capital than regulatory capital".[122] But the markets focused on regulatory solvency and some banks gravitated towards high-risk activities that appeared low-risk under the Basel II lens. Whilst the market risk and counterparty risk elements of Basel II.5 and Basel III are complex and open to debate, they are a better reflection of risk than the previous VaR-based rules of Basel II and result in an output number that works better at an institutional level.

4. Rapid Response to Global Financial Crisis

The glacial development of international bank regulations accelerated superbly during this crisis. Basel II was a decade in the making. The first proposals for Basel III, on the other hand, were published in December 2009 and were in reasonably good shape at that point. Achieving such a milestone in the space of less than two years, bearing in mind the challenges of achieving any level of consensus in an international "club", is a genuine achievement.

5. Maintenance (for the Time Being) of Pillar 2 and Pillar 3

The major breakthroughs of Basel II were the second and third "pillars". These pillars recognise the subjective nature of risk and the need for effective supervision and judgement from the capital markets. Most of the attention of banks and their regulators has focused on Pillar 1 and there was a risk that Basel III would scrap attempts to codify Pillar 2 practices and Pillar 3 requirements. This did not happen. Unfortunately, there remains a risk that it will happen.

4.5.11 Major Issues with Basel III: Top Five

Here are the main criticisms we have with Basel III as a response to the current financial crisis. Chapter 7 sets out an alternative blueprint.

1. Incrementalism and an Excessive Focus on Capital and Liquidity Regulation

Regulators are suggesting that the solution to the regulatory failure that is at the heart of the current financial crisis is more regulation, more capital, more liquidity. In this respect,

---

[121] An assessment of the long-term economic impact of stronger capital and liquidity requirements, Basel Committee, August 2010.

[122] Reform of the global financial architecture: a new social contract between society and finance, Hugo Banziger, Chief Risk Officer and Member of the Management Board, Deutsche Bank.

Basel III is really just a tweaked version of Basel II. It wrongly assumes that the drivers of the crisis were excessive leverage, weak capital bases, poor funding profiles and insufficient liquidity buffers. This ignores the concrete evidence to the contrary: for example, a recent report concluded that low levels of capital were "a principal cause of meltdown" in only 5 of 34 big bank failures.[123] Basel III fails sufficiently to recognize the real drivers, such as massive failures of governance, supervision and risk management. It wrongly believes that a thicker rule book with ever more detail can tame the problem. Of course, regulators want to regulate. Their comments show that they believe higher capital levels will be a panacea:

> Gallingly, on the eve of their collapse, every [failed] bank boasted of capital levels well in excess of the standards of the time. So it should be no surprise when building a more resilient system, the first priority was to strengthen the bank capital regime. Through higher minimums, surcharges for systemically important banks, countercyclical buffers and tougher definitions of capital, the largest banks will have to hold at least seven times as much capital as before the crisis.[124]

Such an approach crackles with irony: it seems to say "the previous regime did not work so let's revise it". It fails to recognise the need for radically different methods and a revolutionary, rather than evolutionary or incremental, approach.

2. Excessive Complexity

Basel III attempted in parts to reduce unnecessary complexity (e.g. collapsing Upper Tier 2 and Lower Tier 2 capital instruments into simply Tier 2). But in most areas, the complexity of rules has increased exponentially. Much of this complexity is unnecessary, serving no clear purpose. For example, what purpose does the threshold approach for deductions from capital (e.g. holdings in financial institutions) serve? And how bizarre is an implementation approach that changes the methodology at the same time as the minimum capital requirement, to such an extent that the capital markets have had to ask banks to disclose a proforma "fully loaded Basel III" capital ratio that can actually be used to assess solvency needs?

One of the world's leading regulators – the Bank of England – is politely pulling the plug. Basel II and Basel III are "a problem for regulators, who cannot really police this complex beast. Increasingly it is a problem for investors in banks, too, who cannot make any sense of the published capital and regulatory ratios."[125] Indeed, there is a clear sign that the international regulatory community is backing away from Basel III altogether: "I have been encouraged to see, over the course of the last few months – perhaps the last six months – that there is an increasing awareness among international regulators that we may have, indeed, taken a false turn. There are moves now afoot within the Basel committee to seek ways of simplifying and streamlining, and to move to a proper, regulatory – rather than self-regulatory – edifice. That may take some time."[126]

3. New Risks: Sovereign Debt, CCPs and Shadow Banking

By looking at Basel I metrics and not thinking about risk, the banking industry committed an act of gross stupidity that led to this financial crisis. Basel III contains three new, powerful

---

[123] Vickers calls for doubling of bank capital levels, *Financial Times*, 8 September 2013.

[124] Rebuilding Trust in Global Banking, Mark Carney, 23 February 2013.

[125] Evidence of Andy Haldane, Bank of England, to the Parliamentary Commission on Banking Standards, Panel on Regulatory Approach, 21 January 2013.

[126] Ibid.

impetuses that contain new risks that have to be adequately managed. The first is the extreme and unnecessary incentive for all banks to build and maintain large credit exposures to their sovereign. Events in Greece and elsewhere have shown us how dangerous this can be. The second risk is the massively concentrated risk that will build up in the centralised counterparties (CCPs). And thirdly, there are clear incentives for risk to migrate outside the regulated banking system into the so-called "shadow banking" system. Just like AAA-rated subprime bonds, these three areas may appear virtually risk-free at present, but there should be no complacency.

4. Timing: Risk of a Credit Crunch?

The current weakness of the economy and the banking system makes Basel III implementation difficult. The economy needs lax lending standards and the banks need central bank liquidity. Markets periodically open up and resume a trend towards normality but the flow of bad news restarts and markets become challenging again. Regulators would rather be building the robust industry of the future with a bull-market backdrop. The consequence of being strict in a challenged market environment is that the rules are being fudged, to create a semblance of compliance. The duality of purpose, one foot on the gas and the other on the brake, is creating a crazy, conflicting banking industry and an economy gasping for correctly-priced credit.

5. Continued Reliance on the Credit Assessment of Either Internal Models or External Ratings Agencies

Basel III has failed to address the fundamental problem of risk subjectivity and asset-level, Pillar 1-type capital requirements. Both internal and agency assessments proved unreliable indicators of risk during the onset of this financial crisis; yet, they still form the bedrock of the regulatory regime. The consequence is that the industry may well move back to non-risk-adjusted capital measures as a primary form of regulation. This would be disturbing.

4.6 RESOLUTION REGIMES

Banks regularly fail. During the period 1921–1933, a total of 14,807 banks failed in the USA.[127] Since then, 4,037 banks have failed, most of them during the "Savings & Loan Crisis" in the late 1980s (see Figure 4.5).

But these bank failures occurred in a highly fragmented market. The greatest number of banks failing in one year was in 1933, when 4,000 banks failed. However, the losses to depositors of these failures represented only 2.15% of total deposits in the system. The establishment of the FDIC has put in place a tidy resolution process for failed banks in a fragmented industry.

The failure of large banks is a different phenomenon. The Financial Stability Board has noted that "the global financial crisis provided a sharp and painful lesson of the costs to the financial system and the global economy of the absence of effective powers and tools for dealing with the failure of systemically important financial institutions".[128]

---

[127] *The First Fifty Years: A History of the FDIC 1933–1983*, FDIC, 1984.
[128] Resolution of Systemically Important Financial Institutions: Progress Report, Financial Stability Board, November 2012.

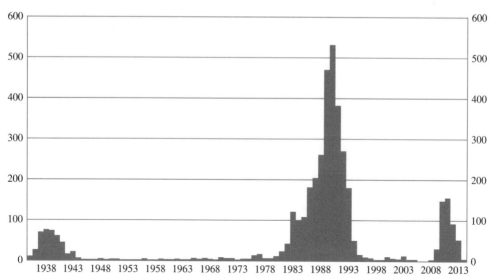

Figure 4.5   Number of bank failures in the USA, 1934–2013[129]

Can Large Banks Fail?

Companies fail when their creditors cannot be paid. For an industrial corporate, this happens due to insufficient cashflow as a result of deteriorating profitability or sales. If no extension of credit occurs, the company will not be able to pay its creditors and will have to seek bankruptcy protection.

Banks fail for exactly the same reasons: lack of cash or lack of confidence. Because of the specific nature of the banking business, the loss of confidence generally precedes the cash deficit. The first sign of trouble is generally a withdrawal of investors or depositors and the intervention of the authorities to provide a stabilising force. In practice, bankruptcy caused by weak capital levels is unlikely, as the bank's counterparties will have seen the problems developing and will no doubt have withdrawn their funding support from the bank, causing it to fail; since all banks are fundamentally illiquid, future solvency problems will lead to a loss of confidence and failure through inability to refinance maturing liabilities.

During the current financial crisis, the authorities have tried to ensure that banks do not go bankrupt. They want to avoid the negative impacts of the bankruptcy of a bank, namely contagion and widespread disruption to the financial system, with spiralling effects on all agents. The Lehman Brothers bankruptcy of 2008 showed the extent of these contagion effects. Instead, failed banks have generally been dealt with through government capital injections and state-backed funding programmes. Vast amounts of taxpayers' money has been put at risk, because the authorities lacked an alternative approach to bank failure.

Resolution instead of Bankruptcy

No-one wants a repeat of Lehman. Equally, however, governments do not want banks to continue to assume that they will be "bailed out" with taxpayers' money. Such implicit government support is an unfair "free ride" for bank owners. But how can a troubled bank avoid bankruptcy if it is not bailed out?

---

[129] From the FDIC database.

The answer is a process called "resolution", an orderly wind-down that avoids the disruptive legal processes of bankruptcy. Resolution regimes are being developed in several jurisdictions as a tool for the management of financial crises, following recommendations from the Basel Committee set out in March 2010,[130] which were endorsed by the G20 meeting in Toronto in June 2010. The Basel resolution framework is a *political* response to the current crisis as much as it is a *regulatory* response. As well as financial stability, resolution regimes are meant to have a fairer outcome, should banks fail, with the owners and creditors of the bank bearing the losses. As an additional benefit, bank governance should be improved, as the removal of the implicit safety net of government support should lead to improved management discipline and greater investor attention to extreme risks.

The framework for resolution regimes comprises 12 key attributes (see Table 4.24).[131]

Drafting of Resolution Regimes: Where do we Stand?

As of early 2013, a handful of countries have a resolution regime in place, though these are far from uniform and only partially compliant and compatible with the latest recommendations from the Basel Committee – see Table 4.25.

Global Resolution Regimes

Since big banks are global and all banks are interconnected, effective bank resolution has a decidedly international flavour. Again, the problems during Lehman's bankruptcy serve as an illustration of the challenge. The policy on international resolution regimes is driven by the Basel Committee[132] and the Financial Stability Forum,[133] to define a consistent approach across jurisdictions that would "make feasible the resolution of financial institutions without severe systemic disruption and without exposing taxpayers to loss, while protecting vital economic functions through mechanisms which make it possible for shareholders and unsecured and uninsured creditors to absorb losses in a manner that respects the hierarchy of claims in liquidation".[134] Resolution is meant to allow for both the continuity of the business (through sale, transfer of business and/or recapitalisation) and orderly run-off.

Legal Challenges

Resolution regimes involve extraordinary powers which will need to be in accordance with existing contracts, constitutional rights and human rights. They may meet a few hurdles. Owners of bank shares, bank securities and deposits at a bank are entitled to the protection of their property rights under the law. Summary confiscation of their property when the institution is not technically bankrupt – which is how they may see the resolution actions – could be resisted on legal grounds. The recent expropriation of SNS subordinated bondholders could provide a test case. Although the Ministry of Finance states that investor recovery is nil, the law allows for possible claims on compensation to the court of Amsterdam, as well as the European Court of Human Rights. The legal process began rapidly.[135]

---

[130] Basel Committee, Report and Recommendations of the Cross-border Resolution Group, March 2010.

[131] Resolution of Systemically Important Financial Institutions: Progress Report, Financial Stability Board, November 2012.

[132] Resolution policies and frameworks: progress so far, Basel Committee, July 2011.

[133] Key attributes of effective resolution regimes for financial institutions, Financial Stability Forum, October 2011.

[134] Ibid.

[135] Judgment on expropriation of Dutch SNS bank, CMS Legal Services, 25 February 2013.

Table 4.24 Resolution regime framework

1	**Scope**	Any financial institution that could be systemically significant or critical if it fails
2	**Resolution authority**	Statutory mandate to promote financial stability and the continued performance of critical functions
3	**Resolution powers**	Broad range of resolution powers, including powers to:
		• transfer critical functions of a failing firm to a third party • convert debt instruments into equity and preserve critical functions (*"bail-in within resolution"*) • prevent derivatives close-outs (subject to safeguards for counterparties) and debt enforcement actions against the failing firm • achieve the orderly closure and wind-down of the firm's business with timely payout or transfer of insured deposits
4	**Contractual obligations**	Maintain segregation of client assets; honour financial contracts Entry into resolution *per se* should not trigger any early termination rights
5	**Safeguards**	All creditors should receive at least what they would have received in a liquidation of the firm. Respect for the hierarchy of claims, where feasible. Right to judicial review to challenge actions that are outside the legal powers of the resolution authority
6	**Funding of firms in resolution**	Funding mechanisms – from private sources – to provide temporary financing to continue critical operations
7	**Cross-border issues**	Cooperative and collaborative solution with foreign authorities and counterparties
8	**Crisis management groups (CMGs)**	CMGs of home and key host authorities for all G-SIFIs to plan action pre-emptively
9	**Cross-border cooperation agreements (COAGs)**	Institution-specific COAGs should be in place between the home and relevant host authorities that need to be involved in the preparation and management of a crisis affecting a G-SIFI
10	**Resolvability assessments**	Resolvability assessments for all G-SIFIs. Authorities can demand appropriate measures to ensure that a firm is resolvable
11	**"Living wills"**	Recovery and resolution plans in place for all systemic or critical firms
12	**Information sharing**	Facilitate domestic and cross-border exchange of information in normal times and during a crisis necessary for planning and for resolution

Table 4.25   National resolution regimes

UK	The Banking (Special Provisions) Act 2008 was used to deal with three situations: Northern Rock, Bradford & Bingley and the Icelandic banks. It was replaced by the UK Banking Act 2009, which introduces the Special Resolution Regime (SRR). This regime gives the Bank of England powers to place failing banks into a state of resolution, once the FSA has determined that a bank is about to fail and the resolution is judged to be in the public interest. The Act has been used to resolve two tiny banks (Dunfermline BS and Southsea Mortgage & Investment Co.). The SRR seeks to protect financial stability, confidence in the banking sector, depositors, public funds and property rights, as well as continuity of access to systemically important functions.[136]
	The Act also amends the powers of the Treasury and the FSA in relation to the Financial Services Compensation Scheme for retail depositors.
Germany	Bank Restructuring Act of 2010 gives the BaFin and the Bundesbank greater responsibility to deal with failing banks.
	Intervention follows a two-step approach. The first step is a voluntary restructuring in which a management restructuring plan is proposed to the BaFin. This plan may include, for example, a request for financial assistance from the government. Should BaFin not agree the restructuring plan, then the second step is triggered, namely the reorganisation process under the responsibility of the BaFin. Measures include shareholders and debt-holders taking losses, change in management, the sale of businesses or liquidation.
	The Act also creates a €70bn stabilisation fund, which can be used for the state recapitalisation of banks and will be financed by an annual tax on banks' profits of €1.2bn.
Denmark	During the current financial crisis, Denmark has introduced a series of support measures, the so-called "bank packages". Bank Package 3 came into force in October 2010 and gives the authorities strong powers of resolution. The case of Amagerbanken A/S in February 2011 demonstrates the workings of the Danish regime. Amagerbanken was in financial difficulty following losses on its real estate portfolio. As continuing write-downs turned the bank's solvency negative, and with no credible management plan, the bank was put into the conservatorship of the government's resolution fund. Shareholders were wiped out and losses were also imposed on senior bondholders and large depositors (above the threshold of guarantee). Initially, these senior investors were given only 58.8% of their principal back, but a subsequent audit revised their claim up to 84.4%.[137]
Holland	The Dutch government has had a busy crisis, with nationalisation of ABN-Amro, the recapitalisation of ING and the troubles at SNS. Unsurprisingly, they have developed powerful resolution tools. The Dutch Intervention Act 2012 gives the Central Bank the authority to intervene and prepare a transfer plan if there are signs of a "dangerous development with respect to its own funds, solvency, liquidity or technical provisions and it can reasonably be foreseen that this development will not sufficiently or timely be reversed". More serious actions, including the expropriation of assets or forced liquidation, can be used if the Ministry of Finance thinks that "the stability of the financial system is in serious and immediate danger because of the situation of the relevant financial firm".[138] The act introduces a tax on larger banks to pay for resolution actions.

(continued)

---

[136] The UK approach to resolution of failed banks in the crisis, Peter Brierley, Head of Policy, Special Resolution Unit, Bank of England, 19 March 2012.

[137] Announcement: Payment of dividend to creditors of Amagerbanken af 2011 A/S, Finansiel Stabilitet, 28 September 2011.

[138] Financial Markets Newsletter – Dutch Intervention Act in Force, Debrauw Blackstone Westbroek, June 2012.

Table 4.25   *(Continued)*

	The troubles at SNS, owing to massive losses on real estate loan portfolios, led to nationalisation of the bank and expropriation of shareholders and all subordinated bondholders in February 2013 with zero compensation. Interestingly, senior bondholders were not touched and their claims remained intact at par. This is reportedly due to the fact that the Minister of Finance did not perceive senior bail-in to be a practical option and that it "should be left to the European legislature to introduce bail-in as a resolution tool".[139]
USA	In the USA, the Dodd–Frank Act prohibits any Federal government bail-out of financial companies (excluding insured depositary institutions) and gives FDIC powers to take action jointly with the Fed in the event of a default likely to affect financial stability. Conversion of debt, ordered by FDIC, is clearly identified as a tool to restore solvency. However, FDIC cannot take ownership of a bank but can organise the sale of the business and separate assets.
European Union	The European Commission has drafted a proposed "Recovery and Resolution Directive", designed to strengthen the banking sector in the European Union through harmonised procedures in place in each member state. This involves the transfer of assets within each banking group to address local tensions on capital or liquidity and the draft of contingency plans with regulators to identify measures to be taken in priority. Resolution measures under this framework should include early intervention and divestment, risk reduction and the appointment of a special manager at the level of the bank. Debt write-down or conversion can be considered when necessary for "a large, complex and interdependent financial institution in a way that protects financial stability and taxpayers' money".[140]

More Power Given to Regulators

Resolution regimes give regulators the authority to intervene at an early stage to avoid a disorderly collapse. This is a new role for regulators, who are traditionally more used to setting rules and monitoring their compliance. From now on, regulators will be able to impose major structural changes on a failed bank, including forcing changes in management, the sale of operations and the imposition of losses on creditors.

Ultimately, it should be assumed that a decision involving the collapse or rescue of a bank involves significant political considerations. This brings a new set of challenges, in particular the fit of resolution actions with the legal and constitutional framework. In a word, when does pre-emptive action become premature and when does the subjective become simply arbitrary or even whimsical? Owners and creditors of banks will need to adapt their investment views to the new reality.

Immediately apparent is the fact that the regulatory toolkit is light on measures to test the viability of an institution. The intervention at SNS in Holland shows us that solvency intervention triggers will necessarily be "soft" rather than hard. For example, on 15 November 2012, SNS reported a core Tier 1 ratio of 8.8%. It had €1.8bn of core Tier 1 capital against €20.8bn of risk-weighted assets. Since Basel II RWAs and capital minima are supposed to be calibrated to a very high confidence level of 99.9% "i.e. an institution is expected to suffer losses that exceed its level of tier 1 and tier 2 capital on average once in a thousand years",[141] it is somewhat of a surprise that on 2 February, Bloomberg reported Jan Sijbrand, the head of

---

[139] Bondholders in heavy weather – the case of SNS Reaal, Matthias Haentjens, Professor of Financial Law, Leiden Law School, 18 February 2013.

[140] Staff Working Document 167, European Commission, 6 June 2012.

[141] BIS, July 2005.

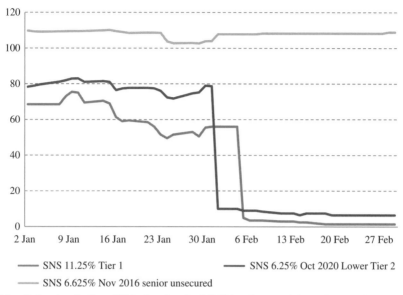

Figure 4.6   Cash price (in € per €100 of notional) of SNS bonds around time of nationalisation (2013)[142]

regulatory operations at the Dutch Central Bank, as saying "there was no capital left in SNS Bank".[143] The accounting and regulatory balance sheets did not reflect the economic reality of the true value of the bank. The more rational and subjective approaches of Pillar 2 will increasingly become the measure to which banks must manage their capital and on which resolution processes are based.

Following the nationalisation of SNS Reaal, credit spreads on other Dutch banks showed little change. This shows that the resolution of a troubled bank does not need to lead to contagion in the entire banking sector.

More Risk for Investors?

Opinion is divided on the net benefits to bank creditors and investors of resolution regimes, which are designed primarily to protect the public and systemic interests.

Bail-out is simply no longer an option. The cost of the financial crisis has been too great. But bankruptcy is also to be avoided. "The differences in outcomes from the handling of Bear Stearns and Lehman Brothers demonstrate that authorities have no real alternative but to avoid the bankruptcy process in the case of systemically important firms."[144] The major feature of relevance to investors in banks – and this includes depositors – is the introduction of the so-called "bail-in". Bail-in is the opposite of bail-out: instead of the state using taxpayers' money to thus stabilise the banking system, it is the claims of creditors that take the hit *before any legal bankruptcy process*.

---

[142] Bloomberg.

[143] Bloomberg, 2 February 2013.

[144] Managing the transition to a safer financial system, Sheila C. Bair, Chairman, Federal Deposit Insurance Corporation.

At first glance, the ability of resolution authorities to impose losses on creditors pre-bankruptcy is a bad thing for investors. But the argument has been put forward that creditors are actually better off under a controlled resolution process than a chaotic bankruptcy procedure:

> Any extra cost of capital should be quite limited because the losses from a bail-in resolution are so much smaller than the losses at risk in a liquidation. A well-designed bail-in process would also be more predictable for creditors than the wide range of resolution outcomes seen in the crisis.[145]

According to Manhattan bankruptcy court papers,[146] Lehman's senior bondholders will end up recovering about 21 cents on the dollar, those with claims on the company's derivatives around 30 cents on the dollar and commercial paper claims between 48 cents and 56 cents on the dollar. Overall, $65 billion will have been recovered and distributed to creditors.

Of course, we assume that investors are to be treated fairly, without discrimination and with transparent rules and procedures. We also assume that decisions are not arbitrary or whimsical.

The counter-argument is that the first signs of trouble at a bank will spark a run that will be more severe than under the current approach, since the banks' creditors are more clearly on the hook. Weaker banks will have more expensive funding than before and the market will be more volatile in times of uncertainty. Interestingly, debt investors have become familiar with taking losses on their exposures to banks in recent years, with many billions of dollars worth of bonds being subject to voluntary liability management exercises (below-par debt exchanges or buybacks). Some of these technically voluntary exercises have nevertheless been extremely harsh on bond investors forced to take losses as part of the "burden sharing principle" according to which investors in failed institutions must take losses before taxpayers' money is mobilised for the rescue. While the majority of the buybacks or exchanges have been voluntary, there have been a number of coercive exchanges such as in Ireland, where investors were offered new bonds at 20% of the value of old ones, or if they chose to resist, a tiny settlement: one investor ended up receiving only €170 for notes which had a face value of €17m.[147]

While senior bondholders will become more accustomed to a risk of write-down, it is likely they will be more picky on lesser credits and direct their investments towards the strongest players. This reallocation of capital to the safest names can have consequences on the stability of the banking system and cause more pain for weaker names, thus reducing competition.

The greatest threat to stability perhaps is in the contradiction we see in having loss absorption features in debt instruments, when these are precisely the tools used by investors to promote management discipline. Under this new regime, failure to repay the debt no longer implies bankruptcy and may incentivise more risky strategies for equity holders, who unlike bondholders continue to benefit from the upside. Moreover, short-term "bail-in" bonds could act as "canaries in the coal mine" with an unintended destabilising effect:

> One potential unforeseen consequence of bail-in capital stems from its shorter tenor and the requirement for frequent roll-over and refinancing. A deterioration in market conditions could impact a bank's ability to refinance effectively, which would potentially reduce the availability of bail-in capital during refinancing periods and reduce a bank's loss-absorbing layers. This in turn could undermine confidence in the bank.[148]

---

[145] From bail-out to bail-in, *The Economist*, 28 January 2010.

[146] *re Lehman Brothers Holdings Inc No. 08-13555*, US Bankruptcy Court, Southern District of New York.

[147] Bond exit consents: No way out?, White & Case, September 2012.

The events of March 2013 in Cyprus have proven a further illustration of the nature of future resolution actions and the mechanisms of credit bail-in. In Cyprus' case, the losses to be borne were deemed to be greater than the regulatory capital bases of the banks. Even if all institutional bondholders were wiped out, the assets of the banks would still be worth less than the remaining liabilities. Therefore, the option of depositor bail-in was pursued. Initially, a broad levy on all deposits was considered, before the authorities settled on a levy only on uninsured deposits over €100,000. This experience should be frightening to depositors, who hitherto treated their bank deposits as immune from financial loss and definitely not susceptible to resolution-style haircuts. In general, we would now expect increased sensitivity of big-ticket deposit balances to bad news and the risk of runs on retail or corporate deposits to have increased, internationally.

Recently, the BIS has floated a specific proposal for recapitalising "too-big-to-fail" banks.[149] In essence, the proposal involves a drastic write-down of the value of the bank's equity, subordinated debt and senior unsecured bonds. Investors in those instruments are to be compensated by being given ownership of the bank, which is subsequently sold. The key element in this BIS proposal is that the investors who are written down do not *share* the proceeds of the eventual sale of the bank, as they would in the case of a dilutive debt-for-equity restructuring. Instead, they are repaid in strict accordance with the prior hierarchy of their claims. To illustrate this, imagine a situation where the regulator deemed it necessary to write off $60 of claims in order for the bank to remain solvent, comprising $20 equity, $20 subordinated debt and $20 senior debt. Let us say that the bank is subsequently sold for $30. The $30 would be distributed as follows: $20 to the investor who had their senior bonds written down by $20, thus their losses are zero; $10 to the subordinated debt investor, who has therefore lost 50% of their investment; and $0 for the equity investor, who has been totally wiped out. This proposal seems fair to investors' respective positions and allows for effective regulatory discretion, since the impact of imposing a conservatively heavy write-down is mitigated by the high recovery values for the senior bond holders. Nevertheless, this approach is not without its challenges. It resembles the Danish approach to bank resolution in several aspects, which has created periodic funding market pressure on Danish banks.

4.7 OTHER CURRENT REGULATORY WORKSTREAMS

The main thrust of regulatory reform has been to improve solvency capital levels and funding and liquidity structures. But the authorities are aware of further changes required beyond these elements. Consequently, there are multiple regulatory initiatives to "complement the existing reforms in order to further address excessive risk taking incentives, complexity, intra-group subsidies, resolvability and systemic risk".[150] A brief summary of the more important ones is given in Table 4.26.

---

[148] Written Evidence in response to call for evidence made on 15 October 2012: Submission from The Association of British Insurers, Parliamentary Commission on Banking Standards.

[149] A template for recapitalising too-big-to-fail banks, *BIS Quarterly Review*, June 2013.

[150] High-level expert group on reforming the structure of the EU banking sector, Erikki Liikanen, October 2012.

Table 4.26 Major regulatory initiatives on the agenda

Market infrastructures	The derivatives market is huge and the risks are not wholly apparent. In September 2009, at the G20 meeting in Pittsburgh, it was agreed that all standardised derivatives should be cleared through central counterparties rather than on a bilateral bank-to-bank basis. The negative contagious impact of the failure of a counterparty could be reduced through centralised margining, collateral management and netting of settlements.
Supervisory approaches	Whilst international regulators have not admitted explicitly a failure of supervision, they recognise there were deficiencies in the overall philosophy and mode of supervision. With this in mind, the Basel Committee and individual countries around the world continue to work on improvements, in particular with regard to the intensity of supervision. Basel has also identified gaps that need to be plugged,[151] for example the ability for a regulator to veto major acquisitions, which was reportedly missing in the UK at the time of the RBS acquisition of ABN Amro.
Macro-prudential focus	International regulators are developing a framework and a set of tools to more effectively manage systemic risks that arise above the level of individual banks. In other words, system-wide problems can develop in the shape of asset bubbles, excessive borrowing, insufficient levels of liquidity and flexibility or high degrees of interconnectedness. Regulators are being encouraged to "lean against the wind". To do that, they need to be able to spot macro-level issues and use their tools to contain them.
Supervision of governance	The Basel Committee has recognised that sound corporate governance is key to a sound banking system. It has set out what it sees as the key principles of governance that supervisors should be ensuring are applied in the banks for which they are responsible.[152] These principles include effective management from a Board of Directors that is competent and well-organised, clear cascading of accountability through the managerial layers, strong control and risk management capabilities led by a Chief Risk Officer (CRO), appropriate compensation structures and robust communication and transparency. Together with international regulators, the Basel Committee is working to detail and implement these principles.
Consumer protection	The current financial crisis has indirectly highlighted the fact that the design and sale of consumer banking products is an area that needs to be improved, to increase the level of "fairness" as well as reducing risk. Consumers need help to make informed decisions to select the correct banking product for their needs and banks need to comply with consumer protection regulation. A host of regulatory initiatives is underway, including the EU's "Markets in Financial Instruments Directive" and the USA's Dodd–Frank "Wall Street Reform and Consumer Protection Act", which has led to the creation of the Consumer Financial Protection Bureau.

---

[151] Core Principles for Effective Banking Supervision, Basel Committee, September 2012.

[152] Principles for enhancing corporate governance, Basel Committee, October 2010.

Transaction taxes	In 2010, the IMF was asked by the G10 to set out a "range of options countries have adopted or are considering as to how the financial sector could make a fair and substantial contribution toward paying for any burden associated with government interventions to repair the banking system".[153] It considered that a levy on size, risk, profit or compensation would be the most appropriate options. The European Commission has proposed the introduction of a "financial transactions tax", which would not only raise funds but also "create appropriate disincentives for certain transactions",[154] thus suppressing trading volumes (by 15% for shares and bonds and 75% for derivatives) and risk. The rate has been set at 0.1% for financial transactions and 0.01% for derivatives.
Compensation caps	At the Basel level, the regulatory principle that has been adopted is simply that an "employee's compensation should be effectively aligned with prudent risk taking".[155] This has led to regulatory developments in pay, especially at the executive level. In the USA, for example, the Dodd–Frank Act is likely to have fundamental impacts on, inter alia, how pay is decided and awarded, disclosure of executive pay and its relation to average pay and clawbacks of pay in case of accounting restatements. In Europe, however, regulators have gone one step further and imposed a maximum level of variable compensation equal to the banker's fixed salary (or two times the fixed salary if shareholders approve).[156] This is widely expected to lead to a rise in salary levels but is intended to have positive risk management benefits. Switzerland too has introduced extra curbs on executive pay, with a ban on one-off bonuses when executives leave a firm or the firm gets taken over, as well as a requirement for binding shareholder votes on executive pay.
Changes to industry structure	Several streams of regulatory development look at restricting or reorganising business activities, in particular those deemed of little social use or excessively high risk. Different countries are developing different solutions.[157]

- The Volcker rule in the USA seeks to stop banks from proprietary trading but allows them to continue market-making activities. It prevents investments in, and sponsorship of, hedge funds and private equity funds.
- The Vickers proposal in the UK recommends that the retail banking activities of a bank are "ringfenced" from the wholesale banking activities.
- The European Commission's expert advice from Erkki Liikanen, the Governor of the Bank of Finland, was that there should be a strict separation between investment banking and retail banking. These should be in separate subsidiaries. The proposals limit contagion within the group by requiring, in particular, that the subsidiaries be self-sufficient in terms of capital and liquidity.

(continued)

---

[153] A Fair And Substantial Contribution By The Financial Sector: Final Report For The G-20, IMF, June 2010.

[154] Implementing enhanced cooperation in the area of Financial Transaction Tax, European Commission, 14 February 2013.

[155] Principles for enhancing corporate governance, Basel Committee, October 2010.

[156] EU tightens up bank lending rules and bonuses, BBC News, 16 April 2013.

[157] Structural bank regulation initiatives: approaches and implications, BIS, April 2013.

Table 4.26   *(Continued)*

	• In France, the ringfencing approach is being introduced for high-risk activities such as high-frequency trading and commodity derivatives. The new French banking law of February 2013 also prohibits a banking group from owning stakes in speculative hedge funds.[158]
	• A new draft law on the separation of retail and some investment banking activities submitted to the German Parliament considers separation of retail banking if assets devoted to proprietary or high-frequency trading and hedge fund financing operations are relatively large in relation to the bank's balance sheet.
Shadow banking	Regulators are working on proposals for the regulation of non-bank financial institutions. Three main workstreams are notable: • The FSB is leading the global framework and attempting to coordinate initiatives at the international level. • In the USA, non-bank Systemically Important Financial Institutions (SIFIs) are being designated and regulations defined. • In Europe, the European Systemic Risk Board is preparing to recommend new shadow banking regulations.

---

[158] The law on the separation of banking activities: political symbol or new economic paradigm? Céline Antonin and Vincent Touzé, OFCE, 26 February 2013.

5

Case Studies

Success is not final, failure is not fatal: it is the courage to continue that counts.[1]

The current financial crisis provides many real-life illustrations of our diagnosis of the banking industry. Some of these are quite spectacular. The management (and mis-management) of the banking industry has moved out of obscurity and become top-line, mainstream news. Several banks have had their troubles chronicled and analysed in public inquiries, which have laid bare the workings of the banking industry and exposed its many inadequacies.

In order to illustrate our diagnosis and inform our proposals, therefore, we are setting out a small number of case studies from recent times. These cases contain interesting lessons on the themes of risk management in banks and their supervision and governance. The themes are recurrent: these cases are not just the stories of individual banks but windows into the structural issues of the entire banking industry.

In selecting the cases, we have attempted to cover a diverse range of situations and business models. We do not try to narrate a comprehensive story, trying instead to extract an insightful thematic description. The cases are not meant to stigmatise any particular bank: the selection has been made on the basis of clarity and relevance rather than the compilation of a "rogue's gallery". But, inevitably, most of our case studies involve banks that have undergone severe stress during the past six years. Some concern banks that have failed and been nationalised or sold off. Others have managed their way through the difficult times with a fair degree of success. We do not make relative judgements on the good and bad points of the banks in question. In general, banks with fewer troubles might claim better governance or risk management processes than failed institutions, but this is not self-evident: absence of failure does not mean absence of risk. Among the cases are the descriptions of the banking industries of two countries – Australia and Canada – that have remained stable and profitable throughout the crisis. We try to assess whether there are positive lessons to be learned from the experiences in those countries. We have chosen cases where there are good public information sources, which chronicle the management and supervisory failures. This appears to give an unintended geographical bias, for example towards the UK, where the authorities have put a lot of "post mortem" studies into the public domain. On the other hand, there are disturbingly few substantive public studies into the regulatory and supervisory failures behind some of the monstrous business models that emerged pre-crisis. We might appear to be absolving those responsible for the disasters from this crisis that remain lightly researched and documented. Again, this is not our intention. The selection is not meant to be representative and the reader should not interpret the fact that there are "missing exhibits".

---

[1] Often attributed to Winston Churchill.

5.1 RBS

The story of RBS offers many interesting insights into the way that risk was being managed by some banks in the run-up to the current financial crisis. The dour Scottish bank had great and acclaimed success following its reverse takeover of NatWest in 2000. There followed an expansionary accumulation of risks in many of the areas that were most heavily exposed to the subprime crisis and its spillover. Just at the point when markets were peaking and maximum risk was about to turn into major losses, RBS led a hostile takeover of the troubled ABN Amro, that was breathtaking in its brazen aggression, complexity and riskiness. As markets turned, the consequences for RBS were collapse and nationalisation.

Growth in Risk

In the years prior to 2007, RBS grew its business rapidly and became a major player in the international banking markets. Its balance sheet grew from £304bn in 2000 to £848bn in 2006. RBS became the European leader in leveraged finance (lending to leveraged buy-outs) and property finance. Its exposure to the structured credit markets was huge: RBS "ranked first among managers of global asset-backed and mortgage-backed securitisations and fourth among managers of global syndicated loans, while among managers of international bonds we moved from thirteenth place to eighth".[2] Profits grew accordingly, rising from £1.8bn in 2000 to £5.6bn in 2006. Though it was compliant with regulation in the run-up to the onset of the financial crisis, the risk appetite of RBS was greater than that of its peers. For example, it ran a Tier 1 ratio of 7.5% in 2006, lower than Barclays' 7.7% or HSBC's 9.4% and with a greater reliance on preferred shares rather than ordinary equity.

Stock analysts and credit ratings agencies were positively disposed towards RBS. Thin capital levels and greater-than-average risk concentrations were noted but did not cause sufficient concern for them. For example, in late 2006, Standard & Poor's noted that RBS "has a sizable U.K. commercial property exposure, but the portfolio is well diversified, with a moderate average LTV ratio and a careful approach to structuring. Only a tiny fraction is considered speculative".[3] S&P rated the bank "AA", with a stable outlook. Interestingly, S&P noted that RBS' capital position was tight and likely to remain weak but was "being managed a little less tightly than in the past" and seemed unfazed in noting the £1bn share buyback programme and increase in dividend payout.

The UK FSA has calculated that, using the new Basel III methodologies, RBS in 2007 would have had a Common Equity Tier 1 (CET1) ratio of 1.97%,[4] less than half of the new bare minimum regulatory requirement. Yet, RBS at the time appeared solvent enough to remain in business, with a reasonable credit rating and sufficient resources to grow and consider ambitious acquisition plans. It was clearly a business model of the time – not an anomaly, but a stereotype.

In addition to low solvency, RBS also ran a risky and aggressive funding profile, relying heavily on the short-term wholesale markets to fund its investments. By way of illustration, RBS was a net borrower from the interbank market of £72bn in 2006 versus only £3bn in 2000.

This level of risk appetite resulted in an institution that would undoubtedly, on its own, have failed during the financial crisis. But organic growth was not sufficient for RBS' growth plans. Instead, RBS bought another risky bank (ABN Amro) at the top of the market, following

---

[2] RBS Annual Report and Accounts, 2006.
[3] Royal Bank of Scotland Group PLC (The), Nigel Greenwood and Michelle Brennan, Standard Poor's Ratings Services, 18 December 2006; reproduced with permission of Standard & Poor's, a division of The McGraw-Hill Companies, Inc.
[4] The Failure of the Royal Bank of Scotland, UK FSA, December 2011.

limited due diligence – information provided to RBS by ABN Amro amounted to "two lever arch folders and a CD".[5] What is more, it used an opaque deal structure and financed the acquisition via mostly short-term debt rather than capital raising. For example, of the €22.6bn that RBS paid for ABN Amro, more than half was funded by debt repayable within a year.

RBS shareholders voted 94.5% in favour of the ABN Amro acquisition, despite the fact that Barclays had chosen to walk away from the deal and the terrible truths of the subprime crisis were becoming patently obvious. But, like many a bride with grave misgivings, walking up the aisle proved easier than cancelling the reception.

Poor Supervision of RBS

The RBS case has highlighted many critical failings at the UK regulator. Whilst the FSA considers that most of these have already been remedied, a recent report from the Parliamentary Treasury Select Committee has criticised the executives responsible within the UK authorities (FSA and Bank of England) for their lack of effective supervision. For example, the politicians considered that "the fact that the Supervision Team was largely doing what was expected of it but was following a deficient supervisory approach, in turn clearly implies however, that the senior management of the FSA who determined those resources, processes and practices must have made design decisions which were, in retrospect, seriously mistaken".[6]

Amazingly, the FSA did not pay much attention to the inherent risks at RBS: "Before the onset of the market disruption in August 2007, the FSA's overall approach involved little fundamental analysis of trading book inventory and did not focus on valuation issues. There were also deficiencies in the market risk capital regime, including its over-reliance on value-at-risk (VaR) models."[7] In fact, the regulatory post-mortem in the case of RBS has exposed the fact that the riskiest situations of the UK banking industry could sometimes be those most neglected: "the flawed concept of a 'regulatory dividend' rewarded firms with less intensive supervision if they could demonstrate effective controls and displayed a degree of cooperation with the FSA that ought to have been a non-negotiable minimum. Reflecting this philosophy, insufficient resources were devoted to high impact banks and in particular to their investment banking activities."[8]

The passive approach of the regulator and a trusting belief in both the all-powerful effectiveness of Basel II and the self-regulatory capability of the capital markets meant that there was, in fact, little supervision of RBS at this time. "The erroneous belief that financial markets were inherently stable, and that the Basel II capital adequacy regime would itself ensure a sound banking system, drove the assumption that prudential risks were a lower priority than ensuring that banks were 'treating customers fairly'."[9]

In particular, though the FSA had misgivings about the acquisition of ABN Amro, they did not lead to any supervisory action, because the FSA did not feel that such actions were in its remit: "RBS did not have to seek the FSA's regulatory approval for the contested takeover of ABN AMRO. Arguably the FSA, if really determined, could have blocked the takeover by other less direct means."[10]

The conclusion regarding the supervisory input into the acquisition of ABN Amro is damning: "In its response to the largest ever cross-jurisdictional acquisition in history, the FSA took

---

[5] Ibid.

[6] The FSA's report into the failure of RBS, Fifth Report of Session 2012–13, House of Commons Treasury Committee, 16 October 2012.

[7] The Failure of the Royal Bank of Scotland, UK FSA.

[8] Ibid.

[9] Ibid.

[10] Ibid.

only limited account of the substantial uncertainties and risks, which were compounded by the restricted due diligence that the firm could perform."[11]

High Levels of Risk Led to Massive Losses

It is hard to know exactly how RBS would have fared without the ABN Amro acquisition. Indeed, it is almost academic. The acquisition of ABN Amro was a natural transaction for the aggressive management of RBS and so it is artificial to remove that transaction from the historical analysis. For what it is worth, RBS states that more than half of its losses related to ABN AMRO-originated portfolios.[12]

RBS losses were in many areas of its business portfolio, not just those related to American subprime assets. The FSA report profiles £14bn of losses in credit trading in 2007 and 2008, £10bn in commercial property lending in 2008–2010 and £10bn in corporate lending in the same time period. Within these numbers, losses in Ireland probably amount to £3bn. It is not clear that all of the losses have now been taken at RBS and current scrutiny from the FSA's successor, the PRA, of RBS' real estate loans may cause further hefty provisions and capital deficits.

As the financial crisis developed and RBS collapsed, public attention turned to the highly-paid Chief Executive, Sir Fred Goodwin. Mr Goodwin was stripped of his knighthood in January 2012. Much of the subsequent media reporting focused on this one man, as if RBS were a fiefdom and its failure the result of one individual. At the same time, the media focused on Mr Goodwin's high pay and generous pension arrangements. The collapse of a bank took on an intensely personal dimension.

The institutional story of RBS has some specific developments, which it is useful to highlight:

- RBS was nationalised in October 2008, when the government injected £45.5bn of equity capital. It currently owns just over 80% of RBS. The government stake was bought at an average price of 50p per share,[13] which is equivalent to 500p once adjusted for the 10-for-1 reverse stock split that occurred in 2012. Around the end of 2012, the RBS share price hovered around the 300p mark, indicating a 40% loss on investment for the government.
- Political pressure is growing from certain directions for RBS to be used as a public policy bank, to direct lending to credit-starved sectors to reflate the economy.
- As part of the recapitalisation, RBS bought insurance from a government "asset protection scheme" (APS). The APS was, in effect, a "bad bank" that isolated the rest of RBS from the potential problems remaining in its portfolio of toxic assets. The total size of the APS for RBS was £286bn at inception and there was a £60bn expected loss on the assets in question. In the end, the macro-economic and market situation did not turn out to be bad enough for the APS to be used and – like any good insurance policy – it did not need to pay out anything. It was wound up in October 2012.
- Alongside several other banks, RBS was implicated in the LIBOR-rigging scandal, and was fined close to £400m. It is also involved in other industry-wide misconduct situations, such as the mis-selling of swaps and credit insurance products.

Lessons to be Learned from this Case Study

The RBS case highlights governance and risk management failures in multiple areas. Its solvency was weak: based on current methodologies, RBS was virtually insolvent in 2006.

---

[11] Ibid.
[12] RBS Annual Report and Accounts, 2008.
[13] Annual Report And Accounts 2011/12, UK Financial Investments Limited (UKFI).

Further, it had an aggressive funding profile and a significant duration mismatch of its assets and liabilities. And its risk appetite was extremely high. These aspects were not tempered by the management, owners, analysts or supervisors of RBS. The aggressive acquisition of ABN Amro was beyond the capabilities of RBS and highlights a lack of supervisory oversight, shareholder governance and market discipline, which should in aggregate have prevented the acquisition from taking place. There was no single flaw in RBS – it took too many risks in too many areas and suffered the consequences when the crisis unfolded.

5.2 DEXIA

Dexia, the Franco-Belgian bank, started as a branch of the state-owned "Caisse des Dépôts et Consignations" before becoming "Crédit Local de France". Pushed by the ambition to extend into other European markets, Crédit Local merged with Crédit Communal de Belgique in 1996 to be one of the first cross-border European banks. A number of other acquisitions followed.

Dexia's business model was focused on lending to the public sector, which was a growing market due to liberalisation and decentralisation of public sector finances. Dexia applied new, sophisticated financial techniques to its business. Securitisation, for example, allowed Dexia to fund its loans to the public sector at very attractive rates, making lending to municipalities profitable. Profitability was further enhanced by financing long-dated assets with short-term funding and taking the risks of such a "maturity transformation". Dexia relied upon a strong credit rating and access to cheap funding.

Dexia expanded its activity rapidly in the early part of the last decade, increasing its balance sheet from €258bn in 2000 to €651bn in 2008 before collapsing following a liquidity crisis in October 2008 and needing to be rescued by the state. The fundamental components of its business model had been torn apart by the financial crisis.

Using Cheap and Abundant Funding to "Go Long" Credit

In an environment characterised by well-functioning and liquid interbanking markets, Dexia's strong credit rating (AA) provided almost unlimited access to liquidity to fund new lending. Public sector loans were primarily refinanced through covered bond programmes, which can be described as a form of "high standard" securitisation (see Section 3.6.5). Dexia was one of the first to set up a covered bond programme after the law of 1999 creating the Obligations Foncières was adopted in France and it seized the opportunity to refinance its public sector loans through the issuance of large quantities of these bonds. Covered bonds enabled the low margin/low risk public sector lending business to become a scalable and profitable business.

Dexia's growth was driven by an expanding risk appetite, dominance of public sector financing, and expansion into new jurisdictions. Dexia's primary covered bond vehicle ("Dexia Municipal Agency") grew to €69bn in size by 2007.

The success of covered bonds as a financing tool was largely driven by the demand from investors across the world (such as insurance companies and central banks) who considered this asset class as an attractive substitute for government bonds, just as safe and with a slightly better return. In reality, during this period, a liquid public sector benchmark covered bond was seen as a high quality, triple-A rated exposure to public sector risk, in other words essentially a risk-free exposure "recreated" by a structured finance vehicle and bearing the stamp of approval of rating agencies.

Table 5.1   Dexia Credit Spread Portfolio as of November 2008 (€bn)[14]

Bank bonds	39%	28.1
Mortgage-backed securities (MBS)	23%	16.6
Covered bonds	17%	12.3
Asset-backed securities (ABS)	6%	4.3
Fully hedged	15%	10.8
Total	100%	72.1

The success of Dexia's strategy in the early years of the last decade led to increased confidence in the business model. Dexia began to expand into other types of risk and created two independent portfolios managed directly by the Treasury and Financial Markets division:

- the €72.1bn Credit Spread Portfolio, which invested in bonds issued by banks (including Lehman, Washington Mutual and the Icelandic banks) and securitisation bonds (see Table 5.1);
- the €91.4bn Public Sector Portfolio, which invested in public sector assets that were not eligible to be included in covered bond programmes, due to the credit rating, the jurisdiction of the assets or the nature of the entity itself.

The risks in these portfolios were not constrained by the need to comply with the criteria for covered bond eligibility. Dexia was able to fund these portfolios through its Treasury operations at low cost and earn a profit on the higher-yielding asset investments. The Treasury and Financial Markets division became a profit centre and Dexia's liquidity risk increased.

A further avenue of expansion was the purchase of the US credit insurer FSA in 2000. FSA was originally a monoline specialised in municipal finance, but expanded into other areas of credit insurance. Using Dexia's strong credit rating, FSA became active in a wider range of credit enhancement transactions, growing the sum insured from $325bn in 2002 to $426bn by the end of 2007.[15] Municipal finance remained the largest exposure, representing two-thirds of FSA's total portfolio, but there was also $12bn of subprime-related RMBS, a far riskier asset class.

Dexia Continues its Course Despite Mounting Losses at FSA and a Deteriorating Environment

As the financial crisis began to take hold, Dexia maintained its strong rating and public sector focused business model; the market's fears were directed towards other banks with more evident exposure to subprime defaults. In fact, Dexia even benefited from a "flight to quality" up until the first half of 2008 and was able to issue public sector covered bonds at levels identical to pre-crisis levels.

Dexia's management seems to have turned a blind eye to market dislocations and mounting pressures on the financial system. Signals seemed to confirm the resilience of the Dexia business model: for example, S&P noted in May 2008 – a year after the crisis began – that "Dexia's low-risk cutomer base, conservative risk policies and culture of risk-aversion have translated

---

[14] Dexia results Q3 2008 presentation – Appendix.
[15] Dexia 2007 Annual Report.

Table 5.2   Breakdown of Dexia liabilities by maturity (€bn)[16]

Maturity		
<3m	134	26%
Between 3m and 1 year	58	11%
Between 1 and 5 years	89	17%
> 5 years	98	19%
Total	513	26%

into a lower risk profile than most its peers".[17] At this time, Dexia continued to expand its operations, buying portfolios (such as £2.2bn of social housing loans from Bradford and Bingley in November 2007) and increasing FSA's market share when all others were scaling back.

In the end, FSA's exposures and losses caught up with Dexia. In the second quarter of 2008, FSA posted a $503m loss. Dexia's support for FSA's solvency and credit strength (essential to continue in business as a monoline credit insurer) were starting to put Dexia's own creditworthiness and earnings under threat. On 23 June 2008, Dexia's decision to extend a $5bn facility to FSA increased investors' fears. Dexia's management attempted to communicate that the overall business model was sound, despite the ordeals of its monoline subsidiary. In summer 2008, they reported "24% growth in underlying results [...] excluding FSA"[18] and predicted that the problems at FSA were down to accounting valuations that "will revert over time",[19] but the market was becoming increasingly nervous. Beyond the losses at FSA, Dexia was having to operate in a market where funding sources were drying up, as investors reduced their exposure to the banking sector.

The nature of its maturity transformation meant that Dexia, more than most banks, was brutally exposed to a liquidity crunch. More than half of Dexia's liabilities matured in less than three months (see Table 5.2).

But by summer 2008, it was probably too late for Dexia to adapt its business model.

First Liquidity Crisis: Liquidity Gap (October 2008)

Dexia's plight can be illustrated by the changes in the income statement of the Treasury and Financial Markets division, which Dexia admitted had been "severely hit by the financial crisis".[20] Income had been decimated and losses were far greater even than historic income (see Table 5.3).[21]

Table 5.3   Dexia key items of the income statement

€m	2007	2008
Income	581	33
Cost of risk	9	716

---

[16] Dexia Annual Report 2007.

[17] Dexia SA, Sylvie Dalmaz and Arnaud de Toytot, Standard & Poor's Ratings Services, 18 May 2007; reproduced with permission of Standard & Poor's, a division of The McGraw-Hill Companies, Inc.

[18] Dexia Q2 2008 result presentation.

[19] Ibid.

[20] Dexia Q3 2008 result presentation.

[21] Dexia investor presentation Q3 2008.

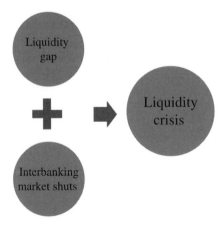

Figure 5.1   Drivers of the first liquidity crisis (October 2008)

The business model relied heavily on a strong credit rating and continuous access to cheap short-term funding. Clearly, viability was being challenged by the deteriorating financial environment. In the days that followed the collapse of Lehman Brothers, in the wake of a freeze on the interbanking market, Dexia was unable to renew all of its required funding volumes and was facing the prospect of a run on deposits.

On 29 September 2008, Dexia applied to the French, Belgian and Luxembourg governments for support. If it were to collapse, the knock-on consequences and contagion would have been catastrophic. The rescue plan included a recapitalisation, new management and a guarantee from the three states to provide funding. Market confidence was restored and a chaotic fire sale of tens of billions of Euros of assets that would have devastated the whole financial system was avoided.

At that time, Dexia's investment portfolio had a negative mark-to-market of €7bn. Dexia management had to choose whether to *do nothing* and wait for the assets' value to recover or *sell assets* at these distressed levels, reducing the risk and the funding needs but crystallising the loss on those assets. The management, blinded by the apparent success of the business model they had created and facing resistance from the business lines, was unable to operate the necessary turn-around and instead opted to sit and wait, hoping for calmer seas after the storm. Massive provision of central bank funding allowed the business to survive from a funding perspective. But by the end of the third quarter, the mark-to-market losses had risen to €11bn. Dexia continued to claim that the "negative MtM of fixed-income portfolio mainly reflects wider spreads and not a deterioration of underlying asset quality".[22] In reality, management had no other realistic choices: the size of the legacy portfolio had made it impossible to reposition Dexia and implement a new strategy.

Second Liquidity Crisis: Downgrading and Increased Collateral Requirements (Summer 2011)
The new management team appointed after the recapitalisation carried out an ambitious programme of deleveraging and de-risking which resulted in a reduction of assets from

---

[22] Dexia 2008 Q3 results presentation – Appendix.

€651bn at the end of 2008 to €412bn at the end of 2011.[23] During this period, Dexia also exited the monoline FSA. More stable market conditions helped reduce the funding gap by reducing reliance on short-term funding and successfully launching long-dated liabilities placed in the market. By the end of H1 2011, €73.4bn of bonds and loans had been sold with limited impact on Dexia's equity[24] and while many challenges remained, the situation appeared to stabilise.

Ironically, it was not the losses on its investment portfolio, nor funding difficulties, that led to a second collapse for Dexia, but a sharp increase in the need for collateral, to cover its derivatives positions, predicated by a fall in interest rates. Dexia's derivatives portfolio was huge (€58bn of assets and €84bn of liabilities on 30 June 2010) and sensitive: for every 1% move in interest rates, Dexia would have to post €12bn of collateral to its derivatives counterparties. Dexia's balance sheet was positioned to benefit from a normalisation of the market environment: tightening credit spreads, a gradual reopening of the capital markets and increasing interest rates once market confidence had returned. Unfortunately, this is not the scenario that played out.

Markets became troubled by a loss of confidence in the Eurozone. Interest rates dropped by nearly 1% during the summer of 2011 as a result. Dexia's collateral requirements increased rapidly. This triggered a chain of events, such as the decision by Moody's to place the rating of Dexia on review for downgrade, citing its belief that "in addition to these funding pressures, Dexia's collateral postings on hedging derivatives have increased due to substantial market volatility. These pressures are likely to have led to a substantial increase in its usage of short-term secured funding potentially resulting in a further squeeze of its available liquidity reserves."[25]

The ratings downgrade further increased the collateral requirements of Dexia, as counterparties were contractually entitled to cover their increasing exposure to higher credit risk. In September 2011, Dexia had a second liquidity crisis and a second rescue by France, Belgium and Luxembourg to avoid bankruptcy (see Figure 5.2).

The governments finally agreed to break up Dexia. Dexia Bank Belgium (a deposit-taking retail bank, now renamed "Belfius") was taken over by the Belgian government and Dexia Crédit Local was put into run-off. Dexia's legacy portfolio still needs to be restructured. Overall, the failures in risk management at Dexia are estimated to have cost taxpayers over €18bn.[26]

Lessons to be Learned from this Case Study

Focused business models can be extremely vulnerable to unexpected changes in the environment. Dexia was one such business model. At its core, the public sector banking model appears low risk, but the thin revenue margins led Dexia to take massive funding risks in order to be profitable. Similarly, the credit insurance business and the Treasury profit centre built large positions in subprime bonds in the bid to improve profit growth. Dexia's management was not aware of the size and nature of the accumulation of imbalances and risks until it was too late to adapt. Perhaps it was always too late: the business model was not only fragile but also proved impossible to adapt to the volatile market environment that characterises the current financial crisis.

---

[23] Dexia 2011 Annual Report.

[24] Dexia 2011 Q2 result presentation.

[25] Moody's report on Dexia, 3 October 2011.

[26] Examen des circonstances qui ont conduit au démantèlement de Dexia, Chambre des représentants de Belgique, 23 March 2012.

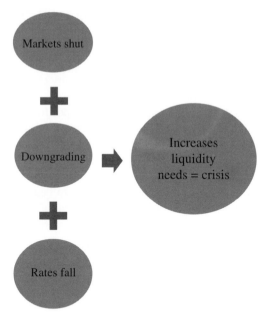

Figure 5.2   Drivers of the second liquidity crisis (summer 2011)

5.3 HBOS

In 2001, the ex-building society Halifax and the 300-year-old Bank of Scotland merged to form HBOS, a "new force in banking" with £312bn in assets and £11bn in equity, annual profits of £1.6bn and a market capitalisation of some £30bn. The new entity was a credible fifth player to challenge the dominant market shares of the UK's "Big Four" banks (Lloyds, Barclays, HSBC and RBS) and its positioning was clear: "HBOS is the most aggressive high street bank operating in the UK."[27]

After the merger in 2001, HBOS became the largest provider of mortgages and loans in the United Kingdom, with around 20% market share. It also had a strong insurance and investment business, but it was relatively small in both the gateway current account product, with only 7% market share, and in business banking, with only around 3% market share.[28] Further, it had minimal presence in wholesale Treasury markets and international operations.

In its 2001 Annual Report, HBOS Chairman Dennis Stevenson stated: "The merger combination gives scale where it was needed, balance sheet and funding support where growth would have been inhibited and a new scale of earnings power driven by product and service propositions that attack the entrenched competition. Rarely can two great brands and two great organisations have combined with so much potential for extraordinary growth."[29]

---

[27] HBOS plc Annual Report and Accounts, 2001.
[28] Proposed merger between Halifax Group Plc and Bank of Scotland, Office of Fair Trading, 11 July 2001.
[29] HBOS Annual Report & Accounts 2001.

Growth and Expansion Abroad

The aggressive business strategy adopted by HBOS was based on rapid growth and was a continuation of the two entities' pre-existing ambitions. While Halifax aggressively marketed its products and provided a superior customer offering in the retail space, the Bank of Scotland side of the business had "been given practically an open cheque book by the bank's board"[30] and embarked on an international expansion drive, which continued post-merger. For example, in 1995 the Bank of Scotland had bought 51% of Bankwest in Australia and the new HBOS mopped up the rest in 2003. HBOS described its growth strategy in Australia as aggressive and boasted about its "aggressively priced products".[31] The aggressive growth platform in Treasury and Wholesale was less evident, at least to shareholders. In fact, HBOS' CEO stated in 2001 that it was combining "two of the most conservative Treasury operations in the City; perhaps best illustrated by the fact that 99% of the investment portfolio assets of the merged entity have credit ratings of A or higher. 86% are AAA credits."[32]

By 2006, HBOS' profit had grown to £5.7bn and return on equity was strong at 21%. International lending was growing at a rate of 24%, including a 46% growth in commercial banking in Australia, 31% growth in Ireland and 33% in Spain (see Figure 5.3). Growth in international markets continued and even accelerated during 2007.

Leverage of the capital base was maintained by growing at a 10%+ rate and buying back £1bn of shares in both 2005 and 2006. The bank was very active in some of the riskiest areas of banking: large, property-related deals; lending to LBOs (leveraged buy-outs) and speculative buy-to-let mortgage lending. It was dominant in all areas of property-related lending and investment, taking equity stakes in property-related ventures in addition to supplying

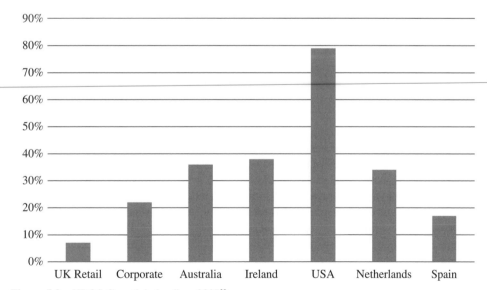

Figure 5.3   HBOS Growth in lending, 2007[33]

---

[30] Peter Cummings, Bank of Scotland Managing Director, quoted in *The Scotsman*, 28 August 2001.
[31] HBOS Annual Report and Accounts 2006.
[32] HBOS Annual Report and Accounts, 2001.
[33] HBOS Annual Report and Accounts, 2007.

Table 5.4   Composition of HBOS' Treasury portfolio, 31 March 2008

£bn	Balance at 31 March 2008[34]		Losses for 2008 (both income and equity accounted)[35]
Covered bonds, certificates of deposits, government bonds etc.	26.9		
Floating rate notes	15.8		2.3
Asset-backed securities (ABS)	39.1		8.5
• US prime mortgages		2.1	
• US Alt-A mortgages		6.9	
• US subprime mortgages		0.1	
• Other mortgage-backed securities		11.6	
• CDOs		6.7	
• Personal sector		5.5	
• Student loans		5.7	
• Other ABS and fair value adjustments		−2.8	
• Negative basis trades (CDS-hedged bonds)		3.3	
Total	**81.8**		**10.8**

traditional banking loans. In a word, HBOS was massively exposed to the property market, which it saw as its natural centre of expertise and competence. Competitors in the UK, Ireland, Australia and other markets noted the amazing business growth that HBOS was achieving and that HBOS was able and willing to lend in situations where, and on terms that, other banks were unable or unwilling to match. And the Treasury operations were building up a growing profit stream by investing in mortgage-backed securities that were highly-rated yet offered attractive yields, though these were to be a major source of losses for HBOS by the end of 2008 (see Table 5.4).

Curiously, HBOS appears to have been adding selectively to its US mortgage-backed securities portfolio. Even though HBOS stated in its accounts that "there has been no increase in net exposure as a result of the purchase of ABS during the year. Any increase in the net

---

[34] Update on Capital, Current Trading, Treasury Portfolio and Outlook, HBOS plc, 29 April 2008.
[35] HBOS Annual Report and Accounts, 2008.

exposure is the result of exchange rate movements in excess of paydowns, fair value adjustments and impairments," the footnote to the accounts that follows this statement indicates that the dollar equivalent amount of US securities rose from \$32.5bn (£16.3bn × 1.99) to nearly \$35bn (£24.3bn × 1.43).[36] If this is the case, it is not transparent and does not appear to have been widely reported.

Businesses that Looked Different but Were Correlated when the Crisis Hit

Management did not perceive the risks building up in the business. The CEO stated in early 2007: "Discussions of corporate credit quality are beginning to have a Groundhog Day theme. There is a certain amount of repetition and, each time we stand up and say it cannot get better, it then does."[37]

The events of 2007 seem to have led to a sense of complacency within HBOS, despite the CEO's assertions as he announced a dividend increase of 18%: "We are never complacent. We intend to prove to you today that HBOS has handled this liquidity crunch very effectively. Not only have our write-downs been very small in comparison to other UK and global competitors, but we are extremely confident that we are emerging from exceptionally tough market conditions with very strong prospects for the future."[38] During that same call, the CFO stated that he remained "comfortable with the quality of our corporate portfolio, which in the case of real estate lending is backed by strong covenants and security over property."[39] Similar descriptions of the high quality Treasury portfolio of nearly £100bn were emphasised by HBOS management.

Stock analysts and credit ratings agencies failed to discern the scale of HBOS' riskiness. Towards the end of 2007, S&P noted that "HBOS is well placed to withstand a more challenging environment. HBOS' strong, diverse earnings provide a substantial cushion to absorb the expected increase in impairment losses in the residential mortgage and corporate segments. Its counter-cyclical approach to corporate lending has been successful to date, but could cause problems if it should weaken its resolute approach to risk management."[40]

In late 2008, the capital markets began to lose confidence in HBOS. The stock price collapsed and borrowing in the markets became difficult. Initially, the problems were blamed on malicious rumours in the market, which the UK regulator sought to quash: "We are satisfied that HBOS is a well-capitalised bank that continues to fund its business in a satisfactory way."[41] As the financial crisis intensified, it became clear that HBOS' troubles were not market technicals but business fundamentals: almost all areas of HBOS' business began to buckle under the strain of huge losses. In the years 2008 to 2011 before it was legally folded into the Lloyds Banking Group, HBOS' official accounts show a cumulative pretax loss of some £30bn.[42]

---

[36] HBOS Annual Report and Accounts, 2008.
[37] HBOS 2006 results announcement transcript, 28 February 2007.
[38] Transcript of HBOS Preliminary Results 2007, 27 February 2008.
[39] Ibid.
[40] HBOS plc, Richard Barnes and Claire Curtin, Standard & Poor's Ratings Services, 31 October 2007; reproduced with permission of Standard & Poor's, a division of The McGraw-Hill Companies, Inc.
[41] FSA statement, 17 September 2008.
[42] HBOS plc Annual Report and Accounts for those years.

Takeover by Lloyds

At the end of 2008, HBOS failed and a takeover by Lloyds TSB was agreed. The history of this disastrous acquisition is still not clear, especially regarding the central issue: was Lloyds TSB unduly coerced into the takeover by government? Many people in the banking industry believe that Lloyds TSB's management was indeed leaned on, but this is refuted by all parties involved. Shareholders were kept in the dark about an emergency £254bn funding line provided by the Bank of England on 1 October 2008 and fully repaid on 16 January 2009: the existence of the facility was only made public on 24 November 2009.[43] Meanwhile, 96% of Lloyds TSB's shareholders voted in favour of the takeover.[44]

Some may view HBOS' losses as the result of being in the wrong place at the wrong time. Any bank with a leading position in the UK property market could expect to lose money in a downturn. But HBOS also lost money where it was in the right place at the right time – the operations in Australia are a good example of this. HBOS had adopted an aggressive strategy to challenge the oligopoly in the Australian banking market via "a differentiated selling proposition based on simple products, aggressive pricing, distinctive marketing and speed of service".[45] In fact, HBOS' business operations in Australia had to be sold off at a loss of £845m; in addition, it has written off on average A\$2bn per year in loan impairments during the years 2009, 2010 and 2011. This figure is at a similar level to that of the large four Australian banks – however, HBOS' Australian operations were *ten times smaller* and so unable to support such write-downs.[46]

Subsequent enquiries into HBOS' demise have documented the weak risk culture at the organisation, as highlighted by HBOS' ex-Head of Group Regulatory Risk, Paul Moore, who criticised the growing sales culture at the bank. The evidence of the top management of HBOS given to Parliamentary committees also shows the top-down problems existent in HBOS in the run-up to – and during – the financial crisis, to the point at which HBOS was close to failure.

Anecdotal evidence suggests that HBOS had a reputation in the market. They were involved in the riskiest deals, to a greater extent than other lenders. Such views have been aired in public: "HBOS corporate were the people you went to if you had some adventurous proposition and you wanted a very quick decision. Wasn't that its reputation? On this idea that HBOS corporate was more cautious than other lenders, I would be surprised if that was really what your peers thought about you – not you personally, but HBOS corporate. They thought the opposite."[47]

The HBOS story continues, in several ways. More than four years after its demise, the authorities are still grappling with the lessons learnt and the correct remedial actions. In April 2013, the parliamentary sub-committee published a damning report, which placed the blame for the HBOS losses partly on the regulator, partly on the markets, but primarily on the senior management: "The losses were caused by a flawed strategy, inappropriate culture and inadequate controls. These are matters for which successive Chief Executives and particularly the Chairman and the Board as a whole bear responsibility."[48] This helps us understand, little-by-

---

[43] Additional information provided to the Treasury Committee by the Bank of England, Bank of England, Tuesday 24 November 2009.

[44] BBC News, 19 November 2008.

[45] HBOS plc Annual Report and Accounts, 2007.

[46] Analysis based on data from the banks' annual reports and accounts.

[47] Transcript of Oral Evidence, Parliamentary Commission on Banking Standards Panel on HBOS, 30 October 2012.

[48] "An accident waiting to happen": The failure of HBOS, Parliamentary Commission on Banking Standards, April 2013.

little, the true nature of the strategy, risk, governance and regulatory failures that led to HBOS' problems, even if the necessary remedies are not immediately clear.

The HBOS business is now part of Lloyds Banking Group. The troubles of its legacy assets and sales practices have now become part of that institution's turnaround story.

Lessons to be Learned from this Case Study

Aggressive banks tend to do well until they do terribly. The risk appetite in such situations can race ahead of the risk-management capabilities of the organisation. Banks that have a deep competence in one area (such as retail banking in this case) should be cautious when expanding into a different industry segment (such as Treasury, commercial property lending or international, in this case). HBOS appears to have demonstrated incompetence in the riskier areas of its expansion. Market distrust was a front-running signal of underlying insolvency: the regulators, ratings agencies and credit analysts failed to appreciate the underlying problems in the HBOS business until it was too late. Unfortunately for Lloyds TSB, the hapless acquirer, they too failed to appreciate the horrendous risks that HBOS had built up.

5.4 HSBC

HSBC is one of the world's largest and strongest banks. Its balance sheet is $2,700bn in size, its equity is $183bn (its market value being approximately the same) and it has 270,000 employees.[49] HSBC is a global, universal bank, as evidenced by the profile of its risk by geography and business unit (see Figures 5.4 and 5.5).

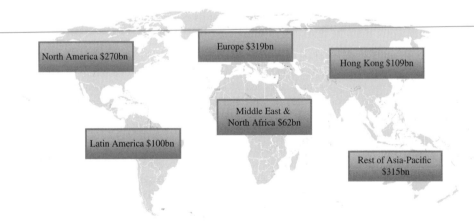

Figure 5.4   HSBC risk-weighted assets by geographical region (Total = $1,155bn)[50]

---

[49] HSBC Holdings plc Annual Report and Accounts, 2012.
[50] Interim Management Statement – 3Q 2012, HSBC, 5 November 2012.

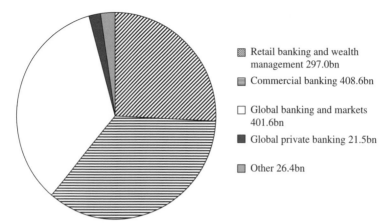

Figure 5.5   HSBC risk-weighted assets by business (Total = $1,155bn)

In fact, HSBC has diversification and conservatism at the heart of its low-risk strategy. Its experiences during the Second World War, when most of the bank's employees became prisoners of war and the bank's survival was down to its "prudent policy of building up large reserves in peace time",[51] forms the historical backdrop to HSBC's conservatism. The need for diversification became a central feature of HSBC's strategy from the 1950s and drove its "three-legged stool" strategy to cover Asia, Europe and the USA.[52]

It is somewhat ironic, therefore, that HSBC's profit warning was the milestone that, for many, marked the onset of the current financial crisis.

Losses on US Mortgages
On 7 February 2007, HSBC informed the market that its mortgage losses in the USA would be significantly worse than the market's assumptions.

> We now expect that the impact of increased provisioning in this area will be the major factor in bringing the aggregate of loan impairment charges and other credit risk provisions to be reflected in the accounts of the Group for the year ended 31 December 2006 above consensus estimates US$8.8 billion by some 20 per cent. This is subject to final review and subject to external audit.[53]

This press release was distinctly more serious than the earlier trading update:

> Challenges continue in the Mortgage Services operations, particularly in second lien and stated income products purchased in 2005 and 2006, which continue to be monitored. Tighter underwriting and pricing criteria have led to a significant reduction in the volume of higher risk mortgages purchased. Outstanding balances within this operation were flat at the end of the third quarter compared to the position at the half year. This slowdown in growth of the Mortgage Services portfolio will of itself lead to higher reported delinquency percentages as the portfolio seasons and will constrain revenue growth.[54]

---

[51] HSBC's history on hsbc.com.
[52] Ibid.
[53] HSBC Trading Update – US Mortgage Services, 7 February 2007.
[54] HSBC Holdings plc – pre-close trading update, 5 December 2006.

How did these losses originate? HSBC acquired the US subprime lender, Household Finance Corporation, in 2003 for $14.6bn and named its lending entity HSBC Finance Corporation. This acquisition ultimately led to losses estimated to be in the region of $50bn. In fact, HSBC Finance Corporation's 10-K accounts show a cumulative five-year provision charge for credit losses of $44.7bn, though it must be noted that the business would have had a high level of credit losses in a "normal" environment: a five-year figure of some $20bn would not have been a huge surprise. In 2008, HSBC wrote off $10.6bn of goodwill relating to its North American acquisitions and noted in its annual review: "HSBC has a reputation for telling it as it is. With the benefit of hindsight, this is an acquisition we wish we had not undertaken."[55]

Why did HSBC acquire Household? In order to grow and diversify its business in the United States. Whilst the decision was not without controversy, as it was in a riskier segment than other HSBC businesses, it is interesting to note that the subprime problems of Household had already been noted in 2002. For example:

> The timing of the transaction is especially unusual given that lending to people with weak credit may be becoming more perilous as the economic recovery falters and personal debt levels continue to rise.[56]

Impact of the Losses Contained

Though the acquisition was ultimately a disaster for HSBC, it had the size, diversification and financial resources to absorb the hit. Despite being a headline-grabber in the early stages of the financial crisis, HSBC weathered the losses well. The share price, which had been hovering just under £10 per share in the run-up to the crisis, reached a "trough" price of £3.60 in March 2009 and has since recovered to more than £7. This compares well to the experience of international peers. HSBC has retained a strong credit rating and is currently one of the highest rated banks in the world, with a rating of AA- from S&P and Fitch and Aa3 from Moody's.

Like many of its peers within UK retail banking operations, HSBC has been embroiled in the scandals around Payment Protection Insurance (PPI) and the misselling of derivatives to small businesses; like several of its international capital markets peers, HSBC has been involved in the scandal surrounding the manipulation of LIBOR. In addition to these problems, HSBC has also had to deal with a serious set of compliance breaches in the USA concerning money laundering and sanctions. As well as having to set aside a provision of $1.5bn in 2012,[57] HSBC has to improve its compliance processes and culture to address "a failure to monitor $60 trillion in wire transfer and account activity; a backlog of 17,000 unreviewed account alerts regarding potentially suspicious activity; and a failure to conduct AML due diligence before opening accounts for HSBC affiliates [...] HSBC's compliance culture has been pervasively polluted for a long time."[58]

---

[55] HSBC Holdings plc 2008 Final Results – Highlights, HSBC, 2 March 2009.

[56] HSBC to Buy a U.S. Lender for $14.2 Billion, Andrew Ross Sorkin, *New York Times*, 15 November 2002.

[57] Interim Management Statement – 3Q 2012, HSBC, 5 November 2012.

[58] HSBC Exposed U.S. Financial System to Money Laundering, Drug, Terrorist Financing Risks, US Senate Permanent Subcommittee on Investigations, 16 July 2012.

Lessons to be Learned from this Case Study
Even the most conservative, competent and experienced institutions can get it wrong. This is most certainly the case with HSBC and its expansion into US subprime lending via the acquisition of Household. But scale and diversification enabled HSBC to take the subprime losses on the chin and stay solid. On the more recent regulatory breaches, we are reminded of the need for tight control and process quality review throughout a banking organisation.

5.5 BEAR STEARNS

Bear Stearns may not have been the largest investment bank on Wall Street, but it was one of the most leveraged. A taste for innovation and risk-taking led Bear Stearns to embrace earlier than others the development of securitisation and repackaging techniques, which created new opportunities in asset management for investment banks in the post-dotcom era. Bear Stearns was one of the first banks to identify the potential of securitising risky mortgages, arranging in 1997 the first public securitisation of "Community Reinvestment Act Loans", which were mortgage loans into poor neighbourhoods. The expertise built in this field allowed Bear Stearns to become a major player in the CDO market in the early 2000s. Bear Stearns was present in all the stages of the value chain: it structured, managed and invested in CDOs. Bear Stearns was known for its aggressive trading strategies, but was well respected at the time, even by rating agencies who praised its "relatively conservative risk profile" and "strong management oversight".[59]

Its biggest problems came in March 2008 through its asset management arm, when the plunge in value of these funds eventually triggered a liquidity squeeze.

Subprime and High Leverage Puts Bear Stearns Funds Under Pressure
Bear Stearns Asset Management (BSAM) was created in 1985 and became a leading player in the CDO business via two highly leveraged mortgage hedge funds worth $18bn, the *High-Grade Structured Credit Strategies Fund* (set up in 2003) and the *High-Grade Structured Credit Strategies Enhanced Leverage Fund* (set up in 2006). These funds delivered steady results and proved popular with institutional investors. Part of the performance of the fund was the result of high leverage: for every $10 invested, the funds would receive $1 from investors and borrow $9 in the market. Investors thus had an exposure to the housing market of ten times

Table 5.5   Volume of assets structured by Bear Stearns' securitisation business in 2003 and 2004[60]

$bn	2003	2004
Agency	61.7	32.8
Of which, retained	1.8	2.6
Mortgage	52.7	73.7
Of which, retained	1.4	1.8

[59] S&P report 9 April 2007 and 22 June 2007.
[60] Bear Stearns 10-K filings 2004.

Table 5.6 Size of repo business in Bear Stearns' balance sheet, 2007[61]

	$bn	% Assets
Securities purchased under agreements to resell	27.9	7%
Securities received as collateral	15.6	4%
Securities borrowed	82.2	21%

their initial investment. In some cases, the leverage on these funds even reached 35 times the invested assets. Leverage was obtained at very attractive conditions through the low-cost, short-term "repo" (repurchase agreements) market (see Table 5.6). Bear Stearns would borrow to purchase CDOs and pledge as collateral other CDO tranches. This enabled portfolio returns to be enhanced further. "The thesis behind the fund was that the structured credit markets offered yield over and above what their ratings suggested they should offer,"[62] BSAM Fund Manager Ralph Cioffi was reported as saying. The leverage and risk-taking meant that a CDO achieved a return of between 15% and 23% annually, a level well in excess of a traditional mortgage rate, but this level did not raise any suspicions or concerns.

The returns of the two funds started to suffer in 2006 as the US housing market started to turn, leading to concern from investors and a rapid decline in their confidence.

Bear Stearns' Reputation Weakened by the Collapse of the Funds
Given the size of its exposure and the leverage in the funds, Bear Stearns had limited options to address a worsening market and a growing crisis of confidence. Initially, Bear Stearns' managers tried to sell the most risky securities, but this only depressed the price of what were already illiquid assets, harming the performance of the funds even further. They had no alternative but to attempt to convince investors to remain in the fund.

The CDO business had become an important component of Bear Stearns' business model. Management did not change strategy despite obvious signs that the US housing bubble was beginning to burst. Bear Stearns even continued to build its exposure to the subprime market in late 2006 and early 2007. Selling CDO tranches had become increasingly difficult, so instead they were repackaged into a "CDO-squared" – a CDO of CDOs – with a credit guarantee from a specialised monoline credit insurer. This strategy seemed to buy Bear Stearns a bit of time, but at the cost of an increase in the risk profile. Despite assertions from Bear Stearns executives that the drop in the housing market would be temporary, in fact it was continuing to deteriorate rapidly.

Confidence evaporated. Bear Stearns' investors and counterparties became ever more concerned with the risks to which they were exposed and the threat of losses to come. The link between the underperforming funds and Bear Stearns' own finances presented a real danger to the bank's credit standing and reputation, threatening its access to repo markets. This was disturbing, to say the least. Given the high dependence on external financing for Bear Stearns' own operations, it was crucial to remain creditworthy and preserve its relationships with major trading counterparties.

---

[61] Bear Stearns 10-K filings 2007.
[62] US Congress, The Financial Crisis inquiry report.

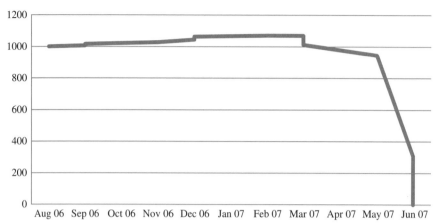

Figure 5.6   Historical Value of Bear Stearns High-Grade Structured Credit Enhanced Leveraged Fund ($ per unit)[63]

In an attempt to stabilise the situation and convince investors not to pull out, on 22 June 2007 Bear Stearns committed its own balance sheet by giving a collateralised loan of $3.2bn. But the funds lost $1.6bn in June and, in July, hundreds of the subprime tranches in their CDOs were put on negative watch by the ratings agencies, in reaction to the continuing deterioration of the housing market. The situation spiralled downwards: expectations of further rating agency actions stoked fears on the value of the assets, leading to panic selling and plummeting prices, with further deterioration in the ability to refinance through repos. On 31 July, both the "High-Grade" and the "Enhanced Leverage" funds filed for bankruptcy, having lost 91% and 100% of their value, respectively (see Figure 5.6).

Deteriorating Asset Quality Threatens Access to Liquidity
The collapse of Bear Stearns' funds revealed to the market that so-called "safe" securities could be of dubious value and the financial system was highly vulnerable to a "death spiral" of accelerated fund redemptions, asset sales, falling prices, loss of counterparty confidence, requirements for more collateral, need to liquidate further the funds' holdings causing further price falls and so on. The effect is similar in nature to a bank run: fearing losses, counterparties such as Goldman Sachs, Lehman Brothers, JP Morgan and Citigroup stopped providing loans to the funds, accelerating the losses and leading to a liquidity crisis.

Contagion Hits Bear Stearns Itself
Beyond the specific case of Bear Stearns, all the dealers in the securities lending market began to revisit their assumptions on the value of the securities that were being lent to them or used as collateral, leading to systemic consequences in the repo market. Volumes dropped as collateral criteria became more restrictive, requiring higher levels of collateralisation or even accepting only government bonds as collateral.

Naturally, after Bear Stearns reported a $1.9bn write-down in November 2007, lenders tightened the criteria on which they were prepared to lend to the bank, charging higher rates

---

[63] Bloomberg.

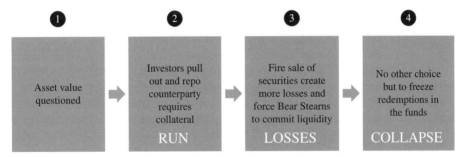

Figure 5.7   Chain of events leading to the liquidity crisis and collapse at Bear Stearns

or requiring more collateral to provide liquidity. Money market funds stopped lending to Bear Stearns and access to the commercial paper became almost impossible. It came to rely heavily on short-term repos, increasing the vulnerability of its operations. Meanwhile, Bear Stearns' exposure to US mortgages remained high at $36bn in February 2008, of which almost $26bn was subprime. Bear Stearns itself came under pressure from the rating agencies and concerns extended into the derivatives market, where Bear Stearns was no longer perceived as a prime counterparty, despite $13,400bn of notional exposure.

All these features began to impact the prime brokerage business, another important pillar of Bear Stearns' business, causing it to lose customer business: assets under management fell from $160bn in April 2007 to $90bn in January 2008. In early 2008, with limited scope to reduce risk and obtain stable funding, the future of Bear Stearns seemed bleak.

The Collapse and Fed Rescue

Moody's downgrading of 15 mortgage-backed securities issued by Bear Stearns Alt-A Trust on 10 March 2008 triggered another liquidity squeeze. Negative rumours regarding Bear Stearns' ability to settle its own trades added to problems. The negative feedback loop continued to worsen. Investors withdrew their funds, with one hedge fund withdrawing $5bn in a single day. Clients reassigned their derivatives to other banks. And several other banks cancelled their credit lines to Bear Stearns, with $500m being pulled by a single bank on 11 March alone.

At this point, Bear Stearns was starting to run out of cash and the Federal Reserve, conscious of the potentially catastrophic damage to other securities firms that a collapse of Bear Stearns would create, responded by putting in place an extraordinary lending facility of $200bn, the Term Securities Lending Facility, designed to give breathing space to the repo market and restore confidence. The next day, Bear Stearns, which was down to its last $2bn of liquidity, received a $12.9bn lifeline from the Fed via JP Morgan. JP Morgan ended up buying Bear Stearns and, as part of the transaction, $30bn worth of Bear Stearns' troubled assets were transferred into a vehicle called "Maiden Lane LLC" owned by the Fed, with JP Morgan investing $1.15bn of subordinated debt.

Lessons to be Learned from this Case Study

Bear Stearns serves as an illustration of the risks of an undiversified business model, in which the performance of subprime-related CDOs was essential to performance and also survival. When the housing market turned, the bank was bound to suffer losses. This business concentration was exacerbated by massive amounts of leverage and extremely vulnerable funding structures. Given such an aggressive strategy, the ability to adapt to a changed macro-economic and market environment was extremely limited. Overall, this case serves as a lesson that risk management is not just about planning for a "base case" – say, stable housing market conditions – but also being resilient to alternative scenarios. Bear Stearns simply wasn't resilient.

5.6 MERRILL LYNCH

Merrill Lynch – created by Charles Merrill and Edward Lynch at the beginning of the twentieth century – built its presence in the international capital markets as a leader in the underwriting and placement of securities through its highly powerful network of investment advisors, known as the "thundering herd". Merrill Lynch played a key role in "bringing Wall Street to Main Street".

A New Business Model, Turning the Page on "Mother Merrill"
The end of the dotcom bubble coincided with a change of management at Merrill Lynch. David Komanski, who had presided over the expansion of the firm as a major underwriter of equity and bonds, retired and was replaced by Stan O'Neal in 2002. The latter drove a profound change in business strategy, exiting low-margin businesses and firing 25,000 people (one-third of the workforce). Unlike his predecessor, Stan O'Neal wanted to position Merrill Lynch as a leader in all areas of investment banking. At the time, Merrill Lynch lagged its key competitors in many areas, such as commodities, private-equity and mortgage securitisation. "Success is often the route of hubris and maybe indulgence; in many respect it's loss of discipline on many fronts," confessed Stan O'Neal proverbially when he took over.[64] It is in this context that Dow Kim, then Co-Head of Global Markets and Investment Banking, identified the CDO business as an attractive growth market. Combining the strength of Merrill Lynch's distribution with the structuring expertise of its capital markets division soon made Merrill Lynch a leader in this field. Revenues in the "Fixed Income Commodities and Currencies" division (FICC), which included CDO structuring, grew 60%, from $5bn in 2004 to $8bn in 2006.[65]

However, the expanding CDO business was faced with a dilemma when the US housing market started to turn in 2006. Merrill Lynch's response was threefold:

- Consider riskier securities.
- Repackage lower-rated tranches of CDOs (into structures known as "CDO-squared").
- Retain a higher portion of the CDOs that could not be placed to outside investors.

In 2006, the disappearance of "real money" investors meant that an ever higher proportion of buyers were CDO managers buying CDOs for their own CDO funds to increase their return. Whilst this concentration made the product even more risky, this did not stop CDO activity, which remained an apparently profitable business and continued to flourish even after AIG stopped insuring senior tranches as the crisis unfolded.

---

[64] Euroweek Stan O'Neal interview, 13 July 2006.
[65] Merrill Lynch 2006 Annual Report.

Table 5.7   Volume of assets securitised by Merrill Lynch[66]

$bn	2005	2006	2007
Residential mortgage loans	58	97	100
Municipal bonds	17	29	56
Corporate, government bonds and commercial loans	16	22	18
Total	91	149	176

Buillding Up of Exposure to Subprime

At the end of 2006, Merrill Lynch's direct exposure to mortgages and ABS had reached $48bn, an increase of $4bn from the year before. But demand for this product slowed towards the end of 2006, as the first concerns appeared on the strength of the US housing market. This led to an increase in the maturity of the mortgages and ABS securities that Merrill Lynch was holding in its portfolio. Merrill's mortgage securitisation machine was still at full steam and continued to add to its risk levels. In 2006 and 2007, Merrill Lynch securitised a total of nearly $200bn of residential mortgages as well as vast amounts of municipal bonds (see Table 5.7).

A decisive step in building Merrill Lynch's leading position in the securitisation of mortgages came with the acquisition of First Franklin Financial Corp in December 2006, giving Merrill direct access to subprime loans and, with it, full control of the mortgage value chain, from origination of the loan, to the structuring, repackaging and distribution. Unfortunately, the change in market conditions that was to come resulted in many of the originated assets being stuck on Merrill Lynch's balance sheet, leading to a rapid and massive build-up of risk and, ultimately, losses.

Net Exposure and Gross Exposure to CDO

Merrill Lynch management was not overly concerned with this build-up of risk. Why was this? We can identify two main drivers. Firstly, the mortgage business was a sizeable revenue contributor, but it was not central to the overall business model, as it was, say, for Bear Stearns. Secondly, many of the retained CDO tranches that Merrill held were rated AAA, which management interpreted as indicating limited downside. These tranches benefited from protection using CDS contracts or insurance from a monoline credit insurer. Whatever the cause for complacency, the effects were staggering: in the face of declining demand, the continuing securitisation activity resulted in an increase in the (notional) value of Merrill Lynch's retained CDO senior tranches from $29bn in May 2007 to $55bn by the end of October 2007.[67]

There is one further explanation for this deadly piling-on of risk, namely the confusion between the *gross* exposure and the *net* exposure to CDOs. At the end of October 2007, Merrill Lynch's exposure in retained CDO tranches was reported as a net exposure of $15bn, but a gross exposure of $55bn. The troubles of Bear Stearns in the summer of 2007 should have alerted Merrill Lynch to the risk related to mortgage CDOs and to the possibility of non-performance of the protection in case of default by the monoline credit insurer. Management appears not have taken this potential ineffectiveness into account, despite it being hinted at in

---

[66] Merrill Lynch 10-K filings.
[67] *All the Devils Are Here: The Hidden History of the Financial Crisis*, Bethany McLean and Joe Nocera, 2010.

Table 5.8   Breakdown of losses in the FICC division[68]

$bn	2007	2008
Write-downs of ABS CDO	16.7	10.2
Write-downs of US subprime mortgages	3.2	10.8
Valuation adjustments from hedge financial guarantors	2.6	10.4
Write-down on subprime securities	0.7	6.5
Total	23.2	37.9

Merrill Lynch's own financial filings: "hedges are affected by a variety of factors that impact their effectiveness. These factors may include differences in attachment points, timing of cash flows, control rights, limited recourse to counterparties and other basis risks."[69]

Losses began to mount during the late summer of 2007. Estimates of CDO losses of $600m at the end of August rose to $1.3bn a few weeks later.[70] As with Bear Stearns a few months prior, Merrill Lynch's inability to sell down its risk positions led to disastrous losses, while increased difficulties in accessing the repo market contributed to weakening the balance sheet.

Record Losses as the Market Turns, Revealing a Massive Exposure to Subprime
The retreat of monoline credit insurers offering protection on super-senior tranches of CDOs during the summer of 2007 revealed the real exposure that Merrill Lynch was facing. Deterioration in the value of super-senior tranches over the summer of 2007 became alarming and led to a write-down of $7.9bn in the third quarter. The mortgage assets continued to be under pressure and, facing a shrinking repo market, Merrill Lynch was forced to reduce its risk and sell assets at a loss. The bank reported a $24.7bn loss related to CDO and subprime losses in 2007, of which $16.7bn related to write-downs on ABS CDOs. The same chain of events continued into 2008 in a deteriorating market, leading to a record loss of $37.9bn – see Table 5.8.

The loss of confidence in Merrill Lynch's credit triggered reassignment of swaps, closure of credit lines and request for more collateral by counterparties, squeezing Merrill Lynch's access to funding.

Loss of Confidence and Liquidity Risk
The amount of short-term funding increased from $100bn to more than $300bn between 2003 and 2007. During the same period, the proportion of short-term borrowing increased from 23% to 31% (peaking at 34% in 2006), weakening Merrill Lynch's balance sheet and increasing further the vulnerability in case of liquidity shock (see Figure 5.8).

Like its peers, Merrill Lynch relied heavily on securities financing (repo). The numbers in Figure 5.9 show the position at the year-end, but also that repo financing was actually higher during the year. For example, the average of repo financing during 2007 was actually $460bn, which is 36% higher than the amount disclosed at year end.

---

[68] Merrill Lynch 10-K filing 2007.
[69] Ibid.
[70] *All the Devils Are Here: The Hidden History of the Financial Crisis*, Bethany McLean and Joe Nocera, 2010.

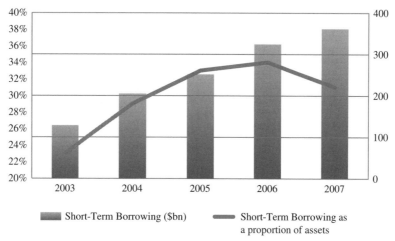

Figure 5.8   Merrill Lynch short-term borrowing[71]

The exposure to subprime had undermined confidence in Merrill Lynch and it became clear to the management at the end of the summer of 2007 that a rescue by another bank was the only option for survival. To this end, Stan O'Neal initiated some discussions with Bank of America's Ken Lewis in September 2007 and later approached Wachovia. These initiatives were rejected by the board, where a sense of disbelief dominated after the revelation of CDO-related losses. Stan O'Neal's tenure at Merrill Lynch ended on 30 October 2007.

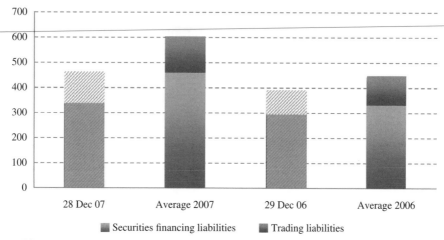

Figure 5.9   Repo – average vs. end of year positions ($bn)

[71] Notice to ML and BofA shareholders, File No. 333-153771, Filed pursuant to Rule 424(b)(3), 31 October 2008.

Merging or Disappearing

A new management team was appointed under John Thain, an ex-Goldman Sachs executive. The clean-up strategy which followed led to the record loss of $27bn for 2008, reflecting the adverse conditions in which the firm was operating. The losses included a $10bn write-down on financial guarantees and the sale of super senior tranches of ABS CDOs with a face value of $30bn for only $6.7bn, for which Merrill Lynch had to provide $5bn of financing to the buyer.[72]

The deterioration of the environment led to the acquisition of Merrill Lynch by Bank of America. The deal averted a contagious collapse. Alone, Merrill Lynch could not survive the loss of confidence, dislocation in the markets and strain on liquidity that was threatening virtually every major bank. The document laying out the reasons for the proposed rescue by Bank of America reveals the level of distress that Merrill Lynch was facing at the time. As a context to the business condition and prospects for Merrill Lynch, it lists the precipitous decline in the share price; the risk of further credit ratings downgrades; the terrible state of the investment banking market in general; the volatile valuations and illiquidity of assets and the problems faced by other, analogous institutions, such as Bear Stearns, Lehman Brothers and AIG.[73]

The "merger" took place officially on 1 January 2009, in a context of mounting losses at Merrill Lynch.

Lessons to be Learned from this Case Study

Merrill Lynch's foolhardy decision to bulk up its CDO business and then to operate along the entire mortgage value chain paved the way for disastrous losses once the decline in the housing market began. Senior management's decision to depart from the historic strategy and franchise and seek out large, risk-free profit streams took the bank into risky territory. The supervisory response to this change of strategy is not clear. High growth rates left behind the organisational ability to assess and manage risk. The sheer size of the exposures at Merrill was staggering – yet management failed to understand the reality of the risks accumulated. This failure was compounded by an inability to recognise the fragility of credit protection from the monoline credit insurers. And credit risks were magnified by aggressive funding structures, such as over-reliance on the repo market. Ultimately, the organisation was also unable to change course to manage the increasing risks in a meaningful way: once the crisis started to unfold, failure was the natural destiny. A high-risk strategy managed as if it were a low-risk strategy grew out of control and blew up the bank.

5.7 AIG

The role of American Insurance Group (AIG) in the subprime debacle begs a legitimate question: how did a venerable insurance company end up playing such a prominent role in a banking crisis?

The Systemic Importance of AIG

The size of AIG's losses, the systemic implications and the size of the rescue package in September 2008 are beyond those of any of Wall Street bank: $13bn of losses in the first half

---

[72] Merrill Lynch Annual Report 2008.

[73] Merrill Lynch's Reasons for the Merger; Recommendation of the Merrill Lynch Board of Directors; Notice of Special Meetings of Stockholders 31 October 2008 SEC File No. 333-153771.

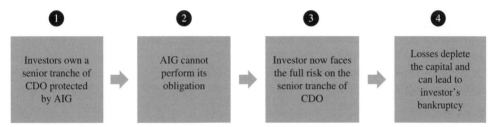

Figure 5.10   Stages in AIG collapse

of 2008, $441bn of CDS written on supposedly risk-free AAA securities, including $58bn of structured debt securities backed by subprime loans. AIG, through its subsidiary AIG Financial Products (AIGFP) had become the counterparty of every player in the structured finance market and its collapse had systemic implications. It was common for investors in super-senior CDOs tranches to require a "credit enhancement" against the risk of default, which credit insurers such as AIG could normally provide at the cost of merely a few basis points. Since AIG enjoyed the superlative AAA rating until recently, the investor would consider that an exposure hedged with AIG was effectively risk-free. Were AIG unable to perform its obligation and pay up for losses incurred, this would affect the risk of the security owned by the investor who will then face a loss. The presence of the credit insurer, in this case AIG, distorted the impression of exactly where the risk was accumulating in the system.

In fact, AIG's collapse was colossal (see Figure 5.10).

- September 2008: $85bn two-year credit facility is extended to AIG via an emergency loan from the Federal Reserve, secured by AIG assets. At the same time, the US Treasury receives warrants for a 79.9% equity stake in AIG, effectively a nationalisation.
- October 2008: Facility extended by $37.8 billion. On 10 November 2008, the day AIG reported a $24.5bn loss, the Treasury decided to purchase $40bn of perpetual preferred shares issued by AIG as part of the Systemically Significant Failing Institutions programme created for AIG inside the TARP. On this same day, the Fed announced that AIG's troubled assets would be transferred into two newly created limited liability companies, Maiden Lane II and Maiden Lane III:
  - Maiden Lane II received a $19.5bn loan from the Fed to purchase $37.8bn of RMBS assets held by AIG in its securities lending portfolio.
  - Maiden Lane III, in contrast, was set up to address the mark-to-market losses on the CDS portfolio through the purchase of the underlying CDOs on which AIG had written protection for an amount of $30bn.

According to the Congressional Oversight Panel,[74] the AIG rescue package used $182bn of taxpayers' money. The bail-out later came under much criticism, but may well have been the only practical response at the time to the all-time record losses of $99bn that AIG posted for the year 2008.

Build-up of a Gigantic Financial Exposure Through AIG Financial Products
As the OTC derivatives market steadily grew before the crisis, AIG found that it could monetise its AAA rating and generate profit by becoming a derivative counterparty. AIG Financial Products, 100%-owned and guaranteed by AIG, was set up in 1998 and gradually became one of the largest derivatives counterparties, with a portfolio reaching $2,700bn in notional

---

[74] Congressional Oversight Panel, 10 June 2010.

Table 5.9 AIG total revenues ($bn)[75]

	2006
General insurance	49.2
Life insurance & retirement services	50.9
Financial services	7.8
Asset management	4.5

assets[76] by September 2008. The build-up of a gigantic derivatives portfolio, notably in CDS, appeared relatively small in the business mix of AIG, since it only accounted for $7.8bn (vs. $49.2bn for General Insurance) or 7% of the total revenues – see Table 5.9. Still, it was the business line that sunk AIG.

AIG's expansion into credit derivatives was fuelled by the development of CDOs designed to repackage subprime assets. The technology needed assets that looked ultra-low-risk. To fit this need, AIG would offer guarantees that would also serve as additional protection for external investors in these tranches and help the subprime repackaging machine; AIG's risk models predicted negligible losses with 99.85% certainty.[77] AIGFP built up CDS exposures of $527bn by end 2007, of which $55bn was written on CDOs containing subprime, as shown in Table 5.10.

Beyond protection offered to external investors on super-senior CDO tranches, another driver behind the development of this activity was the exploitation of loopholes in financial regulation. To put it simply, AIG was not subject to the same regulatory capital requirement as banks, which offered an opportunity for banks to reduce their capital requirements by transferring credit risk to AIG. AIG may have been taking a new risk, but would not be required to put any capital against it. The same amount of risk would remain, but aggregate capital requirements would magically reduce. The most common form of protection offered by AIG was on senior tranches of CDOs and allowed the banks (both in Europe and in the USA) holding these tranches to significantly reduce the regulatory capital they would be required to hold.

Table 5.10 Notional amount of the super-senior credit default swap portfolio in 2007[78]

$bn	Notional amount
Corporate loans	230
Prime residential mortgages	149
Corporate debt/CLOs	70
Multi-sector CDO	78
- o/w exposed to subprime	55
Total	527

---

[75] AIG Annual Report 2007.
[76] US Congress, The Financial Crisis Inquiry report.
[77] US Congressional Oversight Panel, The AIG rescue, its impact on markets and the Government exit strategy, June 2010.
[78] AIG 10-K filing 2007.

Table 5.11   Notional amount of derivatives portfolio[79]

$bn	2006	2007
Interest rate swaps	1,058	1,167
Credit default swaps	484	562
Currency swaps	218	224
Swaptions, equity and commodity swaps	180	179
Total	1,940	2,132

As an indication, purchasing protection from AIG on a super-senior tranche at the cost of a mere few basis points was an attractive transaction, which could reduce capital consumption from 8% to 1.6% of assets. AIG could offer attractive conditions and considered credit derivatives a natural extension of its traditional insurance business into credit risk. The nature of these "regulatory capital" arbitrages was clearly recognised by AIG and grew to reach very high levels: "Approximately $379bn of the $527bn in notional exposure on AIGFP's super-senior credit default swap portfolio as of December 31, 2007 were written to facilitate regulatory capital relief for financial institutions primarily in Europe."[80]

The development of AIGFP was supported by the management and was identified as a healthy source of revenue diversification. It quickly led to the build-up of an enormous portfolio of derivatives of over $2,000bn of notional and an exposure to a variety of assets (credit, currency, commodities, equities, rates) with systemic consequences – see Table 5.11.

AIG had built a portfolio of securities which it would lend to investors in return for cash, investing that cash into fixed-income securities to earn a spread. Through these borrowings, which totalled $69bn at the end of August 2008, AIG had built a direct exposure to CDO and subprime as an investor. It is hard to fathom why, just as AIG was exiting the business of protection of subprime-related CDOs in 2005, it was growing its role in the securities lending market and using the size of its balance sheet to become one of the major players. These transactions created a fragile liquidity profile and exposed AIG to the risk of having to sell the securities in which it had invested or find alternative sources of cash. At the end of 2007, AIG had direct exposure to mortgage-related assets of $140bn and $25bn of direct exposure to Alt-A subprime – see Table 5.12.

Dysfunctional Risk Management and Supervision

2005 was the pivotal year for AIGFP. A rating downgrade is costly for any entity with a large derivative portfolio, as it normally requires the counterparty to increase the collateral against the value of its transactions to secure its obligations and mitigate any risk of its default. For this reason, when Moody's downgraded AIG from Aaa to Aa1 on 31 March 2005, then subsequently to Aa2 on 2 May 2005, it would have been a natural reaction to scale back on the derivative activity and deal with the substantial risk to the business posed by the possibility of a further downgrade. At the same time as demand for CDOs was starting to slow, a number of dissenting voices within AIG started questioning the amount of risk generated from providing CDS protection to subprime mortgage-backed securities.[82] It seemed that certain other, more

---

[79] Ibid.
[80] Ibid.

Table 5.12   AIG available-for-sale securities, 2007[81]

$bn	
Mortgage-backed, asset-backed and collateralised	141
RMBS	90
CMBS	24
CDO/ABS	11
Alt-A	25

nimble, market players knew better than AIG and saw the benefit of hedging against a quickly deteriorating housing market. For example, Goldman Sachs bought protection on its $1.8bn super-senior tranche of "Abacus 2004-1" in the year 2005.

In addition to management failure, the inquiries into the collapse of AIG also revealed a number of issues including:

- Regulatory failure: AIG was overseen by the 50 US state regulators for its traditional insurance business, by the Office of Thrift Supervision (OTS) for Financial Products and the SEC for Asset Management; adding to this complexity, AIG's international operations were under the responsibility of local regulators abroad. The OTS (rather than the Fed) was in charge of the parent company. Designed to supervise thrifts, it lacked the resources for such a complex group and its management later confessed it "did not foresee the extent of risk concentration and profound systemic impact caused by AIG".[83]
- Weak risk management systems unable to monitor the consolidated risk from AIG's complex cross-border operations and ignorant of the correlation between AIG's CDS portfolio and securities lending business.[84]
- Lack of preparedness for the management of the liquidity requirements in its derivative portfolio.
- Complexity of the cross-shareholdings and guarantees within the group and the absence of leadership, which played an important part in the lack of *strategic* reaction to an environmental shift that had sent risk levels soaring.

Despite their apparent similarities (payment of a premium by the buyer of a CDS, protection against losses by the seller), CDS and insurance contracts behave very differently, due to the specific nature of credit risk versus traditional insurance ("property-and-casualty") risk. Normally, an insurance company will set aside enough liquidity and capital to respond to losses according to probability of occurrence. Few property-and-casualty risks are highly correlated. In the case of AIG's credit protection insurance, however, there was a high level of concentration on the mortgage market, especially through senior tranches of CDOs; these proved to be highly correlated, turning when the housing market started to collapse. Maybe the misperception of correlation is why AIG kept expanding its credit protection business after 2005 and why the management of AIGFP chose not to see the consequences of a downturn in the housing market: "It is hard for us [...] to even see a scenario of any kind of realm or reason

---

[81] Ibid.

[82] The Financial Crisis Inquiry report, US Financial Crisis Inquiry Commission, January 2011.

[83] Acting OTS Director Scott Polakoff, US Congressional Oversight Panel, The AIG rescue, its impact on markets and the Government exit strategy, June 2010.

[84] US Congressional Oversight Panel, The AIG rescue, its impact on markets and the Government exit strategy, June 2010.

that would see us losing $1 in any of those transactions."[85] Amazingly, through the whole of 2007, AIG remained confident in its business model and did not seem to be concerned by the risk in its balance sheet. Increasing subprime-related losses at almost every Wall Street bank in Q3 2007 does not seem to have caused any reappraisal or reorientation of the business. Despite a loss of $11.5bn on the super-senior credit default swap portfolio in the 2007 accounts, the confidence of AIG's management seemed intact: "Based upon its most current analysis, AIG believes that any losses that are realized over time on the super senior credit default swap portfolio of AIGFP will not be material to AIG's overall financial condition."[86]

AIG was a well-diversified insurance group that could rely on traditional lines of business to generate revenues. The management belief in the virtue of diversification seemed entrenched until the first quarter of 2008 when referring to the Financial Services as a "strong performer and an important component of AIG's diverse portfolio of businesses", able to "complement [our] core insurance operations".[87] Running a huge risk exposure supported by shareholders' equity of $95bn, AIG had overlooked the amount of risk contained in a relatively small subset of its operations.

A Relatively Small Portfolio at the Source of the Collapse of the Insurance Giant

The Great Fire of London in 1666 started as a small fire in a bakery. The losses at AIG, likewise, have a narrow source, a few specific contracts in the multisector CDO portfolio which brought the whole company to bankruptcy. To put these numbers into perspective, at the end of 2007, the CDS portfolio was $527bn out of a total derivatives portfolio of $2,660bn. Within the $527bn, there was $149bn classified as "Arbitrage CDS" which was responsible for 99% of the losses. Drilling down, the multisector CDO, which was a subcomponent of the Arbitrage CDS portfolio, had a notional exposure of $70bn and was the source of 90% of the losses through no more than 125 contracts (out of 44,000 contracts) – see Figure 5.11.[88]

The Spark in September 2008: Rating Downgrade

For a while, AIG was confident that the losses were only "mark-to-market" and did not necessarily imply a future loss. The issue was more with the collateral requirements following the downgrade of CDOs on which AIG had written protection: since the asset had become (apparently) more risky, it had lost fair value and AIG was required to mobilise collateral to guarantee the protection. According to AIG's filings, the combination of a continuing decline in value of the super-senior CDO and the rating downgrades on these securities during July and August 2008 resulted in a collateral posting by AIGFP of $6bn. "By the beginning of September 2008, these collateral postings and securities lending requirements were placing increasing stress on AIG parent's liquidity."[89]

Events accelerated on 12 September 2008, when loss of confidence shut the access to commercial paper and added more pressure from repo lenders. In this context, warnings of rating downgrade triggered expectations of a liquidity crisis. The collateral amounts, as we saw earlier, depend also on the credit quality of the counterparty who has written the protection. The downgrade from AA- to A- by S&P and from Aa3 to A2 by Moody's was confirmed on 15 September 2008 and immediately translated into an additional need for collateral of $20bn, sealing the fate of AIG. Not

---

[85] J. Cassano, head of AIGFP, AIG Q2 2007 Earnings Call Transcript.
[86] AIG 2007 Annual Report.
[87] Ibid.
[88] US Congressional Oversight Panel, The AIG rescue, its impact on markets and the Government exit strategy, June 2010.
[89] AIG 10-Q filings Q3 2008.

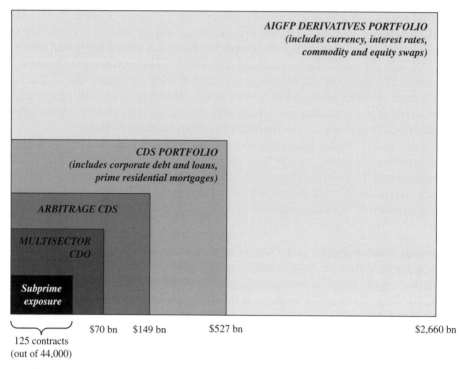

Figure 5.11   Drill-down into AIGFP Derivatives Portolio, end 2007[90]

only was AIG hit by the plunging value of the assets on which it had extended protection, but the rating downgrade had exacerbated its liquidity problems in a fragile market. As a result, the need for collateral increased from only $2bn at the end of 2007 to $32bn in Q3 2008 (Table 5.13).

As if matters could not be worse, in the second quarter of 2008, AIG had written "maturity shortening puts" to allow certain CDOs to be eligible for money market funds (2a-7 funds, to be precise) which carry restrictions on the maximum maturity of the instrument. Offering to buy these instruments would artificially reduce their maturity and make them eligible. These options, which AIG had written for a notional of $9.4bn, were all exercised when the market value of these securities collapsed.

The Abyss and the Rescue

The systemic importance of AIG's liquidity crisis is best represented by the amount of collateral posted to major financial players and which would have represented a loss if AIG had defaulted. It is likely that the losses at the level of each of the counterparties would have triggered a chain of default and global meltdown of the financial system. AIG's collateral posting to credit default swap counterparties included $4.1bn to Société Générale, $2.6bn to Deutsche Bank, $2.5bn to Goldman Sachs, $1.8bn to Merrill Lynch and $1.1bn to Calyon from the period 16 September 2008 to 31 December 2008.

Nonetheless, the conditions surrounding the bail-out of AIG have raised issues related to the use of taxpayers' money to guarantee financial institutions who would otherwise have taken a loss on their subprime exposure.

---

[90] AIG 10-K filing 2007.

Table 5.13 Counterparty collateral demand on CDS portfolio[91]

$bn	Collateral
Q4 2007	2
Q1 2008	9
Q2 2008	13
September 2008	18.9
Q3 2008	32

Lessons to be Learned from this Case Study

AIG built a truly low-risk insurance business that merited a superlative credit rating. Its expansion into banking was less astute. The case of AIG shows us the dangers of "picking up nickels in front of a steamroller", in other words risking disaster while making a small fee with low expected loss. Management failed to anticipate the decline of the US housing market or even take such a possibility into account. Their assessment of risk correlation was all wrong. Their strategy and organisation showed an inability to adapt. More than anything, the AIG case shows us the dangers of blatant regulatory arbitrage, whereby vast risk positions can be accumulated *under the nose of the regulators and investors, not behind their backs*, with little supervision or capital requirements. In the end, the protection offered by the monoline credit insurers was largely worthless, but their presence contributed to the troubles of the banking industry. To avoid "another AIG", we need to ensure that the structural failings of the industry are addressed.

5.8 JP MORGAN

JP Morgan was one of the banks that was weathering well the current financial crisis, its reputation as a "rock" for the financial system staying virtually unscathed, at least until May 2012. JP Morgan is the largest bank in the USA with 259,000 employees, a diversified range of operations, a strong capital base (stockholder equity of $204bn at the end of 2012) and an exceptional ability to grow through external acquisitions. Total net revenue for 2012 reached $97bn and net income $21bn. JP Morgan is the result of many historic mergers and acquisitions including, as a consequence of the subprime crisis, Bear Stearns and Washington Mutual.

This case study focuses on the recent losses at JP Morgan's Chief Investment Office (CIO) division. What distinguishes the losses of the CIO from the troubles faced by other banks is not only that they involve one of the most highly regarded players, nor the magnitude of the losses, but the fact that they occur nearly four years after the calamitous events of 2008 and following many years of supposed improvements in the risk management disciplines of the banking industry. In the words of the *New York Times* editorial board: "Recklessness, tied to speculation in derivatives, still pervades the banking system and still puts the public at risk. [...] JP Morgan saga is a reminder that big banks are too big to fail, to manage, to regulate and to prosecute."[92]

---

[91] US Congressional Oversight Panel, The AIG rescue, its impact on markets and the Government exit strategy, June 2010.
[92] *New York Times*, 21 March 2013.

A Recognised Leader in Risk Management

JP Morgan, one of the world's strongest banks, played a pivotal role in the rescue of many failed institutions during the crisis, either to structure a lending facility for AIG when approached by the US Treasury, or help the consolidation to avoid the bankruptcy of one of its competitors and to stabilise the financial system (Bear Stearns, Washington Mutual).

In contrast to all the failed institutions, JP Morgan was considered a well-run, prudent and well-diversified institution. This expertise, widely recognised by the industry, has won JP Morgan many awards including:

- Derivatives House of the Year (*Risk* magazine, 2012).
- Equity Derivatives House of the Year (*Risk* magazine, 2012).
- Commodity and Energy Derivatives House of the Year (*Risk* magazine, 2012).
- Commodity Derivatives House of the Year (*IFR*, 2011).
- Best Bank for Credit Derivatives and Credit Derivatives Research (*Credit* magazine, 2011).

JP Morgan itself was a pioneer in many of the risk management tools, including the development of the Value-at-Risk (VaR) methodology for trading risk, and offers advisory services in risk management to its clients. JP Morgan's approach to risk is best described with its own words:

> Generally speaking, a robust risk management framework is based on five essential components: a strong corporate governance that diffuses a positive risk culture from the top to the bottom of the organisation, a coherent and exhaustive set of policies and procedures, the technological capability to extract data about the organisation's performance and the risk of its uncertain environment, know-how in measuring this uncertainty, and finally, its ability to monitor risk on an ongoing basis in order to optimise the risk taking process.[93]

Specifics of the CIO

JP Morgan established the CIO as a separate entity in 2005, acting like a dedicated fund manager reporting directly to the senior management. As of 31 December 2011, it had 428 employees, consisting of 140 traders and 288 back office staff.[94]

The CIO's primary responsibility was to balance out some of the credit risk that JP Morgan was naturally accumulating in its role as a lender and actively manage risk-weighted assets (RWA). But it also had the responsibility to manage the excess between JP Morgan's deposits and loans and engage in long-term investments with the objective of generating revenues at the Treasury level. At the end of 2012, the size of the portfolio invested by the CIO amounted to about $360bn. These numbers are consistent with JP Morgan's consolidated balance sheet, which shows an excess of deposits over loans (see Table 5.14).[95]

The CIO is separate from the bank's Treasury and invests excess cash in government bonds, agencies, mortgage-backed securities, high quality securities, corporate debt and other

---

[93] Setting up a sound risk management framework, Romain Berry, JP Morgan Investment Analytics and Consulting, June 2008.

[94] JP Morgan Chase Whale Trades: a case history of derivatives risks and abuses, US Senate, 15 March 2013.

[95] JP Morgan 2012 Annual Report.

Table 5.14   Key balance sheet items: JP Morgan

$bn	2012	2011
Total assets	2,359	2,266
Loans	734	724
Deposits	1,194	1,128
Excess deposits	460	404

domestic and overseas assets.[96] In 2006, the CIO started trading synthetic credit derivatives, which led to the establishment of the Synthetic Credit Portfolio (SCP), whose notional positions grew rapidly from $4bn in 2008 to $51bn in 2011.[97] The SCP was where all the losses took place and was a relatively small subset of the CIO's total portfolio. Most of CIO's other assets comprised of $323bn of available-for-sale securities with an average rating of AA+, as well as $175bn deposited at central banks, all run quite conservatively.[98]

The SCP was designed to protect "the company against a systemic event, like the financial crisis or Eurozone situation"[99] and "generate modest returns in a benign credit environment and more substantial returns in a stressed environment".[100]

The SCP's trades involved a credit default swap index based on the default risk of major US corporations, but its problems were actually to do with the environment in which the transactions were executed, which CEO Dimon described as "flawed, complex, poorly reviewed, poorly executed, and poorly monitored".

The CIO managed a large volume of risk, more than the entire trading platform of JP Morgan's investment bank. Looking at VaR measures as an illustration, the CIO's average VaR was $69m in Q4 2011 and $67m in Q1 2012,[101] whereas the investment bank's VaR was $57m in Q4 2011 and $63m in Q1 2012.

Expansion of the SCP beyond Control

For most of 2011, the SCP was positioned "short credit", which means it would benefit in an environment where credit losses occur, reflecting JP Morgan's views on the economy (economic recession, crisis in the Eurozone, cut in public spending etc.). While these trading positions protected JP Morgan against a deterioration in the credit environment, especially in the more risky segment (High Yield), they also attracted a capital charge and added to the Group's RWA. At the end of 2011, due to an improvement in economic conditions combined with a desire by the senior management to reduce RWA in response to the upcoming Basel 3 regulations, the SCP was asked to reduce its "short credit" orientation and rebalance its portfolio to a more "neutral" position.

---

[96] Testimony of Jamie Dimon Chairman & CEO, JP Morgan Chase & Co. Before the U.S. Senate Committee on Banking, Housing and Urban Affairs, 13 June 2012.
[97] JP Morgan Chase Whale Trades: a case history of derivatives risks and abuses, US Senate, 15 March 2013.
[98] Testimony of Jamie Dimon Chairman & CEO, JP Morgan Chase & Co. Before the U.S. Senate Committee on Banking, Housing and Urban Affairs, 13 June 2012.
[99] Ibid.
[100] Ibid.
[101] JP Morgan Chase Whale Trades: a case history of derivatives risks and abuses, US Senate, 15 March 2013.

Table 5.15   SCP revenues by year ($m)[102]

2008	170
2009	1,050
2010	149
2011	453

At the same time, the management reiterated the importance of generating profit through the CIO trading activities, especially after the completion of a few highly successful bets using relatively low-cost default protection. Anticipating corporate defaults seemed like a low-risk, low-cost, high-reward business and the CIO increased the purchase protection on specific names or indices to position the trading book to generate profit out of the situations it had identified. The profitability of the SCP was volatile at best: for example, almost all the results in 2011 were driven by one single bet, on American Airlines, which netted $400m profit for a total of $453m for the year – see Table 5.15.

The SCP started implementing a rebalancing of the portfolio through the building of an Investment Grade exposure. Putting in place a "long" Investment Grade the "short" High Yield allowed the achievement of a risk neutral position at the end of January 2012. It is unclear whether this superposition of risk helped reduce the RWA metric, but it is certain that it added more risk to the portfolio.

Why did traders at the SCP not simply cancel or significantly reduce the existing "short" High Yield position by purchasing long positions? It would have been more efficient from a pure risk standpoint, but traders at the SCP believed in the benefits of the "short" positioning on the more risky credits to benefit from specific bankruptcies and generate profits.

In the first quarter of 2012, the "neutralisation" translated into an increase of notional of the SCP from $51bn to $157bn.[103] The size of the position achieved was clearly not standard for the market, which normally operates in transactions or "clips" of $250m. Transactions of $500m stand out; anything of $1bn and over clearly moves the market and starts to attract attention. Such large transactions were quite rare, until one counterparty happened to accumulate a very large position, trading several clips of $1bn per day and raising suspicion that it was trying to "corner" the market.

The CIO had entered these positions in an exceptionally short period of time, with $40bn in the month of March alone – see Table 5.16. This started to impact overall market trading conditions. These transactions did not go unnoticed and a number of experienced market participants started to wonder about the identity of the trader, who was soon to be nicknamed "the London whale". A story appeared in the press[104] unveiling the role of JP Morgan's CIO in these trades.

The graph in Figure 5.12 illustrates the sudden increase in the volume of contracts outstanding on the index CX.NA.IG.9, which more than doubled in size from a notional of $60bn to nearly $150bn in just a few months between December 2011 and April 2012, distorting the market and leading other dealers to wonder whether a participant was not simply trying to "corner" the market.

---

[102] Ibid.
[103] Ibid.
[104] London Whale Rattles Debt Market, *Wall Street Journal*, 6 April 2012.

Table 5.16   JP Morgan CIO positions in March 2012 ($bn)[105]

US IG credit index	62
European IG credit index	71
US HY credit index	22
Total	155

The trend continued and, whilst the portfolio may have been described as "risk neutral", it was not balanced and was, in fact, heavily exposed to a convergence of the risk between High Yield and Investment Grade risks. To illustrate this, at the end of 2011, the "long High Yield" position and the "short Investment Grade" position did not move at a similar pace, which resulted in a net loss for the SCP:

Tightening spreads in High Yield:	$575 million loss
Widening spreads in Investment Grade:	$50 million profit
Net Result	*$525 million loss*

During February 2012, losses at the SCP increased by $69m.[106] At the end of March 2012, the mark-to-market loss on the portfolio had reached $718m (see Figure 5.13). Further worsening of the situation and rumours following press articles left no other option to the management but to file an 8-K report containing information about the first quarter results on 13 April 2012, followed by a conference call.

In summary, the decision to reduce risk in early 2012, using the words of JP Morgan's CEO, had "morphed into something that, rather than protecting the firm, created new and potentially larger risks".[107] The losses were not the result of rogue trading, but rather strategies wrongly executed, and raise serious questions of risk management and control of the CIO activity.

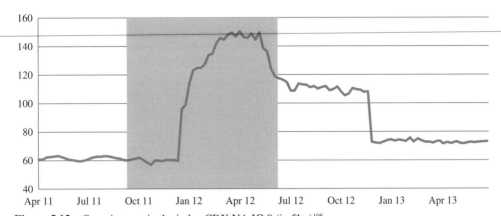

Figure 5.12   Open interest in the index CDX.NA.IG.9 (in $bn)[108]

[105] Ibid.
[106] Report of JP Morgan Chase & Co. Management Task Force Regarding 2012 CIO Losses January 2013.
[107] Testimony of Jamie Dimon Chairman & CEO, JP Morgan Chase & Co. Before the U.S. Senate Committee on Banking, Housing and Urban Affairs, 13 June 2012.
[108] Markit.

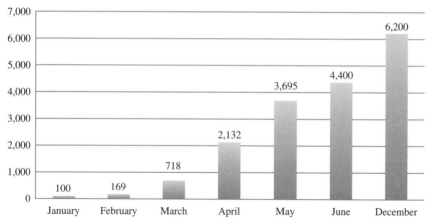

Figure 5.13   Mark-to-market losses of the SCP (2012, $m)

Governance and Risk Management Failures

JP Morgan's CEO further admitted that: "CIO, particularly the Synthetic Credit Portfolio, should have gotten more scrutiny from both senior management, and I include myself in that, and the Firm-wide Risk control function … Make sure that people on risk committees are always asking questions, sharing information, and that you have very, very granular limits when you're taking risk … In the rest of the company we have those disciplines in place. We didn't have it here."[109]

The losses have led to a comprehensive discussion and disclosures by JP Morgan on the failures in conception, execution of the trading strategy and escalation of the issues.[110] But transaction execution and a misreading of the market by themselves would not have produced these effects if the risk control procedures had been more prominent at the CIO, as they were in other areas of the bank. In reality, the controls and oversight of CIO in 2012 seemed weak when compared to the importance and complexity of its activities.

Organisational Issues at the CIO Risk Management

CIO Risk Management lacked the personnel and structure necessary to manage the risks of the Synthetic Credit Portfolio. With respect to personnel, a new CIO Chief Risk Officer was appointed in early 2012. He was still getting to grips with the role at the precise time the traders were building the ultimately problematic positions. More broadly, the CIO Risk function had been historically understaffed, and some of the CIO Risk personnel lacked the requisite skills. With respect to structural issues, the CIO Risk Committee met only infrequently, and its regular attendees did not include personnel from outside CIO.

Risk Modelling

The SCP breached its VaR limits more than 330 times between January and April 2012,[111] but these alerts did not stop the increase of risk. As early as February, the loss using the Comprehensive Risk Measure was estimated at $6.3bn.[112] Traders considered the risk measurement as flawed and challenged the results, which they claim overstated the risk.

---

[109] Ibid.

[110] Report of JP Morgan Chase & Co. Management Task Force Regarding 2012 CIO Losses, JP Morgan, January 2013.

Traders eventually secured the adoption of a new CIO VaR model for the SCP, whose effect was to "immediately lower the SCP VaR by 50%".[113] The old model reported a VaR of $129m during the first quarter of 2012, whereas the new model estimated $67m.

The JP Morgan management task force concluded in its exhaustive post-mortem of the CIO losses[114] that there were six main reasons for the risk management failures:

1. Lack of historic problems meant that CIO was not a focus.
2. CIO was overlooked because it was not a client-facing business.
3. CIO was perceived to be low-risk, dealing only in the best quality instruments.
4. SCP was relatively small within the CIO.
5. Risk measures (such as VaR) were managed down and so risk signals (such as rapid increase in VaR) were suppressed.
6. The risk organisation was poor ("the CIO Risk Committee met only three times in 2011").

Legal Proceedings
In addition to the market losses and reputational damage from the CIO episode, JP Morgan has recently faced legal action for violating securities laws. It has been fined a total of $1bn by various regulators ($300m by the OCC, $221m by the UK FCA, $200m by the SEC/Federal Reserve and $100m by the CFTC). The CFTC referred to JP Morgan's traders' behavior as "recklessly aggressive" in the statement published on 16th October 2013. Legal provisions of $9bn resulted in JP Morgan booking a net loss in Q3 2013.

Lessons to be Learned from this Case Study
These losses may have harmed JP Morgan's reputation, but have never threatened its existence. Ironically, the "London whale" episode has affected the wider banking industry more than JP Morgan itself and given further arguments to proponents of structural measures to curb the trading activities of banks. Clearly, risk is present even in the best run banks. Any long/short strategy carries basis risk and huge market positions can get out of control. Even the best run banks can get it wrong. Management, supervision and oversight of banks can be misguided or blindfolded. In a word, despite the lessons of the subprime crisis, risk in banking has by no means been eliminated or tamed. The truth may be that the risk management and supervisory lessons of recent history have not yet been absorbed or the fixes fully implemented.

5.9 BARCLAYS

During the last 20 years, Barclays has sailed close to the wind. Having survived severe property-related losses in the early 1990s, it built up its risk-management capabilities to become one of the most sophisticated banks in the world. At the end of the 1990s, it lost money in the Russian default and hacked away at its investment banking presence, closing down BZW and allowing the remains to be born again as Barclays Capital, commonly known as "BarCap". It was BarCap that came to dominate Barclays' business, organisation and profitability.

[111] JP Morgan Chase Whale Trades: a case history of derivatives risks and abuses, US Senate, 15 March 2013.
[112] Ibid.
[113] Ibid.
[114] Report of JP Morgan Chase & Co. Management Task Force Regarding 2012 CIO Losses, JP Morgan, January 2013.

Barclays Risk Exposures were High, but it has Survived the Financial Crisis

From an operating profit of £575m in the year 2000 out of a total Barclays Group profit of £3,771m, BarCap grew to £2,216m out of a total of £7,136m in 2006. Whilst the rest of the Barclays Group had grown its profit by a factor of 1.54× over these six years, BarCap's was 3.85×.

BarCap's focus was the business of loans, bonds and derivatives: unlike its competitors, it had no resources in stockbroking or corporate finance. This intense focus enabled it to build a top-tier business and market-leading positions in US mortgages, leveraged finance, CLOs, SIVs and conduits. In its retail business, Barclays had expanded into Spain, Italy and Ireland. In short, Barclays was exposed heavily to most of the businesses that suffered (and are suffering) the most during the financial crisis.

Despite being – arguably – in the wrong place at the wrong time, shrewd management allowed Barclays to avoid nationalisation by the UK government and even use of the Asset Protection Scheme. Instead, Barclays raised capital by attracting new strategic investors (diluting existing shareholders heavily: there was an increase in the number of shares from 6.5bn in 2006 to 12.5bn in 2011[115]) and thus remained independent, against the odds it seemed at some points. The management even had the audacity to acquire Lehman's in the USA.

Sir Mervyn King, Governor of the Bank of England, later told the Treasury Select Committee that Barclays had "been sailing too close to the wind across a wide number of areas".[116] This has now resulted in the downfall of the entire management team in a series of scandals and a consequent strategic review that will no doubt lead to wide-ranging changes.

In April 2007, Barclays announced that it was planning to buy the underperforming Dutch bank, ABN Amro, for €67bn, including the sale of ABN Amro's American subsidiary, LaSalle Bank, to Bank of America for €21bn. The deal would result in an Anglo-Dutch banking group owned jointly by the existing shareholders of ABN Amro and Barclays, headquartered in the Netherlands but incorporated and regulated in the UK. The business combination offered Barclays a "significant opportunity to accelerate our strategy"[117] of consolidation and diversification, alongside synergies of some €3.5bn per annum, justifying the 33% bid premium. The offer was subsequently trumped by RBS, which offered €72bn. Barclays announced that it had obtained commitments from two new strategic investors, China Development Bank and Temasek of Singapore, and raised its ABN Amro offer slightly (to €67.5bn) in July 2007 but withdrew it just over two months later. The ABN Amro bullet was dodged (only to hit RBS later in the year, as the poor state of the ABN Amro asset book became clear).

Now firmly on the acquisition path, Barclays sought to buy Lehman Brothers and played a starring role in the final days of that institution. In the end, the deal was not consummated, but Barclays later decided to acquire Lehman Brothers' broker/dealer operations in the USA, with the associated infrastructure and about 10,000 employees. The operation included trading assets with a then estimated value of $72bn and trading liabilities with a then estimated value of $68bn, and total cash consideration was $250m.[118] The transaction appears to have been very good value, with manageable financial risk for Barclays.

---

[115] Barclays plc annual reports.
[116] BBC News reporting, 17 July 2012.
[117] Combination of ABN AMRO and Barclays, Barclays, 23 April 2007.
[118] Barclays announces agreement to acquire Lehman Brothers North American investment banking and capital markets businesses, Barclays Bank plc, Wednesday 17 September 2008.

A Number of Bold Moves Affecting Reputation

As well as these major acquisitions, of which thankfully only one went ahead, Barclays has been the centre of a series of topical episodes and even scandals during the current financial crisis.

- In 2008, Barclays was forced to recapitalise, to cover losses from the financial crisis and bolster its regulatory capital position. In order to avoid seeking government aid, Barclays turned to strategic investors from overseas to take part in a capital increase, including investors in Qatar. This capital raising is the subject of much controversy and is currently the subject of a criminal investigation by the Serious Fraud Office. Much of the controversy revolves around payments made in relation to capital raising. For example, Barclays noted in June 2008: "Barclays is also pleased to have entered into an agreement for the provision of advisory services by Qatar Investment Authority to Barclays in the Middle East."[119] Later that year, as part of its £7.3bn capital raising, Barclays paid some £300m in fees, including £66m to Qatar Holding.
- Further pressure was put on Barclays' capital position when other banks disclosed losses. For example, "Sandy Chen, an analyst at Panmure Gordon, said the vast loss unveiled by RBS yesterday 'implies that Barclays has significantly further to go in terms of recognising mark-to-market losses, especially on its leveraged loans, commercial real estate, monolines and other structured credits portfolios.'"[120]
- In June 2009, Barclays sold its asset management subsidiary BGI to Blackrock for £8.2bn, representing a gain on sale of £5.3bn. The primary goal was to "realise immediate and substantial value for BGI".[121] This disposal helped Barclays plug its capital hole.
- On 16 September 2009, Barclays announced an aggressive financial restructuring of $12.3bn of subprime-related credit market assets by selling them at "current fair value" to Protium Finance LP. Protium was an SPV run by former Barclays staff and funded with with $450m of equity capital from certain investors and a loan from Barclays of $12.6bn.[122] Because loans are not marked-to-market, the transaction would reduce the volatility of accounting earnings from the portfolio. The egregious financial structure of Protium caused some concern in the industry and Protium was unwound a little over a year later. The Protium transaction "damaged Barclays' reputation in the eyes of its regulators and the market" and was "a mis-judgment by Barclays management and the Board as to the potential damage to the bank's reputation in taking an approach which, as it turned out, tended to confirm sceptical attitudes to Barclays assets and their valuations".[123]
- Alongside several of its retail banking peers in the UK, Barclays was forced to provide redress to customers who had paid for Payment Protection Insurance (PPI). During 2011 and 2012, Barclays took provisions for PPI redress of £2bn.

---

[119] SEC Form 6-K, Barclays plc, June 2008.

[120] *The Telegraph*, 20 January 2009.

[121] Barclays announces receipt of binding offer of $13.5 billion (£8.2 billion) by BlackRock for BGI, 12 June 2009.

[122] Barclays announces the restructuring of $12.3bn of credit market assets, Barclays plc, 16 September 2009.

[123] Salz Review: An Independent Review of Barclays' Business Practices, Barclays plc, April 2013.

- The tax-structuring business (called "Structured Capital Markets" or SCM) has recently been identified as contributing some £1bn per annum to Barclays' revenues.[124] The unit was apparently involved in transactions that employed aggressive – though legal, in the strictest sense of the word – interpretation of the tax rules. Barclays has recently announced, as part of its strategic review, that SCM is being closed, since its activities are "incompatible with our purpose".[125]
- Barclays has also been implicated in the misselling of interest rate hedging products, again alongside several other UK peers. Small businesses were found by the FSA to have been sold products inappropriately and the banks have agreed to make good any losses to customers: "Redress must be fair and reasonable in each case. Redress should aim to put customers back in the position they would have been in had the breach of regulatory requirements not occurred."[126] The provision taken in 2012's financials for the potential costs of redress was £850m.[127] At this stage, it is difficult to assess whether the ultimate bill for Barclays might be far greater.

More recently, Barclays became the first bank to reach a settlement with the authorities on the issue of manipulation of LIBOR. The US Department of Justice noted how Barclays had sought to improve market perceptions by deliberately lowering its reported cost of funding:

> A news article questioned Barclays's liquidity position, in light of Barclays' high LIBOR submissions and its visits to the Bank of England's window, and noted that Barclays's share price had fallen. Senior managers within Barclays expressed concern about the negative publicity. The managers on the money markets desk and in the treasury department who gave the instruction to submit lower LIBORs, which resulted in improperly low LIBOR submissions, sought to avoid inaccurate, negative attention about Barclays's financial health as a result of its high LIBOR submissions relative to other banks. Those managers wanted to prevent any adverse conclusions about Barclays's borrowing costs, and more generally, its financial condition, because they believed that those conclusions would be mistaken and that other Contributor Panel banks were submitting unrealistically low Dollar LIBORs.[128]

The LIBOR scandal gave a very bad impression of Barclays' business practices. Investigations uncovered damning materials, which were published, much to Barclays' embarrassment, such as:

> For example, on 26 October 2006, an external trader made a request for a lower three month US dollar LIBOR submission. The external trader stated in an email to Trader G at Barclays "If it comes in unchanged I'm a dead man". Trader G responded that he would "have a chat". Barclays' submission on that day for three month US dollar LIBOR was half a basis point lower than the day before, rather than being unchanged. The external trader thanked Trader G for Barclays' LIBOR submission later that day: "Dude. I owe you big time! Come over one day after work and I'm opening a bottle of Bollinger."[129]

---

[124] Ibid.
[125] Becoming the "Go-To" bank, Barclays PLC, 12 February 2013.
[126] Interest Rate Hedging Products: Pilot Findings, FSA, March 2013.
[127] 2012 Results, Barclays plc, 12 February 2013.
[128] Barclays Bank PLC Admits Misconduct Related to Submissions for the London Interbank Offered Rate and the Euro Interbank Offered Rate and Agrees to Pay $160 Million Penalty: Statement of Facts, US Department of Justice, 27 June 2012.
[129] FSA Final Notice to Barclays, 27 June 2012.

The LIBOR scandal proved to be a critical blow for Barclays. As well as the immediate fines, totalling some £290m, Barclays faces potential civil suits from aggrieved customers whose products were priced with LIBOR as the reference rate. Most damagingly, however, is the impact on Barclays' reputation and the questions that the scandals raise about its corporate culture and strategy.

Rebounding with a Cultural Change

In July 2012, Barclays witnessed the resignation of Bob Diamond (CEO and President), Jerry del Missier (COO) and Marcus Agius (Chairman). Jerry del Missier had been appointed COO only in June 2012, saying that "we intend to make Barclays the industry benchmark for operational excellence and control in the new economic and regulatory environment. I look forward to working in close partnership with colleagues across Barclays to ensure that we continue to exceed our customers' and clients' expectations at every instance, while delivering on our commitments to our shareholders, regulators and broader stakeholders."[130] These words seem highly ironic now.

Barclays appointed a new CEO, Antony Jenkins, and commissioned the Salz review to explore and address the deep-rooted cultural drivers of its woes. In the middle of 2013, the UK regulator announced that it had identified a substantial capital deficiency at Barclays equivalent to £12.8bn, based on the application of a modified form of the Basel leverage ratio. Barclays has subsequently set out its plans to raise capital (£5.8bn of new stock and £2bn of high quality hybrid capital) and deleverage, in order to improve solvency based on this metric.[131] Some have viewed this regulatory action as a "parting shot" from the outgoing management of the Bank of England, whose reputation had suffered in part due to events at Barclays.

Lessons to be Learned from this Case Study

A sophisticated and respected universal bank managed to escape from the multiple perils that were centred around the markets where it was a leader. Management was able to react and adapt, finding solutions when trouble was encountered. But an increasingly aggressive corporate culture and aggressive financial transactions created risks that eventually led to a change in management and, potentially, strategy. "Sailing too close to the wind" is an exciting but risky business.

5.10 UBS

For many years, UBS was considered one of the greatest and safest banks in the world. In the early 2000s, UBS delivered a steady accounting net income of some CHF6bn, equivalent to an ROE of around 20%. Its market capitalisation peaked at CHF150bn in 2007.

In the decade prior to 2007, UBS' culture of strong risk management was famous:

> UBS has a well-deserved reputation for risk management which can be traced back to its acquisition of the derivatives firm of O'Connor in the mid-1990s. Several of our analyst friends noted that the bank seemed to have dodged all of the major bullets flying about in global banking in the past few years.[132]

---

[130] Jerry del Missier appointed Chief Operating Officer, Barclays, 22 June 2012.
[131] Barclays PLC Announces Leverage Plan, Barclays PLC, 30 July 2013.
[132] *Excellence in Banking – Revisited!*, Steven I. Davis, 2004.

Largely due to this strong risk management culture, on the eve of the financial crisis UBS had credit ratings of AA+ from S&P and Fitch and Aa2 from Moody's. Its credit ratings are now A from S&P and Fitch and A2 from Moody's – a slip of three to four notches. The value of one UBS share has fallen from a peak of CHF80 per share in 2007 to a mere CHF15 in early 2013. The market capitalisation of UBS is now around CHF60bn, despite raising substantial new capital to make up for losses during the financial crisis of around CHF50bn. How did this happen?

A Risky Move into Fixed-Income in 2005 Followed by a State Recapitalisation Two Years Later

The causes of UBS' demise were based around its aggressive push into fixed income products following a strategic review in 2005. UBS already had a strong equities and advisory business – building out fixed income was identified as a priority to bring it into line with other businesses in terms of market position and quality.

The timing of the strategic review was unfortunate. UBS was bulking up in the exact areas that would prove susceptible to turmoil and losses during the period 2007–2009, and particularly those related to the US subprime market.

But it would be wrong to explain away the UBS losses as simply "wrong place, wrong time". In fact, dismal risk management was to blame. Ironically, it appears that the risk appetite of UBS was, in fact, quite low during the subprime crisis. But risk management was ineffective:

> The problem at UBS was not that the Bank's leadership simply ran rampant without any restraint. In fact, the contrary was the case: top management was too complacent, wrongly believing that everything was under control, given that the numerous risk reports, internal audits and external reviews almost always ended in a positive conclusion. The bank did not lack risk consciousness; it lacked healthy mistrust, independent judgement and strength of leadership.[133]

The UBS problems have been well documented and openly analysed. From the excellent diagnosis published by UBS itself and the Swiss authorities, it appears that the risk management failings were grouped around four main themes:

- The UBS business strategy was formulated with an emphasis on business franchise and revenue potential but with no regard to the potential intrinsic and implementation risks inherent in these new lines of business.
- UBS management did not act sufficiently on the warning signs within the subprime market. Instead, these signals were observed and noted, resulting in pull-back in some areas of the business but not in others. For example, "Although the group risk management body was alerted to potential sub-prime losses in Q1 2007, the investment bank senior management only appreciated the severity of the problem in late July 2007. Consequently, only on 6 August 2007, when the relevant investment bank management made a presentation to the Chairman's office and the CEO, were both given a comprehensive picture of exposures to CDO Super Senior positions (a supposedly safe strategy) and the size of the disaster became known to the board. The UBS report attributed the failure in part to a silo approach to risk management."[134]

---

[133] The UBS Crisis in Historical Perspective, 28 September 2010.
[134] The Corporate Governance Lessons From The Financial Crisis, Financial Market Trends, OECD 2009.

- Business lines were provided with virtually infinite sources of funding at subsidised rates, meaning that most investment decisions appeared to be profitable, even though some were merely "carry trades" (meaning the profit generated was no more than the subsidy itself), and could give substantial profit if executed in huge volume.
- Risk information was misleading. Positions were presented to management on an aggregate net rather than a gross basis. Thus, positions that were thought to be "fully hedged" suffered devastating losses. Additionally, several areas of UBS were taking major positions in the US mortgage market, and there was no aggregation of these exposures at the firm-wide level or consideration of whether these positions were desirable.[135]

UBS managed to survive these losses by executing a series of capital transactions, including CHF13bn of new equity in December 2007 from two strategic investors (CHF11bn from the Government of Singapore Investment Corporation (GIC) and CHF2bn from an undisclosed strategic investor in the Middle East), a CHF16bn rights issue in June 2008, the issue of CHF6bn of convertible equity notes to the Swiss state in late 2008 and, at the same time, the sale of some CHF60bn of subprime-related assets to the Swiss state, in order to de-risk UBS' balance sheet. A major restructuring of the business is underway, with a much reduced balance sheet and employee count.

The Challenge of Establishing a Risk Management Culture Remains Intact

UBS retained its focus on investment banking but recently had two significant episodes, highlighting the risks that still remain in its business model.

The first relates to a major fraud. In September 2011, UBS announced that it had lost $2.3bn as a result of unauthorised trading conducted by Kweku Adoboli, a London-based trader in UBS' synthetic equities team in London. The case is reminiscent of that of Jerôme Kerviel (€4.9bn loss at Société Générale, 2008) and Nick Leeson (£800m loss at Barings, 1995). As well as a criminal conviction for fraud and a seven-year jail term for the trader, the Adoboli fraud led to the resignation of UBS' CEO, Oswald Grübel, on 24 September 2011, as he accepted that such gross instances of rogue trading must ultimately be the responsibility of the group CEO. Several other senior UBS executives have resigned over the matter. The regulator in London highlighted the institutional failings that allowed such a fraud to be committed:

> UBS failed to: i. adequately supervise the GSE business with due skill, care and diligence; ii. put adequate systems and controls in place to detect the unauthorised trading in a timely manner; and iii. have adequate focus on risk management systems and to sufficiently escalate or take sufficient action in respect of identified risk management issues.[136]

In turn, the financial press considered the unsatisfactory role of the regulator in such a debacle:

> One question remains: why didn't regulators push UBS to be more careful before financial disaster struck?[137]

---

[135] Shareholder Report on UBS's Write-Downs, UBS AG, 18 April 2008.
[136] FSA Final Notice to UBS AG, UK FSA, 25 November 2012.
[137] *The Economist*, 26 November 2012.

The second episode is UBS' involvement in the LIBOR scandal that came to light in 2012. Along with several other banks, UBS was involved in rigging the market reference rate to make trading gains for its own book. The nature of the manipulation appears to have been worse at UBS than at other banks:

> There was a culture where the manipulation of the LIBOR and EURIBOR setting process was pervasive. The manipulation was conducted openly and was considered to be a normal and acceptable business practice by a large pool of individuals.[138]

The immediate impact of the LIBOR manipulation scandal was a set of fines from international authorities amounting to some CHF1.4bn and the largest ever fine by the UK FSA of £160m. But the longer-term impact is more profound. The LIBOR episode has highlighted cultural and risk management deficiencies that need to be addressed.

On 30 October 2012, UBS announced its financial results for the third quarter of 2012 and took the opportunity to inform the market of its decision to accelerate its transformation strategy, which had been announced in 2011. The acceleration is radical. It was taken by several observers as tantamount to an exit from serious investment banking and is expected to result in similar strategies from other banks.

> Our strategy is centered on our pre-eminent wealth management businesses and our number one Swiss universal bank, complemented by Global Asset Management and the Investment Bank. From a position of strength, we have decided to accelerate the implementation of our strategy. UBS will be unique in the banking industry. It will be less capital and balance-sheet intensive, more focused, highly cash-flow generative and capable of delivering attractive and sustainable returns for its shareholders. [...] UBS will exit lines of business that do not meet their cost of capital sustainably or in areas with high operational complexity. Such areas are predominantly in fixed income.[139]

The reduction in risk capacity in the investment bank is striking. In September 2011, the investment bank had CHF300bn of RWAs, as measured on a Basel III basis. This had fallen to CHF210bn in September 2012, with CHF50bn earmarked for exit. The target for the end of 2013 is set at CHF155bn RWAs for the investment bank, of which CHF85bn will be legacy risks to be exited. In other words, the investment bank by then will be running on a mere CHF70bn RWAs in its core, ongoing businesses. This is at least five times smaller than at its peak and maybe even ten times smaller, in terms of economic risk appetite. The UBS investment bank will have been decimated.

Lessons to be Learned from this Case Study

Despite a strong and established risk management culture, UBS embarked upon a rapid growth strategy at the time when the contextual risk was increasing significantly. Simultaneously – and hardly coincidentally – risk management processes at UBS appear to have been weakened. The bank was not aware of the risks it was running and was unable adequately to manage these risks. Governance from the top down also appears to have been deficient. Senior management seemed to have insufficient oversight and were complacent. Financial transactions and business practices were tolerated and promoted at UBS, to a degree which would not

---

[138] FSA Final Notice to UBS AG, UK FSA, 19 December 2012.
[139] UBS investor relations website.

have been allowed at most other banks. UBS' failings teach us about the importance of risk management at all levels and of all types in a high-growth, risk-taking bank. That said, UBS has pulled through the crisis in reasonable shape. With the assistance of the Swiss authorities, it has recapitalised from multiple sources, de-risked the business and set out a clear path for the future. As well as a case study in disasters being created, it is also a case study in disasters being managed.

5.11 NORTHERN ROCK

Until demutualisation in 1997, Northern Rock was a staid UK building society. Once it had become a plc, it transformed itself into an upstart in UK mortgage finance. The Northern Rock business model was aggressive in several financial aspects and eventually failed spectacularly at an early stage in the financial crisis. Despite a fairly modest size, Northern Rock is an instructive case study in financial (in-)stability and risk (mis-) management and served as a reminder of the importance of liquidity management. It also represents an indelible icon of the woes of the UK banking system, due to the horrific TV and newspaper pictures of patient depositors queuing at its branches to pull their savings to safety – the first bank run in the UK since Overend Gurney in 1866 and the City of Glasgow Bank in 1878.[140]

The Creation of a Wholesale Funded Model
Northern Rock grew fivefold in the decade after demutualisation. Between 1997 and 2006, customer loans grew from £13bn to £87bn and profit grew from £73m to £395m. During the same period, however, regulatory equity capital increased by a more modest amount, from £0.7bn to £1.7bn, yet the regulatory Tier 1 solvency ratio was roughly stable, having gone from 8.7% to 8.5%.[141] In short, Northern Rock had grown its mortgage book far faster than its regulatory capital requirements, by using securitisation on more than half of its mortgage book. This capital "efficiency" and a low-cost marketing model with very few branches enabled an attractive and cheap mortgage product to be offered to customers. By 2007, Northern Rock was writing one-fifth of all new UK mortgages and remortgages and growing at 40% per year.

Securitisation is a valid tool for financing rock-solid loan books efficiently. However, Northern Rock's use of securitisation was aggressive and excessive. Its business model relied heavily upon the securitisation markets being open and accessible. The bank ran a large amount of interest rate and refinancing risk. And a lack of diversification meant that one single shock – a liquidity shock in this case – would render the entire business non-viable very quickly. As liquidity dried up, they were forced to hold on to assets they were planning to securitise.

The FSA supervision was weak, chaotic and potentially even negligent. Supervisors were busy on other matters, such as M&A activity in the UK banking sector at that time (e.g. Abbey, ABN Amro) and implementing Basel II. Northern Rock was not seen as a "high

---

[140] The Run on the Rock, House of Commons Treasury Committee, 24 January 2008.
[141] Northern Rock plc annual reports.

impact" firm. There was little financial analysis in FSA methodologies and so Northern Rock's perilous risk profile was not explored; in fact, the FSA decided to conduct supervisory reviews on a 36-month cycle. When reviews were conducted, the work was over-delegated.

> Although liquidity was included within the February 2006 ARROW visit to Northern Rock's treasury, it was not explored fully; the visit did not, for example, review the firm's stress testing. [...] The intention was to include it in the Pillar 2 ICAAP work, but this was not scheduled until [...] 25-26 April 2007. [...] The objectives of the review did not include wider questions about the implications or adequacy of the liquidity component of firms' business models.[142]

Liquidity Gap, Panic and Bank Run

Northern Rock caused some concern in June 2007, when it issued a profit warning due to shifts in market interest rates, which negatively impacted its interest margins. Nonetheless, it confidently announced a progressive dividend policy the following month:

> [T]he benefits of Basel II enable us to increase our 2007 interim dividend by 30%. Going forward our dividend payout rate increases to 50% of underlying EPS from around 40%.[143]

Global market conditions took a turn for the worse in August 2007. At that time, Northern Rock was preparing a large securitisation deal, which became impossible to execute. It had built up several billion pounds worth of mortgage assets on its balance sheet, which were funded on a short-term basis. Market funding sources dried up and Northern Rock was shortly forced to seek government funding support. Unfortunately, just before the emergency financial support was announced, its details were leaked by the BBC, causing sensation and precipitating a retail deposit run. This was a PR disaster. The head of the FSA noted to Parliament:

> It was extremely unfortunate that the information leaked because it meant that instead of this being put in place as, "This is a solvent institution which has a cash flow problem and the Government is stepping in to make sure that it is saved", it became a panic measure or a response to something that was already in the making. Panic was how it was seen.[144]

As funding conditions continued to deteriorate, Northern Rock sought buyers, but there was little interest unless the government would commit substantial funding (in the region of £30bn) as part of the deal. The government refused to do this and Northern Rock was nationalised on 22 February 2008.

Lessons to be Learned from this Case Study

Northern Rock's lack of diversification in its business model meant that it had little resilience. Its capital ratios did not reflect the massive amount of risk that was building up in the balance sheet. These financial weaknesses combined with poor supervision to form a lethal

---

[142] The Supervision of Northern Rock: A Lessons Learned Review, UK FSA Internal Audit Division, March 2008.
[143] Northern Rock interim results, 25 July 2007.
[144] The Run on the Rock, House of Commons Treasury Committee, 24 January 2008.

combination in a bank which, whilst small, was growing rapidly and was big enough to matter. Diversification, resilience, adequate financial resources and strong oversight of the business are all essential for a bank to survive and prosper.

5.12 BANKIA-BFA

Bankia-BFA is a Spanish banking group that was formed in July 2010 from the merger of seven Spanish savings banks (or "cajas"), including two of the largest, Caja Madrid and Bancaja. Bankia – the main part of Bankia-BFA – was floated on the stock exchange in July 2011 at €3.75 per share, with a total market capitalisation of about €6bn. The creation, flotation and recapitalisation of Bankia-BFA after only one year in existence provide some interesting insights on the property-fuelled banking crisis in Spain and the difficulty that Spanish authorities faced in designing a resolution strategy for the banking sector. It also raises legitimate questions on the way in which the Spanish boom and bust was handled.

Formation of a Real Estate Bubble in the Spanish Banking System
The creation of the Euro, in which Spain participated from its inception, was a driver of a deep transformation of the Spanish economy and, among other things, its banking system. Theories around convergence and Spain catching up with the rest of the more advanced European economies generated a boost in confidence, capital inflows and sustained growth of the economy. Being a member of a large monetary zone opened new fund-raising opportunities that were not available with the old "pesetas"; more specifically, the convergence of Spanish interest rates to the lower Euro rates reduced the cost of borrowing, allowing broader access to borrowing by the population and loans with a longer maturity. Credit to households grew at a rate of around 20% per annum during this period, while the repayment period of mortgage loans doubled, reaching 27 years.[145]

Cheap credit contributed to the formation of a real estate bubble and a boom in the construction industry. Rising house prices contributed to the formation of perceived wealth. House prices rose 10% per year on average between 1995 and 2007, including a spurt of 18% per year in 2003 and 2004. The wealth of Spanish households was concentrated in their homes: real estate represented 83% of total wealth in 2007 (vs. 75% in Italy and 44% in the USA in 2004). Residential housing investment in Spain represented 6.8% of GDP in 2007 (vs. 5.5% in the USA and 5.5% for the European Union) while 13.2% of the workforce were employed in the construction sector (vs. 8% in the USA).[146] Housing stock in the country grew by 5.7m units between 1998 and 2007.[147] This helped stimulate the economy and more demand for housing accelerated bank lending: "… the increase in the value of real estate assets has generated wealth effects on consumption and fuelled the demand for residential investment which has, in turn, been boosted by the increase in the collateral available to secure bank loans."[148]

---

[145] Banco de España Annual Report 2006.
[146] Banco de España Annual Report 2007.
[147] Ibid.
[148] Banco de España Annual Report 2006

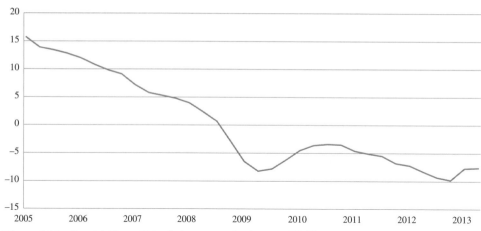

Figure 5.14   Spanish House Price Index, quarterly changes (%) [149]

Real estate quickly became "the only game in town" and the bubble was tolerated by the authorities. Investment in real estate was clearly excessive and fuelled by debt. Still, the choice was made to favour short-term benefits on growth and employment against the risks posed by the fragility of an economic boom driven by an expansion of the construction sector and rising property prices, which were ultimately to decline – see Figure 5.14.

Priority Given to Consolidation and Sovereign Ratings Defence
When the slowdown in housing prices led to a sharp slowdown in construction activity and it became clear that many of the "cajas" had over-extended themselves in real estate lending, the Spanish authorities viewed consolidation as the main tool to remedy the situation. They encouraged mergers of the cajas and set up the "Fondo des Reestructuración Ordenada Bancaria" ("Fund for Orderly Banking Restructuring" or FROB) to facilitate the restructuring of cajas. The Spanish authorities gave two reasons for choosing to consolidate banks first rather than focusing on the root causes of the banking industry's weaknesses: problem loans. Firstly, they assumed that consolidation would reduce the excess capacity in the Spanish banking industry, making it more efficient, profitable and viable. And secondly, a more concentrated banking sector would comprise stronger institutions that were better suited to address the challenges of a deteriorating macro-economic situation.

Spain's approach contrasted with other economies that were suffering from a housing bubble. In Ireland, for example, troubled real estate loans had been transferred rapidly to a "bad bank" called NAMA. This had the effect of recognising the true value of the real estate loans upon transfer, thus damaging the solvency of the banks and of the state. Preserving the credit rating of Spain, still rated AAA by S&P until 19 January 2009 and Aaa by Moody's until 30 September 2010, may have been a reason for delaying a fundamental, financial restructuring of the banking sector and may explain the relatively modest size of FROB's €9bn of capital,

---

[149] Source: SPHSOVY, Ministerio de Fomento – Quarterly changes.

which was not sufficient to meet the recapitalisation needs of the banking sector. The Bank of Spain expressed its confidence in the impact of these mergers: "Now that the new map of savings banks in Spain has been traced out, it is clear that the Spanish banking system remains sound and solvent."[150] By the same token, entities like Bankia would soon be "gaining solidity and raising efficiency, as an essential condition in order to enhance not only the savings bank's competitive position but also their market credibility, increasing the average size of the institutions or groups harnessing synergies".[151]

This confidence was not shared by investors and market analysts, who continued to question the performance of loan portfolios and speculate on the quantum of losses to come. Faced with potentially gigantic needs for recapitalisation, the strategy of buying time, preserving the AAA ratings and delaying decisive recapitalisations, in the hope that the housing market would stabilise and recover, proved to be based on wishful thinking and wasted precious time.

Bankia-BFA Need for Further Capital in 2012

The continued deterioration of the Spanish economy in 2010 and 2011 led to increasing concerns among investors regarding the true quality of Bankia-BFA's loan portfolio. The portfolio was heavily weighted towards real estate: as an illustration, Bancaja's loan portfolio was more than two-thirds real estate in 2010.[152] By May 2012, the state had no other choice but to recapitalise the bank, through the conversion of €4.47bn worth of contingent capital instruments. The downgrading of Spain to BBB+ by S&P on 26 April 2012 and to Baa3 by Moody's on 13 June 2012 prompted a wave of downgrades for Spanish banks.

In May 2012, following the resignation of the senior management of Bankia-BFA, the state was called on for a rescue. An increase in the provisions for doubtful loans led to 2011's earnings being restated from a €300m profit to a €4.3bn loss, sending Bankia shares to less than €0.5 (see Figure 5.15). In the midst of confusing discussions and speculation regarding a rescue package from the EU, and rumours of losses of €4.3bn at the end of August, Bankia-BFA

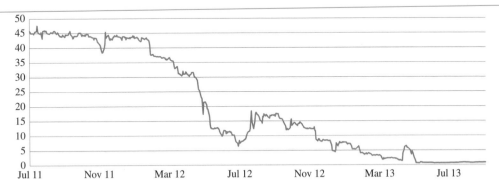

Figure 5.15   Bankia's share price since IPO (€/share)[153]

---

[150] Banco de España Restructuring of Spanish Savings Banks, 29 June 2010.
[151] Ibid.
[152] Bancaja Annual Report FY 2010.
[153] Bloomberg.

was given a state capital injection of €4.5bn in September 2012. Even this rescue package left open the questions of the true economic value of Bankia-BFA and the appropriate level of provisioning.

Failure of the Supervisor

Instead of dealing proactively with losses on banks' real estate loan portfolios, the Spanish authorities chose to limit the impact of the bubble by "breaking the thermometer". Nevertheless, the impact of excessive household debt, rising unemployment and a weak banking system was real and continued to harm the Spanish economy. In the end, the strategy did not work, neither restoring confidence, nor sparing a downgrade of Spain.

The growth in leverage in the real estate sector and the house price bubble were well understood by the Bank of Spain but were explained away by the central bank as natural and sustainable, due to environmental factors:[154]

- immigration flow (5.2m inflow of population between 1998 and 2007);
- increase in the number of households (partly as a result of the rise of single-parent households);
- availability of land and restrictions on construction permits.

Following a similar logic, the slowing of the housing market was welcome as a sign of sustainability, even when the Bank of Spain noted that "household debt continued to expand more quickly than household income, meaning the debt ratio increased once more, albeit more moderately".[155] In reality, the increase in property prices and the real estate boom were another manifestation of a bubble, but little was done about it. Was it in the remit of the supervisor to implement tougher controls on the credit approval criteria and warn banks of the risks? Reports on supervision show some investigations of sub-standard credit approval processes or excessive lending to real estate, but these specific cases on which little detail is provided fall short of a macro-prudential approach that would have curtailed the excessive lending and increased the resilience of the Spanish banking system.

Was "Buying Time" a Value-Creating Strategy in the End?

Unlike other countries, Spanish authorities chose to ignore the losses on real estate lending when addressing the issues of the banking system and delay the time of reckoning, in the hope that the market would strengthen. The reference by Bankia-BFA when reinstating its 2011 accounts to "the difficulties of measuring assets in a highly illiquid market such as the current real estate market in Spain, [the] risk [which] prevails that the carrying amount of these assets will not equate to their realisable value if they had to be sold"[156] captures the opacity in the Spanish banking system and its negative impact on investors' confidence.

To address this, consulting firm Oliver Wyman was eventually commissioned by the Bank of Spain to conduct an independent assessment of the strength of the Spanish banking system, the loss projections of loan portfolios and the resulting capital needs. Their results show an increase of losses from €178bn in the base scenario to €265bn in the adverse scenario for the

---

[154] Banco de España Annual Report 2006.
[155] Banco de España Annual Report 2007.
[156] Bankia Annual Report 2011.

Table 5.17   Loss estimates[157]

(€bn)	2011 balance	Loss – base scenario	Loss – adverse scenario
Real estate developers	227	65	97
Retail mortgages	602	11	25
SMEs	237	25	39

whole banking sector, with a detailed split (Table 5.17) for losses relating to real estate developers, mortgages and SMEs.[158]

The numbers produced were globally in line with analysts' estimates, although perhaps slightly on the low side. In the case of Bankia-BFA, estimated losses ranged between €29bn and €43bn. Bankia shares, which had been floated at €3.75 a year previously, continued to trade below €0.50, raising issues concerning the IPO process, in which more than 350,000 retail investors had participated and were nursing losses. The exclusion of the stock from the Spanish market index on 2 January 2013 worsened the prospects for shareholders and increased the volatility, attracting hedge funds rather than stable buy-and-hold investors. Holders of regulatory capital instruments also took losses, even though the investors in these bonds may have been under certain misapprehensions as to the loss-absorbing nature of their investment and/or the financial health of Bankia-BFA when they made their investment.

Estimates of Bankia losses have been established as shown in Table 5.18.[159]

Burden-sharing, SAREB and EU Rescue Package

Responding to pressure from the EU, at the end of 2012, Spain eventually accepted to adopt a more transparent approach to restructure its banking sector in exchange for a €100bn rescue package to help with the recapitalisation of the banking sector (including Bankia-BFA). The agreement also included the set-up transfer of troubled assets to the "Sociedad de Gestión de Activos Procedentes de la Reestructuración Bancaria" or SAREB. This "bad bank" was created in August 2012, despite longstanding opposition from the Spanish government towards such solutions. SAREB is owned 55% by private sector shareholders, which enables it to be recorded off balance sheet for the Spanish public sector: it does not inflate the crucial debt-to-GDP measure. SAREB uses its balance sheet of €50bn to purchase troubled, mostly real estate-related, assets from Spanish banks in exchange for government-guaranteed bonds. The assets include physical assets (76,000 empty homes, 6,300 rented homes and 14,900 plots of land) and 84,300 loans. In the case of Bankia-BFA, €22.3bn of assets in BFA were transferred to SAREB, including €19.5bn from Bankia.

The terms of the plan negotiated with the EU may help bring back confidence in the Spanish banking sector and improve the governance. A combination of recapitalisation and conversion of debt into equity (liability management) should strengthen Bankia's solvency position, despite a net loss of €21bn announced at the end of February 2013. But investors who have already suffered losses still need to be convinced that there is a credible strategy at the end of this restructuring exercise which has now been under way for three whole years.

---

[157] Oliver Wyman Asset quality review and bottom-up stress test exercise, September 2012.
[158] Ibid.
[159] Ibid.

Table 5.18   Bankia loss estimates

€bn	Base scenario	Adverse scenario
Total losses current credit book	29.4	42.8
o/w real estate developers	12.6	17.6
o/w finished property	2.9	3.6
Existing provisions	19.8	19.8
Capital shortfall	−13.2	−24.7

Lessons to be Learned from this Case Study

Bankia serves as an illustration of the perils of a real estate boom and bust that is allowed to go unchecked by the banking supervisor. More than any other bank, the constituent banks of Bankia had built massively risky concentrations in lending to speculative real estate development and investments. Misplaced confidence, both in the run-up to the crisis and also in the restructuring and the IPO, proved deadly. Mergers and acquisitions proved not to be the answer to the successful restructuring of a troubled banking industry. The Bankia case also shows us how much we rely upon the supervisor to drive the industry's risk agenda and lead the industry in decisive action. Early, decisive action is key – and this did not happen in the case of Bankia.

5.13 AUSTRALIA

The Australian banking industry has weathered the current financial crisis rather well. Though there have been a few scary moments (ROE fell in 2009 to 13%, though it has averaged 16% since the start of the current financial crisis[160]), the industry entered 2013 with a combined market capitalisation well in excess of US$300bn (about the same as that of the entire Eurozone banking industry) and an average credit rating of AA- with S&P. Some observers hold it up as a model for others to emulate, in particular its focus on domestic retail banking and avoidance of over-exposure to US subprime investments. Are there indeed lessons to be learnt from the land often referred to as "The Lucky Country"? Interestingly, the phrase "The Lucky Country" was intended by its author to be scathingly ironic: "I had in mind in particular the lack of innovation in Australian manufacturing and some other forms of Australian business, banking for example. In these, as a colonial carry over, Australia showed less enterprise than almost any other prosperous industrial society."[161] Does this irony from the 1960s also apply to the current day Australian banking sector?

To be fair, a healthy economy generally breeds a healthy banking sector and, in this respect, Australian banks have indeed been lucky. Its economy has been buoyed by strong demand from growing Asian economies (such as China) for commodities. In a world of anaemic economic growth for rich countries, Australia has avoided recession and stagnation – see Figure 5.16.

---

[160] Banks in Australia: Facts & Figures, Australian Bankers' Association website.
[161] Australian Stories, Australian government website.

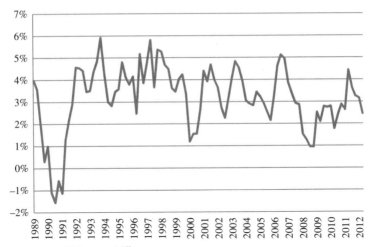

Figure 5.16   Australian GDP growth[162]

Its banking system has a peculiar structure and culture that emanates from a series of influences in recent history.

- In the 1980s, deregulation and competition from new foreign entrants led to excessive risk-taking by incumbent banks, who suffered major credit losses as certain large corporates collapsed.
- Attempts by the Australian banks to expand internationally led to disappointment and disasters (e.g. Westpac losses of A$1,562m in the 1992 financial year,[163] ANZ's value-destroying acquisition of Grindlays in late 1900s, NAB's exposure to UK retail banking sector in late 1990s).
- Following these crises, across the industry "there was a substantial review of the prudential aspects of banking, particularly those concerning credit. An enormous effort was made to reassess credit processes and standards to ensure that it would not happen again. This overhaul happened at all the banks."[164]
- The experiences also shaped government policy to discourage foreign entrants ("any large scale transfer of Australian ownership of the financial system to foreign hands would be contrary to the national interest") and block any mergers between the largest banks (the so-called "four pillars policy").[165] Even though the attempts to improve competition and efficiency, such as the Wallis Report of 1997, purported to open up the industry, in effect, this created the conditions for an oligopoly to establish itself.
- The scandalous collapse in 2001 of the insurer HIH showed the Australian public the damage that mismanagement of the financial industry could wreak. This hardened the conservatism of the banking industry and clarified the need for effective risk management and more

---

[162] Chart Pack, Reserve Bank of Australia, April 2013.

[163] Westpac Reports Profit for 1993 Year, Westpac Banking Corporation, 18 November 1993.

[164] Baptism by Fire: How Adversity Primed Australia's Banking Industry for a Brave New Era, Australasian Institute of Banking and Finance, December 1999.

[165] Mergers Policy in the Financial System, Australian Treasury, 9 April 1997.

common sense: "From time to time as I listened to the evidence about specific transactions or decisions, I found myself asking rhetorically: did anyone stand back and ask themselves the simple question — is this right? [...] There is no doubt that regulation is necessary: peace, order and good government could not be achieved without it. But it would be a shame if the prescription of corporate governance models and standards of conduct for corporate officers became the beginning, the middle and the end of the decision-making process."[166]

Consequently, in the years running up to the onset of the current financial crisis, the Australian banking industry had become a largely domestic oligopoly that was healthily profitable and highly conservative in its strategies and regulation. Aggressive, innovative and niche players did exist, but they were outside the "Big Four". Growth was provided by a doubling of credit levels, relative to the size of the economy (see Figure 5.17). The bulk of this credit growth was to the housing sector. The business model of Australian banks became dominated by their residential mortgage business.

This credit growth was funded largely through wholesale borrowing from the international debt markets. Around one-half of the funding of Australian banks is from the wholesale markets[167] and loan-to-deposit ratios have typically been very high. Australian banks borrow more than the banks *of any country* internationally: around US$300bn in net terms, according to the BIS and IMF.[168]

The Australian banks were largely untouched by US subprime losses. Total losses were, relative to the size of the industry and its profitability, incidental. The largest loss appears to have been National Australia Bank's A$1bn loss on ABS CDO exposures in its nabCapital unit in 2008.[169] Since the Australian banks had profitable growth opportunities at home, they simply had no need to fuel other countries' credit booms.

Since 2007, Australian banks have responded to the tensions in the international capital markets by raising more funds through deposits and/or domestically issued bonds. For example, deposits have risen from 40% of total funding to 50%.[170] Nevertheless, even this diminished reliance upon wholesale funding still represents a risk for the industry. And over the course of the current financial crisis, the "four pillars" have further increased their share of the industry, with several smaller or niche players that were pressured by credit or funding considerations into being consolidated into the big four: for example, St George's into Westpac, foreign-owned upstart BankWest into CBA and Aussie Home Loans also into CBA.

As a result of the domestic focus and the dominance of mortgages in the balance sheet, the business model of Australian banks is highly concentrated and reliant upon the health not only of the Australian economy but also of the Australian housing market. The IMF has recently looked at the issue and the risks involved, opining that "the combination of high household debt and elevated house prices is a risk to banks' large mortgage portfolio".[171] Despite strong macroeconomic housing market fundamentals (e.g. economic growth prospects, immigration and scope

[166] The Failure of HIH Insurance, The Hon Justice Owen, HIH Royal Commission, April 2003.
[167] Banks' Funding Costs and Lending Rates, RBA Bulletin – March Quarter 2012.
[168] Australia: Financial System Stability Assessment, IMF, November 2012.
[169] 2008 Annual Financial Report, NAB Group.
[170] Banks' Funding Costs and Lending Rates, RBA Bulletin – March Quarter 2012.
[171] Australia: Financial System Stability Assessment, IMF, November 2012.

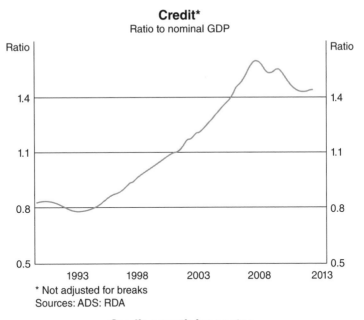

Credit*
Ratio to nominal GDP

* Not adjusted for breaks
Sources: ADS: RDA

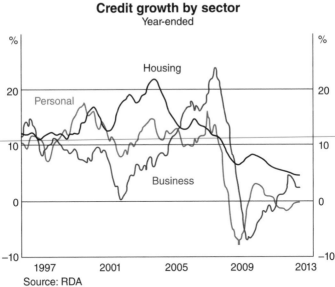

Credit growth by sector
Year-ended

Source: RDA

Figure 5.17   Growth of credit in Australia[172]

for policy rates to be cut in case of need) there is the perennial potential for housing markets to become volatile no matter what the fundamentals, so this aspect is undoubtedly a major risk for the Australian banks. To put this in context, stress tests indicate that the capital resources of Australian banks would remain strong even in the so-called "severe recession scenario".[173]

---

[172] Chart Pack, Reserve Bank of Australia, April 2013.
[173] Australia: Financial System Stability Assessment, IMF, November 2012.

The regulatory regime in Australia has contributed to the resilience of the banking industry. The aforementioned conservatism is demonstrated by a sceptical approach by the regulator towards certain internationally accepted norms for banks. For example, Australian regulatory capital definitions set by the APRA do not apply the Basel "threshold" for deductions of bancassurance stakes, instead deducting all equity investments no matter how small from regulatory capital measures. APRA requires a minimum 20% loss given default for mortgages, versus the Basel standard of 10%. It also requires banks to calculate a risk-weighted asset amount for interest rate risk in the banking book, which regulators in other countries treat as a "soft" Pillar 2 measure. As a consequence of this conservatism, the regulatory capital ratios reported by Australian banks are considerably lower than they would be under a different regulatory regime: CBA, for example, has calculated that its 8.1% Tier 1 capital ratio under APRA's version of Basel III would have been 10.6% if reported under the international Basel III rules.[174] Business models have also been focused by regulation: for example, Australian banks have not set up major capital markets businesses, in part due to the reticence of the regulator. This conservatism is combined with efficient lines of communication between the regulators, supervisors, central bank and commercial banks, as befits a small country with a concentrated, domestic banking industry. Anecdotally, the supervisory approach seems to be intrusive in an equitable way and not just "for the sake of it". Regulations are kept clear and simple: for example, APRA's Basel III documents are far more concise and clearer than equivalents in say the EU. The IMF noted the effectiveness of the Australian regulatory and supervisory approach in its recent assessment:

> APRA takes a proactive, risk-based approach to bank supervision. The approach is principles based and outcome oriented, relying more on directors and management to interpret and apply regulatory principles than on prescriptive regulations. APRA does not prescribe simple regulatory limits, such as LTV ratios or debt-to-income (DTI) ratios; preferring internal regulatory guidance such as on collateralization and serviceability that takes all loan contract terms into account. APRA's notable strengths are demonstrated by its strong risk analysis embedded in the PAIRS and SOARS system, its focus on bank boards' responsibility for risk management, and its assessment of banks on a system wide basis. APRA's on- and off-site supervision is well planned and executed; credit risk management is well developed; and its provisioning requirements typically result in higher reserves than required under IFRS. Moreover, APRA conveys its expectations for the management of specific risks to banks through engagement with bank boards, regular contacts by supervisors and risk specialists, and letters and speeches delivered to the industry. This approach has been broadly effective.[175]

The Australian authorities also appear to have been successful in forging effective formal and informal links with the authorities in New Zealand, which is especially important, given that Australian banks own 85% of the assets of the New Zealand banking system and 15% of Australian bank assets are New Zealand-owned.

Lessons to be Learned from this Case Study
Relative to the recent experience of certain countries, the Australian banking system may seem to be an icon of resilience. The industry structure and regulatory approach – both of which are the conscious product of previous crises – helped Australian banks keep out of the

---

[174] Debt Investor Update For the half year ended 31 December 2012, CBA, February 2013.
[175] Australia: Financial System Stability Assessment, IMF, November 2012.

problems that beset some of their peers in American and European markets. These positive elements could be emulated in other domestically-focused banking industries in small countries, though it is hard to see them working in major international financial centres and the investment banking business. And even in Australia, profound risks (notably, lack of diversification and a reliance on wholesale funding markets) were and are still present in the system: they just have not materialised yet. The major factor behind the good performance of the country's banks is the strong economic performance over the past decade: in this respect, the Australian banks are, indeed, "lucky".

5.14 CANADA

During the financial crisis, Canadian banks were not immune to turmoil. Funding conditions deteriorated, profitability declined and there was even a liquidity freeze in the local Asset-Backed Commercial Paper (ABCP) funding market. Nonetheless, Canadian banks proved to be relatively resilient and there was no need to resort to public funds for capital injections. Now, Canadian banks are recognised as among the safest banks in the world, with six of them in the "Top 25"[176] and the World Economic Forum ranking Canada as having the soundest banking industry for five years in a row.[177] The *Financial Times* enthused that Canada is a "real-world, real-time example of a banking system in a medium-sized, advanced capitalist economy that worked. Understanding why the Canadian system survived could be a key to making the rest of the west equally robust."[178] Are there indeed lessons that can be learnt from the Canadian magic touch?

Of course, the best bedrock for a strong banking industry is a healthy domestic economy. Canada is fortunate to have a young, growing and productive population. Labour force participation rates are among the highest in the world: Canada's rate of 67% compares well with the USA's 64%, UK's 62%, Germany's 60% and France's 56%.[179] It is also rich in resources, which make up around 11.5% of the GDP and half of Canada's exports.[180] Economic growth overall in Canada held up well, with a brief recession in 2009, from which the country has since recovered. GDP is forecast to rise by 1.6% in 2013 and 2.6% in 2014.[181]

As well as a sound economic backdrop, Canadian banks have a heritage that represents a structural advantage, for their industry is an oligopoly based around domestic universal banking.

During the 1980s, retail banks became permitted to acquire brokerages and trust companies. Consolidation of the industry ensued, together with ongoing business diversification, including buying insurance companies and asset managers. By 1998, there were five main banking groups: Canadian Imperial Bank of Commerce (CIBC), Toronto-Dominion Bank (TD), Bank of Montreal (BMO), Royal Bank of Canada (RBC) and Bank of Nova Scotia (Scotiabank).

---

[176] World's Safest Banks 2012, *Global Finance Magazine*, March 2012.
[177] Canadian Bankers' Association.
[178] What Toronto Can Teach New York and London, *Financial Times*, 29 January 2010.
[179] World Bank Database.
[180] Important Facts on Canada's Natural Resources, Natural Resources Canada, 27 July 2011.
[181] Quarterly Economic Forecast, TD Economics, 19 March 2013.

Proposed mergers between BMO/RBC and CIBC/TD, intended to allow the Canadian banks to bulk up and compete on the global stage, were rejected by Paul Martin, the Finance Minister at the time. He ruled that bank mergers were not in the public interest since industry concentration would become excessive, competition would suffer and the federal government would lose some future flexibility in case of the failure of an institution.[182] Thus thwarted, Canadian banks focused largely on retail banking growth within Canada and selective wholesale banking opportunities abroad, where opportunities for specialisation and competitive advantage existed. The acquisition of Canadian banks by overseas investors has been limited by the requirement that the largest domestic banks are "widely held", with no shareholder owning more than 20%.[183]

Despite the broad business mix of the Canadian banks, their retail focus is intense. Big-ticket wholesale banking and capital markets businesses make up only 10 to 20% of total revenues. Mortgages are the predominant risk asset and business line for Canadian banks and it was the nature and the structure of the mortgage market in Canada that played a distinct role in containing the impacts of the current financial crisis for Canadian banks. In particular, Canada did not have the environment for subprime lending to become a major business: although 20% of all mortgages in the USA were subprime in 2007, in Canada they remained under 5% of the Canadian mortgage market and even those loans labelled "subprime" were of far better quality than the US variety.[184]

There were specific reasons why Canadian mortgage customers are less inclined to speculate and more inclined to repay:

- There is no tax incentive to borrow and borrowers in Canada are personally liable for the entire balance of the mortgage.
- Non-bank mortgage originators did not grow in large numbers, unlike the USA.
- Securitisation of mortgages did not become the dominant feature of the market. Although the securitisation market in Canada grew substantially from the 1990s to 2007, ultimately only approximately 25% of mortgages originated by the Canadian banks were securitised (through either RMBS or covered bond programmes) pre-crisis, compared to 60% in the USA.[185]
- Mortgages over 80% of the property's value are required to be insured with the state-owned "Canada Mortgage and Housing Agency" (CMHC). The insurance covers 100% of the mortgage balance in the event of default. The scale of CMHC and the strict standards which it imposed on banks helped to prevent growth in the Canadian subprime market.

Despite a traditional business mix and the soundness of the mortgage business in particular, risks and blemishes were not completely absent from the Canadian banking industry. Unsurprisingly, Canadian banks have significant operations in the USA and cannot fail to encounter problems when the US banking industry goes through a crisis. The bank worst affected by subprime losses was CIBC, which took a $7.3bn hit in its "CIBC World Markets" division

---

[182] Finance Minister Rejects Bank Merger Proposals, Canada Online, 14 December 1998.
[183] Department of Finance Canada.
[184] Why Didn't Canada's Housing Market Go Bust?, Economic Commentary, Federal Reserve Bank of Cleveland, 2 February 2009.
[185] Ibid.

in 2008.[186] Having said that, one of the largest Canadian banks famously exited the subprime business before its rout. "To us, the securities were not transparent and the risk reward relationship was not obvious. These were instruments valued by mathematical models which few people on the planet understood and it wasn't clear to us that the business model was sustainable. So when everyone else was getting in, we got out."[187] The biggest wobble was the freeze in the Canadian ABCP market mentioned above, though this was resolved effectively by means of a negotiated restructuring agreed by industry participants. Current risks centre around the housing market, with several newspaper articles predicting imminent problems, the general view being along the lines of "any hopes of a rebound in housing demand are slipping away and the signs of a significant real estate downturn are everywhere".[188] These views are prudent and cautious: as of January 2013, only 0.33% of bank mortgages were in arrears.[189]

Good business practice by banks is often accompanied by good regulation and supervision of banks. The regulatory and supervisory environment in Canada is characterised by a conservatism that is a hangover from the economic crisis of 1981–1982, when some regional banks in Western Canada failed due to a collapse in the oil price. The framework that resulted from that crisis was "forged out of a series of disasters"[190] and had the new, powerful and authoritative Office of the Superintendent of Financial Institutions (OFSI) at its heart. OFSI is considered to be close to the industry, both physically, with its headquarters located only steps away from the major banks' head offices in Toronto, and also in terms of knowledge and understanding.

OSFI's regulatory rules were generally a little more conservative than international regulations. For example, on capital metrics, the Canadians embraced the risk-adjusted capital measures of Basel II as well as limiting the gross accounting leverage of a bank (total assets to total capital) to a maximum of 20 times.[191] Current adoption of Basel III is stricter and more rapid than the international norm, even though this may cause some headaches for the Canadian banks, since "conservative adoption of Basel III may be putting Canadian banks at a competitive disadvantage relative to many of their global peers".[192] Having the entire banking system under OSFI's authority appears to have avoided some of the regulatory gaps in accountability that have been experienced in certain other countries. OSFI's style of supervision is reported anecdotally as rational, proportionate and commonsensical. It appears to have operationalised its communications message on the importance of good risk management: "Capital is extremely important, but it is not a panacea. An institution will never have enough capital if there are material flaws in its risk management processes. We cannot be lulled into a false sense of security because of some of the significant changes we are making to capital under the recently announced Basel III capital rules. Capital is an important building block, but it is only one of many."[193]

---

[186] Annual Information Form, Canadian Imperial Bank of Commerce, 4 December 2008.
[187] Bharat Masrani, President and CEO, TD Bank, 6 April 2011.
[188] Signs of a Canadian housing downturn are everywhere, *Financial Post*, 5 April 2013.
[189] Canadian Bankers' Association.
[190] How Canada slipped the net of financial crisis, *Business & Finance*, May 2011.
[191] Regulatory Constraints on Leverage: The Canadian Experience, *Bank of Canada Financial System Review*, June 2009.
[192] A New Normal: Perspectives on the Canadian Banking Industry, PWC, 2013.
[193] Capital is not a panacea: Multi-dimensional Oversight vs. Human Nature, Julie Dickson, The OSFI Pillar, Fall 2010.

The global reputation of Canadian bank regulation and economic management in general is nicely illustrated by the appointment in 2013 of Mark Carney as the Governor of the Bank of England, replacing Mervyn King. He is the first foreigner to hold that illustrious post. The UK government is hoping that Mr Carney can bring some of the "Canadian magic" to the UK banking system and economy.

Lessons to be Learned from this Case Study

Canada is not the home of superhuman bankers, regulators and supervisors. Those looking for "magic" may discover that the factors that drive the success and stability of the Canadian banking sector are rather mundane. A strong economy and a profitable oligopoly kept the Canadian banks from over-extending their risk profile. Laws, tax codes and regulations constrained the development of a large, high-risk, subprime lending industry. Conservatism resulting from a recent financial crisis helped to keep the industry focused on good risk management. Common sense from bank management and supervisors alike, combined with strong communication and cooperation, helped to identify and effectively address problems when they occurred.

5.15 SUMMARY OF "LESSONS LEARNED" FROM THE CASE STUDIES

The case studies in this chapter represent a brief glimpse into some illustrations of recent successes, problems and failures in the banking industry. They highlight how some of the themes from earlier chapters play through in practice. Viewed in aggregate, they provide a reasonably good diagnostic of the challenges that the banking industry faces and a few hints as to what "better banking" might be. They certainly show what "better banking" is not.

The fact is that risk exists in all business models, in all countries, in every institution at all times. Risk is not "solved" by capital strength and comfortable funding positions: they may provide a greater degree of resilience, but they are rarely the deciding factor.

Banks naturally sought "capital-efficient" and arbitrage strategies to pursue their profitability and growth objectives, which shareholders required and enjoyed. Most of the time, this was in full view of regulators and owners; in some instances, regulators willingly overlooked risks inherent in various banks. More often than not, these supervisory failures have not been documented: in most cases, we have not been told the concrete answer to the question "how could the regulators have allowed this situation to develop?". The simple fact is that none of the case studies contain episodes where an involved set of owners, management and supervisors could not have spotted the risks and acted to mitigate them.

The supervisory failures at UBS and Northern Rock are well documented. HBOS wore its heart on its sleeve in pursuing an openly aggressive expansion strategy. AIG, in full view of regulators and owners, was able to bulk up its financial products unit, making use of regulatory arbitrage, but ultimately leading it to failure. And RBS's disastrous acquisition of ABN Amro was hardly shielded from scrutiny.

Good governance and risk management set the "winners" apart from the "losers", though massive doses of luck play their part too. This luck, or lack thereof, is evidenced by how quickly many institutions went from being darlings of the market to infamy and ruin. In the case of Bankia-BFA, only a year elapsed between the successful €6bn flotation and a catastrophic collapse.

Fragile business models collapsed spectacularly. For example, Dexia and Bear Stearns both pursued strategies that could only work in stable markets. Their short-term funding structures were assumed to be permanent and resilient: in practice, their excessive maturity transformation heaped extra risks onto an already perilous situation. When the market turned and liquidity faltered, it did not take long for all the pieces to unravel.

Membership of an oligopoly seems to help in keeping bank management away from profit-seeking forays into supposedly attractive, high-risk new businesses. For example, HSBC, operating in a competitive global marketplace, must have thought that their acquisition of the subprime lender Household was a good way to grow their business in the United States, historically a weaker region for the firm. After $50bn of losses, it was apparent that this growth strategy had failed. Similarly, Merrill Lynch made the disastrous decision to own the entire subprime mortgage value chain to feed its CDO business. Growth ambitions proved ruinous for Merrill.

The Australian and Canadian examples remind us that it is possible to maintain healthy, profitable banks. Oligopolies coupled with strong retail franchises have certainly proven strong over the course of the crisis. A strong macro-economic backdrop helps immeasurably and a tight, intimate supervisory model appears to be preferable over some of the more aloof models from other countries. That said, both Australia and Canada were not without their crises and issues. Indeed, there are features of both markets that cause observers to fear for future risk performance.

When a problem does occur, early and decisive action makes a difference – though it does not work miracles. Banks such as HSBC, Barclays and UBS have been battered by the storms of the current financial crisis but have tackled their demons and emerged intact and with good prospects. Lack of remedial action can cause a bank to limp on and bump from one problem to another. Unreformed banks will inevitably cause bigger problems further down the road.

In summary, risk has to be taken: shareholders buy shares specifically to take risk, with the hope that they will be compensated sufficiently. But risk has to be managed. There is no magic formula to choosing the right business strategy, be it geographical or product market selection, though there are prescriptions for the right risk management approach. Headlong growth without control is the feature of most of the problems described in these cases. Lack of management and supervisory attention and a lack of common sense and challenge lead to situations where risks accumulate without being addressed.

Such a lack of care is often accompanied by an aggressiveness and lack of humility, which result in poor risk management strategies or an assumption that risk has been tamed or extinguished. The case of JP Morgan reminds us that this can occur in the banks that might otherwise appear to be among the best managed and at a time when caution and scrutiny should be ubiquitous. These basic failings – and the positive features of the cases that we have observed – can be acted upon to enable change for the better. The last chapters of this book build these observations into a set of proposals for more care, more common sense and, in a word, "better banking".

6
Objectives and Design Principles

If the aim of this book is to talk about "better banking", then we need to consider what we mean by "better" and also *for whom* it should be better.

The events of the last five years have caused immense problems on a global scale. The prosperity of billions of people has been permanently reduced and the future of some entire countries has been blighted. Since this destructive crisis is evidently a financial crisis, we are led to re-appraise the role of finance in our economic system, which leads us to the practical issues of the nature and structure of the banking industry, but also fundamental political and socio-economic questions that may challenge the models of laissez-faire – or at least, market-based – capitalism prevalent throughout much of the world.

To a large extent, the crisis in the banking industry was driven by extrinsic causes, such as fundamental tensions in the world economy as a result of globalisation, developments in communications and information technology, and socio-political changes such as the desire for the extension of home ownership to poorer sections of society. Against this backdrop, there were drivers that were intrinsic to the banking industry, such as growth in size and complexity, mismanagement, insufficient capital, excessive leverage and inappropriate risk-taking. Much of the focus for reform has been on the intrinsic factors. Politicians at an international level (e.g. at the G20 meetings) have tasked the leading regulatory authorities with developing the necessary reforms: unsurprisingly, the regulators have confirmed that the problems can be addressed through an updated regulatory framework. Many of the extrinsic factors are not being considered or addressed. The focus of this book, too, is primarily on the problems that are intrinsic to the banking industry.

At first glance, the ultimate objective of "better banking" must surely be the same as it has always been and always will be. *We require a banking system that is stable and reliable, providing capital and risk management tools to the real economy efficiently and effectively.* But these objectives are too vague to act as design parameters for the banking industry.

We need a more detailed understanding of our goals, in order to have a basis on which to diagnose the shortcomings of the status quo and to be able to propose constructive solutions. We need to define the measures that we will use to define a "better" banking industry. We need to know its role in the economy and in society. In a word, we need to understand *why* we need banks – indeed, *whether* we need banks – and *what* we want banks to do.

Some of these questions are weighty, political and controversial. They can only be covered in brief in this current work. But it is nevertheless worth raising them in this context, partly because there have recently been some serious debates, challenging the accepted wisdom of much that has driven our financial industry during modern times. Examples of the questions that tend to be covered include:

- What is the role of finance and banking in our society?
- Should banking be a smaller industry? What would a smaller industry imply for the users of bank services?

- Can "free-market" economics be applied to banking?
- Who should allocate and price financial resources and manage risk in the economy?
- Should banks be required to meet state-imposed lending targets, as payback for needing support from the state during the crisis?
- What is the risk appetite of society and of investors in a bank?
- To what extent should banks be driven by considerations other than their own profit? How can ethics suitably be married with profit?
- Is there a role for new types of "non-bank" to provide banking services?
- Is the globalisation of the financial services market a necessary or desirable feature? Do we need a global banking regulator and supervisor?
- Should banks have their financial performance capped, like some utilities?
- Do bankers have enough of a vested interest in the downside risks they create? Do they have enough "skin in the game"?
- Do we need more regulation of compensation in banks?
- To what extent is "culture" an issue for banks?

These questions are profound and complex. They are also difficult to answer without laying out some overall observations. Before laying out a "blueprint" proposal for the banking industry, therefore, it makes sense to lay out the design objectives that we are assuming for the industry.

6.1 FREE MARKET VERSUS STATE CAPITALISM

> A democracy cannot exist as a permanent form of government. It can only exist until the majority discovers it can vote itself largesse out of the public treasury. After that, the majority always votes for the candidate promising the most benefits with the result the democracy collapses because of the loose fiscal policy ensuing, always to be followed by a dictatorship, then a monarchy.[1]

Almost all countries in the world – even ones like China that are not liberal, multi-party democracies – operate an economic system where state control, support and intervention is limited and free-market capitalist elements dominate. By capitalism, we mean:

- Private property rights, the right of ownership and inheritance.
- Free exchange of goods and services; open competition and markets.
- Markets not just for goods and services, but also for labour and for capital.
- Use of money as a means of exchange.
- Low level of state intervention and control ("*laissez faire*").
- A sound civil legal system, to enforce contracts.
- Integration into international trade usually symbolised by a membership at the WTO and other international organisations.

---

[1] Attributed to Alexander Frazer Tytler.

Of course, no country or society would want to run a purely capitalist system, since all societies have a desire to provide their members with some degree of centralised control, oversight, "checks and balances", shared services and safety net: in effect, a state apparatus. This applies to all types of activity with potentially negative externalities: for example, with regards to environmental pollution or human rights. Unbridled capitalism is not a desirable or sustainable system for any sector of the economy. Since banking is a business that deals with financial risks, it is clear that the "pure" capitalist model will not address the risks that banks pose to the overall economy:

> Banks themselves do not have an incentive fully to internalize the social cost stemming from their own contribution to system-wide risks.[2]

Different countries choose to have (or have imposed on them, if they are not democracies) differing proportions of state apparatus. In fact, capitalism comes in different forms, reflecting the cultural and historical heritage of the country.

- *China's* single-party political system operates a centrally planned and directed economy, including a state-controlled banking system.
- Liberalism in *the USA* is fundamentally opposed to state intervention while the "pioneer spirit" favours entrepreneurship, individual risk-taking and a higher degree of flexibility and mobility in the workforce. Nevertheless, American political dogmas did not prevent a massive state rescue of the banking system during 2008 and 2009.
- Since the Thatcher years in the 1980s, *the UK* has had a liberal political agenda similar to the USA. Just like the USA, the UK had massive amounts of state intervention in the banking industry during the current financial crisis, with the government taking temporary stakes in several large banks, notably 82% stake in RBS and 40% in Lloyds (the Lloyds stake was reduced to 33% during 2013).[3] These stakes are held on an awkward "arm's length" basis, with a rapid return to the private sector the desired objective.
- By contrast, despite a wave of privatisation in the 1980s and 1990s, the *French* state continues to be interventionist (for example, recently in the auto sector) and protective. In banking, the lending levels of the banks to the financing of the real economy are closely scrutinised by the state.
- For historical reasons, the *German* banking sector is dominated by the cooperative sector, savings banks and the regional "Landesbanks". The share of private sector banks with commercial shareholders (essentially, Deutsche Bank and Commerzbank) is small compared with other countries. This structure lends Germany a special flavour of banking industry and one that has faced several challenges – requiring state bail-outs – during the current financial crisis.

Interestingly, within even the most liberal of market economies, the role of banks and bankers as intermediaries and risk-takers can still be seen in a negative light. Distrust of and dislike for bankers is an ancient phenomenon. More than two thousand years ago, the Greek philosopher Aristotle noted that "the trade of the petty usurer is hated with most reason: it makes a profit from currency itself, instead of making it from the process

---

[2] High-level expert group on reforming the structure of the EU banking sector, Erikki Liikanen, October 2012.
[3] Annual Report and Accounts 2011/12, UKFI.

which currency was meant to serve. Their common characteristic is obviously their sordid avarice."[4] In the Bible, there is an episode where Jesus rants at the money-changers in the Temple.[5] Throughout history, normal people have experienced the pain when repaying debts and have seen the bankers getting rich merely by switching money around, rather than working up a sweat. The balancing side of the argument, namely the benefits of credit, are overlooked. Banking is not seen as *real* work and the income and wealth derived from it is interpreted as greed. In today's troubled economy, the sentiment is intense. Senior politicians can refer to bankers with venom, as illustrated by the UK Business Secretary's reference to bankers as "spivs and gamblers".[6] The recent episodes of egregious behaviour and massive losses in the banking industry have even caused proponents of the liberal, capitalist economy to reflect on the actual workings of such a system: "Bankers are now seen as embodiments of insatiable greed, and are despised not merely by those who are critical of capitalism as an economic system, but also by many who are otherwise well-disposed towards it."[7]

6.2 ARE THERE ALTERNATIVES TO BANKS?

> To the extent that they hive off some of their activity and send it into shadow banking, the next generation of people who will do what I do can worry about that.[8]

Banks are not well-loved at the moment. The popular impression is that banks caused the financial crisis that has had such an horrendous impact on the economy and our personal wealth and wellbeing; banks are not lending enough into the real economy and so households and businesses continue to struggle; bankers are odious people, who are incompetent and grotesquely overpaid. Some commentators have even raised the question of whether we need banks in the first place. In order to form a view on this, we need to consider what services banks currently provide to the economy and to society, then imagine what would happen without those services.

Broadly speaking, the services that banks provide are those shown in Table 6.1.

Now, people who are "anti-bank" are not arguing that those five categories of services are not needed. They generally argue that either (a) new or different types of banks could provide those services instead of the traditional providers or (b) banks add little value to the process of intermediation and can be circumvented (this is termed *disintermediation*). Some of the ideas that exist or have been floated include those shown in Table 6.2.

---

[4] *Politics*, Aristotle.
[5] Matthew 21:12.
[6] Business Secretary, Vince Cable speaking at the Liberal Democrat Autumn Conference, 22 September 2010 and reported on www.libdemvoice.org.
[7] *Central Banking Journal*, JR Sargent, 24 May 2011.
[8] Michael Cohrs, Member of the Financial Policy Committee, Bank of England, quoted in Changing banking for good: Report of the Parliamentary Commission on Banking Standards, June 2013.

Table 6.1 Banking services

Custody of money	Paper money can be convenient, but most people would rather have a bank look after their "at hand" money. People leave their spare cash in their current account, rather than in pound notes and dollar bills.
Payments services	Every transaction in our economy needs to be accompanied by a transfer of funds from the buyer to the seller. Banks traditionally operate the payment system, whether through cash handling, ATM networks, payment cards or electronic transfers. This is because payments are closely tied to the provision of credit.
Provision of credit	Individuals and corporations need to borrow for a variety of reasons. This could be short-term working capital to help them through a period where cash is tight, or a longer-term capital investment (such as buying a house) that is converted into periodic repayments. Banks are intermediaries between those with a need for credit and those with a need for investment.
Investment management	On the other hand, many individuals and corporations are cash-rich and/or need to put money by for future needs, such as a pension. They need to put their money to work. This could be simply by lending it to the bank, which is what a deposit account does. Or, it could be by selecting a longer-term or riskier investment, such as buying bonds or shares. Most people use banks as a source of their short-term financial investments (i.e. deposits). Long-term investments are handled by banks and other types of companies, such as specialised asset managers and insurance companies.
Market-making and risk management	Financial transactions in currencies, investments and risk management tools (such as derivatives) need a matching buyer and seller. Banks faciliate this matching process, either through their own books or on an industry-wide marketplace. Without a market-maker, no-one would know the right level for, say, foreign exchange rates.

Some consider that the use of non-banks represents a solution to the current malaise of the banking industry. For example, Professor Kotlikoff of Boston University has put forward a radical proposal that would turn the entire banking industry into a series of mutual funds. Banks would originate loans and "send them to the [to-be-created Federal Financial Authority] for rating, package them in mutual funds, and sell them to the public. [...] There would still be risk, but it wouldn't be in the financial institutions that put our money to work."[9]

The promotion of non-bank lending has become part of public policy in some countries. In the UK for example:

> in addition to its intention to invest through managed funds, HM Treasury will also consider the potential to invest through other non-bank lending channels. This could include providers of alternative types of finance (such an invoice financing and leasing), and non-traditional lending relationships (such as online platforms, and other ways of directly accessing investors). This would be with the aim of increasing the supply of credit to SMEs and midsized businesses, and helping to increase the diversity of finance options available to businesses in the UK in the longer term.[10]

---

[9] A Modest Proposal: Limited Purpose Banking, Kotlikoff, Assetbuilder, 13 March 2009.
[10] Business Finance Partnership: market engagement, HM Treasury, 6 December 2011.

Table 6.2   Alternatives to banks (illustrative)

Custody of money	Payments providers (see below)
	Stashing physical goods (in times when the value of money is doubted)
Payments services	PayPal
	BitCoin
	Pre-paid credit cards
	Barter (in times when the value of money is doubted)
Provision of credit	Insurance companies
	Pension funds
	Bond market (for corporates)
	Consumer peer-to-peer lenders (e.g. Prosper, Zopa, Ratesetter, Lending Tree)
	Corporate peer-to-peer lenders (ThinCats, Funding Circle, Exchange Associates)
	Vendor finance, captive finance companies (corporates providing finance to their customers, so that the customer is able to buy the goods)
	Friends and family (the oldest form of credit!)
	Deleveraging (the ultimate alternative to bank credit – don't borrow!)
Investment management	Direct investment without a broker
	Peer-to-peer lenders
	Friends and family
Market-making and risk management	Stock exchanges
	Peer-to-peer exchanges (such as Betfair, though no comparable example in financial services comes to mind as yet)
	Insurers in general, but notably monoline credit insurers for credit risk
	Risk retention (i.e. customer bears the risk)

Much of the enthusiasm for new banking models stems from the power that modern information technology offers. Just as the internet has transformed the business model of retailers, travel agents and the music and publishing industries, so might it be able to transform the world of banking services:

> With open access to borrower information, held centrally and virtually, there is no reason why end-savers and end-investors cannot connect directly. The banking middle men may in time become the surplus links in the chain. Where music and publishing have led, finance could follow. An information web, linked by a common language, makes that disintermediated model of finance a more realistic possibility.[11]

These new ways of accessing banking services are provided by what we might consider to be "non-banks", but they are still banking services. We must conclude that whilst we might not need what we see as "*banks*" we do need "*banking services*". But then what should we

---

[11] Towards a common financial language, speech by Andrew Haldane, Bank of England, 14 March 2012.

call companies that offer banking services…?! Is this pure semantics? Surely, if it walks like a duck and quacks, it's a duck. If it provides a banking service, it's a bank.

In a word, non-banks that perform banking activities pose a risk to the financial system in exactly the same way that banks do:

- *Funding and liquidity risk*, if the shadow bank suffers a loss of confidence and experiences periods of customer withdrawals, for instance.
- *Solvency risk*, if it has leveraged its balance sheet and its asset exposures drop in value.
- *Contagion risk* due to the interconnectedness of shadow banks with each other and with the regulated banking system.

The more that society relies upon non-banks, the greater these risks. There is no dimunition of risk by shifting activity onto new entities that have different appearances but the same functions and risks. Similarly, the ability to allow free-market discipline to regulate the market is just as limited as with banks. The end-user (in many cases, the retail depositor) is unable to oversee the providers of financial services, no matter whether they are banks or non-banks. Shifting the risk management burden onto the end-user is simply not acceptable. For banking services and products, the notion of *caveat emptor* is not sufficient. Banking services do not lend themselves nicely to "Wild West" market mechanisms. The Kotlikoff proposal mentioned above, for example, would put large numbers of consumers, small businesses and major corporations on the hook for unlimited risk. This, of course, is unwise. These customers will need an agent of some kind to manage their risk exposures as well as a "Guardian Angel" regulator to ensure their manager is kept in check.

Regulatory attention has turned to the growth in providers of banking services outside the regulated banking industry and the term *shadow banking* has become the standard label. In many cases, shadow banking is merely the development of new, specialised business models that are more efficient or effective than the classic banking model. In several cases, however, shadow banking exploits the arbitrage opportunity provided by the absence of regulation or the presence of an alternative regulatory regime (e.g. insurance).

Shadow banking is estimated to be about half the size of the banking system at present, having grown rapidly in the years preceding the current financial crisis, from $26,000bn in 2002 to $62,000bn in 2007.[12] The non-banks engaged in banking-like activities – and particularly the provision of credit – include those listed in Table 6.3.

As well as non-bank financial institutions, the bond markets represent a major means for bank disintermediation. Corporations can raise money via the bond markets rather than relying on banks to lend them money. This differs by country, depending on historic factors. For example, in the USA, corporations borrow $6,300bn from banks and $6,400bn from the bond market,[13] whereas in the Eurozone, corporations borrow €4,500bn from banks but only €1,000bn from the bond market.[14] Whereas both bonds and loans are debt obligations, they differ in several important respects – see Table 6.4.

---

[12] Global Shadow Banking Monitoring Report 2012, FSB, November 2012.
[13] Flow of funds for non-financial businesses L.101 Q4 2012, Federal Reserve, March 2013.
[14] Euro Area Securities Issues Statistics Press Release (data for February 2013), ECB, April 2013.

Table 6.3 Shadow banking

Type of institution	Banking activity
Pension funds	Globally, there are $20,000bn of assets in pension funds.[15] Half of that figure is in the USA, with the UK, Japan, Australia, Canada and the Netherlands each having $1,000–2,000bn. The average level of pension fund assets relative to GDP is 72% and the OECD considers 20% as being a "mature" pension fund market. Only 13 countries in the world are identified by the OECD as having such maturity. The major Eurozone countries (France, Germany, Italy and Spain) have very few pension fund assets, relying instead on unfunded pay-as-you-go systems. Pension funds have traditionally invested most of their funds in shares, but this has been declining and is now just under half of their total investments; bonds make up about a quarter.
Hedge funds	Hedge funds are a specialised type of investment fund. They have an estimated $2,660bn assets under management.[16] Hedge funds can be grouped according to the overall strategy they pursue, with "equity long/short" the largest category at 22.1%.[17]
Private equity funds	The private equity industry typically seeks to buy companies and turn them around, selling them rapidly and at a profit. Indeed, the industry does not talk about "assets under management", seeing its investment base as a "large pool of unrealized capital that had increased to $1.8 trillion by the end of 2010".[18]
Mutual funds, Investment funds	Specialised funds offer small investors the chance to invest in the capital markets using the services of an expert portfolio manager or, increasingly, a passive investment strategy such as an index-tracker.
	Traditionally investing in listed shares, funds nowadays offer the choice of a broad range of asset classes, including credit instruments such as bonds and loans.
	Total worldwide assets invested in mutual funds: $23,800bn.[19]
Money market funds	Money market funds are a specialised type of mutual fund that offers the investor with surplus cash an alternative to a bank deposit. They are mostly a US phenomenon and make up about $2,500bn of assets there.[20] Though often considered part of the "shadow banking" world, they mostly invest into the short-term bonds ("Certificates of Deposit" (CD) or "commercial paper" (CP)) issued by banks, and so are really an additional intermediation step (for unsecured CP) or part of the overall securitisation chain (for asset-backed commercial paper (ABCP)). Insofar as they invest in short-term bonds issued by corporates, they are an alternative type of investor in corporate bonds: this is considered below as part of the discussion of loans versus bonds.

---

[15] Pension Markets in Focus, OECD, September 2012.

[16] eVestment|HFN, January 2013.

[17] Hedge Fund Industry Snapshot, Citi Prime Finance, February 2013.

[18] Global Private Equity Report 2012, Bain & Co., February 2012.

[19] *2012 Investment Company Fact Book*, Investment Company Institute, 2012.

[20] Ibid.

Type of institution	Banking activity
Insurance companies	Insurers are major investors in the capital markets as well as offering loans directly to individuals and companies. During the recent phase of deleveraging, many bank loan portfolios have been sold to insurers. In several areas, this is due to the regulatory arbitrage between banking and insurance regulations, which means that the cost of regulatory solvency capital and funding can be significantly lower for an insurer, for some asset classes.
	Insurers have an estimated $22,600bn assets under management (equivalent to 12% of global financial assets),[21] with half of their investment portfolio allocated to bonds and loans.[22]
Securitisation vehicles	Like some of the funds highlighted above, securitisation vehicles are often considered part of the "shadow banking" world, but are in fact an additional intermediation step. These vehicles buy portfolios of loans from banks and issue bonds to refinance the loans. See Section 3.6.5.
Finance companies	In general, finance companies provide finance for the lease or purchase of fixed assets. They are often the in-house lending operations of equipment suppliers. Examples include Ally Financial and CIT.
Conduits and SIVs	These are companies set up by banks to arbitrage regulations on solvency and liquidity. In the run-up to the onset of the financial crisis, they offered an opportunity to make leveraged investments and arbitrage the inadequate regulations. Bank-sponsored SIVs took immense funding and investment risk with no regulatory capital requirements: their return on regulatory capital was effectively infinite. See Section 2.4.
Repo counterparties	Repos are a form of secured borrowing. They enable funding and maturity arbitrage, since they allow a bank to raise cash via short-term debt on the back of its holdings of long-term securities.
Monoline credit insurers	Non-banks provided credit protection in the run-up to the current financial crisis. They were known as monoline credit insurers or monolines for short. Examples include AIG, Ambac, MBIA.
Sovereign wealth funds	Sovereign wealth funds (commonly known as SWFs) invest their countries' surplus funds and have aggregate assets under management of $5,000bn.[23]

Non-bank funding markets can prove unreliable. An illustration of this is the pull-back of money market funds' lending to banks in the Eurozone. Because of the funds' perception of the riskiness of Eurozone banks, they reduced their lending to these banks drastically in the second half of 2011 (see Figure 6.1).

---

[21] Global Insurance Industry Fact-Sheet, International Association for the Study of Insurance Economics, 2011.

[22] The Social and Economic Value of Insurance: A Geneva Association Paper, International Association for the Study of Insurance Economics, September 2012.

[23] SWF Institute website.

Table 6.4 Comparison of bank vs bond funding for corporations

Feature	Bank loan	Bond	Comments
Risk assessment	Relationship-based. Also, since the fair value of bank loans is not disclosed, banks may be able to take a longer-term view	Arm's-length In theory, the bond market is an efficient way of allocating capital, but is more prone to panic and volatility	Is relationship-based lending on balance a good thing? Does the benefit of superior customer knowledge outweigh the fact that relationship considerations may pollute risk decisions?
Rated?	Internal assessment by the bank	Yes (generally), public rating from credit rating agency	
Documentation	Can be easily customised	Largely standardised	Bond documents usually incorporate much more information
Size	Any size	Fixed costs (legal, rating agency expenses, syndication fees) and desire from investors for trading liquidity lead to preference for "benchmark sizes" of €500m and up	Loans better suited to small transactions
Flexibility	Loans offer more flexibility in times of stress as they are easier to renegotiate or restructure	Restructuring or amendment of the terms requires a meeting of bondholders. Negotiations tend to be long and costly and, if they are not successful, lead to an Event of Default	Bank loans undoubtedly more flexible
Monitoring	The lending bank retains the exposure and monitors the client and the loan exposure, taking action where appropriate. Most loan agreements contain certain provisos or covenants for the borrower	Monitoring is limited to credit analysts, ratings agencies and events of default/ "credit events"	Bank loan gives more intimate monitoring
Trading	Loans are not listed and are generally not traded. There is a syndication market, where banks share large loans, and a secondary loan market that is private and largely comprises banks selling down large loan positions to other banks	Bonds are listed and traded on the financial markets and pricing tends to reflect more closely the perceived credit risk and liquidity premium	Bonds are more amenable to trading

Feature	Bank loan	Bond	Comments
Secondary price	Loan trading is a relatively inactive market and so prices of loans are more difficult to define	Traded, volatile, transparent	Bonds are easier to value than loans
Market stability	Liquidity gluts and "credit crunches" do occur and can make the availability of bank loans unreliable or excessive	Due to absence of a relationship factor, the bond market is, in theory, relatively rational and risk-sensitive	Both loans and bond markets can exhibit unstable features

The name "shadow banking" has negative connotations, suggesting that the activities of shadow banks are shady and undesirable. Regulators appear to want to extend their supposed fixes for the fundamental shortcomings of banks to the *non-regulated* forms of banking activity:

> Although intermediating credit through non-bank channels can have advantages, such channels can also become a source of systemic risk, especially when they are structured to perform bank-like functions (e.g. maturity transformation and leverage) and when their inter-connectedness with the regular banking system is strong. Therefore, appropriate monitoring and regulatory frameworks for the shadow banking system needs to be in place to mitigate the build-up of risks.[24]

International work, led by the FSB, initially aims at an improvement of transparency in the reporting of shadow banking activities, including for example more disclosures from fund managers to end-investors. The FSB also aims to limit the regulatory arbitrage opportunities by requiring tighter rules on collateral, the promotion of central clearing and changes to bankruptcy law treatment of repo and securities lending transactions.

Measures to control shadow banking are further advanced in the USA. The Dodd–Frank Act contains several provisions to regulate certain areas of shadow banking, such as: increasing the transparency and disclosure of securities lending operations; new rules affecting money market funds' liquidity requirements, to cope with large redemptions; the imposition of more control and collateral rules for repo counterparties; restrictions on the use of ABCP conduits. In securitisations, the originating bank is required to retain a minimum of 5% of a transaction and restrictions on the distribution of securitisation products are introduced to mitigate any conflict of interest between a sponsor and an investor.

Our conclusion is that there *are* alternative to banks but they are, to all intents and purposes, similar to incumbent banks. They are not actually *non-banks*, they are *non-traditional banks*. Whilst they may not be regulated at present as banks and subject to the same controls, they perform similar functions and create the same systemic risks. Society's banking needs require banks to service them and any non-traditional providers of these services need to be regulated using the same principles as for more traditional bank models. The financial industry is too precious and fragile to let trouble in the back door.

---

[24] Global Shadow Banking Monitoring Report 2012, FSB, November 2012.

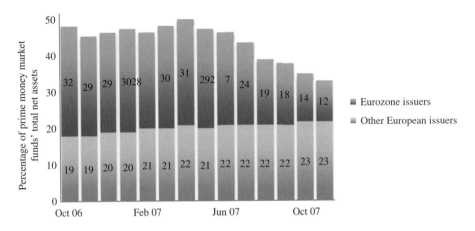

Figure 6.1   Money market funds' reduction in lending to Eurozone borrowers[25]

6.3 BENEFITS AND LIMITATIONS OF FINANCE

> Since the promulgation of Hammurabi's Code in ancient Babylon, no advanced society
> has survived without banks and bankers.[26]

Whilst there are many needs that the banking industry can service, the virtues of finance do, of course, have their limitations. This observation is a truism that *almost* goes without saying, but recent experience suggests that it is sometimes overlooked. If we expect too much from financial services, we are in danger of taking undesired risk, of exceeding our "risk appetite" (see next section).

Banking has the capacity to create wealth and happiness. By matching up the supply of capital (investors) with the need for capital (borrowers), the needs of both parties can be met at a mutually beneficial price and wealth-creating opportunities, such as the building of a bridge across a valley to enable better transport links, can be pursued. The matching up of capital investment needs with capital borrowing needs enables so many productive features of our world: companies can invest in machinery, young people can buy a home, students can pay for their education. Yet, investment projects of dubious value can rarely be transformed into good ideas through waving the magic wand of finance. We now see how banking was used to allow poor people to buy expensive houses by taking out subprime mortgages. On a risk-adjusted basis, the subprime product destroyed wealth: borrowers got kicked out of their houses, investors in subprime lost their shirts and society lost out as the knock-on impacts of the crisis spread. Better banking will lead to economic growth that is superior to the effects of directed lending and subsidies.

Banking has the capacity to reduce risk. Simple financial tools like diversification can be combined with underwriting and risk management expertise to reduce system-wide risk. Banks can facilitate transactions where equal and opposite risks are netted down to zero

---

[25] *2012 Investment Company Fact Book*, Investment Company Institute, 2012.
[26] What good is Wall Street?, *The New Yorker*, 29 November 2010.

(for example, the two sides of a foreign exchange contract). Farmers can sell their wheat in advance at a fixed price and confidently invest in the seed, fertiliser, machinery and labour to get the crop planted and harvested without taking the risk of a price fluctuation causing them a huge loss. Banks can disperse risk around the system so that volatility is reduced. Large, unpredictable risks broken down can become small, low impact risks with a more manageable probability profile. In the jargon, unexpected loss – that is, risk – can be (largely) transformed into expected loss, which is a cost but not a risk. By reducing the unpredictability of outcomes, the spreading of risk reduces the aggregate risk in the system (more precisely, the aggregate *institutional level* risk in the system). This is the basis on which, for example, early mutual insurance companies were founded, such as the "protection and indemnity clubs" used by ship-owners for hundreds of years. However, risk is only reduced in aggregate if any new risks are lower than the ones being mitigated. This is not the case if risk is passed back to the originator in a circular fashion, such as the large amount of subprime exposure that ended up on banks' balance sheets, often hiding in the *liquidity* portfolios. Risk concentrations were passed around the banking system and re-accumulated in new places, creating a new set of risky banks. Risk is not reduced if the initial risk is hedged with a counterparty that is itself risky. Banks who bought subprime securities and hedged them with monoline credit insurers, for example, were merely replacing one risk with another.

Banking can help us manage cycles. We are all familiar with the ways, in which banks can help people through the stages of their life cycle. Bank lending can help a young family, for example, who will then grow wealthier, repay their debts and seek to invest their surplus income in order to provide for their retirement. As they move through the life cycle, they use banking products in different ways to meet their developing needs. In the same way, corporations can use banking services to help them smooth their product cycle, the impact of fluctuations in their business or the investment cycle as new plant and machinery are purchased, installed and become productive. It is less clear whether banking helps society tame the destabilising effects of *economic* cycles. In theory, it can, assuming that the industry is sensitive to risk and provides dynamic feedback to the economy through the price of borrowing, i.e. the cost-of-capital. That would be an anticyclical financial market. If banking were to help us avoid exuberance in booms and nurture our confidence in busts, it would be a powerful economic tool. But, in practice, financial markets and the banking industry tend to follow human psychology and operate in a procyclical way. Immediately before the onset of the "bust" part of cycle, confidence is highest, market prices are at their peak, perception of risk is at its lowest and cost-of-capital is also at its lowest. The market feeds the bubble rather than taming it. Moreover, the banking industry has developed an instinct for arbitrage, finding new approaches to take risk in an unobserved fashion and working against regulation. The market tends not to be self-regulatory. In the following chapters, we consider whether this need always be the case.

6.4 HOW MUCH RISK CAN WE TOLERATE?

Risk is a permanent and necessary feature of our lives. There is no such thing as a "zero risk" economy. Just as society needs banks to take risk in providing credit to wealth-creating opportunities in the economy, so does society need to take risk in allowing a risky banking industry to operate on its behalf. But just how risky should banks be?

At an industry level, several regulators are publicising the fact that they will not be operating a "zero failure" policy. To this end, policies are being advanced for the controlled resolution of banks that fail. In particular, investors are being reminded that they should not expect the state to bail them out. However, it is not enough to know merely that the authorities are prepared to let banks fail; a policy of non-zero failure is not a calibration of risk appetite. Yes, we know that banks will fail and we should live with that fact. What is not clear is how often we expect banks to be failing.

This is a matter of precarious public policy. On the one hand, political considerations can encourage the build-up of risk through, for example, an accommodative monetary policy (current policy of most countries in 2013) or encouraging home ownership (policy in the USA in the early 2000s). Excess liquidity distorts risk, inflates asset prices, lowers yields and plays a decisive role in the formation of asset bubbles, which then burst. On the other hand, risk levels can be kept too low, as happens after the bursting of an asset bubble. Mistakenly, the market perceives risk to be rising and so the availability of risk capital diminishes. Such a "credit crunch" is an example of risk appetite being set too low.

Within individual banks, the concept of risk appetite is meant to help set risk policy and, in a nutshell, help banks avoid surprises. A top-down risk strategy that sets out the limits of acceptability in the risk profile of the bank can be cascaded through the organisation and inform all aspects of the bank's activities in day-to-day operations as well as budgeting and planning. A good, institutional-level definition of risk appetite could be as follows:

> The amount of risk that the institution needs to and wants to take in order to achieve its business plan.

One senior regulator has also defined clearly the role of a risk appetite framework:

> At the heart of a good risk management framework is a clearly articulated statement of the board's appetite for risk. From this can flow the myriad of policies, procedures, limits, reporting and other internal control and assurance mechanisms that make up the entirety of a risk management framework in a financial institution.[27]

To be useful, a risk appetite policy needs to give concrete and quantified guidelines on:

- Concentration by product, geography, client and risk type.
- Sensitivity to economic and market volatility.
- Leverage of the capital base.
- Fraud, malpractice, misselling and other operational risks.
- Reputational risk.
- Political, regulatory and tax risk.
- Management of complexity and growth.
- Catastrophe risk.

When a bank has formulated such guidelines, it needs to identify the best possible way of measuring these risks and then communicate them to investors and embed them into the bank's operational processes, such as business development, underwriting and performance management.

---

[27] Supervisory Lessons From The Global Financial Crisis, John F. Laker, Chairman, Australian Prudential Regulation Authority, 8 December 2010.

If successful, the following types of outcome could be envisaged:

- *During a boom*, investors in the (low-risk) bank would be comfortable with a lower-than-market growth rate, rather than pushing for acceleration in growth.
- *During a period of stress* and industry-wide losses, investors in the (high-risk) bank would accept the higher-than-market-average level of losses that result from the riskier business strategy.
- Investors would *not be panicked by the volatility* in the capital base that results from a more leveraged capital base and would not be surprised by, say, a rights issue to top-up capital levels in the event of losses or high growth.
- Investors would *not be surprised by major losses* in areas where the bank has chosen to absorb the risks involved rather than spend money on hedges or business curtailment.

If all banks had had an effective risk strategy based on an articulated risk appetite policy, it is likely that many of the calamities of the current financial crisis could have been avoided or at least mitigated. Several of the case studies in Chapter 5, for example, are the result of a risk management policy that was riskier in practice than investors (and sometimes even the management) realised. On the other hand, there are several of the troubled banks that were transparent in their risk appetite, even to the extent of labelling their own strategy as "aggressive" (e.g. HBOS, see Section 5.3) and so it would be fair to transfer some responsibility from management, who were executing an agreed strategy, to investors and the regulatory authorities.

There are two links between industry-wide risk of banks and institutional-level risk.

The first is *tail risk*, which comprises the extreme risks that are accepted by the institution that would lead to its failure and so are transferred to its creditors and/or to society. Unfortunately, tail risk tends to be underestimated, with bank managers tending to focus on "normal" or "expected" outcomes. Few banks, for example, had back-up funding plans prior to 2007 and were, in hindsight, running excessive funding risk. We need to have a set of objectives for managing tail risk.

The second is *commercial returns*. Assuming we do not want a system where banking is monopolised by the state, the profits accruing to the private sector owners of the banks will need to be sufficiently attractive for them to invest their capital in the industry. Society's risk appetite may well reduce the risk levels that it is prepared to tolerate from banks, suggesting utility-like returns. But banks are not water companies and good banking practice will not be sponsored through fixed returns on capital. Why do we say this? Because fixed returns imply zero risk and banking is a business that has, at its heart, the transformation of risk. It can only become a utility if we can eliminate risk from the equation. For this to happen, each loan that a bank makes would need to have a highly predictable loss potential with no scope for downside surprises. This *may almost* be the case for some market segments, such as prime residential mortgages, where credit losses across the portfolio are, indeed, highly predictable. In segments such as these, the banking industry begins to resemble a utility: commoditised product offerings, low profit margins offering a minimal return on capital, low-cost business models characterised by standardisation and automation and domination by scale players. But other areas of banking are not as granular or predictable and require banks to innovate and take risk. See Table 6.5.

Therefore, we need to allow the conditions for a risk-constrained yet adequately profitable banking industry, with scope for outperformance from superior strategy and management.

Table 6.5   Comparison of banks and utilities

Utility (e.g. water company)	Bank (if operating properly)
Known business plan	Uncertain business plan
Investment in infrastructure	Risk-taking
Capital for investment	Capital to cover volatility, risk
Regulated tariffs	Regulated risk exposure
Low cost-of-capital	High cost-of-capital
Franchise is key	Franchise is key
Commodity	Value-added service

Interestingly, the industry seems to be able to achieve decent levels of profitability, despite the drop in risk appetite that has led to major increases in capital requirements imposed by new regulations. In fact, the return-on-equity projections of the management of large blue-chip banks appear quite reasonable from a shareholder's perspective (e.g. Barclays "in excess of cost of equity" i.e. 11.5%,[28] UBS 15%,[29] HSBC 12–15%,[30] DNB Nor 12%[31]). These levels would appear investible, if they are achievable and if – a big if – risk is constrained to acceptable levels.

6.5 THE ROLE OF REGULATION AND SUPERVISION

> Government's view of the economy could be summed up in a few short phrases: If it moves, tax it. If it keeps moving, regulate it. And if it stops moving, subsidize it.[32]

The nature of financial services in general – and banking in particular – means that it must be regulated (i.e. subject to a set of rules and principles) and supervised (i.e. monitored for compliance with these rules and principles) *to some extent.* Banks provide services of a social utility, which is so economically stimulating and necessary in normal times, and yet hazardous if applied inappropriately, that it cannot be *completely* subject to laissez-faire approaches and free-market forces. The italic words here show that neither regulation nor the market is the *absolute* controller of the banking system, but instead a balance and a trade-off are required. Finding the optimal solution is not easy, as there tend to be several opposing objectives.

Most people would suggest that a banking industry would be regulated and supervised in a way that was:

- Competent and expert, at least in line with industry practice.
- Effective in allowing the industry to flourish, such that sufficient capital is available and competitive forces improve the industry's services.

---

[28] Becoming the "Go-To" Bank, Barclays PLC, 12 February 2013.
[29] UBS Raises Profitability Target as Ermotti Shrinks Bank, Bloomberg, 30 October 2012.
[30] Investor Day: Capital and Financial targets, HSBC, 17 May 2012.
[31] Norway's DNB slashes dividend, ROE targets, Reuters, 6 September 2012.
[32] Ronald Reagan, 1986.

- Permissive of free-market disciplines (such as profit-seeking) and outcomes (such as failure).
- Effective in stopping activities that could have harmful consequences (or at least mitigating them) and initiating actions that will have beneficial impacts.
- Transparent and clear.
- Consistent and predictable.
- Objective and fair.
- Efficient in the use of both its own resources and also the resources it consumes within the industry and in customers.
- Efficient in terms of timeliness and responsiveness.
- Pre-emptive, if not prescient, and anticyclical, to address problems at their causes rather than their symptoms.
- Adaptable and able to maintain relevance as the industry changes and develops.

Looking at these objectives, it is immediately apparent that tensions exist. How can a system be at once permissive and able to stop negative actions pre-emptively? What is the right balance between effectiveness and efficiency? How can a regulator/supervisor be at once both predictable and adaptable? More broadly, how does shareholder capitalism work in a regulated industry?

The answer is that different societies or jurisdictions will make different choices and end up with different styles of regulation and supervision and, therefore, different types of financial industry. For example, some societies have a low tolerance of earnings inequality and will choose to regulate *levels* of pay in the banking industry quite closely, while others will merely regulate pay *structures* so that excessive risk-taking is not promoted. Global authorities such as the Basel Committee will attempt to impose a degree of consistency across international approaches, especially in areas where there is potential for arbitrage and exploitation of differences with an overall negative impact (for example, money-laundering), but will not remove differences entirely.

In all of the design features, however, there is one constant: banking is not a normal sector. Banks play a vital role in economic and monetary policy. They are susceptible to political meddling and so-called "regulatory risk", the risk that they will need to do something because the authorities require it, rather than it making standalone commercial sense. In a word, banks are to a certain extent organs of the state and regulation is one of the ways that the state can achieve its overall objectives. By way of example, consider the direction given by the UK Chancellor to the Bank of England's "Financial Policy Committee", reminding them: "It is particularly important, at this stage of the cycle, that the Committee takes into account, and gives due weight to, the impact of its actions on the near term economic recovery."[33] Banking is special in all sorts of ways that are positive for management and shareholders, like being able to take deposits and on-lend them to other customers whilst taking a spread on the interest rates paid and received, but it is also special in that it exists only at the behest of the regulator and is therefore significantly reliant upon the regulator in the formulation of its strategies and processes. As a result, banks tend to place more emphasis on "lobbying" the regulators and politicians, in order to ensure that the interests of their owners are represented as policy is formed.

Different business cultures will place different emphases on the relative roles of regulation and supervision. Some societies, for example, tend to place a lot of reliance on written rules and laws that are explicit and prescriptive. The challenge under this approach is to ensure the rules do not become unworkable. They need to be clear, concise and coherent. It could be

---

[33] Remit and Recommendations for the Financial Policy Committee, Letter from George Osborne to Sir Mervyn King, 30 April 2013.

argued that the thousands of pages of regulation in the EU Capital Requirements Directive and in the US Dodd–Frank Act – neither of which is watertight or definitive – are examples of how cumbersome and ineffective a thick rulebook can be. A thick rulebook also has to be kept up-to-date. The alternative is to keep rules to a minimum and instead pursue a "principles-based" style of regulation. This would naturally require a more intimate and intrusive supervisory style and would rely greatly upon the skills and judgement of supervisors.

6.6 THE ROLE OF "THE MARKET"

> I used to think if there was reincarnation, I wanted to come back as the president or the pope or a .400 baseball hitter. But now I want to come back as the bond market. You can intimidate everybody.[34]

Economic developments in most advanced economies in the 1990s were based on the political doctrine that markets were sophisticated, rational, self-interested and self-correcting. This led to increasing deregulation, not only of financial services but also in other industrial sectors such as airlines, energy suppliers and telecommunications.

Basel II was a product of those times. The driving principles assumed that, given a certain minimum level of capital (Pillar 1) and good supervisory scrutiny (Pillar 2), market discipline (Pillar 3) was the most suitable way to steer the shape of the financial industry and this required appropriate disclosure mechanisms. This has been described to some extent in Section 4.4 and is typified in the following statement from Basel:

> A bank that is perceived as safe and well-managed in the marketplace is likely to obtain more favourable terms and conditions in its relations with investors, creditors, depositors and other counterparties than a bank that is perceived as more risky. Bank counterparties will require higher risk premiums, additional collateral and other safety measures in transactions and contractual relations with a bank that presents more risk. These market pressures will encourage a bank to allocate its funds efficiently and will help contain system-wide risks.[35]

The architects of Basel II knew that "the market" had vast amounts of skilled resource at its disposal, far more than the regulatory and supervisory authorities could or should be able to muster. The market was able to process and act on new developments instantaneously, whilst the authorities – with a duty to be comprehensively thorough, consultative and fair – took ages to react. And paramount in their minds was the assumption that the vast sums of money at risk in the financial markets would lead to a degree of self-interest that would automatically and smoothly steer the system towards the right answer.

Unfortunately, in its official pronouncements, Basel II did not develop the concept of market discipline very much, instead focusing exclusively on the disclosure requirements. Market discipline was assumed to follow disclosure:

> Market discipline can only work if market participants have access to timely and reliable information that enables them to assess a bank's activities and the risks inherent in those activities.[36]

---

[34] James Carville, quoted in Greenspan's Rates of Wrath, *Time Magazine*, 28 November 1994.
[35] A New Capital Adequacy Framework, BCBS, June 1999.
[36] Enhancing Bank Transparency, BCBS, September 1998.

In fact, information provision is only one aspect of the requirements for effective market discipline. Just as important are the aspects of incentives, behaviours, discipline and governance.

We now know that these other aspects were poorly understood. In combination, the market mechanisms did not work: "Any competent forensic work has to put the libertarian theory of self-regulating financial markets at the scene of the crime."[37]

The problem is that market feedback can sometimes be self-reinforcing. Since investors and their agents are seeking to avoid losses and make profits, they can exhibit behaviours which might appear vicious, volatile, animalistic, sometimes even irrational. These behavioural traits can lead to chaotic or procyclical market movements. This had not been taken into account by Basel II. Too much reliance had been put on to the mechanisms of laissez-faire capitalism working in a tidy way. The practice of the markets was different from some of the theories and the regulation had unintended consequences. Liberalism had the unintended consequence of allowing arbitrage; self-regulation resulted in self-interest with insufficient systemic care; implicit guarantees, such as the Greenspan put, ironically led to greater instability. The assumptions on the incentives and actions of economic agents were not what had been assumed. This took some of the most esteemed authorities by complete surprise and challenged their beliefs:

> Those of us who have looked to the self-interest of lending institutions to protect shareholder's equity (myself especially) are in a state of shocked disbelief. Such counterparty surveillance is a central pillar of our financial markets' state of balance. If it fails, as occurred this year, market stability is undermined.[38]

In reality, investors can sell or short and depositors can run: there are few other feedback mechanisms. The self-interest of investors and depositors is only rational, but it does give rise to the danger that the "real" or underlying risks are under-priced in a bull market and over-priced in a crisis. It is left to the authorities to provide the regulatory backstop and guard for society's interests by ensuring stability and providing financial safeguards for depositors and taxpayers.

The problem of market discipline even pervades the very aspect on which Basel II had concentrated: information disclosure. In order for the securities markets to price risk properly, they need the requisite information on which to base their actions. Since banking and risk are undoubtedly highly complex concepts both in theory and practice, this aspect of the banking industry is problematic.

> Market discipline, Pillar 3, would also be strengthened by simplified regulatory rules and practices. For investors today, banks are the blackest of boxes.[39]

But is it really possible and desirable to simplify the complexity? The true objective of a market-based banking industry is to enable free-market agents (i.e. risk-taking investors, but also depositors) to have sufficient, comprehensive, relevant information on which to base their investment decisions and influence the companies of which they are stewards. Nostalgists may be fearful of large volumes of data, for example in solvency calculations: "from single figures a generation ago to several million today".[40] But a quest for simplicity may be blind to risk and hence counter-productive. The information available to the investor base may be complex but it must also be usable. That usability – rather than any naïve simplicity – is the real objective.

---

[37] The End of Libertarianism: The financial collapse proves that its ideology makes no sense, Jacob Weisberg, Slate.com, 18 October 2008.
[38] Testimony of Alan Greenspan to the US Committee of Government Oversight and Reform, 23 October 2008.
[39] The Dog and the Frisbee, speech by Andrew G. Haldane, Bank of England, August 2012.
[40] Ibid.

6.7 CONCLUSIONS: PROPOSED OBJECTIVES AND DESIGN CRITERIA

Based on the considerations set out in this chapter, we can propose, in Table 6.6, a set of objectives and design criteria, including some of the necessary trade-offs when objectives conflict with each other, to inform the objective of a blueprint for "Better Banking".

Other commentators will have differing objectives and so it is no surprise that there are many different views on how the banking industry should be restructured. Some, for example, will impose a constraining objective of simplicity on banks, hoping to make the governance of the industry possible by gifted amateurs and semi-professionals. Others may reject the free-market doctrine and seek to increase the level of state control of banks. Of course, alternative perspectives can be perfectly valid in this regard. Our only observation is that different objectives will lead to different blueprints and very different outcomes, in terms of the contribution of the banking industry to the economy and to society.

Table 6.6   Objectives and design criteria

Category	Objective and design criteria
Role of the state	The state should act as a credible backstop to the banking industry, in recognition of the interests of society and the economy in having a stable banking system. Other than providing the regulatory and supervisory infrastructure (see below), this should be its only role. It should not, for example, act as a destabilising force by influencing the lending activity of commercial banks.
Shadow banking	The scope of banking regulation should not be prone to gaps or arbitrage. Unregulated banks and other financial companies – whatever their legal form or label – should be subject to the appropriate supervision; likewise, the regulator should be accountable for financial developments outside the banking sector.
Value of banking; its limitations	Banks should be seen as service and intermediation vehicles to enable our economy to function, to help manage the risks we face and to help mitigate cyclicality. They should be allowed to act in this role on a commercial basis and with adequate supervision.
Risk appetite	The risk appetite of society through the cycle should be clearly gauged. This needs to include measures of macro-systemic and "tail" risk. The banking industry should not be allowed to exceed that limit. If societal risk appetite changes, e.g. through economic stimulus and loose monetary policy, banks and their regulators need to adapt risk profiles.
Role of the regulator	The regulator should act as the "Guardian Angel" of the interests of society and the economy. Regulation should have "brains and teeth", improving the risk management of the banking industry and ensuring that adequate information is placed in the hands of market investors.
	Regulation should promote the right incentives to avoid unintended consequences by developing arbitrage opportunities. It should not prevent innovation when it leads to benefits to the real economy and improvements in financing or hedging of risks.
Role of the market	Regulation should provide the framework for free-market principles to operate, wherever possible. Unacceptable strategies and behaviours should be curtailed by the regulator, where market forces fail to remedy them.
	Market forces should drive competition and efficiency within banks through a competitive landscape that promotes long-term stability over short-term gains.

7

A Blueprint for "Basel IV"

As previous chapters have attempted to show, current initiatives, including Basel III, are unlikely to fix the inherent weaknesses of the status quo banking industry. In order not to simply leave the issue at that and deliver only a sceptical critique, this chapter sets out to give some concrete and constructive "straw man" proposals for the way the banking industry is run.

Rather immodestly, the chapter has been labelled a "Blueprint for 'Basel IV'". That is not meant to imply that the proposals represent a finely honed policy agenda. Instead, they comprise a set of outline proposals, which are not part of current industry reform initiatives. The proposals are centred, naturally, around good risk management. Policy elements from current regimes that do not promote more effective risk management are rejected and excluded. In combination, these proposals should provide a better platform for a sounder and more effective banking industry than the current *modus operandi*. The proposals are based on some basic observations, heartfelt beliefs and a gritty sense of realistic confidence in the ability to be truly better. We believe that they will, on the whole, make sense to industry participants, interested observers and society.

They do, however, require a significant amount of resource, leadership and progress: any framework that assumes that change is simple is unlikely to work. Whether the proposals are too idealistic, naïve or just too ambitious is the subject matter for Chapter 8.

The nine key elements of the proposal are described in Table 7.1.

These elements are explored in more detail in the following sections.

Table 7.1 Key elements of the proposal

1. Risk management	Risk management needs to be upgraded across all parts of the banking industry, ensuring that banks are realistic about the risks they are running and that risk information is not suppressed artificially. Concrete measures such as the adoption of confidence accounting and the implementation of a sophisticated yet standardised *electronic* reporting template would assist. But the solution is more profound and holistic than mere analyses and templates: banks need to put risk management at the heart of their business processes, not the periphery.
2. The "Guardian Angel"	No-one is going to ensure the stability of the banking industry, other than regulators/supervisors. Therefore, supervision becomes one of the most important activities in the industry. The process of supervision needs to become truly *intensive* and *intimate*, with supervisors pulled into the day-to-day operations of the bank. Supervision needs to become a high profile and well-rewarded career, on a par with "front office" banking. The substantial required costs and resources can be paid for by the banks via a charge equivalent to 0.5% of operating income (£5m per £1bn).

(continued)

Table 7.1   *(Continued)*

3. Human capital	Resources and behaviours in the banking industry need to change, in line with the requirement for improved risk management. Top-down management processes need to be improved, with senior management more alert to the risks in the business: a rigorous organisational approach will be required to ensure this, such as our proposed "centurion" model. Pay and culture will need to reflect the focus on risk management: in short, performance management will need to become risk-adjusted.
4. Governance	Society and shareholders need to be more active in managing the institutions on which they rely. The issue of control and governance is a top-down issue. There must be no point at which no-one is responsible and accountable. If governance can be improved, all other problems will be resolved without friction.
5. Capital	The arcane focus on regulatory capital needs to be replaced by an in-depth assessment by the regulator of the level and types of risk that have been assumed by banks and the level and types of capital that are appropriate to that situation. The capital assessment report would be documented and published. In order to provide an objective benchmark of sorts, the Standardised Approach ratio and the leverage ratio can be maintained and published. But the main monitoring tool should be a capital adequacy report from the supervisor.
6. Liquidity and funding	The current Basel norm for liquidity – forcing banks to have large holdings of government bonds – should be replaced by the extension of a committed credit line (like an overdraft) from the central bank of the currency in question. Funding disclosure should be improved through a quantification of the income received by maturity transformation. Guaranteed deposits should be explicitly treated as a deposit with the central bank that is administered by the commercial bank in question: a "quality stamp" will help differentiate such deposits from non-guaranteed bank deposits.
7. The "Pillar 2" mindset	Risk must be treated as a dynamic rather than a static phenomenon and combined with the philosophy that "assets don't have risk, institutions do". With such an approach, deterministic stress testing becomes obsolete and, instead, a "wargaming" capability informs a continuous learning process that identifies institutional pinch-points and prepares the management for non-standard developments.
8. Glasnost: market discipline and Pillar 3	With risk-focused management, the oversight of a "Guardian Angel" and a clear role for deposits, the capital markets should be in a good place to decide which banks are the ones that are most likely to give them a superior risk-adjusted investment performance – assuming readily available, relevant information. Investors will need to be self-interested, employing analysts who understand the risk profile of banks in depth and with credibility. This may require substantial changes to the way that brokers and asset managers operate and staff themselves. Once established, these investment capabilities should enjoy a beneficial feedback loop.
9. Industry structure	Well-managed banks will tend to be large and diversified, though a heterogeneous industry should be nurtured, where possible, with new entrants encouraged and stagnation avoided. Overall, it is market forces that should determine business models rather than regulation, though the supervisor should discourage undiversified, specialised monolines beyond a certain size, due to their higher level of tail risk.

7.1 RISK MANAGEMENT

Reality is far more vicious than Russian roulette. [...] Unlike a well-defined precise game like Russian roulette, where the risks are visible to anyone capable of multiplying and dividing by six, one does not observe the barrel of reality.[1]

Any risk management framework needs to take into account the subjective nature of risk, as described in Chapter 3 "Methodologies and Foundations", and the inherent limitations of risk management as a discipline. To put it simply, you cannot *know* risk, but you can do things to mitigate it and manage it. With that mantra as a starting point, much of the rest of risk management is common sense. So long as risk information is transparent, risk appetite is clearly stated, concentrations are avoided and diversification sought out, risk management is hands-on or intimate and punts on "almost risk-free" exposures avoided, then the outcome is likely to prove acceptable.

This section sets out the principles of a sound risk management regime at the institutional and systemic level.

7.1.1 Valuation Approaches

As described in previous chapters, a crisis of confidence can arise when a bank has loans or investments of doubtful or dubious value. Creditors and depositors of the bank might fear that the assets of the bank will prove insufficiently valuable to be able to repay its liabilities and they, as the providers of those liabilities, will lose money. In essence, a bank becomes "non-viable" when it loses the confidence of its providers of capital.

This situation can occur even if the official accounts appear to indicate that the bank has a healthy level of positive net assets, with the value of accounting assets comfortably exceeding the value of the accounting liabilities. In other words, there is no need for an audited set of financial information to show that the net assets have truly dipped below zero: such a definition of bankruptcy exists only in the textbooks. In fact, due to difficulties in assessing a realistic value to all of a bank's assets, and in particular the limitations of loan book accounting, accounting measures are often a poor reflection of the real value of the balance sheet. This has a severe knock-on impact on market confidence in times of crisis, including the current financial crisis. "The perception that there were large unrealised losses on amortised cost assets was one of the main drivers of the loss in confidence in firms during the crisis."[2] There has to be a better way.

Unfortunately, the debate on accounting (as described in Section 3.2) has polarised into those who are *pro* the use of fair valuation measures and those who are *anti*. This is hardly even a debate: it is more a dilemma, since current regulatory solvency measures and accounting metrics are exclusively mono-dimensional. What is not clear is the objective of valuation, why the asset or the liability is being valued in the first place. Is it assuming a long-term series of cash flows, characteristic of a "going concern" bank, or is it based on a "fire sale" disposal

---

[1] *Fooled by Randomness: The Hidden Role of Chance in Life and in the Markets*, Nassim Nicholas Taleb, 2007.

[2] The prudential regime for trading activities: A fundamental review. Feedback on DP10/4, FSA, July 2011.

of assets and liabilities at today's market prices? A valuation could be radically different, depending upon its basis. If we use the wrong basis, the valuation will be misleading: valuing the assets and liabilities of a failing bank assuming that it were a viable going concern, for example, would overstate its net worth and therefore the risk to creditors and depositors.

Some of the arguments against any fair valuation approaches are that the volatility of values needs to be suppressed. This view sees volatility as unnecessary and undesirable: "Accounting rules should better take into account the need of through the cycle provisioning and develop a longer term view by restricting the use of fair value."[3]

This is a dangerous view, which can ironically amplify market volatility, as fear replaces a sober appraisal. In many situations (think of AAA subprime bonds that were changing hands for 20% of par yet marked in many banks' books at around 80% of par), the accounts stubbornly reflect the purchase price more than any sane appraisal of value. Economic and market conditions can change rapidly and a bank's accounts need to reflect reality. Real-time accounting may not be practical or even desirable, but on-time, realistic valuations are necessary. Some smoothing of market inputs can be useful, to ensure that volatile prices are not given undue prominence just because they are the most recent. Overall, the valuation approach needs to incorporate a realistic view on long-wave and short-wave volatility considerations. Current methodologies do not contain sufficient realism. They do not pass the "common sense" test all the time.

The answer to the valuation dilemma lies in valuation approaches that are richer and more informative and embrace the inherent uncertainties around the valuation of financial assets and liabilities. In a simple version, banks would show an accounting value and a corresponding realistic value in their financial reporting. In many respects, this is already happening for trading assets via new regulatory standards known as "Prudential Valuation Adjustments". Banks could extend the concept to their loan book assets as well, which is where much of the risk and uncertainty currently resides.

To extend the concept further, banks could develop what is known as "confidence accounting", an approach which does not seek to determine a single value for each financial item, but rather a range of values with the estimated probability for each of them. This technique is being developed in the field of weather forecasting, giving people an estimated likelihood of possible weather patterns for the period, instead of a single, most likely, forecast that – despite being the most likely – is wrong most of the time. "The use of a deterministic numeric paradigm in accounting and auditing may well be the root cause of many current problems. Accounting methods could use probabilistic inputs and show resultant outputs as distributions of numbers."[4] It could also extend into scenario-based valuation. Banks could give alternative views of their balance sheet valuations, based on a variety of scenarios, such as fire-sale, run-off or long-term continuation. All assets and liabilities could be included in the analysis – including some that are invisible today, such as:

- Intangible assets, such as customer franchise or brands.
- Future profit streams from existing customer transactions in ongoing businesses (the value of which is referred to in insurance as the "value of in-force" business).
- Staff-related and contract liabilities that would need to be settled.
- Legal liabilities and costs of conduct redress (currently a major topic in the UK due to overhang of future costs of, for example, misselling products).

---

[3] Regulating finance after the crisis, Christian Noyer, Governor, Banque de France.
[4] Confidence accounting: a proposal, ACCA, CISI and Long Finance, July 2012.

Such a valuation would be outside the restrictive framework of international accounting standards. These standards have proven, for banks, to be unsatisfactory and inflexible, to such an extent that the prudential view of a bank's financial health is often vastly different to the accounting view – with the market view proving quite different too. For example, Standard & Poor's has welcomed the prospect of a more sophisticated approach: "When analyzing a bank, an understanding of the range of possible values for financial instruments is as important as the single valuation that a bank includes on the balance sheet."[5]

7.1.2 Role of Internal Risk Assessments

Subjective risk assessment is central to all aspects of sound banking. Internal risk assessments are absolutely essential. One of the greatest advancements of Basel II was that systematic risk assessment was effectively made mandatory for all banks. Whilst the scepticism towards internal ratings-based risk measures has been noted in previous chapters, the current slide towards objective, standardised risk measures is worrying, if it leads to an industry where simplistic regulation drives a risk-agnostic, rather than risk-sensitive, view of banking and risk is seen as an exogenous, unavoidable facet of banking, rather than something that is accepted, absorbed, managed and influenced by the banks themselves.

Only the institution that is holding the risk can ultimately determine the riskiness of the exposure. If banks use risk-weights determined by the regulator or the ratings of credit ratings agencies, then they will have effectively outsourced the risk assessment and underwriting process and be reliant upon the skills and judgements of the fallible third party, namely the regulator or the ratings analyst. More worryingly for the industry, the objective setting of risk assessment will cause homogeneous, herd-like behaviour.

The subjective view of risk allows the institution and the supervisor to engage in a debate on the true risks and sensitivities of a given asset or activity. As well as avoiding the dumb defence of "but it's triple-A" heard so frequently during the run-up to the onset of the current financial crisis, it ensures that risk management is dynamic and diligent. Dropping internal risk assessments may make life simpler in some respects, but it puts new barriers and arbitrages in place. It threatens a return to the days of Basel I (which was, let's face it, the regulatory regime in place during the run-up to the current financial crisis), under which various crude loopholes were exploited to take return-on-reg-cap to the roof while accumulating vastly excessive levels of risk and, in the course of it, destroying shareholder and societal value.

7.1.3 Putting Risk Management at the Heart of Banking

During the reconstruction phase of every recent financial crisis, the banking industry has always vowed to increase the profile and importance of risk management. This has generally failed to work for two reasons.

---

[5] What's Fair Value? Reducing Valuation Uncertainty Could Boost Confidence in U.K. Banks—And Global Peers, Osman Sattar & Giles Edwards, Standard & Poor's Ratings Services, 7 March 2013; reproduced with permission of Standard & Poor's, a division of The McGraw-Hill Companies, Inc.

Table 7.2   Who influences business strategy decisions?[6]

Risk managers have an input but the front office determines business strategy	47%
Risk managers have a significant input but the front office still holds sway over business strategy	34%
Risk managers and front office personnel contribute to business strategy in equal measure	16%
Business strategy is determined solely by the front office	3%

Firstly, the organisational culture of banks has continued to be dominated by the marketing teams of the "front office". The results of a recent survey of banks demonstrate this phenomenon (see Table 7.2). Risk management personnel tend to play second fiddle to the front office in determining business strategy.

Not all problems of the current financial crisis were driven by front office decisions and strategies, it must be noted. Many of them, such as the excessive use of short-term funding to drive profit at the expense of running high levels of maturity risk, were determined by support functions and general management. But still, the point is that not enough business planning and decision-making has the risk aspect adequately covered.

Secondly, the *capability* of risk management has tended to be compartmentalised and concentrated into the risk management *function*. In most banks – and more strongly in the banks that had the most severe failings in risk management during the current crisis – business units try to achieve their revenue and profitability (ROE) goals at all costs, with the risk management function attempting to act as a brake or a balance to the risk/reward assessment. The front office simply doesn't see risk management as its job. Since performance measures tend not to be risk-adjusted, value appears to be being created by the marketing teams of the front office, which therefore attracts a far greater level of compensation and organisational clout; the risk management function tends to have a lesser claim on talent and compensation and so becomes a junior partner in the risk management discussions.

This problem needs to be tackled by *putting risk management at the heart of banking*. Such a simple and obvious necessity will be challenging to achieve unless banks' owners and regulators require it and the governance problems prevalent in the industry can be addressed. Once that is done, the challenge then is to roll out the concept throughout the entire institution and across the industry. This will require many aspects of banking to be redesigned, for example, as shown in Table 7.3.

Risk management capabilities need to be commensurate with the size, complexity and growth of the organisation. Problems can arise if the business races ahead of risk processes, as the head of UBS noted regarding their risk capability: "While it was filled with the best intentions and it had a period when it worked well, it was clearly inadequate once the bank grew to the size and complexity it had in 2006 and 2007."[7]

---

[6] *Using Holistic Information on Risk to Enhance Business Strategies*, Lepus, 2013.
[7] Uncorrected transcript of Oral Evidence taken before the Joint Committee, Parliamentary Commission on Banking Standards, 10 January 2013.

Table 7.3 Putting risk management at the heart of banking

Performance management	Performance measures must move from simplistic, short-term, non-risk-adjusted sales targets to a longer-term value-added approach that takes risk into consideration explicitly and fully.
Strategy and planning	Rapid growth into new business areas tends to result in risk accumulation that is unacceptable. With a firmer focus on risk management, banks will shy away from aggressive growth strategies and M&A conducted on the basis of limited due diligence. Hopefully, efficient market mechanisms will assist in this task by penalising banks with overly rapid expansion plans.
Product design	Management will need to manage product innovation that appears "too good to be true" more carefully. The risk appraisal of new product developments will need to test the performance of products in multiple stress situations to better understand their risk profile. Likewise, the customer angle on suitability and *customer* risk management will need to be assessed: a product that is profitable but nevertheless exposes the customer to risk by definition exposes the bank to risk; *caveat emptor* is not acceptable as a mitigant for risk.
Pricing	Pricing calculations need to take risk into account. Whilst this seems blindingly obvious, in fact few banks consider all aspects of risk (including concentration risk, lessons from "wargaming" and customer optionality, for example) in pricing decisions. Until recently, for example, the cost of liquidity was not often priced into a bank's product design and performance management: it was simply – and erroneously – assumed to be available at the benchmark rate (e.g. LIBOR or fixed rate swaps markets).
Culture	Risk as a concept needs to transform from something boring, tangential and nerdy into a core element of successful banking. Since culture is largely about tolerance and promotion of certain behaviours, banks need to ensure that good risk management is rewarded *as much as good sales* and bad risk management is addressed.
Disclosure	Risk might seem to have a habit of going away if hidden. But in reality it increases if not actively managed. Banks need to adopt a disclosure approach of recognising and communicating risk through a concerted programme of proactive "glasnost" (see Section 7.8). This will lower their cost-of-capital.
Contingency planning	Few banks have contingency plans around anything other than an IT problem or a fire. In fact, the economy and the markets rarely follow a central "base case" and so back-up plans, developed out of wargaming exercises, are essential.

The reward for better risk management will be a better risk-adjusted performance. Importantly, compliance with regulation will be insufficient for shareholder value objectives:

> Most banks have taken steps to improve their understanding of the regulatory implications of their actions. Few, however, have married this perspective to a clear understanding of the economic implications. Banks that have such a one-dimensional view could find themselves in compliance with key regulatory ratios but still far from able to create value on a sustainable basis. [...] Few banks, even among the leaders, have taken concrete steps to integrate a more accurate, comprehensive view of risk into the processes used to guide individual businesses and set the prices of products.[8]

---

[8] Facing New Realities in Global Banking: Risk Report 2011, © 2011, The Boston Consulting Group, December 2011.

7.1.4 Role of Risk Benchmarks

As has been stated many times already, risk is subjective. So what is the role of agencies' credit ratings and of market pricing? The answer is that they both form important reference points, against which the bank's internal, subjective view can be challenged. Since the market comprises thousands of participants, each striving to achieve a decent investment return, it represents a powerful, dynamic risk management system. But markets are prone to excessive swings of exuberance and pessimism, they can be myopic and they can be duped. Similarly, the resources of the credit ratings agencies are skilled credit analysts who generally display expertise and diligence. Their views are likely to be well researched and thought through. But the ratings agencies' views do not represent reliable, actionable investment advice, their methodologies lead to some outcomes that are odd (e.g. the AAA ratings given to some subprime securities), their fee model gives rise to some significant conflicts of interest and they are not visionaries.

External inputs should be treated merely as risk benchmarks and nothing more. They should help highlight risk assessments for further consideration, where the bank's internal assessment differs widely from the market or the ratings agency. But they should not form a hard-wired element of a risk management strategy. Banks and other investors that have a ratings-based investment policy should upgrade it to include internal measures, no matter how simple. For the same reason, we do not see it as appropriate for ratings to be used in regulation as anything other than a rough guide; regulation should also not be "hard wired". Let us recognise, though, that deviations from a benchmark will tend to be closely scrutinised: if a bank's risk policy prefers the risk of a company rated "B" by an external credit agency to one rated "A", then clearly one would expect the policy to be questioned. Likewise, the bank manager who shunned "risk-free" AAA-rated subprime bonds in 2004 is likely at the time to have looked a bit foolish in front of his superiors and in relation to his competitors. Sometimes there is immense pressure to "follow the herd".

7.1.5 Assets Don't Have Risk, Institutions Do

One of the fundamental mistakes that has crept in with the adoption of Basel II is the notion of regulatory capital "charges" on an individual asset level. This was not the intention of the Basel Committee when it introduced the rules. In fact, the intention was for banks to build strong risk management systems and use those to inform the regulatory capital discussion. Whereas Basel II clearly linked the internal risk assessment with the regulatory capital requirement, it also made some approximations and necessary simplifications in the regulatory capital treatment that make it an inaccurate tool at an individual asset level. Regulators were keen to stress this point during Basel II implementation, for example:

> We recommend against using regulatory capital measures as a way of allocating capital internally for business decisions.[9]

However, most banks did not have an alternative risk management methodology. Regulatory capital was maintained as a management metric. Being a management metric, it was

---

[9] Remarks by Matthew Foss, FSA, presenting at the BBA Economic Capital Seminar, 30 November 2006.

managed! Banks focused on risk exposures and businesses that had low regulatory capital requirements. The language of capital moved from "requirements", implying a certain minimum threshold, to "charge", implying an accurate quantification of risk. As the financial crisis unfolded, even those banks that had hitherto employed an economic capital methodology found that newly raised regulatory capital requirements were more of a constraint than the outputs of the economic capital models. Attention moved ever further away from sound risk management to regulatory capital ratio management.

The desire for high regulatory capital ratios and the growing importance of "return-on-regulatory-capital" as a performance measure led to certain business models becoming quite monstrous, as they became overly focused on areas where regulatory rules were deficient. Risk built up and up; several firms with high capital ratios failed disastrously.

The point here is that the notion of RWAs has been overused. The risk to a bank is not the sum of the risk of the individual assets. On the contrary, the risk is more to do with factors that are not captured by the RWA measure: strategy, underwriting standards, responsiveness, diversification, and so on.

Any blueprint for a better banking industry needs to heed this advice. Assets don't have the risk that matters, it's the banks themselves and the way they do business that results in asset portfolios where economic losses can build up.

7.1.6 Risk Disclosure

Bank disclosure has improved a lot over the last five years. As described in Sections 3.11 and 4.4.5, much more relevant and timely information is now available to analysts and investors. However, the ability of these analysts and investors to utilise the information provided is limited by current disclosure regimes.

At present, Pillar 3 reports give investors risk information that is fairly mono-dimensional. The profile of credit exposures is given, the breakdown of regulatory RWAs, the allocation of loan portfolios to internal risk grades. The information is not standardised and often is available only in an electronic format that makes it difficult to analyse the data therein. It is only given once or twice per year and is often out-of-date by the time it is published.

The ultimate goal here is to deliver to investors and to the regulator an electronic template of financial information and risk profile data. In the near term, banks should be forced to provide their non-standard information disclosures in electronic spreadsheet format on their website. At present only a handful provide the information in this way. Once the template is standardised, the electronic format can be improved, moving (say) from Excel format to XML. This recommendation sounds so simple, yet for a reason that is hard to find, it has not yet happened. To be fair, some of the standardised forms used by the Fed and the SEC are a good start for a template. Likewise, the EBA stress tests gave the analyst community important new pieces of data in a standardised format that formed the backbone of many an insightful analysis in the subsequent months.

Some of the data available to the regulator may not be available to investors, though it is not clear that this should be a large subset. There is little risk information in a bank that is genuinely sensitive from a confidentiality standpoint, and the arguments for keeping information from investors are too heavily skewed towards non-disclosure at present.

A good set of static data in a standardised, electronic format would enable analysts to conduct further proprietary analyses, depending on the investor's chosen view. The amount of information that could be handled is large, thanks to the power of modern IT systems. It is wrong that, in this modern era, risk management is being hampered by Luddite views on data analysis. The cynicism of the "keep it simple" camp ignores the view that information is now much more readily handled and the only drag is where there is disclosure that is inadequate in volume, timeliness or format. So, we find nostalgic views of simplistic analyses, such as the lament that for RWAs "the number of calculations has risen from single figures to over 200 million. The quant and the computer have displaced the clerk and the envelope"[10] unhelpful.

Once the industry has managed to implement disclosure templates successfully, it should be provided in "raw" database format, to enable multi-dimensional analyses. For example, the bank may show a table of asset valuations according to confidence levels. It may also show a table of asset valuations by industry sector. If those data were delivered in database format, the analyst would be able to look at asset valuations according to confidence levels *per industry sector*.

The design of the standardised template is beyond the scope of this current work. However, at a high level, data fields would include:

- Detailed income and expense items, together with cash flow reconciliation.
- Risk asset valuations by confidence band, asset type, industry sector, loan-to-value band, currency, geography, provision coverage, maturity, current/maximum exposure.
- Funding sources by type, maturity, currency, interest rate.
- Capital instruments by type and regulatory adjustments to capital assessment.
- Fixed asset and intangible asset details.
- Details of cash, liquidity portfolio and investments.
- Quantification of maturity risk with fully matched funding level (see Section 7.6).

Static data is well served by a template approach to disclosure. However, the disclosure of static data is only a start, for risk is a multi-dimensional concept and only a dynamic assessment of risk is satisfactory. Time is one dimension that needs to be taken into account: the provision of "period-average" rather than just "period-end" balance sheet information should help to end the period-end "window dressing" that occurs at some banks, where banks load up on risk intra-period and shed it on specific dates when they know they are under observation. Further disclosures should reveal the findings of the scenario-based "wargames" (see Section 7.7.2) and a clear depiction of "what risks we take to make this income" on a granular basis, following the "centurion approach" (see Section 7.4.3). It is unlikely that these disclosures can be standardised, although it would be a positive thing if the written reports were to be accompanied with back-up tables and – preferably – databases.

This sounds like a lot of work. It need not be an excessive amount. The banks should have the relevant data in their reporting systems: if not, one has to wonder whether management is able to control the bank with sub-standard information. Analysts and investors will need to upgrade their information processing capacity, or there is a risk that more data will result merely in obfuscation and be counter-productive. It also happens to be one of the "non-negotiables" of a better banking industry. Banks have to disclose better data and investors need to use it. The sloppy ways of old may have been simple but they contributed to the current financial crisis. At any rate, good banks with good disclosure should enjoy a lower cost-of-capital, while their racy peers with inferior risk profiles should be disadvantaged. The lessons of the recent past

---

[10] Capital discipline, speech by Andrew G. Haldane, Bank of England, 9 January 2011.

indicate that markets need confidence and there can be a positive reaction to bad news if markets trust that the financial losses represent a step forward. Ignorance is not bliss:

> We turned out to know much less than we thought we did before the crisis. Key assumptions that underlie risk management models have come under scrutiny. Examples include the assumed normal shape of the risk distribution, the exceedingly short horizons for data records, the blindness to the possibility of herd behaviour, the inability to capture correlations, and the excessive reliance on market prices and past statistical relationships. However, all the financial institutions using similar models did not take similar decisions, suggesting that the problem is larger. The governance process that should support good judgment and decisions failed as much as the models on which people relied. Boards of directors and management of financial institutions were not always asking the right questions, often paying more attention to business volume than to risk management; profits were not analysed, and rewarded, on a risk-adjusted basis; and there were incentives to develop structures and new instruments to circumvent regulation and reduce short-term regulatory costs. Hence, the recent crisis has shown that it is essential to both improve risk modelling techniques to factor in interactions and tail events and rely on judgment and experience to supplement mathematical analysis (not a new concept, but one that had tended to be forgotten).[11]

7.2 THE GUARDIAN ANGEL

> Yes, an angel can illumine the thought and the mind of man by strengthening his power of vision and by bringing within his reach some truth which the angel himself contemplates.[12]

It appears that management, shareholders, bondholders, customers, regulators and ratings agencies might actually not be able to ensure that the banking industry does not fall into weak risk management practices and create the foundations of yet another financial crisis. All of these parties failed in the run-up to the current financial crisis:

> Inadequate supervision and overreliance on bank management, boards and market discipline: Basel II led to the wide-spread use of banks' internal models. However, there was insufficient oversight and challenge of those models. This enabled banks significantly to reduce risk-weighted assets and the real amount of capital held. Newer trading activities were inadequately captured in regulatory capital requirements. Reliance on market discipline failed. Investors demanded increasingly unrealistic returns and banks responded by taking unacceptable risks.[13]

And none of these parties has the resources or the mandate to work closely with the banks to ensure that risks are appropriate.

What is worse is that none of them felt it was their job to take full accountability for risk management on a systemic level, which we now know is the same as risk management on an

---

[11] Minimising the impact of future financial crises: six key elements of regulatory reform we have to get right, Jaime Caruana, BIS.

[12] Catechism of the "Summa Theologica", Thomas Aquinas, Notre Dame University Jacques Maritain Center translation.

[13] High-level expert group on reforming the structure of the EU banking sector, Erikki Liikanen, October 2012.

institutional level. Regulators and supervisors claim to have recognised now that the account-ability should rest with them:

> The historical philosophy was that supervision was focused on ensuring that the appropriate sys-tems and controls were in place and then relied on management to make the right judgement. Reg-ulatory intervention would thus only occur to force changes in systems and controls or to sanction transgressions which were based on historical facts. It was not seen as a function of the regulator to question the overall business strategy of the institution or more generally the possibility of risk crystallising in the future. In the future the FSA's supervisors will seek to make judgements on the judgements of senior management and take action if in their view those actions will lead to risks to the FSA's statutory objectives. This is a fundamental change. It is effectively moving from regulation based on facts to regulation based on judgements about the future.[14]

This is progress, but it is not sufficient. The accountability needs to be increased further and the role and resources clarified. In a word, banks need a benign "Guardian Angel" and this is the supervisor's job. They are the Guardian Angel, rather than the traffic warden. They are the ultimate risk manager (though their presence does not remove the need for risk management elsewhere in the organisation). It is no longer sufficient to expect bank supervisors to act out a game of poacher-and-gamekeeper or cat-and-mouse. Such an adversarial approach leads to inefficiency and – more importantly – ineffectiveness. The supervisory approach will define the culture of the supervisor, the profile of the human resources it develops, the nature of the inter-actions between the supervisor and the supervised bank and ultimately the success of the role.

Strong supervision is a natural extension of the developments in *internal* risk management that began in the early 1990s with the formation of centralised risk management functions, sophisticated information technology solutions and prominent Chief Risk Officer functions. These developments stalled somewhat in the run-up to the financial crisis, as banks became complacent and "sales and trading" overrode risk in the corporate mindset. It appears that the increased emphasis within banks on risk management disciplines is now re-establishing itself. The supervisor must act as an additional layer of the internal risk management function in a manner that is genuinely *intimate* and *intrusive*. These words are not used lightly: they are meant to contrast with the distant, passive and incompetent approaches of the past.

What do the words *intimate* and *intrusive* mean in practice? As an integrated part of the organi-sation, the supervisory team will have access to all information at all times. It will sit on manage-ment committees and receive all management information reports, business strategy documents, new business proposals and performance management analyses. Unlike the internal risk function, it will not operate as a risk "consultant" that advises business units on commercial risk judge-ments. Unlike the internal audit function, it will not merely conduct periodic reviews of process compliance. Instead, the embedded supervisory team will seek to ensure compliance and quality of the risk management capability of the bank *in everyday practice* and compare that with the expected standards. Conceptually, the supervisor should adopt something along the lines of the "centurion approach" (see below) to ensure comprehensive coverage of potential hotspots. At each point in the supervisory process, the team will be seeking to address the following issues:

- What are the areas of rapid growth, high complexity, concentrations?
- To what extent does the bank rely upon non-validated, external assumptions?

---

[14] A regulatory response to the global banking crisis DP09/2, Financial Services Authority, March 2009.

- What vulnerabilities are exposed by Pillar 2 wargaming exercises?
- How clear, comprehensive and timely is the risk information available to management?
- How robust is the risk management process from strategy through to origination, execution, portfolio management, trading, monitoring and problem resolution ... *in everyday practice*?
- Which areas of the business may contain risks that are not being communicated to management, shareholders and the market?
- Etc.

This would be a major change to the status quo. Such topics are far from trivial and the industry is likely to resist a truly embedded supervisory function, ostensibly for reasons of efficiency, in reality due to the inconvenience of such an approach. Quite simply, an intrusive supervisory function will expose areas that could previously have been muddled through by management: an aggressive trade, gung-ho growth in a given business area without real control, an overly optimistic assumption that fails to capture the risks to the bank's resilience under stress. Assuming good internal risk management and clear communication of the firm's risk appetite, there may be little for the supervisory resources to add, but that would be risk nirvana and it is unlikely that any bank in the world is at that point at the moment.

7.2.1 Key Aspects of the Guardian Angel Model

How will this Supervisory Approach have "Teeth" as well as "Brains"?

The Guardian Angel will work with the bank to highlight risks and ensure they are understood by management. They will ultimately be able to recommend sanction to the authorities, but their main tool will be a periodic supervisory report, appended to the financial reports of the bank, wherein the supervisory team will give its full, frank and fair views on the bank in question. In other words, the Guardian Angel will need to be not just intrusive but "extrusive" also. It is difficult to guarantee the competence of bank management or ensure adoption of low-risk strategies. But processes that make incompetence or high-risk strategies explicit are to be encouraged.

The risk clearly is that *subjective* could become simply *whimsical*. It could also become dangerously procyclical, creating additional pressures during times of stress. The subjectivity of the role would mean that several outcomes would depend upon the luck of the draw in which banks get which teams of Guardian Angels. The job of Guardian Angel will not be easy and the authorities responsible for managing the Guardian Angels will need to be skilled in their selection, training and monitoring of this important capability.

What Does Intimacy Mean?

The Guardian Angel should be intimately aware of what is going on in their bank. This closeness means that efficiency should be far greater than the usual arm's-length style of regulation. Currently, the authorities fear that regulation needs to be dumbed down to become practical:

> Robust rules for regulation will of necessity need to be simple or supervisors will be lost in a morass of unnecessary detail.[15]

However, this is not necessarily the case. The intimacy of the Guardian Angel will enable focused assessment of complex situations without getting bogged down in irrelevant detail.

---

[15] Finance: A Return from Risk, speech by Mervyn King, Governor of the Bank of England, 17 March 2009.

They will need to have a sufficient understanding of the bank's operations to know where the "bodies are buried"; their level of ignorance should be far lower than that of current supervisors. Of course, this will require new skills, competence and experience to form part of the job description of a supervisor.

What Does Intensity Mean?

Intensity means hands-on and focused on the necessary level of detail. It does not just mean more. Simply doing more of the same will not bring results. Those countries that had more resources dedicated to supervision were not any better at preventing failures: "The US system of resource-intensive bank examination has been no more successful than the UK's approach in preventing bank failure."[16] Anecdotal evidence indicates that supervisors in several countries had large, on-site teams and still failed to cap the risks of the institutions they were supervising. Likewise, the failures in the current financial crisis do not indicate that light-touch or no regulation was the problem: "It is clear that widespread regulatory failures contributed to the crisis. However, the part of the financial system most affected by the crisis is the most regulated, the banks. So the question of whether we did not regulate enough or we don't know how to regulate financial institutions effectively has not been answered."[17]

Is the Guardian Angel a Shadow Director?

Does the Guardian Angel approach mean that we are asking the regulators to take business decisions, to become what is known as "shadow directors" of the company? Not quite – though the answer could also be "a bit". The answer is not as categorically "no" as some supervisors see their role today: "We certainly told our staff very clearly that they would never get in the position of being shadow directors."[18] In practice, the Guardian Angel role is to live inside the bank as a member of management. Unlike other members of management, the Guardian Angel has the objective of improving the risk management of the bank to the sole advantage of society. Their job is not to second-guess the directors and management of the company as they pursue profits and shareholder value, but rather to reduce the probability of costly failure of the bank. But, indeed, the degree of intimacy required does give rise to several situations where the regulator has to act as a stakeholder, if not a shareholder.

Some have envisaged the role being like a "public protagonist who, on behalf of society, challenges proposals and tests arguments".[19] They see it as akin to having an opposition party in Parliament, to act as a natural countermeasure to unwise or unpopular decisions. It could also be termed a devil's advocate, a role to ensure that alternative perspectives are tabled and obvious truths pointed out: "The industry was in 'silent complicity'; we knew it could not go on…many allowed themselves to feel reassured because the regulators approved of the model of banks not needing much capital…none of them said 'stop'!"[20] On the other hand,

---

[16] The Turner Review: A regulatory response to the global banking crisis, FSA, March 2009.

[17] On the efficacy of financial regulations, Jón Daníelsson, London School of Economics.

[18] Michael Foot, formerly of UK Financial Services Authority, Parliamentary Commission on Banking Standards, Panel On HBOS, 23 November 2012.

[19] *Masters of Nothing*, Matthew Hancock and Nadhim Zahami, 2011.

[20] Inside the Minds of the Money Minders: Deciphering Reflections on Money, Behaviour and Leadership in the Financial Crisis of 2007–2010, Alison Gill and Mannie Sher, in *Towards a Socioanalysis of Money, Finance and Capitalism*, 2011.

we should be aware of the danger that a strong supervisor weakens the management process and reduces management accountability. As an illustration of this point, consider the observation of the Chief Executive of Lloyds Bank with regards to a misselling scandal: "We thought that, with our consistent and constant dialogue with the regulators, we were on the side of the angels."[21]

7.2.2 Creating the Supervisory Elite

The role of Guardian Angel as set out above has to be one of the hardest jobs in banking. It therefore requires resources that are expert, competent and credible. The people in the role need to be able to work with, yet challenge, the senior management of the bank and the notoriously tough traders and front office bankers. This is a challenge but also an imperative:

> Though this issue has not yet gained visibility in the various discussions and reports emerging from the crisis, the question of resources is likely to be crucial in determining whether the reformed regulatory framework can effectively deal with the next financial crisis.[22]

We need supervisors with teeth and brains. This has been recognised: "The PRA will have a larger proportion of more experienced and senior supervisors compared with the past."[23] However, there is a danger that the authorities simply hire lots of expensive people with lots of miles on the clock and it does not translate into competence. Instead, we would argue that, in order to build this supervisory elite, the authorities must be able to compete to hire the crème de la crème to work as supervisors. The challenge is to give the best people the pay, prestige and career path to build a truly competent supervisor. People in the supervisory authorities have to be on a commensurate skill level to the ones they supervise and this is patently not the case today. The skill set is difficult to find. Guardian Angels will resemble a blend of the competence of super-auditors, management consultants, practitioners and financial analysts.

Such resource is likely to be expensive. Some thoughts on how to pay for it are set out below.

The role itself will need free rein to operate intrusively in the institution which they are supervising. They must not be stifled and should focus on strategic risk and management processes, not adherence to restrictive templates. The issue of rotation will need to be dealt with, perhaps through maximum lengths of service at one institution, as seen in audit best practice.

7.2.3 Paying the Bill

With such a talented team to build, supervisors will need the ability to pay staff roughly the same as the banks themselves. Certain authorities appear to have been able to hire excellent staff at very low cost. However, in major financial centres such as London and New York, staff turnover at the supervisors for reasons of pay has been high. So, we assume that the cost of an effective Guardian Angel model would be more than today's costs.

---

[21] Changing banking for good: Report of the Parliamentary Commission on Banking Standards, June 2013.

[22] Minimising the impact of future financial crises: six key elements of regulatory reform we have to get right, Jaime Caruana, General Manager, Bank for International Settlements.

[23] The PRA's approach to banking supervision, PRA, October 2012.

The UK FSA was reportedly paying salaries of £56,473 per head in mid-2010[24] though more recent information shows a fully-loaded staff cost of nearly £100,000, including certain non-salary costs. The average pay in Barclays Investment Bank was £193,000 in 2012.[25] It seems safe to assume that, at present, staff at an investment bank earn about three times more than the supervisor.

As a ballpark and a "straw man", we are assuming that each institution will pay 0.5%, i.e. £5m per £1,000m of operating income to finance the supervisory resource. This would give them roughly 1% of the resource spend of the banks they supervise.

Current levels of expenditure are difficult to gauge and so anecdotal information is all that can be reviewed. In Australia, for example, the APRA has operating expenses of A$120m pa and supervises 898 institutions.[26] This cost is a mere 0.16% of the combined A$73bn operating income of the four big banks. Assuming that half of the workload is driven by the four big banks, it would appear that the supervisory resource in Australia, one of the better regarded regulatory models, costs under 0.1% of operating income.

The UK FSA, on the other hand, had a budget of around £500m pa, of which 31% was for the largest 10 banks.[27] This would equate to around 0.16% of the £100bn operating income of the largest four British banks. If we assume that just over half of that cost is from the largest UK banks, again we arrive at around the 0.1% mark.

The estimates above are heroic and unreliable. We hope, in due course, to be able to work them through in more specificity. But our hunch for the moment appears directionally valid: the cost of supervision is currently very low and the cost of staffing the regulatory elite could be absorbed by a minor incremental charge on banks' operating income.

7.2.4 Cross-Border Issues

For an industry that is half global and half domestic, the regulation and supervision of banks is bound to contain many cross-border issues. The work by the relevant authorities on this topic is neatly summarised thus: *communicate lots and communicate early.* The lessons from Lehman and other failed institutions are that banks are clearly global in their operations and domestic in their demise. Several aspects of a "better banking" approach to regulation and supervision: for example, clarifying that all funds entrusted to the bank – other than "assets under management" as described in Section 7.6.2 – are in fact part of the capital of the institution and will have no prospect of a state bail-out should the bank fail. But cross-border issues will remain, since they are driven by the fiscal aspect of any *potential* bail-out.

Guardian Angels will want and need to have their own domestic approach to supervision. Their accountability is to society and that ultimately means to the fiscal authorities who pay the wage bill and the clean-up costs. International coordination makes a lot of sense but global standardisation, beyond a point, may be unfeasible. Therefore, beyond the simple lesson on communication highlighted above, we assume that the Guardian Angel approach to supervision is likely to be a highly domestic role with a large amount of liaison with other supervisors in other countries of operation and a lead responsibility for the "home" supervisor.

---

[24] FOI1720, FSA, 5 August 2010.
[25] Barclays PLC Annual Report 2012.
[26] APRA Annual Report 2011.
[27] FSA Business Plan 2012/13.

For an industry that is continuously pursuing the goal of global harmonisation and the supposed nirvana of a "level playing field", such a subjective and potentially fragmented approach will sound nightmarish. But, in the quest for hands-on supervision that is effective, we have to make trade-offs and, unfortunately, harmonisation comes second by a long way. This means that multinationals will need to adapt to interfacing with multiple supervisory authorities who may have radically different implementations of a "Guardian Angel" model. Perhaps this is already the case with approaches to Pillar 2, which seem to be nationally defined. We see this as inconvenient but tolerable. In other words, we see harmonisation at the expense of intimacy as an unacceptable trade-off.

Cross-border issues are dealt with further in Section 7.9.3.

7.2.5 The Role of Macroprudential Regulation

Many regulators, supervisors and central banks have latched on to the idea that the regulatory failure contributing to the current financial crisis was due in part to the absence of a macroprudential perspective. Too busy looking at banks individually, they failed to spot the build-up of risk in the system. Hence they see the need to ensure that they also work on "identifying and addressing common exposures, risk concentrations, linkages and interdependencies that are sources of contagion and spillover risks that may jeopardise the functioning of the system as a whole".[28]

This notion is elegant and appealing to an economist but goes against the thread of the Guardian Angel concept. Our proposal instead chimes with the views of the Australian regulator:

> The build-up to the recent crisis resulted more from a microprudential failure than a macroprudential one. The easing in US mortgage lending standards, the growing reliance on short-term wholesale funding, the low risk weights applied to complex and highly leveraged structured securities were all things that an avowedly microprudential supervisor could have – and arguably should have – noticed and responded to. [...] What others think of as macroprudential supervision, the Australian authorities consider simply to be competent supervision.[29]

The identification of "macro-prudential" may have some validity in summarising sectoral issues, such as the desire to introduce centralised clearing of derivatives. The risk is that it diverts attention from the critical "avowedly microprudential" issues and partially rationalises failures at that levels.

7.3 HUMAN CAPITAL

The current financial crisis is the result of a failure of risk management, regulation and governance. To be effective, these fundamental aspects of banking rely on human competence, judgement and action. Intelligence and experience *per se* are not sufficient for effective risk management and governance, as we have discovered: organisational and behavioural aspects also play a part. Real people are at the heart of the banking industry and the current financial

---

[28] Macroprudential Policy Tools and Frameworks: Update to G20 Finance Ministers and Central Bank Governors, FSB/IMF, 14 February 2011.

[29] Macroprudential Policy: A Suite of Tools or a State of Mind?, Luci Ellis, Head of Financial Stability Department, APRA, 11 October 2012.

crisis is very much a human phenomenon. We may think that banking and risk are abstract and statistical in their nature, but they are products of human behaviour: "In all the talk of treating customers fairly, risk-weighted assets, capital ratios, operational risk, control frameworks and the like, we cannot lose sight of the fact that it is people who determine how customers should be served, what risk ought to be taken, and which actions are right (or wrong)."[30]

7.3.1 Competence and Incompetence in the Banking Industry

Management and supervision of a risk-taking entity such as a bank require people of the utmost competence, in other words people who are able to do the job well. As with any corporation, management is the servant of the shareholders and of other stakeholders and is responsible for agreeing and executing the best strategy for the firm. It is accountable for the running of the firm and ensuring that management processes are applied adequately. For banks, the top management is additionally responsible for ensuring sound risk management that is compliant with the applicable regulations, in order to avoid risks that are unacceptable to the system and to society. The supervisor is charged with ensuring compliance and protecting the interests of society, in effect acting as a second line of defence in case management errs. They may also, in the future, be given a more hands-on role of "Guardian Angel", as described in the previous section. The level of competence required to run the banking industry is challenging to develop and is likely to require rewards and compensation for good performance and outperformance (see Section 7.3.2 "Compensation").

Unfortunately, the search for competence in the banking industry finds many negative examples at senior levels in recent history. Whether it concerns the leading supervisors, the boards of directors, senior executives of banks or bank managements, there are numerous examples of people failing to fulfil the role with which they had been entrusted. Concrete examples include:

- Purposefully taking risks beyond the perimeter agreed with owners and regulators ("pushing the envelope").
- Unwittingly taking excessive risks, due to poor understanding of the nature of risk.
- Lacking leadership and accountability, often through over-delegation or leaving organisational gaps in coverage.
- Being ignorant of significant operational details.
- In the most extreme examples, abuse of position.

Apart from the last set, few of the examples of ineffective management and supervision were the result of greed or stupidity alone. We would argue that their incompetence was a result primarily of poor governance structures and other organisational issues. Fixing these issues can increase the *effective* competence of the banking industry.

Positive Feedback Encourages Continuation of Behaviours
Humans react to positive feedback in a way that is hardly surprising: they continue to act in the way that has been praised. Gradually, their professional performance alters to emphasise those aspects that are rewarded by their owners and managers. Before long, certain other aspects of their job have been de-emphasised or neglected.

---

[30] Salz Review: An Independent Review of Barclays' Business Practices, Barclays plc, April 2013.

In the banking industry, pay is the most obvious form of positive feedback, with senior bank executives of banks that later failed through excessive risk-taking being paid millions in performance-related pay before and during the crisis. Other forms of reward are also important, including promotions and (in the UK) the bestowing of heraldic titles by the state.

Whether through financial or non-financial means, rewards indicate to the recipient that their superiors and employers were or are exceedingly happy with their efforts, approach and achievements. If we are to improve competence and fix performance in the banking industry, we need to ensure that positive feedback is reserved for those aspects that are genuinely positively outstanding. In other words, the performance management framework for senior bankers and regulators needs to be improved.

Lack of Negative Feedback Encourages Concentration of Incompetence

Recent resignations and changes in management at the top of many troubled organisations highlight the challenges that an organisation faces in managing poor performance of senior staff. Again, an improved performance management framework is essential. Without negative feedback, managerial behaviours will not improve and competence may gradually decline.

Negative feedback needs to be an ongoing discipline, to enable the owners, directors and supervisors of the bank to influence its behaviours, business decisions and strategic direction. It is not desirable to be able to address problems only after they have occurred. Unfortunately, recent experience from the current financial crisis indicates that negative feedback tends to occur a long time – often several years – after poor decisions have been made. If we were to look at performance-related compensation as a bellwether, we would find that almost all of the failed banks of the last six years paid large discretionary bonuses to discredited staff in the year before the failure of the bank or the departure of the staff in question. The issue of compensation is considered in more depth next, in Section 7.3.2.

The ultimate negative feedback is to dismiss the manager or executive in question. This is considered the ultimate sanction for board directors of failed banks, no matter whether their own actions were specifically to blame for the demise of the bank: "If you are on the board of a bank that fails then you should not be allowed to carry out that role in the future."[31] There is also the possibility to "claw back" pay awards made in the past, as an additional punishment (see Section 7.3.2). This stern approach has some merits, but it may satisfy the desire for revenge more than proving a remedial measure. Our management of people who are not doing their job effectively should aim to root out issues before the point of failure is reached.

Organisational Gaps with no Collective Responsibility

Competence also requires effective action within the organisation. There needs to be a clear and effective system of governance and accountability. In the many *post-mortems* of the causes of the current financial crisis, it is clear that excessively rigid demarcation of accountabilities led to situations where confusion or gaps emerged, with no-one feeling accountable for the "no man's land". This can be observed in supervisory frameworks – such as the UK's "trialogue" arrangement between the Treasury, the Bank of England and the FSA, which managed to leave huge gaps in the industry regulatory and supervisory frameworks – as well as in banks themselves – witness the many abdications of responsibility from senior executives during the recent investigations into the manipulation of LIBOR rates.

---

[31] Delivering effective corporate governance: the financial regulator's role, speech by Hector Sants, FSA, 24 April 2012.

Our proposal on governance is covered in Section 7.4. However, it must be noted in this section that *accountability* is a key component of *competence*, especially for senior staff. Firstly, they need to cover the areas of direct responsibility allocated to them. Secondly, they have the job of ensuring that a "sweeper" role covers miscellaneous issues that may crop up, where there is otherwise a risk of the issue falling between the cracks. Thirdly, they also have the role of ensuring that interface issues for "grey areas" where accountability is ambiguous or unclear are being addressed by others. In all three of these areas, we expect senior bankers and supervisors to flag any issues and concerns that they may have, even if they feel it to be outside their area of responsibility or competence. There is no doubt that most of the senior professionals in the banking industry are highly capable and intelligent, but to be competent, they also have to deliver on the overall goals of their organisations. It is not enough to place blame for failure after the event on others' failings.

Incompetence Due to Lack of Technical Understanding
The incompetence of many of the banking industry's leading lights has given fuel to the debate on whether bankers should be required to have a formal qualification to certify their competence. For example, one of the Parliamentary committees expressed concern "that the Chief Executive of Northern Rock was not a qualified banker, although of course he has significant experience. The Financial Services Authority should not have allowed nor ever again allow the two appointments of a Chairman and a Chief Executive to a 'high-impact' financial institution where both candidates lack relevant financial qualifications; one indication that an individual has been exposed to the relevant training is an appropriate professional qualification. Absence of such a qualification should be a cause of concern."[32]

Several options exist, should the industry choose to implement the requirement for a formal qualification, for example:

- High school level qualifications ("A-Levels").
- An undergraduate degree in a relevant subject (economics, accounting, law).
- MBA (Masters of Business Administration).
- Chartered Banker MBA, pioneered by Bangor Business School in Wales.
- CFA (Charted Financial Analyst).
- Ongoing professional development and skills updating.

The challenge here is to define the most appropriate qualification for the industry's large and varied suite of required skill sets. This challenge is noted by the IFS School of Finance (formerly the Chartered Institute of Bankers):

> One of the reasons for the decline has been that in today's complex financial services industry, that demands increasing specialisation, the term "banker" could be used to describe a range of individuals in a bank performing a very wide variety of different roles having achieved professional qualifications from a variety of professional bodies. The concept of a one-size-fits-all professional qualification for "bankers" is outmoded, unrealistic and probably inappropriate.[33]

---

[32] The Run on the Rock, House of Commons Treasury Committee, 24 January 2008.
[33] Submission from IFS School of Finance (S020), Parliamentary Banking Standards Committee, 24 August 2012.

Despite this challenge, what does seem appropriate is a core set of qualifications to ensure that all staff have at least a basic core understanding of the fundamentals of banking as they relate to a safer and "better" banking industry. The elements of this essential education might include:

- Risk and risk management.
- Regulation and compliance.
- Ethics.
- Customer financial needs.
- Credit assessment.
- Practical economics.
- Reading financial statements.

It does not seem right that people who do not display basic levels of competence in these areas can have a customer-facing, management or director role in a bank.

Technical understanding, though, is not only derived from the classroom or text book – in many ways, it can only be gained on the "front line" of banking. Senior managers and supervisors in the banking industry should additionally be required to have significant hands-on, front-line experience of the industry they are running. This should comprise real work experience rather than mere job shadowing and should cover the relevant functions: customer-facing sales and service roles, trading-floor roles for capital markets, back office functions and support functions. If management ranks, boards of directors and supervisory authorities were staffed with people who had a broader and more relevant skill set, it is certain that the level of *competence* would rise, organisational effectiveness would increase and systemic risk would reduce.

7.3.2 Compensation

Banking appears a highly paid industry. Retail banks have staff who are paid at levels that are comparable with other retail industries. Investment bankers, on the other hand, earn £212,000 on average; average pay per head in a sample of nine European and US investment banks has fallen from 9.5 times the private sector average in 2006 to 5.8 times last year (see Tables 7.4 and 7.5).[34]

Table 7.4   Staff pay at three banks[35]

Bank	Average staff pay 2012	Average bonus 2012
Nationwide BS	£38,000	£4,000
Barclays Investment Bank	£193,000	£54,100
Goldman Sachs	$400,000	N/A

---

[34] Bankers' pay premium is narrowing, *Financial Times*, 25 March 2013.
[35] Annual Reports and 10-K forms.

Table 7.5   Number of staff paid over £1m in 2012[36]

Bank	Number of staff paid £1m+
Barclays	428
HSBC	204
RBS	95
Lloyds	25
Santander UK	19

   These high pay levels are due to two main reasons. Firstly, the job is a professional services job and requires a broad range of academic skills, hard work and initiative. Job security is low and staff turnover is high: in the most highly paid jobs in banking, there are few people who survive more than 15 or 20 years. Secondly, there is a highly leveraged impact of performance, on both the upside and the downside. In other words, doing the job badly can be disastrous, while a job well done can have benefits that are a multiple of the employee's costs. Of course, other professions also have high degrees of difficulty and impact: airline pilots, electricians, surgeons and nurses will attest to the challenges of their jobs, just as much, or more so, than bankers. Some commentators have used professional footballers as an analogy, but this is dubious and in any case could only apply to "star traders" rather than the entire industry. Few other professions create such a stir on the issue of pay. There does not appear to be a broad, popular demand for wage control across the economy. So, why is it that bankers' pay has become such an issue?

   Pay is a matter for the employer and the employee. Throughout our economy, firms recruit, reward and retain their staff with appropriate pay packages and incentive structures. Management sets the compensation for employees and management has its own compensation set by the Board of Directors, who ask shareholders to vote on the pay proposals at the Annual General Meeting. This much is exactly the same for a bank as for any other corporation. What makes banker pay different is that bankers are perceived to be risking the public's money to make a profit and then being paid handsomely as a result of that profit. They are keeping the risks public and the rewards private, so to speak. Such a situation – a free ride for bank shareholders at society's expense – is intolerable, not just for matters of employee pay. Private sector banks and their owners should be made to shoulder the risks that they are running and/ or be charged for access to the societal goods which they exploit.

   Of course, bankers don't pay themselves. As noted above, the level and structure of pay is set by a strict governance procedure that is not unique to the banking industry. Sensationally labelling bankers as "greedy" misses the point: they are paid by their masters and so ultimately any errors in the area of compensation are the fault of the banks' owners, the shareholders. If we protest against huge payouts going to bank executives, we must think hard about the way in which these institutions, which are in the private sector, are governed. Compensation is, first and foremost, an issue of governance.

   By way of illustration, consider the point of the pension arrangements of Fred Goodwin, former Chief Executive of Royal Bank of Scotland. Instead of being dismissed, Goodwin was

---

[36] The 770 Bankers paid at least £1m, *Daily Mail*, 25 March 2013.

asked to leave the company, ostensibly to ensure an orderly handover. This meant that the value of his pension – a pot estimated at between £15m and £20m in present value terms – was almost double what it would otherwise have been:

> If Sir Fred had been dismissed in circumstances which were not characterised as retirement at the request of the employer, he would have received a deferred pension payable at age 60, or, with consent payable at an earlier date but subject to an actuarial reduction. The value of Sir Fred's pension is £703,000 per annum as at 31 January 2009. The approximate value of a deferred pension payable now would be £416,000 per annum.[37]

There has been great debate about who is to blame for such a huge pension being paid to Mr Goodwin. Public outcry led him to voluntarily, though after a long delay, agree to a halving in the pension amount. But was it really his greed that led to the larger amount being awarded? No. His paymasters, including the Chairman of the Board and a government minister, were all involved in him being awarded that amount.[38] Getting pay "wrong" is squarely a problem of governance.

In order for governance to work and compensation to be somehow "correct", the owners of banks – including their supervisors – need to understand the risk-adjusted performance of the business and the extent to which that performance is due to the franchise, the balance sheet and the efforts of staff. An effective performance management framework is essential. Yet, as we have observed in previous chapters, there are many challenges in the financial management of banks, in the areas of risk, capital, liquidity and so on. We have seen case studies where banks have made large profits on apparently low risks, which then turn out to have been highly risky after all. If risk management is weak, management's view of risk-adjusted performance is going to be wrong and rewards will flow to some areas where profitability is actually below the threshold that a fully aware shareholder would demand. At the heart of this compensation debate, therefore, is a problem of risk measurement and management.

See in Figure 7.1 how Merrill Lynch's staff costs tracked its revenues in the years 2004, 2005 and 2006. This was a growth period, with the headcount growing and performance-related pay rising in line with revenues. When losses led to revenues collapsing in 2007, costs barely moved. For many of the staff in the bank, their performance had not deteriorated: the losses were restricted to the activities of a very small number of people. Staff expectations for bonuses remained high and their "market value" – the pay they could command if they switched firms – likewise did not decline. The pay required to retain staff was dictated by the "going rate", rather than the actual performance of Merrill Lynch. For the same reasons, when revenues went negative during the troubled year of 2008, again staff costs stayed stubbornly high. And pay in 2012 was about 50% higher than the pre-crisis revenue levels would indicate. It shows how the pay in investment banking can display a certain amount of hysteresis: elastic as revenues increase and inelastic when revenues drop. It also shows the high cost of running an investment bank in difficult market conditions. The current cost levels of Merrill Lynch (reportedly around $20bn) take up 75% of revenues and mean that the bank's profitability is weak.

---

[37] Letter from Miller Mclean, Group General Counsel and Group Secretary, RBS, to the Chairman of the Committee, 2 March 2009, published on www.parliament.uk.
[38] Lord Myners given "full disclosure" about Sir Fred Goodwin's "enormous" pension, *The Telegraph*, 31 March 2009.

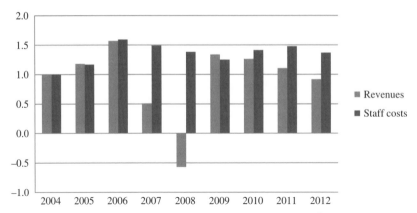

Figure 7.1   Merrill Lynch revenues and staff costs (indexed, 2004 = 1.00)[39]

The absolute level of pay is an area for public consternation. When the public gets a peek at how the banking industry operates – generally during the collapse of a bank, a fraud trial or a discrimination case – they are not impressed. A bank really does seem like a state-backed casino. Despite their claims to brilliance and huge rewards, bankers come across as incompetents and apologists. Aggregate pay levels in the banking industry had become excessive. In fact, the financial services industry has been shown to have contributed "60% of the increase in extreme wage inequality"[40] observed in the early years of the twenty-first century.

Some of this excess is now being reversed and pay in banking is now moving slowly towards a more "normal" level, even if it remains higher than average. For many years, the banking industry sucked in an inordinate number of talented graduates and trainees, at the expense of manufacturing and science. For example, in a recent study on physics graduates in the UK entering employment, 18% were found to have gone into finance,[41] which was the second-most popular destination after education and "respondents with first-class degrees were the most likely group to be working in finance and those with lower-second or third-class degrees were the most likely to be working in education". The same study also found that physics graduates from the most prestigious universities made up most of the entrants into finance.

The main area for public gripe regarding pay is the overwhelming sense of unfairness. The public is angry when highly paid executives preside over colossal failures that have negative implications beyond their own institutions. They detest the payment of bonuses when banks are loss-making. And they do not understand the logic for generous – in fact, off-the-scale – payoffs and pension arrangements for failed and disgraced bankers.

No discussion on the controversy over banker pay is complete without addressing the issue of bonuses. Bonuses make up 25% of the wage bill in banking, versus 7% for the economy as a whole.[42] The phrases "banker bonuses" trips alliteratively off the tongue and is used by those outside banking to describe an industry that is out of control. In the understanding of most

---

[39] Merrill Lynch 10-K forms.

[40] Bankers' Pay and Extreme Wage Inequality in the UK, Centre for Economic Performance, April 2010.

[41] The Career Paths of Physics Graduates: A Longitudinal Study 2006–2010, Institute of Physics.

[42] Bankers' Pay and Extreme Wage Inequality in the UK, Centre for Economic Performance, April 2010.

people, bonuses are a discretionary payment that is awarded for outstanding achievement. They are generally modest – a month's salary, say – and are definitely not awarded for below-standard performance. Understandably, the public is angry when bank staff are paid bonuses that are multiples of an already large salary and in circumstances that resemble abject failure more than outstanding success. Bonuses are, on the one hand, a form of profit-sharing left over from the days when banks were run as partnerships. On the other hand, they are a useful form of variable compensation that can be used to give flexibility on costs and to incentivise staff to perform in the right way. There is a semantic problem of what a "bonus" represents. This needs to be clarified. Does it represent performance-related compensation for the individual or profit-share of the institution? But the reliance of the banking system on bonuses as a major compensation tool is unique, antiquated and often counter-productive. In the absence of reliable risk management metrics, bank staff have been incentivised to arbitrage the rewards system and this has led to a riskier banking industry: there are numerous examples of management blindly pursuing volume targets, revenue targets or accounting profit targets with little regard for the risks of their activities.

The irony is that most bonuses are not seen by staff as bonuses but as a moderately variable element of pay. Staff have accepted relatively low salaries and have developed an expectation that their "top-up" bonus, often linked to performance measures over which they have little control, will make the difference. They are not partners in the business, as they have no say in the direction of the business. They do not have "skin in the game" as they are not putting their own personal capital at risk, but rather the capital of their owners and of society. Rarely does the financial performance of their individual sub-businesses have much to do with individual out- or under-performance, instead being driven as much by exogenous or franchise factors. Despite the vast amounts shelled out in bonuses by the banking industry, the science behind the process is sketchy. In short, the bonus should form no greater a part in the compensation of bankers than it does in an engineering company or a supermarket chain.

One Swedish bank, Svenska Handelsbanken, reportedly does not pay bonuses and is often quoted as an example of an alternative approach. Instead, staff are given a share in a trust called "Oktogonen". In his book on Handelsbanken, Niels Kroner describes Oktogonen as embodying "the bank's visceral dislike for risk-taking, its focus on concentrating on customer satisfaction over profits, and its emphasis on long-term orientation". He adds: "As the system has been in place for a very long time, there is simply no expectation of any special remuneration for doing the job well. Staff know that they will get a competitive salary and a very generous pension from the Oktogonen foundation once they retire."[43]

Bonuses are increasingly seen by outsiders as a profit-share pool, rather than a tool to drive individual performance. This is disturbing and implies that talent will migrate away from struggling banks and/or demand high fixed salaries – indeed, this is probably already happening. Staff are alert to the fact that bonuses can prove to be politically "up for grabs":

> The obvious place to look for the funds required is the bonus pool, sums of money that executives are expecting to be added to their salaries for 2012. [...] To many RBS managers, who had nothing to do with the Libor scandal, this would seem very unfair. [...] It would be even more unfair, however, for the fine to come out of taxpayers' pockets.[44]

---

[43] As reported in *The Guardian*, 17 September 2012.
[44] We shouldn't pay a penny of RBS's fine, Andreas Whittam Smith writing in the "i" newspaper, 16 January 2013.

To remedy the problems of being paid for failure and to reflect the fact that losses can take years to realise, the authorities have recently demanded that bonuses are deferred over multiple years, paid in large part in instruments that have risk-sharing features (such as shares) and are subject to "malus" or "clawback" should future performance of the bank deteriorate. Some banks (e.g. Crédit Suisse) have even paid part of their bonuses to employees in the form of high-risk, "toxic" debt instruments, the risk of which would otherwise have remained with shareholders. Whilst these features may seem to make good sense, the logic of extending such arrangements beyond senior management and key risk-takers is questionable. More fundamentally, the system will only ever adjust to realised risk and will continue to reward risky behaviour that does not lead to realised losses; conversely, it will penalise good behaviour in times of macro-economic difficulties or when executing a strategy that fits with a high-risk appetite of the bank's owners.

More recently, the concept of bonus caps has come to the fore. Having proposed in 2012 that "the impact of further restrictions (for example to 50%) on the level of variable income to fixed income ought to be assessed",[45] the cap on variable pay is now being implemented in the EU. As anticipated, banks are seeking ways to retain the ability to pay their top staff handsomely, through raising fixed salaries, making those fixed salaries more "dynamic" by having annual salary changes and even by moving staff to positions that are not covered by the restrictions.

Capping compensation does not address the lack of risk management incentives in the banking industry. Aside from the opportunities for arbitrage, it does nothing to create the incentives for a productive, yet risk-savvy workforce.

Our proposal is for a compensation policy that is based on the same commercial principles that are used by any other company in any other industry. Banks and their boards should be able to direct rewards to those areas where they feel it will have the most impact on the long-term, risk-adjusted performance of the bank. In particular, it seems desirable to have to following features:

- Salaries commensurate with the job at hand, with no expectation of bonus payment for performance at expected levels. Bonuses should not form a major part of compensation for most roles in a bank.
- Nevertheless, a small element of performance-related pay, in order to incentivise good behaviour and performance on a risk-adjusted basis. This to be assessed based on a multi-factor scorecard, of which risk should be major component.
- For senior executives with strategy-setting responsibilities, payment in shares of the bank, with long-term lock-up terms and clawback provisions.
- For general managers of the banks below executive board level, the introduction of "partnership points" to reflect performance and seniority. A general profit share for this cadre of managers should be paid out relative to the points of each of these managers.
- For senior staff in risk management positions, payment in subordinated bonds, with long lock-up terms.
- For traders taking open risk positions and engaged in proprietary risk-taking, the introduction of a partnership structure within joint stock companies.

---

[45] High-level expert group on reforming the structure of the EU banking sector, Erikki Liikanen, October 2012.

- For sales staff with clearly identified client and product portfolios, the payment of commission according to a formula based on: sales volumes beyond an agreed budget (risk-adjusted, of course) and subject to broader performance measures and customer suitability and satisfaction metrics.
- All compensation structures to be presented to the shareholders' Annual General Meeting, in order to ensure appropriate governance process.

We recognise that such an approach would be complex to administer. But once established, it should enable a superior risk-adjusted performance for the bank, which would reap benefits for all. By aligning pay incentives with the true objectives of the bank, the scope for overpaying for poor performance and the potential for incetivising the wrong type of behaviour is reduced.

7.3.3 Culture

Most people think that "culture" is a soft and vague word, but in fact it represents the tangible underlying driver of most of the symptoms of a troublesome banking system. The wrong culture can lead, for example, to bank employees taking excessive risk to achieve short-term accounting profit at the expense of the bank's genuine goal, to be successful on a sustainable basis and over the long term. Culture is a set of *behaviours*: the way in which business is done, the attitude towards customers, the nature of teamwork, the way in which rewards are given. All these factors make a real difference to the riskiness and effectiveness of a bank.

What are some examples of poor culture?

- In some banks, ethics were poor and customers were mis-sold products that were unsuitable for them and occasionally ruinous to them.
- Some banks incentivised traders to take massive risks that were not transparent and led to major losses for the bank and for society.
- In certain banks, management culture was brutal, discouraging challenge and quality control, thus allowing risks to build up.
- And some bank executives and leading figures in the authorities were lauded for their achievements in the face of abject failure and incompetence.

In order to make *culture* more realistic, it can be seen as the product of the *values* of the bank and can be tested either through *examples of reward and censure* but also through a *sniff test* or a *daylight test*. In other words, culture can be observed through the outcomes of real-life management processes.

Values can be seen as the real goals of the institution. Making lots of money for oneself does appear to be the personal goal for many employees in the banking industry and they are often prepared to find loopholes in operational systems in order to take huge punts with the bank's money for personal gain (the case of Kweku Adoboli at UBS being an obvious example, though less egregious cases happen on a daily basis in their thousands across the sales and trading functions of the industry, as bankers scramble to hit financial targets). But the problem is not simply one of unashamed greed. Instead, those employees genuinely believe that accounting profit maximisation is their goal. The real values of the institution are not formulated, communicated, understood or enacted. How else would one expect the individual to act? Anything else may well feel to them as a contradiction of their job description. Likewise, the leaders of the financial authorities no doubt genuinely feel that they were acting in good faith as they more-or-less fulfilled their strict job descriptions, while allowing the banking industry to spiral out of control. If we could get people to focus on the actual goals and *values* of their institutions, rather than the narrow accounting-based performance measures they have been allocated, then the chances of success would increase.

Examples of reward and censure are the key test of a culture. If salespeople are paid hand-somely for hitting sales targets, despite deficiencies in other aspects such as teamwork or risk management, then their behaviours will be emulated and the consequence is likely to be a higher risk level and lower organisational effectiveness. Some banks operate a "no jerks" policy, whereby lack of teamwork is not tolerated; others have used "public hangings" to remind staff of the importance of requirements such as regulatory compliance. But in general, banking suffers from a sales culture that tends to reward aggressive and selfish behaviours and a focus on short-term accounting profit metrics. Again though, this is not a bottom-up prob-lem, but rather the result of a simplistic focus on misleading earnings metrics by shareholders.

Institutions might use a "sniff test" or a "daylight test" to assess whether particular behav-iours and transactions make sense and fit with the goals and values of the institution. Looking at a given situation and asking "What would my customers/the public think if we told them about this?" can be a good test of ethics. If we're not proud of it, if we can't justify it, perhaps we shouldn't be doing it.

Over the coming years, we may learn more about the specifics of *culture* and how the bank-ing industry might improve its culture, in order to reduce risks and improve effectiveness. Barclays offers a good case study in this respect. As a result of failings in its business strategy, Barclays replaced its entire top management team and is undertaking a comprehensive review of its *culture*. It commissioned an independent consultant (Anthony Salz, a lawyer) to conduct the review, based on the following objectives:

> The culture of the banking industry overall, and that of Barclays within it, needs to evolve. A number of events during and after the financial crisis demonstrated that banks need to revisit fundamentally the basis on which they operate, and how they add value to society. Trust has been decimated and needs to be rebuilt.[46]

In its terms of reference, the Salz Review gives some steer as to what his understanding of culture comprises:

> Culture is generally defined as "the instinctive behaviours and beliefs characteristic of a particular group". Changing a culture, therefore, requires at least three things:
>
> - Affirming the key values and operative beliefs that guide the behaviour of everyone in an organisation – these are deep-seated and tend not to change without direct intervention.
> - Ensuring that the actual behaviours of those who represent the organisation are consistent with those values (and are so regarded by those who come in contact with the bank); and
> - Ensuring that vital reinforcing mechanisms, such as visible leadership examples, formal and informal systems and processes, policies and rewards, are aligned with those values, operative beliefs and behaviours.[47]

---

[46] The Salz Review of Barclays Business Practices – Terms of Reference, 29 August 2012.
[47] Ibid.

Most of the thrust of the Barclays Salz Review is that culture was at the root of Barclays' failings and needs to be fixed. Academic views on what constitutes culture are relegated to the appendix. Instead, the review gives a practical twist to the issue:

"Culture" and cultural change have become somewhat of buzz words amongst those faced with delivering change in banking. The reality of course is that changing culture should not be a goal. The goal should be to change the tangible things about what the service does for customers and how people will do their work; gradually, this will change the culture. Fundamentally changing how we work (beliefs, behaviours, structures and systems) is the more challenging part and takes time.[48]

This approach seems realistic. Culture is a description of how the various management processes in a bank operate in practice. If we are to foster an appropriate risk culture, there need to be clear management processes relating to risk in all aspects of the bank's operations.

7.4 GOVERNANCE

Remember, Roman, that it is for thee to rule the nations. This shall be thy task, to impose the ways of peace, to spare the vanquished, and to tame the proud by war.[49]

Governance is a concept that is sometimes difficult to grasp, but pervades many of the problems and solutions considered in this book. The concept of governance embodies ownership, control, responsibility and accountability; it also underlies our approach to transparency, communication, performance management and compensation. If governance does not work effectively, a suite of problems will manifest itself. During the current financial crisis, it has been observed that "there were fundamental shortcomings in financial institutions' governance, of which the current risk management shortcomings are just a symptom".[50] On the other hand, if we can get governance right, many of the other troublesome aspects of the banking industry will more-or-less fall into place.

7.4.1 How Does Governance Work in Theory?

Everything has an owner. In capitalist democracies, such as we mostly live in, the relatively slim organs of the state are owned by society, the people (be they voters, citizens or taxpayers). The civil servants in the monetary, regulatory and supervisory authorities related to the banking industry are employed by society. In other words, the banking system is ultimately in the hands of the people. Whilst this may appear rather daunting, it is the system that we have chosen to adopt. In terms of governance, the highest form is the democratic process comprising the ballot box and the court of public opinion.

---

[48] Salz Review: An Independent Review of Barclays' Business Practices, Barclays plc, April 2013.
[49] Aeneid Book VI, Virgil.
[50] Beyond the crisis: the Basel Committee's strategic response, Nout Wellink, former Chairman, Basel Committee.

Of course, banks themselves are generally owned by private sector shareholders. These private sector banks rely upon the infrastructure provided by the rest of society (such as the rule of law), the special privileges franchised out to them (notably the ability to collect deposits) and, potentially, the financial support in stressed situations from the central bank. They are not entities that exist and operate in an unfettered free market. To this extent, they need to be governed, not only by their owners and shareholders, but also by the regulatory authorities. This aspect of governance – we call it effective regulation and supervision – has been covered in the previous sections.

Effective governance passes accountability upwards and control downwards. The owners are ultimately accountable for the performance of their banks. As owner of the economy, society is ultimately accountable for its success or failure. Society or "the people" cannot blame "bankers" for a financial crisis. Likewise, shareholders cannot complain if they lose their investment due to shoddy management decisions: they employed the management.

Shareholders need to govern the institutions they own. For this, they appoint a Board of Directors, which is accountable for the high-level direction of the bank and to which the bank's management reports. They set the strategy, sign off on pay levels, decide on acquisitions and ensure that management processes pass scrutiny. Their work is essential in protecting and nurturing the shareholders' investments and interests.

In turn, the bank's management appoints middle management, and so on. Ultimately, the customer places his or her business with the bank. They then benefit from the privileges of the customer – to choose, to switch, to complain – as well as the *caveat emptor* (or "buyer beware") responsibilities of the customer.

There simply is no point at which no-one is clearly responsible or accountable; and at each point, the management node immediately above shares the responsibility and accountability (see Figure 7.2). If our governance is working, then society profits from an excellent banking industry and shareholders earn an attractive return. If our governance is less effective, then society gets hit and shareholders see their investment decline in value.

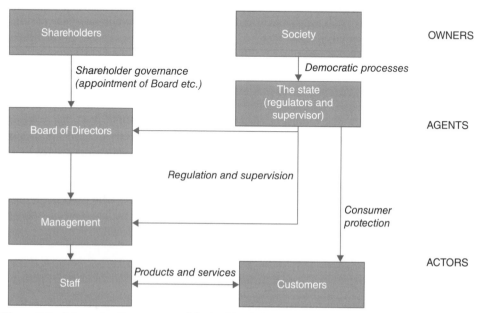

Figure 7.2 Schematic of governance of the banking industry

Yet, despite the theoretical workings of shareholder governance, it has been insufficiently effective over the past decade: "Shareholder engagement is still very limited, for example when it comes to strategic managerial decisions. All in all, there has been marginal capital market discipline prior to the crisis."[51]

7.4.2 Improving Governance of Banks

There are few large banks where the top management has put in place a management infra-structure that is comprehensively competent and able to steer the organisation confidently, in terms of compliance, risk management, the serving of stakeholder interests and shareholder value creation. Note by the way that this is not an empirical observation, only an impression formed through years of working in the industry. Recent events, for example the scandal around misreporting of market reference interest rates such as LIBOR, have shown us that even when institutions claim they are fully reformed, there may well be inappropriate activities that continue. UBS gives us an example where the lack of perceived risk led to complacency and a lack of challenge. Regarding UBS, the Chair of the Parliamentary Commission on Banking Standards was driven to observe that "the level of the board's ignorance seems to be staggering to the point of incredulity",[52] without noting that his own organisation was also blissfully ignorant of many of the undesirable goings-on in the banking industry and also had an important governance role.

Top management needs to put in place structures that give the necessary amount of transparency and control. This sounds simple, but is incredibly hard to achieve. One tool to help achieve it might be the "centurion approach", whereby the business is decomposed into a hierarchy of 100 nodes, based on gross exposure/transaction volumes, economic risk, revenues and economic profit. This rigorous profiling of the bank will enable management to keep firmly on top of the upsides and downsides of their business. The combination of measures is meant to ensure that low-risk, low-margin businesses do not get neglected, as they often contain substantial tail risk. Likewise, forcing management to see exactly where they are earning revenues will bring small, risky and lucrative activities out of the shadows, where the question "how are we making money here?" can be well understood. Many of the activities that caused major losses in recent years were not properly understood, but would be captured by the "centurion approach".

Indeed, much of the discussion about "breaking up the banks" has been centred on the issue of control and simplification.

> Better structures in these banks will help regulation, help get the taxpayer off the hook, help supervision and help the management of these organisations. In the same entity, in some cases, they were doing such a wide array – whether geographically wide or in terms of products and services – that the complexities of management and the lack of awareness at the top of these banks, which you have seen very vividly, had certainly become a major issue. However, one cannot wave a magic wand and split overnight these large institutions into nice, discrete units that can be happily managed and run. This is complicated, costly, difficult business.[53]

---

[51] High-level expert group on reforming the structure of the EU banking sector, Erikki Liikanen, October 2012.

[52] Uncorrected transcript of Oral Evidence taken before the Joint Committee, Parliamentary Commission on Banking Standards, 10 January 2013.

[53] Sir John Vickers to the Parliamentary Commission On Banking Standards, 16 January 2013.

As a consequence of the lessons being learnt from the current financial crisis, there are many proposals that have been put forward as potential ways to improve governance at banks.

There are proposals on ownership models, director competence, compensation structures and the nebulous "culture" (see Section 7.3.3). These solutions are interesting but insufficient by themselves to make much improvement to the quality of governance. For example, there are moves to ensure that bankers' pay is deferred over a long period of time and linked to the ongoing financial performance of their bank. The theory is that, if banks were run as partnerships, then governance might work better. But evidence from the years 2008 and 2009 does not prove the theory. The management teams of some of the biggest failures had major share ownership of them. For example, CEOs such as Dick Fuld of Lehman and Jimmy Cayne of Bear Stearns "were prepared to gamble with the bank, even though they owned a large part of it [...] we should question the automatic assumption that aligning the owners' and shareholders' incentives is sufficient for responsible management. Culture, it seems, matters as much as share ownership."[54]

To the existing proposals, we would add some additional proposals that are explained in this book, namely shareholder engagement through introducing "glasnost" (Section 7.8), the "Guardian Angel" concept (Section 7.2) and the "centurion approach" (in the following section). We would also highlight the hope that, over time, market forces will force banks' governance models to learn from the past and adapt, with superior models being rewarded with financial outperformance.

7.4.3 The Centurion Approach

Given that accountability needs to be clear, in order to have effective governance from owners down to front-line workers, the question arises how to implement management processes that operationalise this accountability? In too many cases over recent years, yawning gaps in management process have led to oversights, errors and confusion. As the UBS case study in Chapter 5 shows, these management failures can occur in banks considered among the world's best. And the LIBOR scandal has shown us that there are few banks where the management can sleep easy at night, safe in the knowledge that behaviours are appropriate and risks are being managed. A rigorous management framework for accountability needs to be introduced.

The "centurion approach" is based on the simple premise that bank boards, executives, officers and managers should be expected to know what is going on in their area of responsibility. Since no manager is superhuman, responsibility must be delegated, but in a tightly controlled fashion. A pyramidal, watertight risk reporting framework needs to be institutionalised.

In the "centurion approach", each 1/100th (or 1%) of the bank is separately documented and understood. If a bank has £1,000m of exposures, can we break it down into £10m chunks for description? If it has £100m of revenues, can we describe them in £1m chunks? If not, something is amiss. Managing or supervising a bank without the ability to scrutinise at the 1% level is not acceptable. Allowing concentrations to build up in miscellany is perilous. Neglecting minor contributors to the business can lead to small monsters developing.

At each level of management, the 1% rule is observed. Each manager acts as centurion for his or her department. So, the manager responsible for £60m of revenues and £5,000m of exposures should be required to manage his or her department in segments down to each £0.6m of revenues and £50m of exposures. The 1% is across multiple dimensions: revenues,

---

[54] *Masters of Nothing*, Matthew Hancock and Nadhim Zahami, 2011.

costs, exposures (gross, net and risk-weighted), staff numbers, customers, profits. Risk assessments need to address each 1% of the business, even for businesses seen as low risk. Over-prioritisation of risk management has led to several second-order problems during this current financial crisis, as small fires have grown into large ones due to lack of attention. Managers are responsible for ensuring that risks are highlighted, including areas where gaps are perceived. Those gaps need to be explicitly addressed at the next level up.

If the "centurion approach" sounds like a lot of work, that is because it is. But it is not meant simply to mean "more" risk management and bureaucracy. It is meant to introduce fresh rigour into the management and governance processes of banks that have been tested and found wanting. Time and again, most recently in the JP Morgan CIO debacle (see Section 5.8), we have seen how the most esteemed management can let risk build up out of sight because they stopped asking questions about aspects of the business that seemed to be a low priority. "In the very complex modern financial world you can have an inordinate amount of risk on your books and actually not know that you have it. And even a CEO, who is extremely talented and brilliant and cares deeply and works really hard, can still miss it."[55] Organisations need more rigour to ensure that cracks do not develop.

We advocate the "centurion approach" as one way of introducing such rigour and clarifying accountabilities. It served the Roman army well during its days of empire-building: it has something to offer today's banking industry.

7.5 CAPITAL

> What alone was wanting to the realization of a vast fortune, he considered to be More Capital. Those were the two little words, more capital.[56]

The answer to many of the banking industry's woes appears to many to be "more capital". But it is far from clear whether more capital *per se* holds the answer to improving the resilience of banks.

If we were to take a cynical attitude, we might say that solvency requirements work roughly as follows:

- The bank uses reasonable assumptions based on historic patterns to model the variability of losses in the businesses it runs and the assets it holds.
- The regulator verifies the capital model and agrees the minimum level of capital that the bank must hold.
- Little of this risk assessment needs to take into account current reality or likely developments; the degree to which they need to take into account unlikely future developments is also subject to debate.
- The capital requirement is met through a measure of capital that is based primarily on the net accounting assets of the bank, calculated using valuations of assets and of liabilities that can be far from the current, observed market value or a hypothetical yet realistic value.

---

[55] Bethany McLean, Author, on BBC TV's *Bankers: Fixing the System*, May 2013.
[56] *Great Expectations*, Charles Dickens.

In practice, none of this is going to be "true", of course. There are so many things that deviate from norms and to such a significant degree, it is fair to say that capital is an indicative measure at best and an inaccurate or even meaningless measure at worst.

7.5.1 The Role of "Capital"

Banks should have the financial resources to ride through a period of stress without needing public sector bail-outs or proving unable to repay the funds entrusted to them by depositors and creditors. These financial resources should come from the owners of the bank and from other creditors, who are quite aware of the risks they are running and the fact that their funds are invested in the business and are subject to losses if the bank goes through a period of stress. In short, we are saying that banks need "capital" and the entrusted funds that are not "capital" need to be protected, in such a way that they are practically risk-free.

This approach to "capital" is not controversial, though the way in which it is applied gives rise to many differing opinions and approaches. The Basel accords contain examples of the arcane and ineffective results of codifying capital requirements for banks. The proposal below seeks to offer a constructive improvement in this area.

7.5.2 Principles-Based Solvency Regulations

Just as risk is difficult to define, so is capital. They are both "blobby" in definition and attempts to solidify this "blobbiness" inevitably lead to complications, contradictions and inelegance.

Since current regulations give a fixed definition of risk, capital and solvency, there has developed an entire sub-industry devoted to "regulatory capital optimisation", namely devising instruments and transactions that reduce the need for capital or the cost-of-capital. Much of this has genuine economic substance, changing the risk profile of the bank for the better or finding risk-bearing resources that are better suited to the risks in question and hence more efficient. For example, a hedge fund may have a constructive view on commercial real estate and be able to provide an effective hedge on a bank's loan portfolio at a cost that is lower than the equivalent cost of financing that risk with the bank's own shareholder capital. However, some of the "optimisation" of capital consists of arbitrage of regulations, finding loopholes and pushing legal definitions. By giving an objective, rules-based standard for solvency assessments, the current solvency frameworks may have the unintended consequence of encouraging banks to manage to the regulatory solvency metrics and increase their real, economic leverage in the process.

An alternative approach would drop the reliance on a simple, ratio-based solvency requirement. It could be far more effective to adopt a "blobby" – or, technically speaking, "principles-based" – regulation on capital and solvency. The regulatory and supervisory authorities would be responsible for assessing the risks inherent in each bank's business profile and risk asset portfolios. They would then determine whether the bank's current level of capitalisation was sufficient and form a qualitative opinion on the strength of solvency. Both the risk assessment and the adequacy of capital resources would be documented and published in a solvency assessment report, which would be updated quarterly or, exceptionally, on an ad-hoc basis.

In essence, the formulaic Basel "Pillar 1" approach to solvency regulation would be downgraded, being replaced with a "Pillar 2" style approach that is subjective, judgemental, comprehensive and arbitrage-proof. Of course, the switch from rules-based solvency measures to principles-based measures does involve the demise of simple solvency indicators. It would also highlight the need for a high quality, intelligent supervisory model: applying principles and making judgements is harder than putting numbers into statistical models. These would be the casualties and costs of progress and there are many who would not be willing to make such sacrifices.

7.5.3 Need for Capital

There is no need completely to jettison the bottom-up, objective measures of Pillar 1 as a means of taking a first step towards solvency assessments. In fact, the analysts of the supervisory authorities will need to take accounting data (gross and net of hedges and provisions), risk "buckets" to enable segmented analysis and the bank's own internal risk assessment and pricing models to feed their own work. But the assessment of the need for capital will need to add several important pieces of information: realistic valuation adjustments on trading and banking assets of the bank; concentration and sensitivity analyses; learnings from wargaming exercises; and adjustments for "unknown unknowns", for example in periods of rapid business growth.

The output of these analyses is *not* a level of capitalisation at which the regulator/supervisor would be comfortable. They cannot define the "blob" of capital required to match the risks of the institution in a single number or set of numbers. Instead, they will assess the actual or proposed capital of the bank and give an opinion on whether that is sufficient.

7.5.4 Supply of Capital

An assessment of the capital resources available to absorb losses in a stressed scenario needs to incorporate a dynamic analysis of how the resources of that bank would behave in a stress, rather than merely a static accounting presentation filtered through a set of regulations.

Some people think of capital as an asset (akin to reserves) or a liability (money entrusted by shareholders), but in fact it is both: accounting equity is the same as accounting net assets (gross assets minus debt). Therefore, bank capital resources can be thought of as the excess value of the bank's assets over its non-capital liabilities (essentially, its deposits and senior funding notes). The accounting presentation is not quite realistic enough to be suitable for prudential purposes, so a definition of capital could be derived from the accounts as shown in Table 7.6.

Clearly, this is a complex and dynamic assessment. The complexity reflects reality and is necessary: a simplistic view of capital is not useful for managing or supervising a bank. Since the regulator/supervisor is not attempting to derive a single capital number nor to publish a ratio (see below), the sum of all these parts is largely meaningless. Some of the components may well have a higher quality than others, but there is no need to apply a quantified weighting or "haircut". Neither is there a need for a defined stress or run-down scenario, the famous and artificial distinction between "going concern" and "gone concern" capital.

As well as existing sources of loss-absorbing capital, the bank's ability to handle stresses, raising capital and shedding risk, is of paramount importance. Real-life stress scenarios show us that access to capital is as important as capital itself and constitutes a real resource to improve resilience and maintain stability. Likewise, the ability to reduce risk in a stress, by stopping production, syndicating and hedging positions, selling businesses and bolstering

Table 7.6   What is capital?

Accounting net assets	A good place to start.
minus accounting goodwill	Accounting goodwill is simply the difference between what was paid for an asset and what it was then worth. It is a balancing item and needs to be removed.
plus or minus adjustments to get to a "realistic" valuation for individual components	In adjusting for realism, a range of probable values will be used ("confidence accounting", see Section 7.1.1).
plus liabilities that are clearly designated to their investors as "capital"	Any liability that does not carry the expectation of senior, *pari passu* treatment is loss absorbing in its nature and forms part of the capital resources of the bank.
plus the value of business streams that are not represented on the balance sheet	Future earnings streams can be used to offset future losses. Both are uncertain but both need to be considered. Uncertainty should be reflected in the assessed "quality" of the value: dollar-for-dollar, future earnings are not worth as much as a pile of cash today. Timing is key and timing risks (such as the risk of early losses and late profits) need to be factored into the assessment of capital quality.
minus any contractual obligations or potential liabilities that are not on the balance sheet and have not already been considered in the need for capital assessment	As well as onerous contracts that need to be fulfilled, banks need to recognise the impact of future downside risks on their capital resources.
plus the value of any latent or contingent sources of capital	Banks may have the ability to raise capital during a stress via support from strategic shareholders, for example. This is a soft factor and a lower quality source of capital, but is real nonetheless.

customer collateral buffers, is vital. Comitted staff who are have significant proportions of discretionary variable pay (or rather, low levels of fixed, contractual pay) can also represent a source of valuable capital at a time of stress. These aspects are sometimes termed "capital liquidity" and they are especially important for businesses where the need for capital has, for whatever reason, an in-built volatility.

7.5.5 Role of "Hybrid" Capital

In case the above philosophy were not totally clear, the proposal outlined is totally accommodating of all types of at-risk and loss-absorbing financial resources, including those that have fixed income or mezzanine qualities.

- *Fixed Income:* Capital instruments that carry an expected or capped investment return that is payable whenever the bank is in good enough shape to pay it. The sole proviso is that distributions are not paid if the regulator's assessment of the solvency of the bank indicates that the bank is too weak to pay distributions in cash.

- *Maturity:* Some investors value a dated security. In the interests of solvency, the maturity should be "the longer, the better", though there is no real reason to insist on perpetual maturities and preclude long-dated instruments.
- *Mezzanine:* Sources of capital can be structured, tranched or subordinated in relation to each other, so long as they are clearly taking the risk that insulates the depositors and senior creditors. Financial resources invested in the bank's business and clearly "at risk" are a source of solvency and stability, even if there are other investors who stand to lose more in an insolvency or failure scenario.

This approach towards hybrid capital disagrees with the view that hybrid capital instruments failed to absorb losses during the current financial crisis. Suspension of distributions is a form of loss absorption, even if the accounting representation indicates otherwise. If distributions can be suspended indefinitely, then there is no real liability to the bank and its solvency and stability are preserved. Of course, any "must pay" instruments can represent a real burden on the bank and so are of dubious solvency value.

In a similar vein, the concept of "contingent capital" is rather weak in Basel III. What we are seeing as "contingent capital" issuance is actually a form of subordinated debt with some rather wooden, late stage conversion triggers. What is really needed as a source of high quality, standby equity is a form of pre-funded and pre-underwritten rights issue available to the issuing bank *at any time* and at management's discretion. The investor would receive a decent fixed income coupon prior to conversion and shares at a discount of, say, 20% to the market value at point of conversion. Such instruments would be genuinely high quality and efficient in the capital structure of banks. They should be introduced and promoted.

Basel III is struggling with the design and treatment of hybrid instruments, largely because regulators are overly focused on the accounting treatment, legal form, triggers and conversion features. Some of the debates in the industry on this topic are arcane, especially when considering what actually happens at point of trigger and conversion. A more rational and realistic approach, as outlined above, makes more sense. It has the added advantage of being less prone to arbitrage (regulator-friendly) and more flexible in structure (investor-friendly).

Hybrid capital is an important source of risk capital for the banking industry. Much of the world's investment capital is steered towards the bond markets because bond investors are seeking a predictable, "fixed income" source of cash flow. This preference for bonds characterises, for example, most pension funds and insurance companies. The equity markets offer a less predicatable source of income and are, consequently, less suitable for those investors. This constrains the size of risk capital that the equity markets can provide the banking industry. It is vital, therefore, for banks to be able to tap the fixed income (bond) markets for risk capital. The banking industry needs effective hybrid capital instruments of a fixed income nature if it is to improve solvency and resilience, enabling healthy and safe growth.

The major counter-argument to the need for hybrid capital is the argument that the capital structure of a bank does not matter. This point of view draws on two supporting points: firstly, that banks had more equity until a couple of decades ago and managed to provide decent products and shareholder returns; and secondly, that the Modigliani–Miller theory proves that the debt:equity mix of a corporation does not change its overall cost-of-capital. We do not agree with the assumptions behind these arguments. To the first point, the banking industry of yesteryear was a very different model that was severely restricted in what it covered. For example, it did not and could not enable the mortgage market of modern times, which has brought the potential for home ownership to millions of people throughout the world. There simply is not enough equity capital sitting around to provide large volumes of mortgages without banks leveraging themselves with a decent amount of debt. Secondly, the theoretical arguments of the Modigliani–Miller theory have practical limitations, meaning that the *capital structure of a bank does matter.* Equity capital levels below or beyond a certain range are inefficient. In other words, the blended cost-of-capital has a "sweet spot". Any inefficiencies resulting from imposing the wrong capital structure will be industry-wide and hence passed on to the end-customer, leading to a worse situation for society. In fact, the broadening of the definition of "capital", as set out above, enables lower levels of risk in the banking system while at the same time giving an efficient cost-of-capital for the assumption of that risk.

7.5.6 Life without Capital Ratios

Investors and analysts worldwide are yearning for a solvency capital ratio that is simple, transparent, comparable and meaningful.

Why is this? Equity analysts are seeking to spot capital surpluses and deficits, in order to model dividend flows and rights issues, which are the major drivers of fundamental stock valuations. Credit analysts are trying to spot those banks that have the most resilience and ability to service their debt fully and on a timely basis. For both of them, the need for capital is largely driven by regulatory considerations. This is because they view capital purely in regulatory terms: it is defined and required by the regulator. If the regulator requires banks to have more capital, then more capital is needed. Few observers look at capital on an economic basis, and even fewer would be able to answer the question "if there were no regulatory capital requirements, how much capital would the bank need?"

How would people cope without regulatory capital ratios? Well, they would have the regulatory assessment of capital adequacy (qualitative but detailed and fact-based) as well as a raft of new information that would enable them to make a much more informed assessment *themselves* of the economic or realistic solvency of a bank. In many ways, this is what S&P has done in its "Risk-Adjusted Capital" or RAC methodology, rejecting regulatory solvency ratios as subjective and incomparable, replacing them with a proprietary S&P ratio, the "RAC ratio" (see Section 3.10.2 for a brief description).

In fact, ratios are dangerous. Since they are a highly inaccurate representation of the true solvency of a bank, they will systematically underestimate the true solvency of certain banks and overestimate the solvency of others. The fact that several banks have recently gone to the wall, causing heavy losses for taxpayers and creditors, while still reporting healthy capital ratios, is testament to this danger. Back in 1988, the Basel Committee did not claim that the Cooke ratio was a sound assessment of a bank's solvency, merely that it represented a decent benchmark for international operating minima for commercial banks. By dint of banks' aggressive arbitrages and the overuse of the Cooke ratio by investors, it gained a life of its own and spawned the sport of ratio management. Twenty-five years on, with a wealth of advances in the banking industry and the capacity of information technology to improve our understanding of complex financial businesses, together with a financial near-collapse in recent history to inform our policies, we can hopefully move on from vain attempts to distil risk and resources into one, simple ratio. If not, we may be guilty of a deeper deceit, that of thinking that we can definitively measure and therefore "know" risk. Unfortunately, risk is blobby and our best measures will be qualitative.

7.5.7 Minimum Capital Standards

Despite this strong belief in the danger of largely meaningless ratios, the market may wish to use "quick and dirty" capital measures nonetheless. They could be used with care as performance indicators, for example. Therefore, as a compromise proposal, the industry could maintain the current unweighted leverage ratio (regulatory capital to accounting assets) and the risk-weighted Basel III "Standardised Approach" (SA) solvency ratio. Since their use would be restricted and indicative, rather than binding, their definition should be kept as simple as possible. We apply the principle of Occam's Razor, namely that the simplest explanation is the one to be favoured in the face of a problem.

This approach – essentially a rejection of the Pillar 1 element of Basel II – is gaining ground now amongst regulators. For example, Andrew Haldane of the Bank of England is quoted as saying that Basel III, and indeed the Basel II regime that preceded it, was too complex and should be ditched.[57]

Some experts have proposed that the industry should adopt a minimum capital standard that is both simple and low, a kind of backstop to ensure that extreme levels of leverage do not emerge. This appears unnecessary, though again, as a compromise, if the industry feels uncomfortable without a minimum, it may wish to adopt one. A Basel III "Standardised Approach" ratio of 8% would have the benefit of nostalgia for Basel I, even though the measurement methodologies are very different; similarly, a leverage ratio of 3% should not cause too many problems.

Regulators are already using multiple measures of solvency, in recognition of the fact that none is meaningful by itself. The logic here is that multiple indicative measures should be more useful than one or two "hard" measures:

> At the recent Prudential Regulation Authority (PRA) launch conference (October 22nd), David Rule (Director, International Banks Division, Prudential Business Unit, FSA) emphasised, during Q&A, that the PRA's prime objective was to ensure banks are adequately capitalised and will use a combination of Basel-standardised, Basel-IRB, simple leverage and banks' internal models to assess risk and capital requirements. From a regulatory perspective, this is a pragmatic approach. However, it is likely to increase rather than reduce opacity for investors in understanding and comparing capital requirements across the sector.[58]

On the other hand, some commentators suggest that high capital levels are a preferable solution. They assume that the debt/equity mix of a bank's liabilities is unimportant. To improve creditworthiness, banks simply need to raise more equity "*by issuing additional shares and selling them to investors*. If the additional funds are used to make new loans, the higher capital requirements will actually allow the banks to lend more rather than less. Banks that do not have access to a stock exchange can increase their equity by reinvesting their earnings."[59] There is a certain elegance to the "loads more equity" arguments and they are gaining in popularity at present.

Our counter-arguments are that, firstly, capital requirements can never replace risk management discipline and, secondly, that equity sources are not infinite. So long as implicit

---

[57] UK regulator says changes afoot for "too complex" bank rules, Reuters, 21 January 2013.

[58] Written Evidence in response to call for evidence made on 15 October 2012: Submission from The Association of British Insurers, Parliamentary Commission on Banking Standards.

[59] *The Banker's New Clothes*, Anat Admati and Martin Hellwig, 2013.

guarantees are removed, as should already be the case with "bail-in" regulations, all funds invested in the bank are loss-absorbing in principle and therefore they form a tranche of the risk capital of that bank. Whether they are in the form of shares of the bank or a fixed-income "hybrid" should be of no concern to the supervisor from a risk management perspective: they do the same job in insulating depositors from losses. The nature of share-based investments means they are unsuitable for most investors, who prefer the bond market instead. And multiple tranches can result in superior monitoring from investors, assuming they act to preserve the value of their investment.

7.5.8 Disclosure of Capital Assessment

Based on the "Guardian Angel" supervisory model, we envisage the risk assessment and the adequacy of capital resources being documented and published in a solvency assessment report. In this, the supervisor would compare the actual level of financial resources in the bank to the risks that the bank is running. This would be a multi-dimensional (or "blobby") assessment but could be summarised in an overall verdict on economic solvency along the lines of "very well capitalised", "well capitalised", "adequately capitalised", "inadequately capitalised" and "poorly capitalised" or simple grades (A, B, C, D, E). The lower grades would require a management comment on capital-building initiatives planned. The solvency assessment report would be updated quarterly or, exceptionally, on an ad-hoc basis.

This proposal is not too far from current reality and best practice. The Pillar 2 approach to solvency assessment is gaining ground in several countries and we can see the emerging primacy of capital measures that go beyond Pillar 1-style ratio management in the UK's ICG (Individual Capital Guidance), Ireland's PCAR (Prudential Capital Adequacy Review) and Danish Pillar 2 add-ons, to name but a few. Some of these solvency assessments are beginning to use multiple dimensions in the valuation of a bank's assets, the inclusion or not of future profit streams and the scenarios which the bank is planning. Few of the assessment exercises are transparent or published in a detailed format, but we expect full disclosure to become the norm.

7.5.9 Resolution of Failed Banks

What to do when a bank is deemed to have a financial position that is not appropriate to its continued operation? In other words, how to deal with failed banks?

The topic of resolution of failed banks is not a major focus of this book. Most of the ideas on bank resolution have already been considered and integrated into regulation by the authorities, as they see fit. The reader is directed to some of the excellent overviews of the topic that have been published by national, regional and global regulators as well as by institutions such as the IMF. In general, the policies that have been adopted appear rational and effective. Major progress has been made in ensuring that the financial resources of banks are effective in insulating creditors and depositors from the impact of losses and that troubled banks are placed into the resolution process before systemic contagion can occur. The authorities have spent an inordinate amount of time attempting to define specific solvency "triggers" for failure and resolution, but thankfully have allowed themselves discretion to act even when reported solvency is above those trigger levels.

Legal obstacles to resolution in advance of technical bankruptcy are being addressed. The concept of "bail-in", in cases where losses extend beyond the resources that are considered regulatory capital, has become widely accepted and its nuances have been explored (for example, the way in which large and small depositors can – or cannot – be forced to take losses, in the case of Cyprus). Public authorities are adamant that they will not put society's money at risk in propping up failing banks. In effect, the bail-in policies make it clear that all the resources of the bank – up to and including retail customer deposits – are investments in the bank and are liable to be lost if the bank should fail disastrously.

Indeed, there is a hope that the harsher and more explicit resolution regimes that are being established will lead to indirect benefits in the corporate governance of banks:

> Holders of bail-inable debt will have the incentive to monitor banks more closely, which contributes to reining in excessive risk-taking provided that (i) national authorities take the necessary action when needed, and (ii) investors are actually able to scrutinise banks.[60]

The by-product of reducing the prospects of a bail-out by introducing bail-in and effective resolution powers is that the sensitivity to risk that is referred to in the quotation above will, over time and as investors and depositors become acquainted with the operation of the rules, lead to a more volatile banking industry. The rush to the exits will begin earlier and with more energy. Yet again, fixing one problem will lead to an unintended consequence.

7.6 LIQUIDITY AND FUNDING

Liquidity and funding are highly problematic elements of banking. Most of the time, they are infinite, elastic and cheap. They are perceived to be mundane and non-strategic. Then, during a period of crisis, we are reminded that they are the life-blood of the banking industry: when they dry up, banks struggle and weaker banks fail. Liquidity and funding are phenomena that are difficult to observe and even more difficult to understand. For this reason, they have been neglected, with regulatory reform, such as the current Basel III proposals, taking so long and proving so contentious.

7.6.1 Liquidity

In a crisis, the only source of true liquidity is the central bank of the currency in question (say, the Federal Reserve for dollars, the ECB for euros, the Swiss National Bank for Swiss francs and the Bank of England for sterling). Yet liquidity regulations essentially require banks to hold a large amount of "high quality" government bonds, which can then presumably be sold to meet cash flow needs, or as a last resort, pledged at the central bank in exchange for cash.

Where the central bank operates on behalf of the government in question and can issue money in domestic currency at the government's request, this may appear a valid approach. The problems with using government debt as a source of liquidity for the banking industry are that:

- The government security carries a liquidity risk of its own (for example, not all US government securities are highly liquid). There is not necessarily a buyer for the security in size, at the right price and at all times.

---

[60] High-level expert group on reforming the structure of the EU banking sector, Erikki Liikanen, October 2012.

- A government bond has market, maturity and related interest rate risk. All of these can cause a loss of value on the security.
- Government bonds carry a not-always-insignificant credit risk. This is one of the reasons why credit spreads are not zero and there is wide divergence in spreads between different sovereign issuers of differing perceived credit quality. For example, holders of Greek government bonds have just suffered major financial losses on their holdings.
- Governments do not always need to borrow in sufficient size to provide a ready stock of assets for liquidity purposes.
- The interest income provided by government bonds in bank liquidity portfolios is largely illusory – banks are forced buyers, the coupon barely compensates for the risks outlined above and the negative carry involved is effectively a tax on banking activity. On its part, the government receives a false signal, when it finds ready buyers of its debt in the domestic banking industry.
- Most importantly, forcing banks to hold government bonds weakens both the government and the banks in question, as it ties their fates inextricably together. This has been demonstrated in several Eurozone countries recently (notably Greece, Ireland and Portugal).

In summary, the holding of government bonds as a liquidity reserve should be discouraged. But is there an alternative? We believe there is. The predominant form of liquidity reserve should be in the form of a facility with the central bank.

The provision of a committed credit facility (in effect, an overdraft) from the central bank of the currency in question is one of the liquidity tools that has been adopted by the Basel Committee in its liquidity rules within Basel III. The option was designed largely to meet the needs of banks in countries like Australia, whose supply of government debt is not large enough to meet the liquidity needs of the banks: total government debt in issue is only A\$427bn (or 28% of GDP)[61] and 70% of that is held by international investors,[62] whereas the liquidity buffer needs of the banking system are likely to be around 40% of GDP.[63] Banks in Australia pay a commitment fee of 0.15% per annum for the provision of the facility.[64]

The fee for the obligatory overdraft is a tax on banking activities that carry liquidity risk. But it is society that genuinely "owns" liquidity through its ownership of the currency, hence it is only right to rent out this social good (for a fee) to those who utilise it.

From a risk perspective, the provision of the facility should be the same as having banks hold government bonds of ultra-short duration. Such bonds would have virtually no credit, market or maturity risk. They would be useless for the government as a source of funds and so would pay a zero coupon. They would represent a "negative carry" cost for the bank, which would of course need to raise the funds to buy the bonds. The fee for the committed facility should be equal to the cost of negative carry for the bank. Liquidity is provided on a standby basis rather than a funded basis, but the costs to the bank are the same and the system eliminates the reliance upon the government as a source of risk-free investment and removes the temptation to take risk in a liquidity portfolio.

The other area for improvement is the assumption regarding the quality of retail deposits, in terms of cash flow during a stress scenario. Liquidity measures set out in Basel III pre-

---

[61] World Economic Database, IMF, April 2013.
[62] Reserve Bank of Australia website.
[63] The Committed Liquidity Facility, Guy Debelle, Reserve Bank of Australia, 23 November 2011.
[64] Ibid.

sume that high quality (guaranteed, historically stable and non-aggressively priced) retail deposits are "sticky" and will exhibit limited outflows during a crisis. As described in Section 4.5.6, the assumption is that 3% of retail deposits are assumed to be withdrawn, 5% of small business deposits and 40% of large corporate deposits. This is not an unreasonable assumption, but nor is it a watertight fact: retail investors can and do withdraw their funds in large volumes during a crisis, even if they carry a solid guarantee. We saw, in 2007, a retail run on the Northern Rock in the UK, much of which was the withdrawal of funds that were guaranteed by the UK's deposit guarantee scheme. It is reported that 5% of Northern Rock's deposits were withdrawn on one day.[65] In Cyprus in early 2013, the freezing of deposits – and imposition of a loss of principal for large deposits, which had earlier been a proposal to "haircut" all depositors, large and small – serves as a reminder of the fragility of the value of a bank deposit.

From a liquidity management perspective, our proposal is to remove the confusion and ambiguity around the nature of retail deposits by making them *explicitly* a deposit with the central bank that is administered by the commercial bank in question. This is described in more detail below.

7.6.2 Funding

Funding considerations relate to preventing cash flow crises ("runs") on banks, which precipitate their collapse and lead to systemic contagion. Runs are caused by a loss of confidence in the bank, which exposes the maturity mismatches of the bank.

Irrespective of the *legal* maturities or the assumed *behavioural* maturities, what matters in bank runs is the *actual* maturities of a bank's loans and investments relative to the *actual* maturities of its funds. The actual maturity mismatch can be far greater than the legal mismatch, since customers can legitimately expect their term deposits to be available to them prior to their legal maturity, or the behavioural mismatch, which measures the historic behaviours of demand depositors under a different set of circumstances. Assets will also have an actual maturity, as customers will often require a rollover at legal maturity, if they are unable to refinance elsewhere; drawdown assumptions on customer credit and liquidity facilities will also need to be factored in, based on actual rather than contractual commitment.

A bank has no funding risk if the *actual* maturities of its assets and its liabilities are matched across all currencies and time periods. History shows us that no bank can be certain of maintaining such a perfect profile under all scenarios. Banks undertake a maturity transformation role and must, therefore, manage their funding risk.

As a disclosure item, we would suggest that banks share with the market a quantification of their funding risk, expressed as the incremental interest expense that would be incurred to remove all funding risk on a legal maturity basis as well as on alternative *actual* maturity bases. For example, a bank with a 25-year loan at an interest rate of 10% funded with 5-year term funding that costs the bank a spread of 6% would appear to have a net interest margin of 4%. If the bank's 25-year funding spreads were 9%, however, it would be informative to see the funding risk quantified at 3% and the Zero Funding Risk Net Interest Margin (ZFR-NIM) would be 1%. Such a measure would enable the market to observe the income derived from maturity transformation.

---

[65] Rush on Northern Rock continues, BBC News, 15 September 2007.

A further concept that could be applied to help observe maturity risk is the so-called "mark-to-funding" approach for asset valuation.[66] Using this approach, the value of a bank's assets would depend upon the maturity of its funding profile. Assets that are notionally funded with short-term liabilities would be valued at their current market price, no matter how drastic; assets whose notional funding is longer-term could be carried at a long-term fair value based on reasonable assumptions and the current disposal price of the asset in the market can be ignored. The effect of this would be to highlight the increased volatility in the solvency of banks with short-term funding bases. This has to be preferable to the imposition of arbitrary minimum funding standards and the use of arbitrary accounting conventions for valuation. Such a concept would mesh well with the risk-based methodologies for asset valuation (such as "confidence accounting") outlined in Section 7.1.1.

In addition to the risk measures outlined above, there is also a need to consider the role of deposit funding more carefully. For many banks, retail deposits form a major part of their funding base. They are assumed to represent a long-term ("sticky") funding base, even though they are mostly demand deposits, repayable instantly or at very short notice.

To strengthen the liquidity and funding structures of banks, such deposits need to be upgraded, such that they become a truly stable and permanent element of the banking system. In fact, they should become de facto a deposit with the central bank, administered by the commercial bank in question and guaranteed by the central bank in question. For the avoidance of doubt, in the Eurozone, we mean the European Central Bank. Such deposits should carry a clear "quality stamp" (akin to the "kite mark" used to show that consumer goods have been approved by the quality checks of the British Standards Institute) to make it clear that they are "assets under management" rather than an investment that might bear losses at some point. This quality stamp could be applied to all manner of deposits, corporate and retail, small and large. Assuming the central bank in question has control of the currency, there is no need for a pre-funded deposit guarantee fund. The charge to banks for utilisation of such "quality-stamped" deposits would need to be set and would be risk-based, according to the outputs of the periodic risk assessment conducted by the regulator.

The simple fact is that small retail depositors are *always* going to be bailed out. Populist politics, on which democracy rides, give an implicit guarantee to the small clients of banks, no matter the formal legal status. The recent events in Cyprus underline the importance of protecting small, retail depositors. Better to make this explicit and do away with the pretence of the current system.

If such a system were adopted, who would provide maturity transformation? The answer to this is threefold.

- Firstly, depositors could be encouraged to place their funds on term deposit, presumably at similar but slightly lower rates than a government bond of similar maturity, reflecting the superior credit quality of the central bank over the government in question. Within Europe, this credit quality gap – and hence the pricing differential – could be somewhat wider.
- Secondly, where the depositor prefers to place their money on demand deposit, they would receive a commensurately lower deposit rate and the central bank can use the statistically-driven assumptions of "stickiness" to determine an estimated *actual* maturity that is probably quite long (and far longer than it would have been for a commercial bank, since there is no reason for there to be even a mild run on the central bank).

---

[66] The Fundamental Principles of Financial Regulation, Brunnermeier et al., 6 January 2009.

- And thirdly, the entities who borrow the funds from the central bank (the commercial banks and the indebted government) can run a certain amount of maturity risk/transformation themselves, by borrowing on a short-term basis from the central bank, in order to fund assets with a longer duration.

Non-guaranteed deposits could be marketed, with the clear label of "investments", a higher interest rate and a clear absence of any government guarantee. They would not be subject to the "moral hazard" that has plagued the banking industry for too long, with creditors assuming an implicit government guarantee, often to the detriment of the state's finances. They would effectively be subordinated to the guaranteed deposits, absorbing losses in case of bank failure once other, more junior, sources of regulatory capital are exhausted. A clear bifurcation of the funding base into guaranteed and non-guaranteed will make risk, accountability and pricing very clear.

7.7 THE "PILLAR 2" MINDSET

For too long, banks and their regulators have focused on mild "stress tests" as a way of assessing financial resilience. Such stress tests are highly deterministic – they take a given situation and model the outcome on the bank's profitability and losses. Rarely are they sufficiently harsh to really test the institution to destruction; the severity of input assumptions generally drives the severity of outcomes. The outcome of a stress test is along the lines of "if this macro situation happens, here's what will happen to our bank". They can also be gamed, with banks encouraged implicitly to follow the same strategies that are treated more favourably under the stress tests.

As the unexpected twists and turns of the current financial crisis show us, risk does not always play to the central scenario nor even to the "adverse" scenario. Increasingly, banks and their regulators are looking at the impact of unlikely events or "tail risk". "Assessments of the balance sheet consequences of tail macroeconomic risks are now in the bloodstream of financial policymakers. They also appear, belatedly, to be entering the bloodstream of financial firms. That is real progress."[67] But despite the undeniable progress, the industry is stuck in the mindset of the single scenario stress test.

Wargaming is a different approach, with different objectives and superior utility.

It is our unshakeable view, if not a concrete fact, that risk has to be assessed at the institutional, rather than the individual asset, level and on a dynamic, rather than a static, basis. This view was reflected in the spirit of the second pillar of Basel II, which was unfortunately neglected during implementation and has been neglected during the formulation of Basel III. Part of the proposed blueprint, therefore, is to reinvigorate the focus on Pillar 2 in bank risk management and regulatory/supervisory processes. In fact, the proposal is that Pillar 2 risk and capital assessments will form the focus of supervisory efforts.

---

[67] Small Lessons from a Big Crisis, speech by Andrew G. Haldane, 8 May 2009.

7.7.1 Putting Scenario Assessment at the Heart of the Risk Management Process

Treating risk as a dynamic concept introduces the slightly awkward requirement of multi-dimensional risk assessments. We are forced to reject (or at least supplement) the deterministic, Pillar 1-type approach, wherein each risk asset has a risk-weight and each element of capital has a value. This concept is not new:

> Under observation, the financial system changes. When models are put to use, the financial system changes. Therefore, attempting to systematically forecast prices or risk using past observations is generally impossible. […] If we don't understand how the system works, generating numbers may give us comfort. But the numbers do not imply understanding.[68]

It is surprising that the guardians of the financial system, therefore, operate with such a "Pillar 1" mindset, where risk is knowable and deterministic models tell us the answer. We should rather treat a bank as a living organism, which manages risk and responds to changes in the environment. It is not a passive, closed-end fund of assets that follows a single "base case" path. Its riskiness is the inverse of its resilience and its resilience is driven by its ability to cope with unexpected outcomes. The risk assessment of a bank should be the risk assessment of how a bank fares under different scenarios, how adept it is at facing various stresses and ultimately of how good it is at remaining operational and viable in the face of duress.

Scenario management should form the heart of the risk management process. Bank managers in all divisions should be thinking about the risks that they originate and manage and how those risks contribute to overall institutional riskiness. If banks adopted such an approach and implemented it deep into the organisation in the form of holistic management thinking, then risk management would be much improved and the riskiness of the banking industry would reduce. How would this manifest itself in practice? Well, for example, business strategies that rely on benign or "expected" conditions would be scrutinised more closely, diversification, risk mitigation transactions would become more commonplace, management decision processes would be sharpened and the resources of risk capital, liquidity and optionality would be more highly valued.

> In areas such as nuclear power, chemical engineering, air transport and the military, deep scenario analysis is at the heart of the risk assessment process, consuming a huge amount of time and effort. Such analysis is almost unheard of in finance. It was certainly lacking in the months leading up to the subprime crisis of late 2007 and 2008.[69]

7.7.2 Wargaming Instead of Stress Testing

Regulatory stress tests are highly deterministic "fire drills", based around a single scenario and designed to be passed or failed. The recent Dodd–Frank stress test in the USA in March 2013 can serve as an illustration. It contained a "severely adverse scenario", in which the USA's 18 largest banks modelled the impact of a major shock to economic activity and asset prices: a real GDP decline of 5%, rise in unemployment rate from 8% to 12%, slowdown in inflation to 1%, a collapse in stock markets of 50% and a drop in real estate prices by 20%. The results

---

[68] On the efficacy of financial regulations, Jón Daníelsson, London School of Economics.
[69] The forgotten pillars of Basel II, *Risk* magazine, 10 January 2013.

Table 7.7 Dodd–Frank Act stress testing 2013, Minimum stressed Tier 1 common ratios, Q4 2012 to Q4 2014. Federal Reserve estimates in the severely adverse scenario[70]

Bank	Actual Q3 2012	Minimum during stress period	Difference
Ally Financial	7.3	1.5	5.8
American Express	12.7	11.1	1.6
Bank of America	11.4	6.8	4.6
BONY Mellon	13.3	13.2	0.1
BB&T	9.5	9.4	0.1
Capital One	10.7	7.4	3.3
Citigroup	12.7	8.3	4.4
Fifth Third Bancorp	9.7	8.6	1.1
Goldman Sachs	13.1	5.8	7.3
JP Morgan Chase	10.4	6.3	4.1
KeyCorp	11.3	8.0	3.3
Morgan Stanley	13.9	5.7	8.2
PNC	9.5	8.7	0.8
Regions Financial	10.5	7.5	3.0
State Street	17.8	12.8	5.0
SunTrust	9.8	7.3	2.5
U.S. Bancorp	9.0	8.3	0.7
Wells Fargo	9.9	7.0	2.9
Average	**11.1**	**7.4**	**3.7**

showed that – under this scenario – the largest American banks would have to take loan provisions of some $317bn as well as capital markets losses of over $100bn. Of course, much of this would be covered by the banks' pre-provision revenues, net of costs, which would be $268bn, even after "losses related to operational-risk events and mortgage repurchases, as well as expenses related to disposition of owned real estate of $101 billion".[71] Overall, the capital bases of the banks would be eroded by $194bn, knocking the average Tier 1 common solvency ratio down from 11.1% to 7.4%. The relative assumptions in the stress test would hit different banks in different ways, largely as a function of their business mix. As the specific bank results in Table 7.7 show, the capital markets houses fare the worst.

Interestingly, media reports suggest that the stress test calibration appears to be somewhat negotiable: "After last year's embarrassing failure, Pandit and other [Citigroup] officials vowed to talk more with the Fed about how it would be scored this year, particularly for potential losses on emerging markets assets, which are less well-known by regulators."[72] More

---

[70] Dodd–Frank Act Stress Test 2013: Supervisory Stress Test Methodology and Results, Federal Reserve, March 2013.

[71] Ibid.

[72] Citigroup asks to spend $1.2 bln on stock buybacks, Reuters, 7 March 2013.

interestingly, the results of the Dodd–Frank stress test are being used to assess which banks are deemed to have surplus capital and can thus engage in distribution of capital to shareholders via dividends and share buybacks. This is disturbing: no-one is claiming that the stress scenario represents a likely scenario, yet it becomes central to the banks' capital planning.

Running a single-scenario stress test only tells us how banks would fare in that given scenario. The results are therefore unlikely to surprise, as they are a direct reflection of business mix. A differently calibrated stress test would give a different set of outcomes. We have no reason to believe that the scenario that has been chosen is a reasonable one to consider, either in terms of overall severity or in terms of the mix of losses that result. In a perfect world, the results of a deterministic single-scenario stress test will be seen as interesting, illustrative and informative, nothing more. Unfortunately, in reality, there is every reason to suspect that banks will seek to "game" the stress test, altering their business profile to suit that particular scenario, even if it means weakening themselves to other potential scenarios. Moreover, the scenario acquires an importance and meaning in practice (i.e. it is assumed to show which banks have "enough" capital) that is far beyond what it actually represents.

Wargaming is a different approach, with different objectives and superior utility. It is a technique developed by the military in order better to prepare for a campaign. Instead of defining a small number of defined scenarios and ensuring the institution is equipped to deal with those scenarios, wargaming takes many scenarios and assesses where the weak points of the institution lie. A view can then be formed on whether to commit resources to address the weaknesses.

Wargaming is used, for example, to prepare for space missions. The astronauts do not *only* undertake the training and carry the tools for a straight-down-the-middle, base-case operation. They rehearse under multiple scenarios, none of which is necessarily seen as precisely "probable" or "improbable" but merely to give them the experience of understanding the potential approaches when something goes wrong. This may drive the decision to, say, carry an extra 10mm spanner or, since risk management does not always mean risk reduction, carry one less fire extinguisher. The team learns about the system in which it operates, the resources and skills they need and how they might expect to cope with events that come out of the blue. Simply by thinking and working through multiple scenarios, they can identify where they would like to be positioned in terms of risk and how they could optimise their response should unexpected developments occur.

Such scenario testing is an important risk management activity, but it is not part of the risk management capability of many banks. There is evidence that some sort of wargaming has been used by the supervisory authorities, for example the 2004 exercise in the UK to assess how they might cope with the failure of a large bank. That particular wargame highlighted the need for a special bankruptcy procedure for banks. Disappointingly – and with disastrous consequences for the UK's banking industry – the authorities failed to implement such a procedure. Other lessons also went unheeded: "In spite of appreciating the vulnerability of Northern Rock and HBOS three years before the very public run on the Newcastle-based lender made headlines around the world, regulators did not subject either to closer supervision."[73] In 2006, European financial regulators also went through a wargaming exercise, which simulated the collapse of a large European bank with operations in several countries.[74]

---

[73] Chilling plausibility of bank's "war game", *Financial Times*, 30 May 2009.
[74] Europe simulates financial meltdown, *Financial Times*, 9 April 2006.

On an individual level, we can imagine employing wargaming to improve our personal lives. Let's take an example. What do I do if little Johnny has an accident at school and has to go to hospital, while I'm at work? If we run ourselves through this scenario, we might learn something: the distance between school and work is unacceptably great, we don't have the mobile phone number of our boss stored in the phone memory, the mobile phone is flat or we haven't renewed our medical insurance. These are not negatives, they are *learning points*. Rather than helping us cope better with that single scenario, the run-through allows us to consider other arrangements that need changing. They can lead us to re-appraise more strategic aspects of our lives: do we live in the right place, does work tie us down, do we have our administrative files in order? Or even, to charge the mobile phone more often.

Corporate wargaming generally takes the form of competitive simulation.[75] Groups of competitors form themselves into opposing teams and play through a simulation, integrating the feedback from the opponents' actions and decisions, as well as changes in the macro environment thrown in by the games' administrators and adjudicators. The impact of extreme changes can then be assessed. For example:

- What would you do if your main competitor slashed the price of its products to try to spark a price war?
- How would a company deal with a shock event, say the arrival of a disruptive technology or the closure of a key export market?
- What if the top management team defects to a competitor or gets stranded abroad by a volcanic ash cloud?
- What happens if it snows all summer?

Corporations that undertake wargames might learn of their deficiencies in contingency planning, their unnecessary over-reliance on key product markets or supply chain elements, their lack of flexibility in business strategy and their lack of control over front-line business operations. In a word, they understand their risks better by playing with the business in a simulated environment.

The wargaming approach is already used extensively in disaster recovery and operational contingency testing, which has been an area of focus for banks following the lessons of recent terrorist attacks. Wargaming would also be a superb tool for banks to improve their risk management in other areas. But it would also be a supervisory tool, for the authorities better to assess the resilience of the institutions for which they are responsible. The lessons from wargaming would also assist in understanding the macro systemic dynamics of the banking system. For example if, when faced with the closure of a key wholesale funding market, all banks plan to increase retail deposit market share through better remuneration of deposits, increased marketing and cannibalisation of insurance products, then it is clear that, in aggregate, the plans are not feasible. This dynamic perspective on macro issues is more powerful than the current focus on asset bubbles.

Fortunately, we live in an era with information technology that offers us the processing power to be more analytical and consider more variations than previously. Whereas simulating the balance sheet of a large banking group under a single, given scenario would have been

---

[75] *Wargaming for Leaders,* Herman, Frost and Kurz, 2009.

daunting in the year 2000, now we are able to be much more demanding of the analytical aspect of scenario analysis. So long as we do not fall into the trap of thinking that statistical models have strong predictive powers, we can enhance the risk management capabilities of banks through wargaming.

7.7.3 Communication of Pillar 2 Findings

Pillar 2 absolutely must be communicated, if we believe that Pillar 2 is important as a risk management discipline and investors need to understand the riskiness of the banks in which they are investing. The arguments that the modelled performance of the institution under alternative scenarios is somehow secret are unfounded.

Of course, the Pillar 2 approach to risk is somewhat innovative and will require a change in the mindset and the capabilities of investors too. They will, for example, need to:

- Recognise that their job is to understand and assess the risk management capabilities of the banks, in which they invest.
- Feed back to management the risk appetite for which they, as owners of the institution, ultimately are responsible.
- Favour banks that are better at risk management, part of which is reflected in Pillar 2 processes.

Assuming a competent supervisor, the bank will not be able to unduly "game the wargame", nor should they. Banks should not be seen to pass or fail Pillar 2 tests, nor should Pillar 2 necessarily result in a penalty "capital add-on". Instead, the core of Pillar 2 should be a feedback to the bank itself on the main vulnerabilities and strengths, which should serve as a management tool for improvement.

Investors should share the Pillar 2 feedback via a Pillar 2 report, which goes through in detail the nature of the wargames conducted and the learning points from them. There is nothing deterministic in the scenarios chosen, so the specific management actions and resulting outputs don't matter *per se*. The best Pillar 2 reports will show a bank that is able to be presented with a really tough situation, adapt to it readily and with the pre-existing resources available and identify the weak points that the scenario assessments identify. There will be Pillar 2 reports that will contain defeatist arguments such as "funding markets will of course never close" or "real estate is a one-way bet": these reports will show the banks that are fragile and doing nothing about it.

We can only imagine what would have happened if investors had had access to comprehensive Pillar 2 reports in 2006. One possibility is that investors would have had a better view of the dynamic risk profiles of the banks and their resilience to potential shocks. The reports would have highlighted weak spots which management chose to tolerate. Investors then could have formed their own view on the likelihood of those vulnerabilities being tested and made a more informed investment decision. Risk and risk appetite would have been more closely matched. In reality, however, an extensive and dynamic wargaming programme that is publicly disclosed would be more likely to have led to management action. It would have tempered some of the hidden risks in the system. The lessons from the wargames would have informed management of unacceptable vulnerabilities in their businesses, which investors would not tolerate or which would have caused the bank in question's perceived creditworthiness and market value to fall. In short, they would have reduced risk in the system and mitigated some of the causal factors of the current financial crisis.

7.7.4 The Modular Approach to Risk Assessment

Since risk is complex and banks are daunting, systematic and modular risk methodologies will assist in breaking down the problem into its constituent parts and allowing the management, the supervisor and the investor to form a view. Some of the catastrophic decisions taken during the current financial crisis have been taken as a result of inability to understand and manage large and complex situations. Broad-brush appraisals are sometimes necessary, but a rigorous drill-down is needed for a more effective understanding.

We have already put forward the "centurion approach" as a way of ensuring thorough coverage of risk management and effective governance (see Section 7.4.3). Under this approach, management discipline will be ensured at the level of each 1/100th of the bank. Additionally, there is a need for a systematic breakdown of key themes and risk management focuses. One modular approach that has much to commend it is the "CAMELS" approach, used in the USA by the FDIC and the Federal Reserve. CAMELS is an acronym of the main areas of attention by the supervisor:

C – Capital adequacy
A – Asset quality
M – Management
E – Earnings
L – Liquidity
S – Sensitivity to market risk

The CAMELS framework is used to derive a confidential supervisory rating:

> The results of an on-site examination or inspection are reported to the board of directors and management of the bank or holding company in a report of examination or inspection, which includes a confidential supervisory rating of the financial condition of the bank or holding company. The supervisory rating system is a supervisory tool that all of the federal and state banking agencies use to communicate to banking organizations the agency's assessment of the organization and to identify institutions that raise concern or require special attention. This rating system for banks is commonly referred to as CAMELS.[76]

Each part of the CAMELS rating has component elements for the supervisor to address. The Asset Quality part, for example, has the following components:

- quality of underwriting, credit process and underwriting standards;
- volume of process errors;
- management capability in credit and risk management;
- volume and profile of delinquent or low-profile loan exposures;
- provisioning levels;
- off-balance and "synthetic" credit risk;
- quality and diversification of the loan and investment portfolios;
- risks from capital markets operations (e.g. inventory and counterparties);
- degree of asset concentrations;
- quality of policies and procedures;
- robustness of internal controls;
- quality of IT systems.

---

[76] The Federal Reserve System: Purposes and Functions, Federal Reserve, August 2011.

The CAMELS framework has operated with reasonable success in the USA and is now an established tool. Other countries have similar approaches: the UK, for example, had a framework called ARROW, which is the acronym for Advanced Risk-Responsive Operating frameWork. And ratings agencies have their own methodologies for credit assessment of banks (see Section 3.10). These systematic frameworks work well as checklists, but they need to be supplemented with other "checks and balances". The following five areas of investigation and assessment should be included in any risk assessment of a bank, whether by management or by supervisors:

1. Special focus on and scrutiny of business areas of high growth, with a "devil's advocate" approach to the apparent and latent risks of those areas. Many of the problems in the current financial crisis were in business areas of high growth, where management had limited experience and the supervisor had limited visibility of historic performance.
2. Clear exposition of the drivers of profitability. Which features of the business make it profitable for the bank? This scrutiny would expose flawed business models such as misselling of unsuitable products (e.g. PPI in the UK) and assumption of excessive risks (e.g. monoline credit insurance of structured finance).
3. Understanding the drivers of complexity and volume. This is especially necessary in businesses that have a high level of operational risk (e.g. payments clearing) or notional volumes (e.g. derivatives). Unneccessary complexity can cause unnecessary risk.
4. Gathering of market intelligence, market feedback and "mystery shopper" exercises. The risks of a bank are sometimes more evident from an external perspective. Market practitioners and customers may have a more informed view than management or the supervisor.
5. Areas of high or growing market share, which can be indicators of risk concentrations or risky, off-market behaviours. For example, any bank that is beginning to dominate a market segment at the expense of competitors may well be misunderstanding the risks of that segment.

7.7.5 Risk Appetite and Reverse Stress Testing

Reverse stress testing is an elegant way of matching Pillar 2 risk assessments with risk appetite. Banks simply need to tell their owners and investors "here's what would need to happen to make us fail". Just as an engineer defines the strength of their bridge by showing how many tanks it could carry, so does a bank define its risk resilience under Pillar 2 by showing how bad it can get before it fails. A reverse stress test defines the boundaries of resilience and can then be assessed by management, investors and supervisors. They can form a view of whether the reverse stress test indicates a position that is acceptable or not, according to their appetite for risk.

As with wargaming, the outputs of a reverse stress test are unlikely to be a simple pass/fail. Feedback from the test is likely to result in management actions to improve (or, in cases where the bank is assessed to have more scope for risk-taking, reduce) the level of resilience and the degree of stress that the bank is able to endure before failing.

Reverse stress tests are now required by regulators as part of Pillar 2 stress testing. In the UK, for example, the regulator requires banks to "identify a range of adverse circumstances which would cause its business plan to become unviable and assess the likelihood that such events could crystallize".[77] In a similar vein, the EBA gives guidelines about using reverse stress tests "to overcome disaster myopia and the possibility that a false sense of security might arise from regular stress testing in which institutions identify manageable impacts".[78] Sadly, there are few examples in the public domain of the outputs from regulatory reverse stress tests and the actions that they have prompted.

Understanding the boundaries of resilience is essential to gauging risk appetite. There is nothing worse than a bank with risk-averse shareholders who thought it was bomb-proof getting blown away at the slightest problem.

7.8 GLASNOST: MARKET DISCIPLINE AND "PILLAR 3"

> Without glasnost there is not, and there cannot be, democratism, the political creativity of the masses and their participation in management.[79]

In the late 1980s, the leader of the Soviet Union, Mikhail Gorbachev, adopted the policy of "glasnost", to open up the Soviet system to scrutiny and popular public involvement. Glasnost was translated into English as the rather passive "openness". In fact, its meaning may be closer to the more active noun "publicity" and could even have tinges of "criticism". It is very hands-on, at any rate. Gorbachev was actively engaging the people in the government of their nation. The act of opening up and publicising the workings of the state led to increased accountability of Soviet apparatchiks, civil servants and politicians.

The banking industry needs to adopt a policy of glasnost too. Our system will not work effectively without market discipline. It is imperative that investors must play a highly active role in the functioning of the banking industry. Without that, the industry will be inefficient and ineffective.

In order to improve market-based feedback on the banking sector, *more, relevant risk-based* information must be made *readily available*. The first point will require the regulator to publish its own risk assessment of each bank (see Sections 7.5.8 and 7.7.3), while the second point necessitates the publication of detailed financial information in a standardised, electronic database format (see Section 7.1.6).

The provision of the information does not imply that regulators are giving a recommendation to investors. Rather, they are providing a useful information collation, processing and analysis function. Along with audited financial information, the regulatory assessment report provides a bedrock of accessible and *usable* information to investors. The data they provide will allow investors to track the metrics they see as insightful and supplement those with extra, probing, proprietary analyses and soft judgements on aspects such as underwriting standards. Investors will also be responsible for conducting the "sniff test" that ultimately lies at the bottom of most investment decisions.

None of this is terribly new or innovative. The concept of market discipline was enshrined in Basel II's third pillar ten years ago. But by focusing on *engagement* rather than mere

---

[77] Stress and Scenario Testing, FSA, December 2009.
[78] CEBS guidelines on stress testing (GL32), CEBS/EBA, 26 August 2010.
[79] Mikhail Sergeevich Gorbachev, 1986.

disclosure (covered already in Section 7.1.6), the power of market discipline can be harnessed. The differences from current practice would be significant:

- Pent-up demand from investors for a better market discipline model, due to recent memories of painful losses.
- More differentiation between good and bad bank strategies.
- Risk assessment of the "Guardian Angel" supervisor made public.
- Better information and use of information than before.
- Removal of implicit systemic support, which made investors lazy.
- Creation of the conditions for risk-based stock analysts to prosper, rather than the current focus on short-term earnings.

The last points are rather startling. Many of the most egregious losses of the current financial crisis happened in full view of investors. There was less complexity and misunderstanding than is sometimes portrayed. Despite the clamours for sackings and revenge on management, investors were clearly neglecting their duties. The openly aggressive HBOS strategy serves as an example:

> Many of the principal causes of the HBOS failure and the weaknesses in its business model were known to financial markets. Public disclosures by the Group showed the pace of asset growth, key distinctive features of the Corporate Division's assets (including the exposures to commercial real estate, leveraged finance and equity and joint ventures), the pace of the International Division's growth and its concentration in commercial real estate, and the overall Group reliance on wholesale funding. Nevertheless, the financial markets as a whole, including shareholders, debt-holders, analysts and rating agencies, also failed to discipline the company's growth until it was too late. When they did, the Group had become a serious threat to financial stability.[80]

This underlines the necessity for improved investor and market engagement in the supervision of the banking industry. Supervision by the authorities is not sufficient in itself. The market cannot blindly follow the judgements of the supervisor in deciding to which institutions their investment capital should flow and, anyway, that is not the job of the supervisor. The supervisor's "Guardian Angel" approach supplements and catalyses market-based supervision and vice versa. They share the same high-level objective – a healthy banking industry – but not necessarily the same opinions. The diversity of approaches will keep each other alert in the spirit of the classical quotation *"quis custodiet ipsos custodes?"* or "who is guarding the guards?"

This section on market discipline places great faith in the robustness of market principles. Investors will need to adjust to the lessons of this current financial crisis and markets will need to adjust to find a new equilibrium. Some of the weaknesses of our market economy will have been exposed and the system as a whole will come out stronger from the crisis. This faith is not a rock solid faith, however. The truth is that market discipline needs to be nurtured by the various stakeholders and agents of the capitalist system – such as the regulatory authorities and the popular media.

---

[80] "An accident waiting to happen": The failure of HBOS, Parliamentary Commission on Banking Standards, April 2013.

7.9 INDUSTRY STRUCTURE

As a result of the damage inflicted by the financial crisis, there is intense pressure on the authorities to mitigate the dangers caused by the banking industry – and, to a certain extent, inflict punishment on aspects of the industry that appear incompatible with its perceived social goal – by imposing structural changes to divorce "high street banking" from "casino banking", to constrain the size of the biggest banks deemed "too big to fail", and to re-erect national barriers in an industry that had become highly internationalised. Hardly a public debate can be heard without people baying for the "break-up of the banks".

This section looks at the structural issues of business mix, size and internationalism, independently in turn. At this point, however, it should be noted that most of the structural changes being sought are the product of a knee-jerk legislative urge that has become popular with politicians and journalists, combined with a disturbing mis-appraisal of the causes of the current financial crisis and an ignorance as to the nature of banks' service provision, especially as it relates to wholesale banking. The argument here is not that the status quo structure of the banking industry is perfect, just that the solutions being tabled in a serious way (they are being written into law in several major countries) are the wrong ones. And the risk is that this causes unnecessary inefficiencies, a false confidence in the effectiveness of the new structures and potentially even the introduction of new and counter-productive risks from the measures themselves.

7.9.1 Different Types of Banks

There has been scepticism for a long time about mixing up different types of banking in one entity. This was mostly from the USA, as a result of the experiences of the Wall Street Crash. The Glass–Steagall Act of 1933 forced deposit-taking banks and securities dealers to be separated, so that retail deposits were not used to speculate on the capital markets. Glass–Steagall was largely repealed in 1999 by the Gramm–Leach–Bliley Act, allowing deposit-taking banks to once more own securities firms (but note that the part of Glass–Steagall that prohibited insured banks themselves directly underwriting, dealing, or market making in corporate debt or equity securities was not repealed by the Gramm–Leach–Bliley Act and remains in effect[81]). Outside the USA, the universal banking model, where deposit-taking, lending and capital markets activities are often integrated in the same bank, continued to be the norm.

The current financial crisis has caused people once again to consider separation of activities as a way of making the banking system less risky. Such proposals – the Volcker rule in the USA, the Vickers report in the UK, the Liikanen report for the European Union – are summarised in Table 7.8, produced by the BIS.

There are major differences between these alternative approaches to structural reform of the banking industry, as Table 7.8 highlights. But there is also confusion on which aspects of banking need to be made less risky: "while the Vickers report argues for more stringent capital requirements for the protected activities, on importance grounds, the Liikanen Report argues

---

[81] Written Evidence in response to call for evidence made on 15 October 2012: Submission from Davis Polk & Wardwell LLP, Parliamentary Commission on Banking Standards.

Table 7.8 A stylised comparison of selected structural reform proposals[82]

	Volcker	Liikanen	Vickers
Broad approach	**Institutional separation** of commercial banking and certain investment activities	**Subsidiarisation:** proprietary and higher-risk trading activity have to be placed in a separate legal entity	**Ring-fencing:** structural separation of activities via a ring fence for retail banks
Deposit-taking institution may:			
– deal as principal in securities and derivatives	No	No	No
– engage in market-making	Yes	No	No
– perform underwriting business	Yes, in response to client/counterparty demand	Yes	Restricted
– hold non-trading exposures to other financial intermediaries	Unrestricted	Unrestricted	Restricted (inside the group)
Holding company with banking and trading subsidiaries	Not permitted	Permitted	Permitted
Geographical restrictions	No	No	Limitations for ring-fenced banks in the UK to provide services outside the European Economic Area

for potentially more stringent ones for the trading business (and possibly for real-estate related lending), on risk grounds."[83]

Whatever their differences, the various structural reform proposals are based on two fundamental tenets:

- Firstly, that capital markets activities are odious speculation of no social or economic utility: the label "*casino gambling*" was used and has stuck.[84]
- Secondly, that separation of wholesale banking from retail banking will result in a business model for the banking industry that is superior to the integrated, universal banking model.

We disagree with these hypotheses.

---

[82] Structural bank regulation initiatives: approaches and implications, BIS Working Papers no. 412, April 2013.

[83] Ibid.

[84] Cable says Diamond appointment highlights bank worries, BBC, 8 September 2010.

Role of Wholesale Banking

Wholesale banking is perceived to be riskier and less important than retail banking: "The basic rationale for the structural measures is to insulate certain types of financial activities regarded as especially important for the real economy, or significant on consumer/depositor protection grounds, from the risks that emanate from potentially riskier but less important activities."[85] Senior figures in the regulatory authorities talk about wholesale banking as if it should be closed down, since the current financial crisis "caused a severe retraction in terms of taking risk and attitudes towards taking risk. There's no doubt that of course that spilled over from those sectors of risk-taking that we don't want to see in the future into the basic credit creation functions of the economy."[86]

But wholesale banking is *not* an industry segment entirely bereft of social value. It serves the Treasury operations of major corporations. It provides the ability for consumers and small businesses to manage their risks in relation to currencies, interest rates and supplier credit. It acts as a mechanism for global capital to flow and find the most effective applications. Banks can only provide fixed-rate mortgages or foreign currency transactions because they have trading desks willing to "make the market". A world without market-makers would rely upon exactly equal and opposite customer needs, which never happens. (Imagine it: I need to buy $1,000 with my euros on the 19th February and another customer needs to sell their $1,000 for euros on exactly the same date, with the bank merely introducing and administering the trade. Unlikely.)

Some of the segments of wholesale banking may appear egregious: for example, the huge $647,000bn beast that is the OTC derivatives market, or the tax arbitrage business, which seeks to help companies reduce their corporate tax bill. But the problem with these activities is not where they sit, it is their nature and size. If wholesale banking were indeed of low or negative utility, it would not make sense to allow it to continue. The owners of the bank would surely not want to run such a business. "A volatile, capital-hungry non-client facing business, consistently earning sub-cost of equity returns has no place in a bank, whether inside or outside the ring-fence."[87] From the regulator's perspective, the goal should be to control this sector not alienate it.

Is a Segregated Business Model Less Risky?

If it were wholesale banking or trading activities that had characterised the causes of the financial crisis to the exclusion of all others, then clearly that would be the segment of activities to be purged. However, this is not the case. It is not the wholesale banking sector, nor the "universal banking" sector that was the cause of the current financial crisis. Various business models failed. Indeed, high street banks with few wholesale activities were among the worst casualties of the financial crisis (e.g. HBOS, Northern Rock, Caja Madrid/Bankia, Countrywide). This has been noted by multiple observers (see Table 7.9).

Is a Segregated Industry Easier to Run?

A universal banking model offers the benefits of business line diversification, whereas a segregated model does not. The IMF has recently pointed out that, in a segregated industry

---

[85] Structural bank regulation initiatives: approaches and implications, BIS Working Papers no. 412, April 2013.

[86] Andrew Bailey, PRA/Bank of England, on BBC TV's *Bankers: Fixing the System*, May 2013.

[87] Written Evidence in response to call for evidence made on 15 October 2012: Submission from The Association of British Insurers, Parliamentary Commission on Banking Standards.

Table 7.9   Observations on business model risks

Observer	Observation
European Commission	"Traditional (retail) banking activities can be the source of crisis, in particular if insufficiently regulated banks with weak internal controls engage in excessive lending."[88]
London School of Economics	"Distinctions between utility banks and casino banks are arbitrary and losses can occur everywhere. Narrow banks are inevitably less diversified, less stable, and less resistant to a crisis. Splitting banks up along business lines would be a mistake."[89]
Banque de France	"The current crisis showed the resilience of a universal banking system."[90]
Association of British Insurers	"Universal banking is not viewed by most investors as an inherently broken model. Whilst accepting that it will happen, investors so far are unconvinced about the real benefits of ring-fencing and/or separation and are sceptical about the benefits relative to the operational costs and disruption."[91]
	"Most investors so far are broadly of the view that the universal banking model was not the root cause of the financial crisis. Moreover, many banks that failed during the crisis were 'narrow' banks and indeed would be inside the ring-fence rather than outside. This would be true in the UK of all of Northern Rock, Bradford & Bingley and Alliance & Leicester and, arguably, most of HBOS. Within the UK, banking cycles have been closely correlated to real estate valuations and 'bubbles' rather than to investment banking cycles or structural limitations or weaknesses within universal banks."[92]
Parliamentary Commission on Banking Standards	"Whatever may explain the problems of other banks, the downfall of HBOS was not the result of cultural contamination by investment banking. This was a traditional bank failure pure and simple. It was a case of a bank pursuing traditional banking activities and pursuing them badly. Structural reform of the banking industry does not diminish the need for appropriate management and supervision of traditional banking activities."[93]

structure, "the reduction in diversification benefits can be substantial. The returns from retail, wholesale and trading activities of banks complement each other, allowing for greater diversification benefits. Furthermore, the inability of banks to move capital and liquidity to where it is most needed may amplify idiosyncratic risk to the group level."[94]

---

[88] High-level expert group on reforming the structure of the EU banking sector, Erikki Liikanen, October 2012.

[89] On the efficacy of financial regulations, Jón Daníelsson, London School of Economics.

[90] Regulating finance after the crisis, Christian Noyer, Governor, Banque de France.

[91] Written Evidence in response to call for evidence made on 15 October 2012: Submission from The Association of British Insurers, Parliamentary Commission on Banking Standards.

[92] Ibid.

[93] "An accident waiting to happen": The failure of HBOS, Parliamentary Commission on Banking Standards, April 2013.

[94] Creating a Safer Financial System: Will the Volcker, Vickers and Liikanen Structural Measures Help?, IMF, May 2013.

Despite this, many of the arguments for business model segregation are based on concerns on how diversified banking groups are managed and supervised. In other words, the daunting complexity of large, modern banks is a reason to consider breaking them up. Their whole-sale banking activities in particular are treated with suspicion. Wholesale banking is "more opaque, difficult to monitor and supervise, and more remote from core banking services" and "separation of activities is the most direct instrument to tackle banks' complexity and inter-connectedness".[95]

There is also a suspicion that banks are over-indulgent of their risky, wholesale arms and run risks that are obscured by implicit intra-group subsidies. UBS, for example, has high-lighted the fact that trading desks could obtain large amounts of funding at subsidised rates as one of the drivers for its subprime losses: "more demanding internal transfer pricing require-ments could have made several cash positions unattractive."[96] On the other hand, it could be argued that risks in the capital markets in 2006 and 2007 were underestimated not only in universal banks such as UBS but also in specialist investment banks.

Segregation may not be the panacea that certain people think it is. The issue of implicit subsidies, for example, may simply apply to risky banking activities in general, not just those related to the capital markets. This may have distorted decision-making and capital allocation, giving a preference for riskier activities:

> Our view is that at present there is a cross-subsidy from explicit and implicit government guaran-tees across all elements of bank operations; this reduces the perceived cost of capital of the riskiest activities, and increases perceived returns from those activities. Ensuring that a solid ring-fence is in place would remove this cross-subsidy and encourage all the banks to apply an appropriately varied cost of capital across all their activities, removing an inappropriate incentive to take risks which are not warranted.[97]

So, perhaps the subsidy also applied within retail banking business models such as North-ern Rock and Bankia, not just trading activities.

Ultimately, the issues of complexity and cross-subsidisation are not solved by re-arranging the pieces in a different order. Complexity does not go away, it is merely shifted somewhere else: the supervisory challenge of a broken-up industry is at least equal to the existing challenge. And seg-regation does not *per se* remove the misleading subsidies that can cloud good risk management.

As the BIS has observed recently:

> Limiting the permissible range of banking activities may help reduce systemic risk, but that is not likely to be a silver bullet. The limits will do little to reduce the complexity of banks, and even if they simplify the firm-level organisation of banks, their impact on system-wide risk is ambiguous.[98]

Structural Measures and Market Forces

Our hope is that market forces will shape a better banking industry, rewarding business models that provide good returns on manageable risk profiles. This *could* result in an industry that has

---

[95] High-level expert group on reforming the structure of the EU banking sector, Erikki Liikanen, October 2012.

[96] Shareholder Report on UBS's Write-Downs, UBS AG, 18 April 2008.

[97] Written Evidence in response to call for evidence made on 15 October 2012: Submission from Hermes, Parliamentary Commission on Banking Standards.

[98] 83rd BIS Annual Report 2012/2013.

a different structure to today's. For example, investors might prefer simpler, more utility-like banks: "A number of large investment institutions have minimised their exposure to the banking sector, but might be tempted to return to providing capital to banks which look more like utility providers of retail and small company banking services, in other words, to banks within the ring-fence."[99]

If regulation defines the structure of the banking industry, there will be two unintended consequences. Firstly, rigid measures will be ineffective and inefficient. Changing a bank's scope of activities should instead result from "bank-specific measures arising from resolvability assessments instead of constituting an across-the-board application".[100] Secondly, the industry could end up optimising around regulation. Banks will look the same, because alternative strategies will be less efficient from a regulatory perspective. Herd-like behaviour will increase, markets will become more volatile and cyclical and systemic risks will grow. A prescribed industry structure may lead to oligopolistic behaviours, which might have some appeal from a stability point of view, but are unlikely to lead to a value-creating financial sector in the long run. Oligopolistic structures appear neat and safe, but they misallocate capital and damage the longer-term prospects of an economy.

Instead, free-market forces will dictate the appropriate business models for banks. "Indeed it will be interesting to observe market reaction to the distinctive business and structural models that will emerge post regulatory reform. Capital will flow to the preferred model."[101]

Improving a risk profile can surely be achieved by banks themselves. There is no need for regulation to prescribe such measures. Indeed, regulation should ensure that the banking industry is dynamic, competitive and heterogeneous. "Regulation has not been neutral in fostering increasingly, if not homogenous, clearly converging business models. Profit recognition rules and capital consumption associated with some investment strategies did play a role. A key issue going forward is that financial regulation needs to safeguard diversity in financial system."[102]

Market forces should be able to allocate capital more accurately and nimbly than regulation and this is already happening, as evidenced by the recent announcements on strategic refocusing by banks such as UBS and Bank of America. It is the job of the markets to determine the right strategy for each bank and reward those companies that manage to get it right. If it is true that the market is rewarding companies for pursuing overly risky goals, then is it the job of the kindly regulator – who openly admits to finding the complexity of the situation daunting – to correct the situation?

In summary, it would be wrong to assign pariah status to wholesale banking and to decree that the synergistic goals of the universal banking model are illusory. The problems that Likannen, Vickers and others are seeking to address through breaking up large, universal banks could and should be mitigated through other means more effectively. A mild form of "ring-fencing", such as clear identification and separate capitalisation of speculative, proprietary trading activities or investment in hedge funds, should be tolerable and may assist banks in

---

[99] Ibid.

[100] Creating a Safer Financial System: Will the Volcker, Vickers and Liikanen Structural Measures Help?, IMF, May 2013.

[101] Written Evidence in response to call for evidence made on 15 October 2012: Submission from HSBC Holdings, Parliamentary Commission on Banking Standards.

[102] Regulating finance after the crisis, Christian Noyer, Governor, Banque de France.

their tasks of risk management. But anything more stringent may risk reducing the social utility of banking, increasing the number of institutions and hence the complexity of the banking industry, while simultaneously promoting homogeneous and oligopolistic behaviours, introducing temptations to arbitrage as well as new frictional costs and reducing the focus on risk management inside the supposedly safe, "ring-fenced" entities. Given the current momentum of regulation, it is a shame to say that several of these risks are likely to be realised.

7.9.2 Too Big to Fail

Isn't it rather disturbing to have a single bank, whose assets are equivalent to the level of the annual economic output of the entire nation in which it is headquartered? This is the case for, among others, Credit Suisse, Deutsche Bank, HSBC, ING, Nordea, Santander and UBS.[103] Wouldn't it be nice to have a banking system that is completely fragmented, with hundreds of small banks, each of which is completely dispensable in the case of idiosyncratic crisis? These are the questions posed by the "too big to fail" dilemma. The answers require a view on diversification, efficiency, heterogeneity and correlation – see Table 7.10.

Up to a point (defined by competition concerns), a concentrated banking industry should be preferable in terms of risk management and resilience. The regulator should not seek to prefer any given level of fragmentation or concentration, instead steering the industry by the application of strong risk management standards.

But doesn't this approach leave many banks that are "too big to fail"? Isn't it preferable to have banks able to fail and surely that means banks have to be small? We would disagree with many of the viewpoints on this topic and would instead make the following arguments as regards size of individual banks:

- Banks *of any size* should not be allowed to go bankrupt through the normal corporate bankruptcy regime: the attendant risks to financial stability are too large.
- Instead, banks *of any size* need to be well managed, regulated, supervised and – should they run into problems – have these resolved. The examples of Northern Rock and SNS Reaal illustrate the facts that small banks can't be allowed to fail.
- Size can be a good thing in banking. It enables risk diversification, management competence and scale economies. Small banks can benefit from a more responsive management model. Both small and large banks should be tolerated and supervised closely.
- Complexity needs to be managed with adequate management and regulatory resources. In order to have effective, "intimate" supervision, the level of supervisory resource is likely to be proportional to the size of the bank.
- Regulatory capital requirements that stipulate higher minimum risk capital requirements for larger banks are misguided. In fact, all things being equal, smaller banks are likely to need to operate with more capital per unit of "Pillar 1" type risk, due to relative lack of risk diversification.
- A fragmented banking industry with a large number of smaller firms of variable management quality is not preferable to a concentrated banking industry with a small number of large, universal banks that are diversified, well run and well regulated.

---

[103] Just How Big is the too Big to Fail Problem?, Milken Institute, March 2012.

Table 7.10 Considerations regarding "too big to fail"

Diversification	Larger institutions will have a better chance of withstanding a shock in one business area, as they can theoretically balance out the impact of that shock with the stable capital and earnings of the other business areas. This assumes that larger banks are indeed more diversified across a range of risks. Clearly, this is not always the case, as even large banks can have a business mix that is not diversified. HBOS, for example, was active in many business segments but managed to have problems in almost all of them, since it had adopted an aggressive, even cavalier, risk strategy across the board, and had problems even in the markets that were inherently healthy, such as Australia.
Efficiency of banks	People who fear that banks are too big tend to believe that, beyond a certain point, there is no incremental benefit of scale in banking. In Europe, this was the conclusion of the European Commission's expert report: "Although there is no agreement in the literature on the maximum efficient scale of banking, the available estimates tend to suggest levels that are relatively low compared to the current size of the largest EU banks."[104] In the USA, the FDIC has noted a similar finding: "Notwithstanding expectations and industry projections for gains in financial efficiencies, economies of scale seem to be reached at levels far below the size of today's largest financial institutions."[105] Yet, in reality, it is common for large banks to pursue acquisition strategies in order to improve scale economies or "synergies"; they tend only to be limited by competition constraints. Bank shareholders and bank analysts warm to acquisitions that have a clear and achievable cost synergy (and, to a lesser extent, revenue synergy) target and will bake the profit enhancement into their valuation models, if it appears credible. Even if the scope for efficiencies is dubious, it should not be for the regulator to define that scope.
Efficiency of supervision	It is not clear whether it is any easier to supervise a large number of small banks or a small number of large banks. Many of the features of the current financial crisis in some countries (e.g. USA) indicate that a fragmented industry is preferable, but in some countries the crisis is very much a small bank crisis (e.g. Denmark, Spain) and other crises in the past have been very much dominated by small bank problems (most notably, the Savings & Loan crisis in the USA in the late 1980s, which saw more than 1,000 small banks fail[106]). Common sense and first principles would indicate that the supervisor will benefit from having a smaller number of institutions with the professional management processes and systems that require greater investment and hence a broader revenue base.
Heterogeneity	Banks in a given system need to be different from each other and respond differently to crisis situations. If banks pursue similar business strategies, then they will be exposed to the same risks in the same way and will all have problems simultaneously. "Problems may arise when many small banks operate similar businesses and are exposed to common shocks ('systemic as a herd')."[107]
Correlation	Banks are generally linked to each other, not only through financial exposure but also through a mutually owned industry reputation. A run on a small bank can be catastrophic for the entire system. In a fragmented banking system, although the chance of a single bank failing is higher and the direct impact lower, there is the potential for the failure of a small bank to undermine confidence and spark off a systemic crisis.

---

[104] High-level expert group on reforming the structure of the EU banking sector, Erikki Liikanen, October 2012.

[105] Managing the transition to a safer financial system, Sheila C. Bair, Chairman, Federal Deposit Insurance Corporation.

[106] S&L crisis of the 1980s, Reuters, 15 March 2007.

[107] High-level expert group on reforming the structure of the EU banking sector, Erikki Liikanen, October 2012.

7.9.3 Cross-Border Issues

The current financial crisis has been a huge backwards step for the internationalisation and globalisation of banking. Despite progress in the fields of technology, popular culture, communication and even political integration, the recent losses in banking have forced a re-domesticisation of the industry. Is this a problem? Yes, because customers' needs are not solely domestic. Many consumers and most corporations have international banking needs and it is highly disruptive to them to have loosely integrated financial markets. The one area where cross-border banking is of more questionable utility is the continued existence of tax havens and money laundering centres, those "shady places for shady people". These offshore centres cause a lot more financial transactions to be transacted across borders than is necessary and introduce risks into the process as a result. But it is not in the scope of this book to propose a fix for offshore banking, aside from ensuring that bank management and supervisors are wary of financial structures with an offshore component of any complexity. Despite this area of reservation, the benefits of international banking are undoubtedly positive for the economy but hard to quantify. One piece of evidence, a study by the European Central Bank, shows that financial integration within the European Union was responsible for a recurring fillip to annual economic growth of about 2%.[108]

Ironically, the re-domesticisation of banking markets is now happening within the EU. Not only has "the crisis has put a halt on the integration process in the EU banking market"[109] but also local regulators are requiring foreign banks to maintain local balance sheets that are well-funded and well-capitalised. A further irony is that the world's largest banking acquisition, the purchase of ABN Amro by the RBS-led consortium in 2008, was meant to herald an era of international M&A activity to build multi-domestic and subsequently global banking franchises. A few have begun to emerge in retail banking (e.g. Santander has major operations in Spain, Portugal, Brazil and the UK; BNP Paribas in France, Italy, the USA, Luxembourg and Belgium). But the banking industry will need to re-invent its risk management capabilities before major globalisation trends can re-emerge.

At the root of the problem is that fact that "banks which are global in life are national in death".[110] By this we mean that banks are headquartered and regulated in one country but operate and take risks all over the world. If they run into trouble and need to be bailed out to preserve financial stability, then the bill is footed by the headquarter country for the entire global operation. Three-quarters of the recent losses of the major UK banks were related to their non-UK balance sheets.[111] To stop bail-outs happening, the authorities have increased the level of regulation and introduced so-called "bail-in" laws (see Section 7.5.9), which enable regulators to force losses onto not only shareholders and holders of regulatory capital instruments but also the senior bondholders of the bank, which was not possible before. To limit the risk of contagion around a bank's global operations, the concept of "subsidiarisation" has been introduced. This requires a bank's

---

[108] Finance and Growth in The EU: New Evidence from the Liberalisation and Harmonisation Of The Banking Industry, Diego Romero De Ávila, ECB, September 2003.

[109] High-level expert group on reforming the structure of the EU banking sector, Erikki Liikanen, October 2012.

[110] Reshaping banking: The retreat from everywhere, *The Economist*, 21 April 2012.

[111] Deleveraging, Ben Broadbent, 15 March 2012.

operations in each country to be run on a standalone basis, with their own legal entity, capital and funding. The global banking group is then a federation of discrete local entities. Such a model is used by some of the world's largest multi-national banks, such as Santander and HSBC.

Even in the federal organisation model, the regulation and supervision of the entire global group is a key activity. International regulators have agreed a *modus operandi* in which the lead regulator in the headquarter country coordinates the activities of, and shares information with, regulators in other countries. This model was termed the "home/host" approach to regulation and was an integrated approach, with the bulk of the global regulation being controlled by the "home" regulator. The financial crisis has tested the "home/host" approach to breaking point. Local regulators are beginning to demand that foreign banks meet local requirements. Most importantly, the USA is considering moves that would require European banks operating in the USA to have a separately capitalised legal entity in the US to conduct their business there. This amounts to forced federalism and would increase significantly the financial resources needed by Europeans for their US businesses. The EU may choose to remove any competitive imbalance for European banks by requiring similar measures for American banks in Europe.[112]

The regressive trend in regulation of cross-border banking is disturbing. So many features of banking only make sense in a globally integrated model. Even simple asset and liability management (ALM) processes across currencies become tortuous if they have to be done with multiple regulatory frameworks and legal entities. In Europe, it is now evident that full banking union is the only logical consequence of the single currency and there are moves afoot to extend the integration process into a shared deposit guarantee scheme and a single, Eurozone-wide regulator. The nitty-gritty technical details of administering the banking industry have thrown up the big issue: a single currency does not make sense without greater – even full – political and fiscal union.

So, the need to protect *local* taxpayers and *local* society from the consequences of the actions of foreign banks is paramount, but leads to tensions and contradictions along the way. At this stage, deep into a painful financial crisis, the urge to re-domesticise will prevail over the push for global integration. The trend towards global integration will inevitably start again, once the economic cycle progresses and confidence returns. All industries – car manufacturers, airlines, oil companies, mobile phone networks, power utilities and branded fashion goods, to name but a few – face these issues of working across national boundaries and multiple standards. Financial services is probably the most amenable to global integration, due to its intangible nature. We are a long way from having a global regulator, but it is the inevitable long-term solution for a naturally global industry.

7.9.4 Ownership Structures

Does it matter who owns a bank? In theory, the ownership model is important as a source of capital, confidence and culture. In practice, various ownership models exist (see Table 7.11) and none appears to be clearly superior or inferior to the others.

---

[112] Bernanke Warned by Barnier That Bank Unit Rules Risk Retaliation, Bloomberg, 23 April 2013.

Table 7.11   Ownership models

State-owned banks	State-owned banks tend to be found in economies with a relatively undeveloped financial system and where state intervention in the economy is prevalent. As economies develop and liberalise, such banks are often privatised. The gradual privatisations of Sberbank and VTB in Russia are a good example of this. The other reason for state ownership is as a consequence of nationalisation following the failure of a bank, a recent example being SNS Reaal in Holland. In such cases, state ownership is a temporary measure during stabilisation and restructuring, with the state seeking to withdraw from its ownership role once circumstances allow.
	In general, governments are bad owners for banks. The lack of commercial imperatives tends to lead to poor operating efficiency, low levels of innovation, weak risk management, misallocation of resources and corruption or favouritism. State-owned banks can also distort competition in the banking market, due to their unique privileges. On the other hand, state-owned banks can be good at channelling subsidised financial resources to projects for the "greater good" and they can also be important anchors during times of crisis.
Mutual banks	Many banks started out as mutual organisations, owned by their customers. Members of a mutual bank could be depositors or borrowers, or both. Traditionally, they were united by a common bond – generally, by living in the same town. Similar models include cooperative banks and credit unions, which might technically not be mutuals but in practice are very similar. Despite a demutualisation surge in the 1980s and 1990s, mutual banking remains alive and kicking in most countries in the world. For example, the European Association of Cooperative Banks claims 4,000 members. Some of the largest banks in the world are mutuals: for example, Crédit Mutuel in France, Rabobank in the Netherlands, Nationwide Building Society in the UK.
	Mutuals are not profit-oriented organisations, pricing their products at the keenest possible prices for their members' benefit. They only need profits to build and maintain their capital base; they do not distribute profits to their members in the form of a dividend. The capital base of a mutual is effectively orphaned. The past members of the mutual, who have contributed to the capital base through subscription or capital-accretive product pricing during times of growth, do not charge for their capital-providing services. Since it demands no financial return, the base cost of a financial product at a mutual is lower than for other types of bank.
	Smaller mutuals will often band together in groups in order to gain from scale economies. A central service company is set up, owned by the individual mutual banks, and provides processing and IT services, central branding and marketing support, sophisticated wholesale products and access to the capital markets. For example, at Rabobank, the central entity is Rabobank Nederland, which serves the 140 Rabobank constituent banks throughout the country.[113] The individual mutual banks often enter into a pact of mutual support, enhancing the creditworthiness of the group. These large groups are federations rather than banks in themselves.

(continued)

---

[113] A smart design is half the job, Rabobank, 30 June 2011.

Table 7.11   *(Continued)*

Mutual banks *(continued)*	Mutuals can be very well-run and successful. The fact that they do not need to grow or strip capital out of the business to give to hungry shareholders means that their strategies can be very patient and risk-averse. Indeed, they need to be, since they are not always able to raise equity with ease, in case they need to fill a capital gap that has been caused by losses, for example. Mutual product pricing can often be superior to that of a bank that needs to price in a return on shareholder capital. Intimate ties with customers can lead to superior brand perception, customer satisfaction and risk performance. The superior financial performance potential has been empirically documented, for example in the Liikanen report.[114] This is not to say that the potential superiority of mutuals to other types of banks is realised in practice. In fact, mutuals can sometimes be less innovative, efficient and responsive than privately-owned banks. They are, of course, prone to the same mistakes as banks with private shareholders. The recent challenges at the Co-Operative Bank in the UK are testament to this. The Co-Op merged with the Britannia Building Society in 2009 to form a "super-mutual", but in 2013 was forced to float on the stock market, in order to fill a capital hole caused by historic lending to the commercial real estate sector.
	Mutuals can sometimes have severe governance problems, since there is a risk that monitoring by members is less effective than the scrutiny that is applied to publicly-traded banks. The disastrous experiences from reckless real estate lending that many of the the Spanish Cajas have experienced is a good example of the weak governance and management structures that can plague mutuals.
Privately-owned banks	The most common form of ownership, as with companies in other sectors of the economy, is to be owned by private shareholders. This can be in the form of a partnership or a PLC (public limited company). In turn, PLCs can have either private sources of ownership or have shares that are listed and traded on an exchange and are thus widely held. By far the most common form of private bank ownership these days is that of a listed PLC, though the events of the current financial crisis force a consideration of the relative merits of partnerships and non-listed private sector banks as ownership models.
Listed PLC	The listed PLC is under constant scrutiny from investors, with the share price acting as a visible bellwether of the bank's success and shareholders taking an active role in the governance of the firm. On the one hand, this is good, as it keeps management on their toes; on the other hand, market pressures can hinder contrarian strategies and reward short-termism and excessive risk-taking. Many of the failed banks of recent years were stock-market darlings, with highly rated shares and feted management teams. During a crisis, the share price itself can act as a negative signal, with a share price crash often creating panic by itself and the evaporation of market confidence in the bank in question. In short, the market is not always the best manager.

---

[114] High-level expert group on reforming the structure of the EU banking sector, Erikki Liikanen, October 2012.

Private PLC	Private PLCs are not listed investments and are owned by a limited number of shareholders. Because of this, they tend to be far smaller than their listed peers. Private equity has a more intense linkage between management and the owners and is more able and willing to pursue difficult, niche and contrarian strategies. For this reason, the private PLC ownership model is well suited to high-risk start-up or turnaround situations.
Partnerships	Recent events in the capital markets have caused certain commentators to call for the partnership model to be revived. Partnerships are felt to be more accountable, since management has its own money on the line. But they are also far more restricted in their access to capital. The partnership model is unlikely to be a valid construct for widespread application in the modern financial system. However, there are certain behaviours, frameworks and management processes that can usefully be borrowed from the partnership model and applied to a PLC model. At present, many of the developments in senior executive pay at PLC banks are based on similar structures in partnerships.

We would argue that one should be wary of an industry blueprint that pre-supposes or favours a given ownership structure. In all likelihood, an industry with a diverse set of banks and a broad range of ownership models is likely to be more resilient than one with a prescribed form. Different aspects of different models appear to offer good elements for certain segments of the industry: mutuals for traditional retail banking provision, listed PLCs for the large universal banking platforms, partnerships for niche advisory and capital markets work, private equity for turnaround situations. Good risk management, including appropriate governance, should be – must be – a common feature of all ownership models.

8
Challenges

The proposals set out in the previous chapter attempt to give fresh ideas to the debate on how to improve the banking industry. The insights behind them are based on a mixture of theory and experience and are meant to be implementable. Nevertheless, some of the proposals may appear far-fetched to certain banking specialists and maybe even naïve to some others. Whilst disagreeing with such scepticism, we do recognise that genuinely radical and creative solutions will face some profound challenges, which this chapter analyses and discusses. Whether these challenges are so great that they result in the blueprint being impossible is difficult to know. The authors believe that they are not insurmountable. If it turns out that they are "deal breakers", then our lament is simply that the banking industry is confined to its historic *modus operandi* and financial crises will continue to plague banks and the societies they serve. Our heartfelt hope is that this is not the case and the blueprint – or something like it – can be realised and made effective.

8.1 INDUSTRY ENTRENCHMENT

Grandiose stuff, but I suspect we will have to think big to get ourselves out of the mess we find ourselves in.[2]

In most systems, the status quo tends to dominate and survive by constructing barriers to entry. Concepts are deep-rooted, change is incremental and progress is evolutionary, rather than revolutionary. The banking industry behaves in this way too.

Following the near-collapse of the banking industry around the time of the Lehman Brothers bankruptcy, the need and appetite for change was large. As described earlier in this book, the hyper-rational capital markets reacted to the crisis by withdrawing their liquidity from the banking industry and central banks were forced to step in and bolster the financial system. The ensuing regulatory backlash, embodied by the Basel III regime, is not vastly different from the pre-existing Basel II regime: as stated earlier, we viewed it as an updated version of Basel II rather than a new regulatory paradigm worthy of the "Basel III" label.

This conservatism is natural rather than sinister. Regulatory initiatives tend to be resourced by people with a deep understanding of the rules and an expertise that easily becomes a vested interest and a preference for non-revolutionary approaches. Those with strategic accountability

---

[1] Albert Einstein, 1932.
[2] Some Comments On The Current Scene And Its Antecedents, UK Economic Affairs Committee, supplementary memorandum by Peter Cooke, 1 February 2009.

for the running of the industry – whether regulators or senior bank executives – have tended to blame unfortunate oversights that can be remedied, rather than the essence of the industry's governance and risk management frameworks. When improvements in the industry are discussed, the terms of engagement are so entrenched that the only logical outcome is a tweak to current structures and processes.

> The implicit theory [...] is that the recent crisis happened because regulatory standards were not quite complex enough, because the extensive discretionary authority of bank supervisors was not great enough, and because rules and regulations prohibiting or discouraging specific practices were not sufficiently extensive. That theory is demonstrably false.[3]

Despite the falsehood of this approach, it remains the dominant approach. The authors of Basel III are the regulators who were responsible for the operation of the previous Basel II regime. They do not see fundamental deficiencies with that regime and the frameworks it contains. They are tweaking the Basel rules to try to make them work, rather than revisiting the overall framework.

As a result, the banking industry is, at present, implementing Basel III with the following unchallenged components:

- IFRS or GAAP accounting valuations used with little interpretation or challenge.
- Intense focus on capital stock as a tool for stability, rather than risk management (or, to put it differently, the use of Pillar 1 in preference to Pillar 2).
- Increasing complexity of bank regulations that has moved from the laborious to the arcane.
- Regulatory resources focused on administration and enforcement rather than application of common sense and challenge; still massively under-powered to supervise their banks effectively.

Implementation of the blueprint outlined in Chapter 7 would be an affront to this natural conservatism. It would require a genuine sea-change in the established processes and technologies of the banking industry. Let us consider, for example, the adoption of a capital adequacy measure as set out in Section 7.5. The current regulatory model at Basel and in individual countries would struggle to embrace such a flexible and subjective measure. The mindset of RWAs and capital ratios that are assumed to have some sort of objective meaning does not cope comfortably with the concept of an impressionistic capital assessment. Their challenge would be that banks need to be treated fairly and with a degree of objectivity and precision: rules have to be clear and algorithmic. This requirement is indeed an obstacle – but it must be overcome, since it is the wrong approach to risk. Risk is simply not objectively knowable or it wouldn't be risk!

There will be winners and losers and many conflicting agendas to resolve. Vast sums of money and personal and institutional reputations will be at stake. Finding a decent, never mind optimal, solution in the midst of such a politicised context may appear improbable. Senior figures have noted that "profit maximisation and level-playing field considerations naturally stand in the way of prudence and risk prevention"[4] and that "we should not expect too much of regulation. Conventional judgment is a safe haven for bankers and regulators alike. It is not easy to persuade people, especially those who are earning vast sums as a result, that what looks successful in the short run is actually highly risky in the long run."[5]

---

[3] Meaningful banking reform and why it is so unlikely, Charles W. Calomiris, 8 January 2013.

[4] Regulating finance after the crisis, Christian Noyer, Governor, Banque de France.

[5] Finance: A Return from Risk, Mervyn King, Governor of the Bank of England, 17 March 2009.

8.2 HUMAN BEHAVIOUR

Created half to rise and half to fall;
Great lord of all things, yet a prey to all;
Sole judge of truth, in endless error hurl'd:
The glory, jest and riddle of the world![6]

A major challenge to improvements in the risk management of the banking industry is the inbuilt behaviour of human beings. Humans tend to be bullish and blind to risk at the top of the cycle, creating asset bubbles, mispricing risk and under-pricing capital. When cycles turn from boom to bust, human behaviour overshoots in the opposite direction: risk appetite diminishes and liquidity dries up. Due to the nature of the financial system, this cyclical "fear and greed" is self-reinforcing, causing swings in asset prices and financial gains/losses that are generated purely by the cyclicality itself. In a word, humans exhibit procyclical behaviour (see Section 3.8).

This psychological misbehaviour is difficult to tame. Despite numerous historic examples of bubbles, our personal better judgement and the regulatory authorities who look after us consistently fail to deflate the next bubble, instead convincing us that "this time it's different". Famously, the British Chancellor announced in 2007 that "we will never return to the old boom and bust".[7] In fact, the popularity of booms makes them stubbornly difficult to tame. "The record of the past indicates that the temptation to 'let the good times roll' is deeply embedded in the political economy of regulation."[8]

Recent developments in behavioural finance consider the realities of human behaviours towards financial risk: how do humans actually make financial decisions? The findings are intriguing. Traditional models that assumed efficient markets and perfectly cold, rational human actions are discredited. Rather than being strange, the supposedly irrational behaviour of humans can be described accurately and consistently. Examples include those listed in Table 8.1.[9]

Collectively, these behavioural aspects can explain many of the challenges that we face in attempting to stabilise and improve the financial industry. Some of the fascinating areas to be explored include:

- What are the examples where we have proactively popped bubbles or tamed the cycle?
- Will banking crises continue to happen, as we are focused on fixing the exact cause of the previous problem?
- Aren't we doomed to take on excessive risk just at that point where we don't perceive it?
- What motivates people in the banking industry?
- Is history repeating itself ("greed and fear")?

Better risk management may help, in that it requires people to be more *aware* of the risks they are assuming. Merely acknowledging that undesirable outcomes are possible will remove the false confidence that risk has been tamed and the situation is under control.

---

[6] *An Essay on Man*, Alexander Pope, 1733.
[7] Chancellor of the Exchequer's Budget Statement, 21 March 2007.
[8] The new approach to financial regulation, speech by Andrew Bailey, Bank of England and PRA, 1 May 2013.
[9] *A Survey of Behavioral Finance*, Nicholas Barberis, 2003.

Table 8.1 Examples of behavioural finance

The inability for professionals to act on arbitrage opportunities, if their clients want to follow the trend	This has been called "a separation of brains and capital".[10]
Overconfidence and the inability to deal with very small and very large numbers	People underestimate the frequency of rare events. Apparently, what people view as 98% certain is actually only about 60% certain.
Optimism and wishful thinking	People can be unreasonably optimistic regarding their abilities and prospects. Apparently, over 90% of people think they are above average at things like driving and sense of humour.
The "gambler's fallacy"	If a coin toss has resulted in five heads in a row, some people think that the outcome of the next toss is clear, whereas it is not. Tellingly, some think it is certain to be heads while others think it is sure to be tails!
Belief perserverance	People cling to an opinion or theory too tightly and for too long after contradictory evidence comes through.
Anchoring of values	People's initial view is hard to shake and their subsequent estimates stick stubbornly close to it. For example, retail investors often refuse to sell shares below the price at which they were bought, despite that being a largely meaningless benchmark.
Non-linear attitudes to risk	People are willing to spend good money on a lottery ticket or an insurance policy, both of which have a payout ratio of around 50% of revenues. The chance of winning a huge amount, or avoidance of a disastrous loss, is worth the probability-adjusted loss of wealth.
"House money" effect	People are increasingly willing to gamble when they are ahead. Losses are less painful when they are cushioned by prior gains.
Momentum	People love a rising stock. Retail investors tend to "buy high and sell low", contrary to professional advice.
Positive feedback and the greater fool (or castle-in-the-air[11]) theory	In short, investors can be happy to buy something for more than they think it is worth, in anticipation of being able to sell it later to other investors even more optimistic than themselves.
	Investors are not "making superior long-term forecast of probable yield of an investment over its whole life, but foreseeing changes in the conventional basis of valuation a short time ahead of the general public".[12]

[10] The limits of arbitrage, A. Shleifer and R. Vishny, *Journal of Finance*, 1997.

[11] *The General Theory of Employment, Interest and Money*, John Maynard Keynes.

[12] Ibid.

Table 8.2   Yields on US securities, 22 January 2013[13]

Bond	Yield	Breakeven yield	Yield 3 yrs ago
2 yr Treasury	0.24%	0.54%	0.79%
10 yr Treasury	1.84%	2.23%	3.61%
30 yr Treasury	3.03%	3.26%	4.53%
Investment Grade Corporate	2.75%	3.50%	4.52%
High Yield Corporate	5.90%	7.57%	8.75%
AAA 10 yr Muni	1.67%	1.94%	3.00%

The human need for predictability and control is central to a psychological account of panics. Confidence in a system such as a financial market results when investors believe they understand how things work, which leads to a sense of predictability (Einhorn 1986). This sense of predictability gives investors a feeling of control, which then legitimizes further opportunity seeking (reaping benefits while avoiding catastrophic losses) that is often riskier than it is perceived to be (Hertwig et al. 2004). We argue that events that destroy this sense of predictability and perceived control trigger panics, the feeling that crucial control has been lost and that the future is unpredictable, and hence, dangerous. Resulting behavior, including a retreat to safe and familiar options, aims to minimize exposure to such danger until a new model of how things work has been established.[14]

We are currently experiencing a period of increasing confidence on the back of a period of panic. There has been a snapback of risk appetite. "For the first time in a few years, there is room to imagine not a perfect future, but a brighter and less unstable couple of years in which the private credit cycle starts to reinforce growth, and growth starts to reinforce the credit cycle."[15]

This can be illustrated by some interesting data from an economic research team, which shows the investment yield on American securities in early 2013 (see Table 8.2), in relation to historic levels and also to an estimated "breakeven" yield. The inference is that investors were mispricing risk. They were not getting the returns that their risk exposures merited.

In order to deal with such exuberance, regulators somehow need to be empowered and have teeth, not just during occasional crises but during the longer-term periods of stability and pre-crisis bubble formation. This is going to be hugely challenging. Some commentators have used such a worry to assume that regulators will need more rules rather than more discretion. Their fear is that discretionary tightening in boom conditions will prove impossible.[16]

The opposite could also be argued: regulators need to avoid hiding behind a rule book and exercise their role as the "Guardian Angel" of society. The way to avoid being seen as "spoiling the party" is not to mechanise the regulatory process (which would, at any rate, be arbitraged through loopholes and clever structures) but to increase the quality and reputation of supervision.

---

[13] The biggest pictures, Bank of America Merrill Lynch Global Research, 28 January 2013.
[14] A Psychological Perspective of Financial Panic, Anat Bracha and Elke U. Weber, Federal Reserve Bank of Boston, September 2012.
[15] Long-term pessimism, short-term frothiness, and the recovery in world wealth, Cardiff Garcia, *FT Alphaville*, 22 January 2013.
[16] The Fundamental Principles of Financial Regulation, Brunnermeier et al., 6 January 2009.

8.3 PERFORMANCE MANAGEMENT FOR GOOD RISK MANAGEMENT

The person who imposed locks on cockpit doors gets no statues in public squares.[17]

Since risk is difficult to observe, it is difficult to measure. This leads to a situation where the performance measures used to judge banks – and internally to judge the performance of people, products and businesses – tend not to be risk-adjusted. The case studies in Chapter 5 highlight a few cases where accounting profit was initially strong but the accumulation of risks led ultimately to massive financial losses.

Most banks and bank analysts have a strong focus on the accounting income statement as the key financial performance management tool. There are many examples where positive feedback is given by performance management frameworks to decisions that appear profitable at the time of execution but are bad on a risk-adjusted basis (for example, investing in a subprime mortgage). This can breed a sales culture that is difficult to dislodge. Revenue generation can be prioritised over risk-adjusted value creation. In some cases, banks and bankers are rewarded for taking risks, while the bank (and its shareholders) do not *sufficiently* promote reward for good risk management.

This is because it is challenging for performance management frameworks to recognise good, risk preventative behaviours. The problem begins with the owners of the bank, the shareholders. They are often excessively interested in profit growth and can fail to penalise banks when they take excessive risks. The knock-on effect is that some bankers who took high risks were supported by their boards, shareholders and regulators (again, there are numerous examples in Chapter 5). Contrarian behaviours that fail to catch the revenues of a boom are subject to negative performance feedback.

The author of *The Black Swan* makes a valid point in the quote that begins this section. If someone had had the bright idea to lock all cockpit doors on aircraft prior to the hijackings of 11 September 2001, would they have been praised and rewarded? There is no *apparent* victory in a problem averted. As regards banking, he raises the pertinent question: "Who gets rewarded, the central banker who avoids a recession or the one who comes to 'correct' his predecessors' faults and happens to be there during some economic recovery?"[18]

The examples of insightful investors who were ahead of their time but contrary illustrates this point. During the exuberant dotcom boom towards the end of the twentieth century, there was Tony Dye at Philips & Drew, who was vociferous about the over-valuation of dotcom stocks at the turn of the century:

> P&D's comparative performance was knocked for six and Dye, once regarded as one of the City's foremost investment gurus, was hounded out of his job. But only days after Dye quit, the tech bubble burst. Markets went into reverse and P&D's performance against its rivals began to rally.[19]

Jeffrey Vinik was the manager of Fidelity's Magellan Fund, who decided to move out of technology stocks into bonds in late 1995, leading to Magellan underperforming the market in the short-term, even though the strategy was proven correct by the subsequent dotcom crash. Vinik left Magellan in 1996.

---

[17] *The Black Swan: The Impact of the Highly Improbable*, Nassim Nicholas Taleb, 2008.
[18] Ibid.
[19] The fall and rise of Phillips & Drew, *London Evening Standard*, 20 January 2002.

8.4 TIMING

> Make me chaste, just not yet.[20]

Is now the right time to be fixing the banking industry? Most of the public policy in place is devoted to boosting capital levels by restricting capital distribution to shareholders. New resolution policies are coming into force, which aim to make bank failures less contagious. Funding pressures have been eased through massive liquidity injections by central banks and the continued provision of credit to the economy is being supported by subsidised lending schemes, such as the UK's "Funding for Lending Scheme" (FLS). Risk build-up due to these policies is being overlooked and other looming risks (such as a slowdown in the Chinese economy or the outbreak of war in the Middle East or Korea) are being ignored. Any genuinely radical changes to the banking industry could threaten the much-desired economic recovery. We now need a pragmatic, bubble-pumping banking sector and the "great deleveraging", as well as the fundamental rebuilding of a better banking system, might need to wait.

The regulatory authorities are not blessed with the time and resource to dutifully consider what the future regulation and supervision of the banking industry should look like. There is, frankly, no bandwidth for the design of a framework that will be long-lasting and robust. Unlike in the years leading up to the introduction of Basel II, the tone is intensely pragmatic and incremental. The industry elite that was running the show during the boom years is largely still in place. Now is not the time for thoughtful radicals to gain credibility and status, indeed this cadre will take a long time to develop footholds. Nor is society ready to consider the fundamental issues of design for their banking system: they want an end to recession and a rebirth of confidence and investment. The coincidence of huge *fiscal* problems (partly due of course to the banking crisis) and *deep political* issues (such as the future of the EU and the Eurozone) do not help focus the mind on banking reform. Recessionary politics are proving unsuitable for long-term reform programmes beyond certain populist actions (such as the introduction of bonus caps).

As the economic cycle swings slowly towards growth and normalisation, there is a risk that banking reform will slip off the top of the agenda and the pressures for change will diminish. Banks will once again become boring and invisible to the public and to politicians. If that situation materialises, reform will drift. When is a good time to develop the right reforms and achieve the right mix of stability, patience and ambition? It is not clear when that time might be, but the current timing is not ideal, and as the English tourist asking directions from Tipperary to Cork is told: "You wouldn't want to start from here …"

8.5 A POSITIVE CHALLENGE: TECHNOLOGICAL AND SOCIAL PROGRESS

Most of the challenges above appear to be quite negative for our hopes for the banking industry. Yet there is one major development that seems to offer new hopes and opportunities. The rise of new technologies, in particular the internet and the spread of popular computing, has occurred at the same time as certain shifts in our social structures, such as increasing levels of

---

[20] *Confessions*, St Augustine.

literacy, productivity and prosperity. The solution to the current woes of the banking industry does not lie in nostalgic simplifications of the past, but may rather be built upon more public interaction with banks, more information flow combined with technological analytics and the development of new risk management disciplines to exploit these new opportunities.

What does this mean in practice? Well, since the frictional costs of information and processing have dropped virtually to zero, then all manner of capabilities are made possible:

- Detailed disclosures of risk information, including confidence accounting and database (rather than fixed table) provision.
- Peer-to-peer lending, as exemplified by retail platforms such as Zopa, LendingTree and RateSetter.
- Improved, more intense, governance and management structures, such as the "centurion approach" proposed in a previous chapter.

And social changes should lead to a significant increase in financial literacy, in other words the ability of people to understand how finance works. In this way, we can hope that popular engagement in the banking industry is a positive and constructive element rather than a negative and obstructionist one. In a shareholder democracy, we rely upon grass-roots understanding of how finance works to shape policy and bring the authorities and management teams to accountability. With better popular understanding, we would have less faith in "get rich quick" schemes and more ability to accept short-term pain for longer-term gain, for example in planning for pension provision.

These developments have to be good. They represent one of the main hopes for a positive correction to the constant trend for financial crises. Even if the advances of recent generations are unable to guarantee world peace and the abolition of poverty, they may at least be able to mitigate the causes of problems in the banking industry.

9
What Next? A Call to Arms

> There's no question that this search for yield is reappearing, people are now actively taking more risk to get a higher return.[1]

Our concluding chapter highlights the need for action to fix the banking industry. Basel III is not the answer to the faults exposed by the current financial crisis. Major risks remain unaddressed and the solution is not an incremental tweak to the *ancien régime*. Instead, a comprehensive overhaul of regulation, supervision and risk management is required to deal with the fundamental, inherent and dangerous nature of market-based financial services. The answer to the transport bottlenecks of the nineteenth century was not a faster horse but the motor car. Basel III is, frankly, the equivalent of a faster horse. We need to start detailing the blueprint of the motor car.

The conceptual challenges set out in the previous chapter are immense. Even if they can be overcome, the practical challenges of implementation would be immense too. The recommendations set out in Chapter 7 would result in changes to organisations, job descriptions, processes, systems and financial structures. Reconstructing an entire industry along fundamental lines is not to be undertaken lightly. That said, we are not put off by the implementation challenges. Many of the concepts of "better banking" are already in use in certain banks and supervisory models; some of the proposals would reduce the complexity and resource requirements of banking by removing legacy structures, such as foot-thick rule books; any rigorous cost/benefit analysis would be heavily weighted towards the benefit case, due to the reduction of risk.

Our guiding philosophy has been a confident "can do" attitude. The changes to the banking industry need to happen, even if it is along different lines from the ones we propose. If we are wrong and the conceptual and practical challenges prove insurmountable, then society may have to "make do and mend". In that case, society has to recognise that it is not in control of the banking industry. Society may need to accept the fact that financial crises will continue to re-occur in the future. Alternatively, society may decide that the benefits of modern banking are illusory and we should reinvent an old-fashioned banking industry that is apparently simpler, smaller and easier to control. Such an approach would not be immune to banking crises – as described towards the beginning of this book, crises have occurred throughout history – but it might mitigate some of their more disastrous effects. It would also mean that society would need to forgo the features and benefits of modern banking: getting a mortgage would be harder, saving for retirement would be riskier, economic growth would slow. Instinctively, this does not feel like the right approach. It seems nostalgic, Luddite and incompatible with the rest of our modern, liberal and enlightened economy.

Pushing radical reform in a troubled macro-economic environment and in the face of a powerful, entrenched industry status quo is not easy. Society may desire revenge over reform and the industry may devote its resources to a self-interested lobbying process. These

---

[1] Andrew Bailey, Bank of England, on BBC TV's *Bankers: Fixing the System*, May 2013.

challenges – challenges of acceptance – are our real foes, even if we have a conceptually valid, implementable framework. This book has been written as a means of making a small amount of progress to address these challenges.

Risk is at the heart of all of the considerations in this book and risk management is the theme of our proposals. There was a massive build-up of risk in the years running up to the current financial crisis. Not enough was done to manage that risk. No single constituent of the system was entirely to blame – in fact, the crisis is a crisis of the entire system. If we have not addressed the weaknesses of the system, which is the central hypothesis of this book, then risks remain and new risks – the unintended consequences of policy actions – will arise. This is, indeed, happening.

The seeds of the next financial crisis are being sown today already. We cannot predict when and where the problems will arise. But we can identify factors that contribute to a potential for uncertain outcomes on the downside. At a high level, these factors include:

- Unprecedented monetary easing, which has led to historically low interest rates and a glut of policy-induced liquidity. No-one understands the way in which the economy will cope with these policies in the longer term.
- Consequently, massive exposure of the banking industry and the broader economy to interest rate risk. Any rise in interest rates would cause severe losses for bond investors and lead to high levels of borrower defaults.
- Evident lack of discipline among bond and equity investors, as risk appetites are increased in order to meet return targets in a low-yield environment. The "thirst for yield" that was evident in 2006 has returned. For example, the Markit iTraxx Europe Crossover index (which includes 50 equally weighted credit default swaps on the most liquid sub-investment grade European corporate entities) went from 779bp in September 2011 to 410bp at the end of May 2013. High yield isn't yielding as much as it might.
- Continued forbearance towards banks that are non-viable in a commercial sense. Government capital injections have not yet been fully privatised and central bank funding levels remain high. For example, the ECB was still lending €667bn to credit banks at the start of October 2013.[2]
- Multiple overrides to sound policy frameworks that then tend to become permanent features of the system and weaken it. The 0% capital requirement applied to EU government bond holdings is one example.
- Build-up of risk in the push for central clearing of securities and derivatives. Central counterparties are thinly capitalised and the new approach is trapping large amounts of collateral.
- Ambiguous treatment of retail depositors through bail-in proposals and actions (e.g. in Cyprus). The resulting risks of retail deposit runs are growing, even if not fully apparent.
- Disturbing developments on the political front, with increasing risks associated with international military action and the shambolic government in the USA (Federal shutdown) and Italy (coalition instability).

The biggest latent risk is the risk of inaction through over-confidence. At present, markets are bullish: in February 2013, the Dow Jones Industrial Average (DJIA), a key measure of confidence in the future profitability of the economy, got back to its pre-crisis high of 14,000,

---

[2] European Central Bank.

which had last been seen in October 2007. By mid-May 2013, it had continued its climb and reached a level of 15,300, some 10% higher than the pre-crisis peak, and was still at this level in October 2013. Little of this new-found confidence is driven by fundamental appraisals of the economic situation and the risk profile of investments; much is driven by "technicals", the need to invest and the relative price of investments. A bull market leads to two negative effects for the goal of better banking:

- Investors interpret their positive returns as evidence that risk has diminished: *risk management appears less important.*
- The horrors of the financial crisis appear to have abated and we can return to a period of "normality": *the imperative to reform is diminished.*

Both of these stances are disturbing. We should not "waste a good crisis". There are valuable insights fresh in the memory, which will recede as we get further into any recovery and ultimately be lost. It is the task of all interested members of society – who will bear the burden of the next financial crisis, without doubt – to bring influence to bear in their own way, through the ballot box, consumer action or political engagement.

There is a zero possibility that there will be no further financial crises. The impact of the forthcoming ones will be determined by the action programme that is put in place now. For the banking industry, we believe that the answer lies beyond Basel III. A fresh approach is needed, but that will need interested parties to overcome any natural myopia and complacency. The key need is for a broader and fuller public debate on the reforms that are required and the trade-offs that need to be made. This book has attempted to provide a "toolkit" to enable and inform that debate. In this way, by improving our understanding of the need for improvement in the areas of risk management, governance and regulation, it will, hopefully, contribute to the development of "better banking".

Glossary & Jargon Lookup

ABCP Asset-Backed Commercial Paper, a type of ABS with short-term (under 270 days) maturity

ABS Asset-Backed Security, the bonds resulting from a securitisation of loans

AFS Available For Sale, an accounting classification for certain assets, indicating that the intent for holding them is short-term trading rather than long-term investment

ALM Asset and Liability Management, the process whereby a company attempts to manage the profile of its funding and its investments to get the right risk and return

Alt-A A type of US mortgage where the risk is considered to be in between prime and subprime

Bail-in Rescue of a financial institution by imposing losses on shareholders and bondholders

Bail-out Rescue of a financial institution through the use of public funds

Balance sheet The schedule that shows the accounting value of a company's assets and liabilities on a specific date

Bank capital A bank's own funds, which are not subject to repayment and are computed by deducting liabilities from assets. Beyond this simple definition, there are various types of capital – regulatory capital, economic capital and rating agency capital, for example – all using slightly different definitions for different purposes

Basel Committee for Banking Supervision (BCBS) A specialist part of the BIS that deals with issues relating to the regulation and supervision of banks

Basel I An international capital accord formulated in 1988, which set out for the first time a standard for minimum bank capital levels

Basel II A revised and far more sophisticated version of the Basel capital accord; Basel II, formulated in June 2004 and implemented in most countries around 2007–2008, was meant to be better than Basel I because it was more risk-sensitive

Basel II.5 Amendments to the market risk component of Basel II, introduced in 2009 as a response to the experience of the current financial crisis and as a precursor to Basel III

Basel III Another iteration of the Basel capital accord, first published in December 2010 as a response to the experience of the current financial crisis. The Basel III standards are being implemented in most countries at present

Basis point (bp) One one-hundredth of one percent (i.e. 0.01%)

Bear market Market conditions characterised by weak confidence and low or falling prices

BIS The Bank for International Settlements, headquartered in Basel, Switzerland. Sometimes referred to as the "central bank for central banks"

Bubble Acceleration in the rise of asset prices, increasing the gap with their fundamental value

Bull market Market conditions characterised by strong confidence and high or rising prices

CAPM Capital Asset Pricing Model, a methodology that purports to give the minimum acceptable return of a security by looking at its price volatility relative to the overall market and other factors

Carry trade Typically, when an investor takes funding at low cost and invests into an asset with a higher yield, thus earning a "spread" or "carry"

Casino banking A derogatory term widely used to describe banking activities that are related to the capital markets and meant to imply that those markets are equivalent to gambling and have no social value

CCP Central Counterparty, a clearing house that manages and settles securities and derivatives trades between capital market traders, becoming (in the words of the BIS) "the buyer to every seller and the seller to every buyer and thereby ensuring the future performance of open contracts"

CDO Collateralised Debt Obligation, an investment that is a portfolio of bonds and is often tranched. A "CDO-squared" is an investment that is a portfolio of CDO tranches

CDS Credit Default Swap, a derivative contract whereby the buyer pays a periodic premium and receives payment if the reference entity defaults

Centurion approach An organisational framework loosely based on the structures used by the Roman armies in ancient times

CFTC Commodity Futures Trading Commission, the regulator of the futures and options market in the USA

Clawback The cancellation of deferred bonus amounts or forced repayment of bonuses already disbursed

CMBS An MBS formed from mortgages to corporations or commercial landlords

CoCo Contingent Convertible bonds, a form of security that converts into equity shares upon some form of trigger occurring. There are also CoCos where the principal claim is written down or written off upon trigger

COE Cost of Equity, a notional return that shareholders require from their investment in the company, below which they should in theory demand their investment back for reinvestment elsewhere

Confidence In risk modelling, the probability assumption

Correlation The degree to which the performance of financial assets follows a similar pattern. A low level of correlation between asset performance can be used to achieve risk diversification in a portfolio

Coupon The periodic interest payments on a bond

Covered bond A bond that is linked to a portfolio of loans in the same way as ABS, but with recourse to the issuer if the loans are not sufficient to repay the bond

CRD IV Capital Requirements Directive version IV, also encompassing the associated CRR: the basis of the implementation of Basel III in the European Union finalised in 2013

Credit crunch A sudden reduction in overall market credit provision, generally with negative knock-on effects

Credit rating The short-hand code, such as "AA", for the assessment given by a credit rating agency on the relative probability of timely servicing and repayment of debt

Credit risk The potential for a lender to lose money if the borrower does not pay their interest or repay their principal

CRR Capital Requirements Regulation, part of the EU's CRDIV reform package (see above)

Default Failure to pay interest or principal repayment on a loan or bond

Derivative A financial contract that has payments linked to a reference item, such as interest rates, currency rates or stock prices

DGS Deposit Guarantee Scheme, an arrangement whereby depositors in failed banks have money repaid to them by the scheme, whilst other creditors have to rely upon the bankruptcy process

Discount rate In investment appraisal, the rate used to adjust for the fact that near-term cash flows are generally worth more than cash flows further out into the future

Dodd–Frank The Dodd–Frank Wall Street Reform and Consumer Protection Act, the basis of regulatory reform of the banking industry in the USA

D-SIB and D-SIFI Domestically Systemically Important Bank and Domestically Systemically Important Financial Institution

EAD Exposure At Default, an estimate of future actual exposure (including, for example, the drawn amount of a variable loan facility such as an overdraft) at the time of borrower default

EBA European Banking Authority, the EU body responsible for ensuring "effective and consistent" regulation and supervision for banks in the EU

ECB European Central Bank, the central bank for Europe's single currency, the Euro

Economic profit A management (rather than statutory) accounting item that represents the notional profit generated by an activity once a notional charge for the riskiness of that activity is applied

EL Expected Loss, the average loss from an exposure based on estimates of probability (PD), recovery (LGD) and level of exposure (EAD)

Fair value The realistic, rational and unbiased value of something, which can be highly subjective, even if liquid market prices are readily available. Similar to – but not the same as – mark-to-market

FCA Financial Conduct Authority (UK)

FDIC Federal Deposit Insurance Corporation, the body that supervises and provides deposit insurance and resolution services to most of the banks in the USA

Fed Federal Reserve System, the central banking system of the USA

Financial system All entities (banks, States, brokers, clearing houses) dealing with financial instruments globally

Fixed income Instruments, such as bonds and loans, that have contractual payments (of interest coupon and principal), as opposed to equity, which offers a discretionary and variable income to investors

Flight to quality Strong demand from investors for safe assets away from risky assets in reaction to increasing uncertainty in the system

FSA Financial Services Authority, the regulator of the financial services industry in the UK, now replaced by successor bodies including the PRA

FSB Financial Stability Board, an international body that is meant to coordinate the various national and regional supervisors of financial institutions

FSR Financial Stability Report, a document produced by central banks on a periodic basis to highlight risks and developments in the economy and the financial system

Funding The term used by banks to describe their sources of money, with which they provide loans and make investments

GAAP Generally Accepted Accounting Principles, the standard guidelines for financial accounting unless IFRS has been adopted

GDP Gross Domestic Product, a widely-used metric that indicates levels of economic output

GGB Government Guaranteed Bond, a bond issued by a bank that has been guaranteed (in return for a guarantee fee paid by the issuing bank) by the government

Glasnost A policy of openness, debate and engagement introduced by Mikhail Gorbachev in the Soviet Union in the late 1980s to enable change and foster accountability

Glass–Steagall US legislation, introduced in the 1930s to separate deposit-taking, commercial banking activities from capital markets businesses. It was effectively repealed in 1999

Going concern Continuing to trade normally

Gone concern Being wound down, run off or liquidated, either as a result of resolution (by the supervisor) or bankruptcy (by the liquidator)

G-SIB and G-SIFI Globally Systemically Important Bank and Globally Systemically Important Financial Institution

Haircut A reduction of some sort, for example in repayment amount or collateral eligibility

Hedge fund A type of specialised asset manager or investment fund

HQLA High Quality Liquid Assets, the asset holdings deemed by the regulator to be suitable to form the liquidity buffer

HTM Held-To-Maturity, an accounting classification for certain assets, indicating that the intent for holding them is long-term investment rather than short-term trading

Hybrid capital Regulatory capital instruments with some features that are equity-like (such as loss absorption) and some that are debt-like (such as fixed coupons)

IAS International Accounting Standards, the predecessors of IFRS; some of the current IFRS standards still bear the prefix "IAS"

IFRS International Financial Reporting Standards, the standard guidelines for financial accounting used in most countries and set by the International Accounting Standards Board (IASB) since 2001

Illiquid Not liquid; having poor liquidity

IMF International Monetary Fund

Interconnectedness Mutual reliance on each other of the multiple contacts between all financial institutions forming the financial system and the risk of contagion or knock-on effects

Investment grade A credit rating of BBB- or better

IRB (AIRB, FIRB) Internal Ratings-Based (Advanced IRB and Foundation IRB), the most sophisticated approach to calculating minimum solvency requirements for credit risk under Basel II and Basel III. Banks use their own internal calculations to define the capital requirements of their exposures. Under FIRB, banks give their own estimates of default probabilities (PD); under AIRB, other aspects are modelled, including LGD

Junior tranche or ranking A low position in the payment priority, relative to senior notes or tranches, and therefore higher risk

LCR Liquidity Coverage Ratio, a metric introduced in Basel III to act as a standard for banks' liquidity

Lender of last resort A convention, whereby the central bank has the ability and resources to provide funds to banks in times of stress

Leverage The amount of debt (as opposed to equity) in the capital structure. A highly leveraged firm relies heavily on debt to finance its investments

Leverage ratio A regulatory metric, being implemented globally in Basel III, that compares the regulatory capital of a bank with the size of its exposures, without applying any "weightings" to adjust those exposures for perceived riskiness

LGD Loss Given Default, the loss suffered by a lender when a borrower defaults, after taking into account the recovery value of seizing pledged collateral

LIBOR London InterBank Offered Rate, a benchmark interest rate used as a reference point for the pricing of many loans and derivatives

Liikanen Report High-level expert group on reforming the structure of the EU banking sector, Erikki Liikanen, October 2012

Liquid Having good liquidity (see below)

Liquidity The ability to meet financial commitments on a timely basis and/or the ability to sell something (to "liquidate" it) in size, rapidly and without forcing the price down

Liquidity crunch A sudden reduction in overall market liquidity, generally with negative knock-on effects

LTRO Long Term Refinancing Operation of the ECB (generally, 1 to 3 years)

Mark-to-market The practice of valuing an asset in the accounts at a level based on the current market price of that asset. In practice, highly problematic to define and controversial to apply

Market risk The potential for a bank to lose money on its open trading positions should the capital market price levels move against it

MBS Mortgage-Backed Security: the bonds resulting from a securitisation of mortgages. Can be RMBS or CMBS

Money market The part of the capital markets that deals with loans and bonds of very short maturity

Monoline credit insurer An insurance company specialised in providing financial protection against borrower default

Negative carry A carry trade (see above) where the an investor's funding costs more than the yield on their investment, and so the "spread" or "carry" is negative

Notch One move on the credit ratings scale: for example, from AA- to A+

NSFR Net Stable Funding Ratio, a metric introduced by Basel III to enable better regulation of banks' funding structures

OCC Office of the Comptroller of the Currency (USA)

OECD Organisation for Economic Cooperation and Development

OIS Overnight Index Swap, an interest rate derivative

Operational risk The potential for a bank to lose money when something in its operations goes wrong: fraud and misconduct are recent examples

OTC derivative Over-The-Counter derivative, a derivative trade that is conducted directly between two parties, without the use of an exchange platform

OTS Office of Thrift Supervision (USA)

P&L Profit and Loss, an alternative name for the income statement in accounting

PD Probability of Default, the estimated probability of the borrower failing to service or re-pay their debts during a given period

Pillars The three building blocks of Basel II (and Basel III): Pillar 1 Minimum Capital Requirements, Pillar 2 Supervisory Review, Pillar 3 Market Discipline

PIT Point-in-Time, a way of calculating PDs that reflects current economic conditions (as opposed to TTC)

PLC Public Limited Company, the most common legal form of large companies and banks, with public share ownership and limited liability

PRA Prudential Regulation Authority, the UK regulator of financial services

Price-to-book The ratio of the stock price to the per share value of the bank's net assets or accounting equity. Used as a key value metric by analysts and investors

Prime mortgage A mortgage to a borrower of high quality. Exact definitions vary, though standard definitions are in use in the USA

Principal The amount of money outstanding or invested

Procyclical Something that not only reflects the inherent ups and downs of the economy ("cyclical") but actually magnifies them ("procyclical")

RAC Risk-Adjusted Capital: a metric used by S&P to assess the relative solvency of banks on a comparable basis

Regulator The authority responsible for setting the rules for the industry

Repo Technically, a sale-and-repurchase agreement. In practice, a form of short-term secured borrowing

Reserve A term with many meanings that are sometimes confused with each other. The term can refer to: cash deposits with a central bank; or provisions earmarked in the accounting balance-sheet against potential future losses; or elements of a bank's accounting equity (e.g. retained earnings are often termed "reserves"). To be clear: equity reserves are not the same as cash reserves

Resolution Powers given to an authority to wind down a bank in case of failure, without the need for formal bankruptcy procedures

Reverse repo The other side of a repo. A form of short-term secured lending

Risk The potential for bad things to happen unexpectedly

Risk-free rate The return from a notionally risk-free investment, such as a government bond. Recent turbulence in the government bond markets has caused problems in assessing the risk-free rate

Risk-weighting A factor applied to a risk exposure, to reflect its relative perceived riskiness (see "RWAs" below)

RMBS Residential Mortgage Backed Security, an MBS formed from mortgage loans to homeowners

ROE Return On Equity, a widely used metric for bank profitability: defined as net income to shareholders divided by average shareholders' equity

Run A sudden and often chaotic withdrawal of funds from a bank

RWAs Risk-Weighted Assets, a regulatory measure of the total risk of an institution, used to set minimum capital requirements

S&P Standard & Poor's, a credit ratings agency

SCAP The 2009 Supervisory Capital Assessment Program, a stress test run by the Fed on 19 US banks

SEC Securities and Exchange Commission (USA)

Securitisation The process of transforming individual loans (or receivables such as royalties) into publicly traded bonds, generally through pooling and tranching

Senior tranche or ranking A high position in the payment priority, relative to junior notes or tranches, and therefore lower risk

SIB and SIFI Systemically Important Bank and Systemically Important Financial Institution, jargon used to describe banks and other financial institutions where problems could have a knock-on effect throughout the financial system and so are deemed "too big to fail"

SIV Specialised Investment Vehicle, a company not subject to banking regulation that funds itself on a short-term basis and uses the funds to buy long-term assets (often subprime related RMBS or CMBS)

SME Small and Medium-Sized Enterprise, a commonly used acronym for small businesses

Solvency Measure of the financial strength of a financial institution based on the level of capital

Sovereign debt Debt issued by a national government

Spot A transaction carried out at current market price and for immediate settlement (as opposed to a forward transaction)

Spread The difference between two levels

SPV Special Purpose Vehicle, a legal entity set up to achieve a specific financial objective

Standardised Approach The least sophisticated approach to calculating minimum solvency requirements for credit risk under Basel II and Basel III. Banks apply fixed risk-weightings to various asset classes in order to determine

Strawman An outline proposal for discussion and development

Stress A period of challenging economic conditions leading to losses for banks

Stress test A simulation exercise used by management and regulators to assess the solvency of a bank and its resilience to stress

Sub-prime mortgage A mortgage to a borrower of poor quality. Exact definitions vary, though standard definitions are in use in the USA

Supervisor The authority responsible for overseeing the banking industry and ensuring compliance with regulation

Swap A derivative contract that requires an investor to pay one stream of cash flows and receive a different stream. For example, the agreement could be to pay a fixed interest rate and receive a floating interest rate

SWF Sovereign Wealth Funds, asset managers set up by some countries to manage their budget surpluses

Systemic risk Risk that appears insignificant at the level of the individual institution but, when viewed across the entire financial system, becomes significant. Examples include systemic risk due to interconnectedness, lack of heterogeneity or industry concentrations

Tail risk Extreme downside risk that is both severe and highly unlikely to materialise

TARP Troubled Asset Relief Programme, established in 2008 to stabilise the US financial services industry through equity injections and purchase of securities

Tranche A "slice" of risk that is junior or senior to other tranches

Triple-A/AAA The highest possible credit rating, representing an annual default probability of some 1-in-5,000

TTC Through-The-Cycle, a way of calculating PDs that is meant to reflect average economic conditions (as opposed to PIT)

Unexpected Loss (UL) Loss beyond the level of expected loss. To quantify UL, a calibration of confidence is needed

Universal banking Those banks that combine a broad range of customer and product businesses, covering retail banking, business banking or commercial banking, investment banking and capital markets operations

Vickers Report Final Report: Recommendations, Independent Commission on Banking, September 2011

Volcker rule A section of the Dodd–Frank Act that imposes strucutural limitations on banks' riskier activities

Wargaming The use of multiple simulation exercises to learn about how complex systems (such as a military campaign or the banking system) might behave under different assumptions and generate actionable learning points to improve the performance and resilience of that system

XML Extensible Markup Language, a way of building a standard format for electronic information to make compilation, comparison and analysis easier to automate

Disclaimer Regarding Excerpts from S&P Materials

Standard & Poor's Financial Services LLC (S&P) does not guarantee the accuracy, completeness, timeliness or availability of any information, including ratings, and is not responsible for any errors or omissions (negligent or otherwise), regardless of the cause, or for the results obtained from the use of ratings. S&P GIVES NO EXPRESS OR IMPLIED WARRANTIES, INCLUDING, BUT NOT LIMITED TO, ANY WARRANTIES OF MERCHANTABILITY OR FITNESS FOR A PARTICULAR PURPOSE OR USE. S&P SHALL NOT BE LIABLE FOR ANY DIRECT, INDIRECT, INCIDENTAL, EXEMPLARY, COMPENSATORY, PUNITIVE, SPECIAL OR CONSEQUENTIAL DAMAGES, COSTS, EXPENSES, LEGAL FEES, or LOSSES (INCLUDING LOST INCOME OR PROFITS AND OPPORTUNITY COSTS) IN CONNECTION WITH ANY USE OF RATINGS. S&P's ratings are statements of opinions and are not statements of fact or recommendations to purchase, hold or sell securities. They do not address the market value of securities or the suitability of securities for investment purposes, and should not be relied on as investment advice.

Please see material referenced in footnotes 132 and 138 in Chapter 3; footnotes 3, 17 and 40 in Chapter 5; and footnote 5 in Chapter 7.

Index